RISE OF KOREAN LANGUAGE PROGRAMS IN U.S. INSTITUTE OF HIGHER EDUCATION: A NARRATIVE HISTORY

KLEAR-RILI Studies in Korean Language and Linguistics

THE KOREAN LANGUAGE EDUCATION AND RESEARCH CENTER &
THE RESEARCH INSTITUTE OF LANGUAGE AND INFORMATION

RISE OF KOREAN LANGUAGE PROGRAMS IN U.S. INSTITUTE OF HIGHER EDUCATION: A NARRATIVE HISTORY

Edited by Hye-Sook Wang

KOREA
UNIVERSITY
PRESS
고려대학교
출판문화원

Korea University Press
82-2-3290-4234 (Tel.) 82-2-923-6311 (Fax)
http://www.kupress.com kupress@korea.ac.kr
145, Anam-Ro, Seongbuk-Gu, Seoul, 136-701 Korea

Published November 2015

ISBN 978-89-7641-883-8 93710

EDITORIAL STATEMENT

The Korean Language Education and Research Center, Inc. (KLEAR) in Honolulu, Hawai'i, and the Research Institute of Language Information (RILI) at Korea University initiated the KLEAR-RILI Studies series in Korean Language and Linguistics in 2013 in order to promote studies on the Korean language worldwide. This multi-volume series is aimed at publishing, through the Korea University Press, scholarly manuscripts, written mainly in English, which deal with the linguistic structure, change and variation, language use, teaching, and learning of the Korean language.

It is well known that a large number of important studies conducted in overseas institutions of higher education on a variety of aspects of Korean have remained unpublished, being unable to find an appropriate international publisher for the obvious reason that an in-depth study on a specific area or issue in Korean generally fails to attract wide international readership. Under these circumstances, our goal is to cover a broad spectrum of research areas, capture state-of-the-art studies on Korean language and linguistics, and expeditiously bring significant research findings to light.

The KLEAR-RILI series accommodates not only monographs, anthologies, and edited books, but also, from 2015, revised versions of outstanding doctoral dissertations that are written in English. The series accommodates theoretical, descriptive, and applied studies on the one hand and both formal and functional approaches on the other.

One cataclysmic change in the history of the teaching of Korean as a foreign language is the unprecedentedly rapid growth of student enrollments in Korean language classes around the globe during the past fifteen years or so. In the United States, Korean has shown the largest increase in student enrollment among all modern foreign languages. This dramatic increase in enrollments in Korean calls for extensive pedagogical research in order to better serve the diverse needs of the ever-increasing population of learners of Korean. The KLEAR-RILI series is prepared to publish such pedagogical works, as well.

Ho-min Sohn
KLEAR President &
Professor of Korean Language and Linguistics
University of Hawai'i at Mānoa

Seok-Hoon You
RILI and the Korea University Press Director &
Professor of Linguistics
Korea University

ACKNOWLEDGEMENTS

Making this book has been a long process. As any product of concerted effort by a group of close to twenty people, the effort required comes only naturally. When this idea was born in my mind while I was completing my term as the president of the America Association of Teachers of Korean in 2006, I certainly did not anticipate it would take almost a decade to make this a reality. I am only elated and grateful that it did not slip away and was buried somewhere without any tangible product.

I always believed in recording things. This project is a fruit of that belief. As I have devoted two decades of my professional life to educating American college students in Korean language and culture, I felt it was my duty to reflect upon many decades of history and evolution of Korean language and culture education in America as a member of this group. I was reassured in my conviction when I realized that there was no such document in the field.

It would have been ideal if all the schools with Korean programs were invited, but it would also have been practically very challenging, if not impossible. As the first step, it has to be small and is only the start of a larger project. I hope that those institutions, which were invited but were unable to participate this time have another chance in the future.

Those schools whose stories were included in this book were selected based on a few criteria including the length of the program's history, the size of the program measured by student enrollment, number of faculty members, whether the program has a major or minor in Korean, and so on. While the title of the book is Rise of Korean Language Programs in U.S. Institute of Higher Education: A Narrative History, Defense Language Institute is included despite the fact that it is not a regular college. I decided to include DLI because of its unique place in Korean language education in America. DLI is one of a few institutions that serve large numbers of so-called "non-heritage" learners of Korean who learn the Korean language for very distinct purposes.

Specific instructions were provided to the authors when they accepted my invitation to participate in the project with respect to its background, purpose, and goal, and the expected focus of the writing. However, as the readers will soon find out, some authors focused more on the history while some authors offered more on current state for different reasons. The specific information provided also varied quite a bit in each piece. Various factors must have led them to determine their respective pieces. One thing is clear, though. I am confident that readers will gain a good sense of how the field in general struggled and succeeded, and how each program evolved over time.

I am indebted to countless people from the beginning to the end of this process. I would like to express my sincere appreciation to all of the chapter authors who graciously agreed to share the stories of their institutions, squeezing time out of their already busy schedule and putting up with my constant deadline reminders. I salute their unparalleled dedication to our profession. My heartfelt thanks go to Professor Ho-min Sohn for being a role model for everyone in the field, and for the support of the Korean Flagship Center of the University of Hawaii at Manoa for which he serves as the Director. I am very pleased to see this book published as a volume of the KLEAR-RILI Studies in Korean Language and Linguistics. I am also grateful to Kurt Moriber and Ah-Young Song for their editorial assistance (Kurt during the middle stage and Ah-Young for final publication editing), and Dr. Soohee Kim for her invaluable feedback on the draft of my Introduction to the book. Thank you to Professor Seok-Hoon You, Director of the Korea University Press, Mr. Wonki Kim, Mr. Chul Kim, and Mr. Jaehyouk You of the

KUP who worked very hard to bring this manuscript to the world. I thank them deeply.

I thank my family, my husband and my daughter Marisa who put up with me for so long while I worked on this project. You are my ultimate joy and source of inspiration. Thank you.

Finally, I wish to acknowledge that this project has been supported by the grants that I received from the Academy of Korean Studies for two years from 2011-2012, Competitive Research Grants 2011-R24, 2012-R24. It pushed me to go on when things became hard, and I am truly grateful for its support.

Hye-Sook Wang
Spring 2015, Providence, RI

Contents

Contents

INTRODUCTION

The History and Evolution of Korean Language Programs in U.S. Colleges and Universities

Hye-Sook Wang
Brown University

1. Background

Korean language education in the United States dates back as early as 1934, when Columbia University first started teaching the language.[1] For over eight decades, Korean language programs in U.S. institutions of higher education have undergone a unique evolution, separating it from Korean programs in other parts of the world. America is not the first foreign land where seeds of Korean language education were planted, but it now has the highest number of schools running Korean (Studies) programs and students learning the language.

According to Cho (2005a, 252), the history of Korean language education overseas is analyzed in three major stages: "The Jump-start Period" (1940-mid 1980s), "The Take-off Period" (mid 1980s-late 1990s), and "The Period of Growth and Expansion" (after the late 1990s). While this division may not accurately reflect historical trends found in the rest of America, it nonetheless provides a very useful general framework for understanding the evolution of Korean language education history overseas. In America, only a handful of schools (viz., the University

1 There have been conflicting reports as to which school (Columbia or University of California at Berkeley) started the Korean language instruction first. According to Columbia University website (http://www.columbia.edu/cu/ckr/about.html) retrieved on October 9, 2014, Columbia offered the first Korean course in 1950. However, the current site (http://www.columbia.edu/cu/ckr/kstudies.html) retrieved on June 3, 2015 says that "In 1934, Dr. Eungpal Yun, Minister of the Korean Methodist Church, taught the first Korean language course at Columbia." Columbia University regrettably could not be included in this book due to the program's inability to participate.

of California-Berkeley, Columbia University, Harvard University, the University of Hawaii, the University of Washington) offered Korean language courses before the 1960s. It was not until the 1980s when Korean language education in America began to enjoy a considerable level of popularity. The period between the mid-1980s and the early 1990s was a critical turning point in the development of Korean language programs in the U.S. A number of external and internal sociopolitical factors contributed to this change.

First, the popularity of the Korean language and subsequent Korean program development were bolstered by Korea's elevated status in the world economy. Various economy-related indexes support this finding of Korea's improved image from a war-torn, impoverished country during the 1950s and 1960s to a country under dictatorships during the 1970s to a country as a rising star in the global stage, along with a fast-growing economy. In addition, Korea was receiving much-needed publicity through the winning of 1988 summer Olympics bid several years before the actual hosting of the event.

Second, enrollment of second-generation Korean American students at colleges and universities notably increased. A great many first-generation Koreans immigrated to the United States during the 1970s, as a result of the Korean government's enactment of Overseas Immigration Law in 1962, which had been accelerated by an unstable and turbulent political situation during the Park regime. America was an ideal destination for many Korean immigrants not only in moving away from frustrating domestic situations but also in finding a better place for their children's education. The emergence of second-generation Korean American students became noticeable as they reached the age of college matriculation towards the mid-1980s and the early 1990s. Korean families were negotiating their children's struggles with identity development and communication issues that many immigrant families typically face.

Third, the promotion of bilingual and foreign language education in America in the government's language education policy spurred the boom of foreign language learning, including Korean. Regardless of the motivations behind such policies, colleges and universities were one of the big beneficiaries. With these factors working favorably towards the development of the Korean language programs by the early 1990s, the establishment of more Korean language programs was further boosted by the rapidly growing popularity of the Korean popular culture called “Hallyu” (the “Korean Wave”), which swept through many countries in Asia and spread to other continents at the end of the 1990s and the early 2000s.

Starting small in a few institutions and in a perpetual state of limited stability for many decades, Korean programs and Korean language education in America now in the early part of the 21st century has a very different look and caliber in terms of schools offering Korean classes and the kinds of students interested in these programs. However, the current state of affairs is a product of many decades of work by all who were involved, and its history and evolution need to be examined in order to better understand the entire process.

2. History and Evolution

2.1. BEGINNING OF THE PROGRAMS

Among the 17 schools whose histories are included in this book, four schools offered small-scale Korean language courses around the 1940s: the University of California-Berkeley (henceforth UCB, 1943), the University of Washington (henceforth UW, 1944), the University of Hawaii (henceforth UH, 1946) and Yale University (1947). UCB became the frontrunner in terms of offering quality Korean language instruction through the devotion and sacrifice of a faculty member named Bong-Youn Choy, who volunteered to teach Korean out of sheer patriotism. Still, the early interest that UW and Yale showed in the Korean language seemed to be derived from America’s changing strategies in world affairs. For example, UW started Korean language instruction as part of the needs of the Navy program and Army Specialized Training Program,[2] and Yale started Korean language instruction with the sponsorship of the federal government, through which Air Force students could take courses.[3]

During the 1950s and 1960s, only Harvard University (1952) and Indiana University (1962) were added to the list of schools offering Korean language courses, which was followed by a recession period in the 1970s.[4] After nearly two decades of inactivity, the 1980s saw an addition of a relatively long list of schools, which opened the door to Korean language instruction for a much wider audience. These schools were the Ohio State University (1981), Stanford University (1984), the University of Pennsylvania (1984), UCLA (1985), the University of Chicago (1985), and the University of California, San Diego (1987).[5] As stated before, the changing sociopolitical situation (i.e. remarkable economic development of South Korea achieved during the 1980s and planned hosting of Seoul Olympics) is likely one of the main reasons for the notable growth of Korean language programs during this period. While each school must have had its own motivation for starting its respective program, growing interest in Korea surely contributed to the rising popularity of the Korean language in America.

The last major group of institutions including Princeton University (1991), Rutgers University (1992), the University of Minnesota (1993),

---

2 Even though Stanford started the regular Korean language course offerings much later, in 1984, Korean was also "taught intermittently as part of the Army Specialized Training Program." (See the Stanford chapter in this book.)

3 Although Yale started early, there was a long intermission until the program officially started in 1990.

4 Brigham Young University is believed to have begun their program during this period but was unable to participate in the project. Cho (2005b) notes that a few other schools (e.g. University of Illinois at Urbana Champaign, University of Kansas, and University of Pittsburgh) also started during the 1970s, and that a total of 11 schools were offering Korean language classes by the early 1970s (p. 54).

5 Although not included in this book, Brown University (1987), George Washington University (1982) and State University of New York at Buffalo (1984) also started during the 1980s. Both GWU and SUNY-Buffalo were invited but were unable to participate.

and SUNY-Binghamton (1994) began their Korean programs in the early 1990s. These schools have a much shorter program history, but they have grown into, at least from the perspective of student demand, major Korean language programs with high enrollments. In the following sections, different aspects of program evolution and development will be discussed in more detail.

2.2. BIRTH OF THE PROGRAMS: KEY PLAYERS AND CONTRIBUTORS

The story of each program tells us that there were always key players at its inception and throughout its development. Many of them worked single-handedly to build their programs despite the enormous challenges, especially considering there was very little understanding of the significance of Korea as a country or of its language, history, and culture in college curricula. Generally, a new program came often from a concerted group effort by concerned students, faculty members teaching courses related to Korea, school administrators (e.g., department chairs), or community leaders or organizations.

The role each party played in establishing their respective program varied from school to school. Several schools (e.g., SUNY-Binghamton, Stanford, UPenn) started their Korean language courses at the initiation of students,[6] presumably of Korean descent, who were trying to connect to their roots by learning Korean. Since students are the most important clients at a university, their voices are less likely to be ignored, and their actions are more likely to be taken seriously by the school administration, although their petition does not necessarily materialize in the form of a new program.

In the case of Indiana University, it was the university administrators who so enthusiastically devoted themselves to starting a Korean program. Indiana's story is even more intriguing and worth noting when the location of the school is taken into consideration. At the time the

6 The story of Duke University, while not included in this book, is an excellent example of how crucial and powerful student initiation can be in starting the program (Kang 2005, p. 487).

program began, and even now, Midwestern (i.e., non East or West coast) towns have not been heavily populated with Korean immigrants and have thereby lacked a strong Korean community. In the early 1960s, when only a handful of schools were running small-scale Korean language programs, Indiana University joined this pioneer group with the vision of dedicated administrators (especially department chair), who understood the importance of the Korean language in the context of East Asian studies. Indiana University also ran the Korean Language Summer Institute (as part of the East Asian Summer Language Institute) for 13 years (1985-99), which was the only college program in North America for students who wanted to focus on the Korean language during the summer.[7] Faculty members who taught at the Indiana summer school are former or current leaders in Korean language education.

Rutgers University is another good example of how school administrators' enthusiastic support was the main driving force behind the successful launch of a program. While both Indiana and Rutgers started their programs with the support of administrators, only Rutgers could take full advantage of its location, which is near a large Korean community, especially in the early development of the program. The role of the Korean community in both establishing and sustaining a Korean program appears to be substantial, as seen in the Rutgers case. The University of Pennsylvania is also a beneficiary of the support of a local community, particularly from notable individuals. Even though in many schools, heritage learners are not the majority in Korean language classes any longer (which will be discussed further in a later section), the community connection created by heritage students is still important.

Faculty members spearheaded and played a pivotal role in starting Korean programs at institutions like Ohio State University, University of California at Berkeley, UCLA, Harvard, and the University of Hawaii. These schools will be discussed again in a separate section. The faculty's role can be critical not only in launching a program but also at a

7 Middlebury College has just established the school of Korean language to begin instruction in the summer of 2015, but in its west coast campus of Mills College.

time of crisis, as so powerfully exemplified in the cases of the University of Washington and Ohio State University. When the program at UW was facing a major crisis of potential discontinuation, "a collaborative letter by 18 faculty members ensured the continuation of the program against the university's 'intent to desert [it] when the Army Specialized Training Program ended'" (quoting Soohee Kim from her chapter). Instead of a collective group, often a single faculty member faced an uphill battle with the university administration, as was the case at OSU. Closing an unviable and unpromising program was one of the most easily conceivable cost-saving measures on the part of the university, and the Korean program was unfortunately one of the targeted eliminations. The author of OSU chapter, Danielle Pyun, wrote "Professor Yung-Hee Kim then stepped forward and fought to sustain the Korean program. She talked to the president and dean of the university in person, pleaded for support from students and the Korean community in Columbus, Ohio, and petitioned the university to keep the Korean program alive. In addition, she flew to Korea, met with government and academic authorities and OSU alumni to drive fundraising efforts, and called for financial support from the Korea Foundation." Having survived through tough times, these programs became even stronger, growing into some of the largest Korean language programs in the nation. As a saying goes, "the land becomes firmer after a rain." Hardship sometime brings a sweet fruit when dealt with right.

2.3. FINANCIAL SUPPORT FOR KOREAN PROGRAMS

Funding unarguably is the most crucial issue related to an institution's ability to start a new program, develop and expand it, or simply sustain it. Each school manages to use various sources of funds, both internal and external, to varying degrees, some more successful than others. Certain schools were fortunate enough to be self-sufficient, while others had to seek external grants diligently for the addition of every single position. Major external grants from which most schools benefited came from Korean government agencies, namely the Korea Foundation (hereafter, KF) and more recently the Academy of Korean Studies (hereafter, AKS), while some schools also received other grants from U.S. agencies (e.g., Ford Foundation, Freeman Foundation). These funding agencies have been particularly instrumental in starting Korean programs at many institutions. The list of beneficiaries is long, and almost every school appears to have received support at some point in their program history, either as seed money or in the form of matching funds.

Since its foundation in 1991, the Korea Foundation was the most influential funding organization for more than two decades in support of faculty positions in various institutions around the world. According to the KF website, 113 faculty positions were established at 76 institutions in 12 countries as of 2014,[8] as it has responded to growing needs, which have in part arisen from the popularity of Korean studies overseas. A good number of these positions were awarded to institutions in America (81 positions in the U.S. and Canada), a few of which were Korean language faculty positions (about 10 percent, either lecturer or tenure-track). OSU created two tenure-track positions with the grants from KF, one of which was for the language program, whose position holder has recently become tenured, and Yale created a lecturer position for the Korean language with KF grants.[9] While the focus of KF's support seems to have shifted to other regions of the world after many years of experience and demonstrable impact in North America, it is still one of the major sources of funds for Korean programs in America.

In more recent years, AKS has assumed some of the tasks for which the KF had been solely responsible for a long time. SUNY-Binghamton has received a grant of $1 million from AKS in 2011 for carrying out various projects. Similarly, the Nam Center for Korean Studies at the University of Michigan has also received a grant of $1 million from

---

8 Retrieved from http://www.kf.or.kr/?menuno=147 on October 20, 2014.

9 Other schools that have been supported exclusively for a Korean language position (i.e. not combined with Korean language and culture or Korean language and literature) include SUNY-Buffalo, University of Michigan, Rice University, University of Maryland-College Park, University of Maryland-Baltimore County, and Pittsburgh University.

AKS, although their piece is not included here. Both awards were made through the Core University Program for Korean Studies (CUPKS) that AKS had launched in 2006. University of Washington is also a two-time winner of this grant.[10] Other recipients include Harvard, UCLA, UCB, and USC. The duration of funding is five years (three initial years and two additional years), and continued distribution of funding is expected through the CUPKS program. However, this program focuses on already established institutions with firm infrastructure for Korean studies[11] and good track records, thereby limiting other institutions in eligibility and accessibility. Moreover, the support for Korean language is minimal since the program's goal is to promote a comprehensive Korean studies program, of which the Korean language is only a part. However, small programs, which need temporary teaching support, can still benefit from visiting lectureship programs that the KF and AKS both offer. Irrespective of how the support money is mostly spent, the KF and AKS are the two biggest and most reliable sources of funds, which have made enormous contributions to not only shaping but also sustaining today's Korean programs in American institutions of higher learning.

Private donors are other external funding source. They are usually successful alumni of the university or community leaders who have vested interests in the university. Notable figures include Sang-yong Nam of the University of Michigan (The Center for Korean Studies was named after him in 2010) and James Joojin Kim of the University of Pennsylvania, who donated $6 million to the school's Korean Studies Program. Dongsoon & Mija Im's donation to UCLA Korean program, in conjunction with the Henry Luce Foundation grant, enabled the university to create a program in Korean Christianity studies. There are other people from the Korean community who played a vital role in helping other Korean programs (e.g., Paul Shinn at the University

10 Data retrieved from http://ksps.aks.ac.kr/default_eng/page_pj_list.php?1dx=105 on October 21, 2014.

11 One of the qualifications is that the applicant institution should have a graduate degree program in Korean studies with more than two full-time Korean studies faculty.

of Washington). These individual gifts have brought real momentum to the development of Korean programs, which can lead to successful applications for other external grants.

Apparently, some schools are more fortunate than others to be able to obtain single or multiple external grants. However, even when schools receive financial support from the KF or AKS, or any other sources of funds, what is crucial is each institution's commitment, support, and careful planning and execution, because it is ultimately their responsibility to continue to develop the program after the funding period is over. Once established with seed money from external grants, a Korean program needs to prove to the school administration that it can grow into a viable program that is deserving of investment over other programs.

2.4. ADMINISTRATIVE STRUCTURE

As the stories show, almost all the Korean language programs included in this book follow the department-based model in terms of administrative structure. The vast majority are housed in East Asian-related departments: East Asian Languages and Literatures (e.g. the University of Hawaii, Ohio State University, Yale University), East Asian Languages and Cultures (e.g. Indiana University, the University of California-Berkeley, University of California at Los Angeles, Rutgers University), East Asian Languages and Civilizations (e.g. the University of Chicago, the University of Pennsylvania, Harvard University), or East Asian Studies (e.g. Princeton University). A few programs find their homes in more broadly named departments such as Asian Languages and Literatures (e.g. the University of Minnesota, the University of Washington). The Binghamton University Korean program is part of the Department of German, Russian, and East Asian Languages, and the Department of Asian and Asian American Studies; Korean language courses at the University of California San Diego are offered through the Department of Literature and the Department of Linguistics. Stanford University is unique in that the Korean program (with other foreign languages) is housed in the Stanford Language Center, which is not affiliated with any academic department. In looking closely into the history of the schools, some Korean programs have gone through quite a metamorphosis (department restructuring, name changes, and so on), while others did not experience a great deal of change since the inception of their programs.

Unlike other foreign language/literature or area studies departments, Korean language programs are usually one of three major parts of an East Asian studies department, along with Chinese and Japanese. However, they are almost always the smallest except for the University of Hawaii and UCLA, which have the two largest Korean programs in the nation, and possibly in the world. At the University of Hawaii, the Korean language program is larger than the Chinese program but smaller than the Japanese program due to a traditionally strong presence of Japanese. At UCLA, the Korean language program "offers the largest number of language courses among all Asian languages" (quoting Sung-Ock Sohn from her chapter). Since these three programs at most schools are housed under the roof of one East Asian studies department (EALL/EALC/EAS), Korean programs are often in competition with Chinese and Japanese programs for allocation of limited resources. A Korean program, as the last addition to a department with long-standing Chinese and Japanese programs, is smaller, has fewer faculty members, and consequently has a weaker voice. From a school administrator's perspective, an East Asian studies department can also be viewed as a single department, without the need to distinguish between three separate programs. Thus, resource allocation is usually determined within the department, and decisions are usually not made in favor of Korean programs.

While the competition within a department is already fierce, competition with other foreign language and literature or area studies programs on campus makes the battle even tougher. Under this added burden, chances of starting a new program are slim, and sustaining an existing program is demanding if the program has to rely solely on institutional funding and support. Nonetheless, the department-based model has various advantages, offering "the best conditions for a unified vision of curriculum development and innovation, integration of the program into that of the department, coordinated administration, reliable financial support, availability of faculty expertise, and overall sustainability" (Bokamba, p. 40). However, it would be at the institution's discretion as to determine where language programs belong, leaving little to no decision-making power to the Korean program itself. Given these circumstances, the key for a Korean program is to find a way to integrate itself on a more even footing with the Chinese and Japanese programs within the department, and to take advantage of all the benefits that the department can provide. In addition, sustaining a good relationship with a Korean studies center or East Asian center would be desirable, if there is any such entity on campus.

2.5. KOREAN LANGUAGE PROGRAM AND THE CENTER FOR KOREAN STUDIES

Despite the fact that the 1970s was a relatively dark period during which few Korean language programs were established, several Korean studies centers were born, including The Center for Korean Studies at the University of Hawaii (1972), The Center for Korean studies at University of California at Berkeley (1979), and The Center for Korean-American Studies and Korean Studies at the University of California at Los Angeles (1979), which later became the Center for Korean Studies (1993). Following these centers, later came the Korea Institute at Harvard (1981), the Center for Korean Research at Columbia (1988), the Nam Center for Korean Studies at the University of Michigan (1997), and the Center for Korean Studies at University of Pennsylvania (1997), which was renamed as the James Joo-Jin Kim Program in Korean Studies in 2011 in honor of his generous gift to the center. The Center for Korean Studies at Binghamton University and the Institute for Korean Studies at Ohio State University are the most recent additions to this list, in 2010 and 2011 respectively.

As we have seen, the beginning of Korean language programs preceded the establishment of Korean studies centers in virtually all cases. For example, the CKS at the University of Hawaii was founded in 1972, nearly 30 years after the first semester of Korean language courses. The same is true for Harvard University, where the first Korean language courses were offered in 1952, while the Korea Institute was founded only some 30 years ago, in 1981. UC-Berkeley's Korean program started in 1943, but it was not until 1979 when CKS was established. It must have been a natural course of events, as the offering of Korean language courses might have prompted the need to develop a full-fledged Korean studies program with the establishment of a center for Korean studies. Generally, the language program that is housed in the department has goals, missions, and an administrative structure different from those of a corresponding area studies center.

Stories suggest that the majority of Korean studies centers follow the "department-center model," although some schools appear to run a smaller-scale center with a different name (e.g., Korea Institute at Harvard, Institute for Korean Studies at OSU). In this 'department-center model,' Korean language instruction is provided through a Korean language program in the relevant department (related to East Asian or Asian studies), with courses on literature and culture in a narrow sense (sometimes including history), whereas other non-language, literature, and culture courses (most often in the social sciences, e.g., sociology, political science, international relations) are offered through various other departments. This is partly due to a departmental identity reflected in its name and structure, as it is usually focused on language, literature, and culture/civilization. Such departments confer either minors or majors in Korean mostly for undergraduate students. Graduate degrees in Korean are awarded from other units, which are the homes of faculty members of other subjects, unless the graduate degree is conferred in Korean linguistics or Korean language education, as in schools like University of Hawaii and UCLA.

Since the degrees are awarded through the departments, the centers play more of an auxiliary role than purely academic one. Faculty members who are hired by their home departments based on their disciplinary training and areas of scholarship but teach Korea-related subjects (e.g., a Korean sociologist from a sociology department) constitute the membership of the center, unless they are hired directly by the center. Depending on funding sources, they can be jointly appointed by their home departments as well as by the CKS due to their regional focus on Korea, or they simply are center members while holding full FTEs in their home departments.

Korean studies centers share similar missions and functions, regardless of size. They promote all aspects of Korean studies and function as Korean studies hubs for intellectual exchange and collaboration for affiliated scholars. Specifically, they host visiting scholars and a myriad of Korea-related activities and events (e.g., film festivals, colloquia, seminars, conferences) independent of but occasionally in conjunction with the department. A center can also play the role of a liaison, connecting the various sectors in government, society, and community with academia. Some centers (e.g., University of Hawaii CKS, University of Washington CKS) publish Korean studies journals. More importantly, centers provide necessary support for faculty and students. As such, the presence of CKS can significantly promote Korean studies in general, and centralization of resources makes planning and execution far easier and more effective. A center can also play a significant role in submitting funding applications, adding more weight and premium to their qualifications. Additionally, since a department is usually more structurally rigid and limited in its activities, the center can go beyond. Moreover, given the organizational structure of most departments to which Korean programs belong, resources should be shared among the member programs of the department, whereas centers are concentrated only on Korea. The fact that CKS can host more visiting scholars from various disciplines than the department normally can is also an added advantage of having a center.[12]

Among the schools whose stories are heard in this book, most big programs have Center for Korean Studies. What is also noted is that

---

12 Policies admitting visiting scholars vary from school to school, and from department to department, which need to be investigated further. However, the capacity of the department hosting visiting scholars in any given year is generally limited.

the bigger programs with centers receive and take advantage of grants repeatedly. A good example is the Academy of Korean Study's Core University Program for Korean Studies (CUPKS) grant that was mentioned earlier in the financial support section. While it may be seen as a stretch to claim that the presence of CKS is a necessary condition for successfully obtaining external grants, especially those from the Korean government, it nonetheless would be reasonable to say that those schools with CKS certainly have an advantage and a better chance for receiving grants based on these records. This reality unfortunately deepens the phenomenon of "the rich getting richer and the poor getting poorer." It is not clear what comes first — big programs garnering more grants or more grants making the program bigger — but it looks as if CKS is a prerequisite for becoming a major Korean program.

Each institution adopts the right structure to fit their institutional goals and meet their needs, but establishing a close relationship and maintaining good communication between the department and the center is essential for the success of a Korean studies program in any institution. Stories indicate that at some schools, the communication between the two units is minimal and that the bond is not as strong as expected. Also, schools whose Korean language program heads are faculty members of a center seem to get more deeply involved in the center life than those schools whose Korean program heads are not professorial faculty and/or not affiliated with the center.

Needless to say, the relationship between a school's Korean language program and Korean studies center is crucial for developing a strong and viable Korean studies program. As Sohn (2011) compellingly argues, language is a basic but indispensable tool for area studies research, and thus language training is a prerequisite for Korean studies. It can also be an object of research at the same time, making it a subfield of general Korean studies. In the same way that students of Korean studies need language training as their foundation, students learning Korean language also need to learn more about Korean history, culture, and society to make their language learning complete and more effective. In this respect, language learning and content learning are in a reciprocal relationship, complementing each other, as Korean language program and Korean studies program rely on each other to create a synergy. Moreover, Korean language programs without content integration of Korean studies programs are not only limited in their potential development but also will likely encounter more challenges during times of trial.

2.6. THE BIG FOUR KOREAN LANGUAGE PROGRAMS: THEIR SUCCESS STORIES AND LESSONS TO BE LEARNED[13]

There is little debate that the University of Hawaii at Manoa (UHM henceforth), UC-Berkeley (UCB), UCLA, and the University of Washington (UW) have run the biggest Korean (language) programs in the United States, leading the field. Understanding the current state of affairs and the driving forces behind the success of these programs will shed some light into the development of other programs and thus warrants further examination.

UHM, UCB, and UW all started Korean instruction during the 1940s, far earlier than most other schools as pioneers of the field, each of them having nearly or over seven decades of history. Whereas it took many decades for these three schools to grow into what they are today, UCLA quickly emerged as the largest Korean program within a short period of time since the program's foundation in 1985. Despite a surprisingly late start compared to other large programs discussed in this section, UCLA took full advantage of its location and support from the university.

Location is one of the main reasons and common denominator for the success of these programs, although UW seems to be somewhat different from the other three (UHM, UCB, UCLA) in the sense that Seattle is not as heavily populated by Korean immigrants as Hawaii, Los Angeles, or San Francisco and that UW serves more non-heritage learners than

13 Due to the school's inability to participate in the project, other big programs (e.g. BYU, Columbia, University of Michigan) are not included for discussion here. These schools are chosen for further discussion based on a number of criteria: overall student enrollment, presence of CKS, number of courses offered, major/minor in Korean, graduate program, tenure track faculty positions, and so on.

heritage learners. However, they have all benefited tremendously from being near large populations of Korean immigrants. In these schools, large enrollments in Korean classes are direct reflections of the Korean American population in these areas. Hawaii was the first U.S. state where the first cohort of official immigrants from Korea landed in early 1900. Los Angeles and San Francisco are two other major destinations of Korean immigration whose Korean populations are the highest in the nation.

The fact that these are all state universities also places them in advantageous positions in terms of enrollment, since the vast majority of Korean classes have been taken by Korean Americans. Unlike private colleges and universities, which are generally smaller in size, state schools serve far more students, and a substantial portion of them are Korean American students. Even though these programs have had to withstand many obstacles and a series of uncertain times, especially due to heavy reliance on state budgets, their proximity to areas filled with Korean populations must have been hugely advantageous for the growth of the program. According to the authors' reports, annual student enrollments for Korean language programs in the academic year 2010-2011 were over 1,000 at UCLA, 950 at UHM, 668 at UW, and 464 at UCB (which was increased to 635 in 2013-2014). While enrollments fluctuate to some degree at UW and UCB year to year, it continues to grow at UHM, exceeding 1,000 during the 2011-2012 academic year (1051 to be exact).

The importance of the location of these schools in terms of growth becomes even more salient when looking at the case of Indiana University. The IU Korean program is the first program opened among the schools in the East-Midwest, established purely by the efforts of the department. It has been serving mainly non-heritage learners. The program was forced into a dormant stage from 1971 to 1982 and was on the verge of collapsing more than once during the program's history due to lack of enrollment. The author of the Indiana chapter, Hyo Sang Lee, acknowledges that the IU Korean program started based on "legitimate disciplinary and cultural value, not as a demographically motivated service," but the school lacked the "pushing power of the demographic base of the Korean community and Korean heritage learners," unlike some of the bigger programs.

UW stands very strong with respect to the number of Korean majors and minors the program produces. The growth has been truly remarkable. According to Soohee Kim's report in this book, UW has produced a significant number of Korean majors and minors in the last decade, and the number is rapidly increasing. Six majors between 1987 and 2006 have soared to more than 30 majors and minors in 2011. What is also notable is that UW Korean program is claimed to be the third largest program serving non-heritage learners.[14] UHM, since its establishment of the B.A. program, is also sizeable in terms of undergraduate majors and minors. As of fall 2014, it has 58 Flagship-track students and 69 regular-track students.

As for training graduate students, UHM and UCLA are the two powerhouses in the Korean language and linguistics. UHM has already produced 25 PhDs and 14 MAs since 1987, and UCLA trained 14 PhD students in Korean linguistics alone since 1996. Undoubtedly, the presence of two distinguished scholars of Korean linguistics and Korean language education, Ho-min Sohn at UHM and Sung-Ock S. Sohn at UCLA, made this possible. UHM currently enrolls 33 graduate students (18 PhDs and 15 MAs), and UCLA has 30 as of fall 2014, making them the largest graduate programs in Korean language and linguistics in the nation and maybe in the world. The graduates of these two schools have been obtaining the majority of positions in Korean language programs elsewhere. Among the four giants, UCB has yet to establish Korean majors and graduate program, as it only confers minors in Korean. As UCB chapter writer Kijoo Ko notes, it is unfortunate that such a major program like UCB does not have a full-blown degree program. The fact that the Korean program director position has never been a tenure-track professor position might have to do with this situation. As

14 At the time of this writing, UW enrolls approximately 100 non-heritage learners and 20 heritage learners in the first year class. The other two big programs that register high non-heritage enrollments are BYU and University of Minnesota.

a matter of fact, while the two programs (UHM and UCLA) are headed by professorial faculty members, as mentioned in the earlier section, two other programs (UCB and UW) are directed by non-professorial faculty members. Whether the status of faculty members responsible for directing or coordinating the program has any impact on the general development of the program remains to be further discussed.

Another common feature that these programs share is the existence of a Korean studies center, which seem to suggest that the role of the center is crucial to the success of the Korean program in general (the relationship between the two units is already addressed in 2.5.)

As discussed, the success of these programs can be explained by a myriad of factors, anything from funding to desirable locations. However, one conclusion is certain. At the core of their success are dedicated faculty members. Ho-min Sohn at the University of Hawaii began his career as an assistant professor in 1972 and is still working tirelessly after more than four decades of service; Michael Rogers served for UCB for 34 years from 1953 to 1987; Peter Lee at UCLA from 1987 to 2007; and Fred Lukoff (1977-1989) and James Palais (1968-2001) at the University of Washington.[15] While some of them were more involved in the language program than others because of their expertise, they not only laid the foundation of their programs but also nurtured them during their tenures. These Korean programs would not be what they are today without these dedicated individuals, their insight and vision, tireless work, unparalleled enthusiasm, and enormous devotion. Their legacy continues.

2.7. NOT-SO-BIG BUT SOLID: STORIES OF OTHER SCHOOLS

Whether big or small, there are common patterns in the history of every program. However, it is also true that each program was developed under its own environment and presents its own unique characteris-

15 Although not included in the four big schools, Edward Wagner of Harvard (1958-1995) and Chong-Sik Lee of the University of Pennsylvania also deserve well-earned recognition.

tics. Indiana University is an interesting example in that the program was borne out of the American administrators' genuine interest in and perception of Korea as an integral part of East Asian studies, which led to the institution's full commitment to the program without help from any external funding resources. Furthermore, securing a tenure-track position in the Korean language in the early 1990s was very rare and is also telling. IU also separates itself from other major programs in that non-heritage learners far outnumbered heritage learners from the beginning of the program, which is not a result of the recent changes in student demographics that almost all Korean programs are seeing.

Like IU, the University of Minnesota is another institution that enrolls a very high number of non-heritage learners, a trend that has never changed since the program's establishment in 1993.[16] While the two giant programs, Defense Language Institute and Brigham Young University, almost exclusively serve non-heritage populations for specific purposes (DLI for military personnel and BYU for religious people), Minnesota stands unique in that a significant portion of these non-heritage learners were comprised of adopted Koreans, especially towards the beginning. "Minnesota is home to the largest Korean adoptee population in the United States," according to a scholar cited by the program director, Hangtae Cho. The vision of the Korean language program director and the department chairperson at the beginning made the current success of Minnesota Korean program possible, as they took full advantage of their geographical location. The program's strategic decision and early efforts in building curriculum and developing instructional materials helped the program not only sustain itself but grow surprisingly quickly, even when the number of adopted Korean learners drastically decreased (in proportion to other groups of learners) in recent years. The program was already equipped with tools needed to adjust to instructing different groups of non-heritage learners with diverse

16 While graduate students or part-time instructors first taught the Korean language through the School of Continuing Education in 1993, the Korean program was officially established when it became part of the Department of Asian Languages and Literatures in 2000.

backgrounds. Minnesota recorded 385 students in Korean language courses during the 2011-2012 academic year, of which 90 percent was non-heritage learners.

Harvard (1952), Yale (1990), Princeton (1991), Stanford (1984), Chicago (1985), and UPenn (1984) are all prestigious private universities in the nation. With the exception of Harvard and Yale, which started Korean language instruction much earlier, others did not start their programs until the mid 1980s and early 1990s. Also, Harvard and Yale had two great figures, who grandfathered their respective Korean programs; Harvard owed much to Edward Wagner, as Yale did to Samuel Martin. Other schools did not rely as heavily on any single faculty who was as influential as Wagner or Martin (the author of the Harvard chapter Sang-suk Oh divided Harvard's Korean language program history as the "Wagner period" and "Post-Wagner period," reflecting Wagner's influence in the program). Rather, these other programs were built gradually by a number of faculty members. These schools are generally smaller than many state universities (especially the ones discussed earlier) in terms of not only the entire student body but also the students enrolled in Korean courses. UPenn is the largest of all in this cohort, enrolling around 180 students in Korean classes annually over the past several years; the number for other schools ranges from 55 to 135, placing Harvard near the high ceiling and Yale near the bottom, with Chicago and Princeton in the middle group (between 100 and 120) on average.

What is notable about this group is that many of these Korean language programs are directed by non-tenured/tenure track faculty and have a mutually supportive relationship with a Korean studies program through other entities, like the Center for Korean Studies. The size of the programs varies from one tenure-stream faculty member teaching a few content courses in his/her disciplinary expertise (usually literature and culture) to several faculty members covering a wide array of Korea-related topics including literature, culture, film, history and society. However, the fact that all of these programs provide high-quality language training with the students through a well-established Korean language program suggests that Korean studies in these schools have a solid grounding and infrastructure for more potential growth.

Ohio State University also claims a special place in educating students learning Korean. OSU started the program in 1991 and serves 120 students in any given quarter. It offers non-language courses on Korea through other academic units, namely the Institute of Korean Studies, which functions similarly to a center. A few dedicated faculty members (e.g., Yung-Hee Kim and Chan Park) who are not language specialists steadily built the OSU Korean program. Being one of few schools that were able to establish a tenure-track professor position in the Korean language with the funding support of the Korea Foundation, the OSU Korean program seems to be well poised to further grow, especially after the tenure of the Korean program head. Professor Y. Kim's departure for UHM was a major loss for OSU, but the program has become more stable.

Even though somewhat overshadowed by other giant UC schools, the Korean program at the University of California at San Diego (UCSD hereafter) is by no means small. Like many institutions, it went through a phase of uncertainty after the program's establishment in 1989, but it became quite stable after the arrival of the current program director in 2000. The Korean program serves 220-250 students per quarter on average and awards graduate degrees (both MA and PhD) in Korean literature. Two non-language tenure-track/tenured faculty positions are fully or partially funded by the Korea Foundation, which accelerated the formation of Korean studies on this campus, in conjunction with Korean Studies Initiative launched in 2010.

Similar to UCSD, Rutgers University (Rutgers hereafter) is also a big state university located in an area where there is a strong Korean community, thus serving a large number of students of Korean descent. Rutgers' Korean program awards a minor and a graduate certificate in Korean. Like UCLA, Rutgers began its program surprisingly late in 1992, considering its location and demands, but it demonstrates much potential to become a major Korean studies program and a mecca of Korean language teacher training as it began an accelerated teacher certification program and a Master of Arts in Teaching (MAT) in Korean in 2008.

Binghamton University (SUNY-Binghamton) is a showcase example of how a program can develop quickly within such a short period of time. Starting its Korean language program as late as 1994 and Korean studies program in 2000, the program now offers a minor (2006), major (2010) and an MA degree (2011) in Korean. The successful funding from three major external grants, including one of each from the Korea Foundation and the Academy of Korean Studies, the willingness of institution's administrators to expand the Korean program, and a faculty member's excellent leadership were the main contributing factors for its success.

3. Eight Decades of Korean Language Education in America: Looking Back for Looking Ahead

When looking back at the 80 years of Korean language instruction history through the stories of 17 U.S. higher education represented in this book, it is clear that the program has developed by leaps and bounds, but most dramatically since the 1980s. In the following, four major events are highlighted and discussed in more detail for the purpose of providing a broader context of the field.

First and foremost, quantitative growth in terms of the sheer number of programs that offer Korean language courses as well as overall student enrollment should be addressed. According to various sources (R. King 2006, H. Sohn 2011), more than 100 colleges and universities in the U.S. currently offer Korean language courses.[17] The overall student enrollments in Korean courses in U.S. colleges have also seen a dramatic increase over the past 10 years or so. The most recent MLA report released in February 2015 shows that the total enrollment in Korean has gone up from 8,449 in 2009 to 12,229 in 2013, showing 44.5 percent

---

17 Precise statistics are unavailable, but Sohn (2011) claims that the number is approximately 130 to 140.

increase. The increase between 2002 and 2006 was 37.1 percent, while that of 2006-09 was 19.1 percent. This designated Korean as the highest language increase and elevated the status of Korean as the 13th most popular language by enrollment among all reported foreign languages. However, the size and caliber of Korean programs differ, depending on several factors. Some have long-established programs that offer a minimum three-year sequence of language instruction (beginning-intermediate-advanced) on a regular basis with a solid curriculum. Others are still in the early phases of development and are attempting to gain necessary internal support from their institutions, from the Korean government agencies through external grants, and from the surrounding Korean communities where their institutions are located. Starting a new program from scratch poses various challenges, but developing and sustaining an existing program is equally challenging, and this has been a major concern for many schools throughout the evolutionary process.

Another notable achievement was the development of instructional materials. More specifically, it is the launching and completion of a Korean language textbook development project, led by Ho-min Sohn and sponsored by the Korean Language Education and Research Center at the University of Hawaii. This was a long-term project over the period of more than 10 years (1994-2006),[18] funded by the generous support of the Korea Foundation. A total of 20 textbooks for various Korean language courses were developed, including five years of a Korean language instruction sequence, and many of them are widely used in various Korean programs in U.S. institutions. A survey conducted by the American Association of Teachers of Korean in 2007-2008 shows that approximately 75-80 percent of participating schools in the survey adopted the *Integrated Korean* series developed through this project.[19] The adaptation rate was highest for first-year and second-year courses. Before this project, the options for textbook selections for teachers were

18 *Korean Language in Culture and Society*, the last book in the series, was published in 2006.

19 Information retrieved from http://www.aatk.org/www/html/textbooks.html

extremely limited. Teachers were left with few choices but to use textbooks published by Korean universities (with Korea University, Sogang University, Yonsei University being the most popular three) written for learners in Korea. Lack of pedagogically sound materials specifically geared towards learners in U.S. universities had long been an obstacle for effective instruction for seasoned or novice teachers alike.

First-year (Beginning) and second-year (Intermediate) textbooks have gone through a revision process in recent years, after more than ten years of publication of the first edition. Issues that were raised in the first edition were addressed in the second edition; the second editions of the beginning textbooks were published in 2010, and the second editions of the intermediate textbooks were published in 2012. Even though a few other textbooks are available in the market (e.g., *College Korean*, *Modern Korean: An Intermediate Reader, You Speak Korean* and others) for the first two years, advanced level textbooks (viz., for fourth- and fifth-year courses) are even more limited. Because of this, the *Integrated Korean* sequence makes an even deeper contribution to upper-level instruction for those who choose to use this book. There is no doubt that the field of Korean language education has made an enormous step forward with the completion of this ambitious project. Its impact on Korean language education in America is significant, although one may argue that the domination of one textbook in the entire field is not desirable.

The establishment of the American Association of Teachers of Korean (hereafter AATK) in 1994 was a major event in Korean language education in America. Despite the fact that the field was growing rapidly, with more schools offering Korean language instruction and consequently more teachers hired, there was no professional organization for Korean language teachers. The birth of AATK truly advanced Korean language education in America to the next level through scholarship, networking, collaboration, and advocacy.[20] First and foremost, promoting

20 Historical background of the foundation of the AATK can be found in "Presidents' Panel: Reflections upon 10 years of AATK History" in H.Wang (Ed.), *Korean Language in America*, Vol. 10 (2005), pp. 119-139.

research and publishing it through its journal, the *Korean Language in America*, was a worthy and tangible contribution to the field. It started as proceedings of an annual conference but changed into a collection of selected papers through peer reviews, then finally evolved into the official journal of the organization in 2008, beginning with volume 13. Another major breakthrough is made with the publication venue, which has remained as a local publication, but the Pennsylvania State University Press has become the official publisher of the journal starting in early 2015 with volume 19.[21]

Second, as the sole professional organization for Korean language education in the United States for college teachers,[22] AATK has increased the visibility of Korea and has advocated the Korean language as well as its teachers in America. AATK was invited to join the National Council of Organizations of Less Commonly Taught Languages (NCOLCTL) as an organizational member from the beginning, and it successfully established the Korean Language Special Interest Group (SIG) of the American Council on the Teaching of Foreign Languages (ACTFL) in 2006. Both the NCOLCTL and ACTFL are the two largest foreign language advocacy organizations in America.

Third, annual workshops and conferences have been at the heart of teachers' ability to learn from other colleagues, update their knowledge of the most recent language education theories and practices, exchange information, and network with fellow educators. AATK has successfully held 18 annual conferences so far (as of 2014) without any interruption since its foundation in 1994 except for one year (1998), when only professional workshop was held due to a funding issue. Together with the efforts of leadership and members of the organization, continued financial support from the Korea Foundation again made this possible.

---

21 Since it turned into a peer-reviewed referred journal, Hye-Sook Wang (Brown University) has served as the editor-in-chief until 2012, when the current editor-in-chief Susan Strauss (Pennsylvania State University) took over the job.

22 The membership is open to secondary school teachers, and the group is represented by one executive board member. However, the overwhelming majority of the membership is college teachers.

Moreover, psychological benefits, though invisible and implicit, of the existence of this organization for the teachers cannot be simply put into words. Many teachers who felt isolated and marginalized in their respective schools and programs before joining AATK found others with whom they identified and were subsequently able to correspond and connect. AATK had approximately 50 members in the beginning,[23] but it has grown into an organization serving more than 200 registered and active members within 20 years. The place it holds and the role it plays for Korean language education in America will become only more important in the years to come.

Lastly, creating Standards for Korean Language Education is another major endeavor that is well underway in the field and important for AATK in particular. The project was launched in 2008, when the task force team was first formed after the annual conference of the AATK at SUNY Binghamton, and has been in progress since. The Korean language is one of the twelve foreign languages taught in America for which there was a developing framework for national standards. The "Standards for Korean Language Learning" document was published as a chapter of the *Standards for Foreign Language Learning in the 21st Century*, an outcome of the work that the task force team had completed. Based on this basic framework, several groups of teachers are currently developing a standard curriculum for all levels (first- through sixth-year classes, and a separate heritage class), aiming at a 2015 completion date for level-specific sample lessons. This project is overseen by three former presidents of the AATK (Hye-Sook Wang at Brown, Hyo Sang Lee at Indiana, Young-mee Yu Cho at Rutgers) and two OPI Korean language certificate testers (Sahie Kang at DLI, Hee-Sun Kim at Stanford). Progress reports have been made, and the outcomes of the projects-in-progress have been shared in AATK annual meetings at Stanford University in 2012, at Michigan State University in 2013, and at Boston University in 2014, soliciting members' feedback and

23 According to 1994 AATK directory, 88 members were listed but many of them are believed to be inactive.

suggestions to be reflected in the ensuing development process. Once this is completed, a new milestone will be set in teaching the Korean language in America.

4. Looking to the Future: Challenges and Prospects[24]

While each Korean program started and evolved within its own unique environment, the challenges and issues that each Korean program has faced and will face do not seem to differ greatly. Unresolved issues still remain, while new issues are emerging as a result of the changes in teaching environments. Some issues are more general in nature and can be applied across the programs, while others are more program-specific. These will be discussed from both non-pedagogical and pedagogical perspectives.

Funding by all means is at the top of non-pedagogical issues, especially for state schools, which rely mostly on the state budget and are thus vulnerable to economic conditions in the country and the world. The overall stability of any Korean program is dependent on funding to a significant extent, and breaking a vicious cycle may not come across easily. Lacking or insufficient funding adversely affects all developmental aspects of the programs - establishment, growth, and sustainment, which are intricately interconnected. Lack of funding results in a lack of faculty positions, especially tenure-track professorial positions, which in turn result in limited numbers of Korea-related content course offerings and ultimately the instability of the Korean language program. This situation eventually leads to fewer students in Korean classes, difficulties in establishing Korean degree programs, and challenges for the training and production of future Korean specialists in the long term. A lack of professorial positions will also limit the probability that Korean specialists will be chosen to serve in powerful positions such as

24 In writing this section, the author shares views expressed in S. Sohn's chapter on UCLA in this book, and those in H. Sohn's paper (2011).

department chairpersonships, positions that indeed could exert strong influence in making important decisions regarding Korea.

While most programs have been heavily relying on Korean government funding not only to build the foundation of but also to advance their programs, the future of funding is uncertain, especially in light of the fact that the KF has reduced the level of support for American institutions in recent years. Moreover, the total amount of fund that the KF has been operating with is considerably smaller when compared to similar funding agencies for Chinese (e.g., Confucius Institute) or Japanese (e.g., Japan Foundation), which support similar tasks, as shown in the table below. This means that any institution that needs an external funding will have to compete fiercely. However, the creation of faculty positions with internal funding from institutions can hardly be expected and would result in an uphill battle in spite of the rising recognition of Korea on the world stage, and the prospects do not seem to be all that positive. Alternative sources of funds should be sought, and new strategies should be tried.

Table 1. Comparison of Main Funding Agencies among China, Japan, and Korea for Similar Tasks (Source: *Donga Daily*, May 24, 2014)

	Korea Foundation (Korea)	**Confucius Institute (China)**	**Japan Foundation (Japan)**
Year of Establishment	1991-	2004-	1972-
Annual Budget (approximate)	35 million (2013)	225 million (2012)	242 million (2011)
Overseas Offices	7 offices in 6 countries	Over 400 CIs (in colleges) in over 100 countries, over 500 CIs (in elementary, middle and high schools) as of 2012	21 overseas offices in 19 countries

As discussed before, community is one invaluable source of support for many schools. However, the corporate world is another source that has been missing in this picture to date, as pointed out by King (2006). While many Korean companies (e.g., Samsung, LG, Hyundai, Kia) have become truly global companies whose names have become household names in America, their participation in and contribution to the promotion of Korean studies in a tangible and consistent manner has been virtually non-existent, with a few exceptions such as the University of Chicago program supported by the SK group, and Stanford University supported by Tong Yang Group. Although it was to their credit that these global companies made very positive impacts on improving the image of Korea, which eventually led to drawing many more students to Korean classes, more active involvement from the corporate sector has yet to be seen.

Second, securing financial, administrative, and moral support from each institution is crucial. As we have seen in stories from several schools, administrators with vision and devotion proved to be extremely valuable. For those who do not have such luck, we need to educate departmental personnel and school administrators to better understand the role Korea plays on the world stage, the uniqueness of Korean culture that distinguishes it from Chinese and Japanese cultures, and the necessity of and demand for the balanced development of Korean studies in a given department. In fact, the majority of school administrators does not seem to be very knowledgeable about Korea and are reluctant to invest any resources into Korean studies. More serious effort should be made to inform and educate the administrators who can make important decisions for Korean studies programs. Two examples prove that this strategy would bear significant fruits: The heads of the Korean programs at SUNY-Binghamton and the University of Minnesota managed to travel to Korea (Binghamton) and to the KF Washington Office (Minnesota) with their school administrators and subsequently garnered grants from AKS and KF.[25] As the saying goes, "seeing is believing,"

25 Although not included in this book, Emory University is another excellent ex-

and introducing Korea to high administration firsthand can make a huge difference. Once such momentum is achieved and investment is made, further development in the form of matching funds and sustained support from the school will follow.

Third, a closer collaboration between the Korean language program and the Center for Korean Studies (Korean studies program) is pivotal and thus strongly recommended. As discussed in section 4, the majority of the major Korean language programs have a Korean studies center. According to some reports, the establishment of a center dates much later than the beginning of Korean language instruction, which seems to suggest that the success of a language program is at the foundation of further expansion of Korean studies. Language can be a tool but it is not simply an instrument itself. It can provide a solid foundation for studying a nation's history, culture, and society by enabling students to read original materials written in Korean as well. Increasing opportunities for engagement in more language-related activities (e.g. lectures by guest speakers who are linguists, organize small workshop for language teachers, etc.) is also possible in centers.

Fourth, several authors discussed the role of students and student organizations on their respective campuses for the promotion of Korea and Korean studies. Students' participation in the beginning and development of the Korean program proved to be effective, as discussed before. This might be particularly true at schools that have few to no Korean faculty members. In fact, many stories in this book reveal that a collective movement by an active and enthusiastic group of students was powerful enough to convince the school to offer new Korean language courses and eventually led to the official beginning of the program. On the one hand, it is important that each faction — faculty members, students, administrators, and community leaders — plays its role the best it can. On the other hand, networking, orchestrating, and collaborating with these people is key to the successful development of a program.

---

ample that proves the effectiveness of this strategy. The newly established Korean program is growing remarkably well with the strong support of the university's president, who visited Korea before the program's establishment.

There are many pedagogical issues that the field of Korean language education in general and the Korean language program in particular will most likely face. Heritage and non-heritage learner issues have been daunting for many Korean programs whose classes were dominated by heritage learners before the numbers of non-heritage learners began noticeably increasing. As the Korean language has become less of a language for heritage learners and more a language for non-heritage learners, responding to an ever-increasingly diverse student population is becoming a serious challenge. Some schools were able to find means to deal with this situation more effectively than others by implementing the so-called "two-track system," which separates the two groups of learners according to their ethnic and linguistic backgrounds, thus accommodating their differing needs. UCLA pioneered this system in the early stage of its program in the 1990s, and more programs are adopting it once staffing needs are met. Whether or not this system achieved the anticipated results is worthy of a close investigation, but it is considered the most viable solution to the challenge at the present. Moreover, the issue of what to do with programs that do not have sufficient teaching staff to run a two-track system still remains. There are clear indications that the number of non-heritage learners will continue to rise (many authors in this book report on this change and the results of the survey that the author of this introduction conducted in 2009 and 2015 also support this), and the Korean programs will be further pushed to shift from heritage instruction to non-heritage instruction, not only in instructional methods and materials but also in program management.

Related to this issue, the diversification of students' background appears to be a major change that will require due attention from the programs. As already stated, the learner profiles used to be rather simple and homogenous until about 10 to 15 years ago but have become far more complex. The first visible difference is manifested through the overall increase of non-heritage learners and decrease of heritage-learners. However, when these two groups are closely examined, there are more complexities, especially regarding instruction. Heritage learners present various differing needs depending on their family backgrounds/environment, the degree of their exposure to Korean language and culture, and motivation before they come to college. As third-generation Korean Americans enter Korean studies, there are more heritage learners who are no different than non-heritage learners from a linguistic perspective. Moreover, some schools (e.g., Stanford, Princeton) report that they are seeing increasing numbers of international students, many of whom had left Korea before they entered middle or high school, a trend detected recently at a number of prestigious private universities. While they are native Korean speakers, they certainly need to work on achieving superior level Korean skills (especially in formal or academic writing) and to be able to discuss sociopolitical issues that are pertinent to Korean society. Courses will have to be developed to address the needs of this group of students as well. The Princeton Korean program, for instance, does address this issue deftly and sets a nice example in this respect.[26]

In addition, non-heritage learners are also from various ethnic and cultural backgrounds. Asian Americans — both from East Asia (especially China) and South Asia — make up a big portion of the non-heritage learner group, thanks to the influence of the "Hallyu." There are now virtually all kinds of hyphenated-Americans, whom the programs rarely saw in the past, including Latino Americans and African Americans. According to the Korea Foundation's "Global Hallyu Data 2013," which was posted on its website in January 2014, the number of "Hallyu" fans in the world has reached 9.3 million and "Hallyu" fan clubs nearly 1,000 (compared to 6.7 million fans and 783 fan clubs of 2012). Of particular note is that America ranked second with 1.25 million fans, following Asia and Oceania with 6.8 million in terms of "Hallyu" fans. On the other hand, as for fan clubs, America ranked at the top with 464, leaving Asia and Oceania behind with 234. What is also notable is the incredible growth of "Hallyu" fans and fan clubs in Africa and Middle East; the number of fans tripled and fan clubs almost doubled. While still small in number compared to other groups, half-Koreans or 'Hapa students' from

26 Hi-Sun Kim (2013) discusses the impacts of a growing number of Korean international students on Korean language teaching in U.S. universities.'

interracial marriages and adopted Koreans are added to this group.[27] It would be quite challenging to develop courses and programs to meet the needs of these learners from very different backgrounds, but it is a reality that every program must learn to manage. There are also increasing number of students who study two Asian languages (e.g., Korean and Japanese or Korean and Chinese).

Although more relevant to bigger programs than smaller programs, an imbalance between the program's capacity and the growing demand can cause a serious discord. The fact that more students are interested in and willing to learn Korean is very encouraging. However, if teaching staff and other resources cannot catch up with growing student interest, temporary solutions are sought by either increasing the course cap to accommodate more students (which is not ideal or desirable) or by forcing the program turn students away. Program heads are forced to make strategic decisions on perceived long-term goals and short-term benefits. High enrollment caps jeopardize the quality of instruction and place more burden on instructors, as more students also mean more work for the teachers. The overburdening of faculty members will, in all likelihood, adversely affect both their teaching and the students' learning at the same time. Placing over 20 students in a language class, as some schools reported, is detrimental to optimal learning. Institutions who have large graduate programs — though not necessarily a Korean program — and/or a Korean studies center find themselves in a better position than those who do not, because they have a better pool of personnel resources. Hiring someone who is not professionally trained to teach language courses entails its own risks, but it can be an alternative when a long-term solution is not viable. In fact, quite a few schools in reality rely on graduate TAs to run the program. Ultimately, teaching assistantships can be more readily obtained than regular positions.

Enrollment issues in upper level classes — mostly third-year through fifth-year courses but even in second-year courses at some schools — is another serious problem that concerns many program heads. The

27 For a detailed discussion on biracial Koreans, see Wang & Liu (2014).

impact of "Hallyu," discussed in the previous paragraph, was further accelerated by Psy's enormous popularity over the past a few years. In addition, many schools' language requirement policies have contributed to high enrollments in the first two years of instruction.[29] Any noticeable enrollment changes for the upper-level courses, however, have not been detected. Although generally upper-level classes are usually much smaller than the lower-level classes in any foreign language, and students' motivations for studying Korean differ (as do students' reasons for discontinuing after a certain level), a healthy upper-level enrollment could mean a better prospect for Korean studies. This is closely related to the establishment of a Korean major or minor. It would be undeniable that producing Korean specialists is critical for the advancement of Korean studies in the long run, and equipping them with a superior level Korean language proficiency is a pre-requisite for this. At present, the Korean Flagship Program run by the University of Hawaii since 2002 (Certificate Program, B.A. Program, and M.A. Program) is at the forefront of training students to achieve professional-level proficiency in the Korean language and turn them into Korean specialists, but more for practical jobs than for academia. Their curriculum is geared toward accomplishing this goal.[29]

Other challenges also exist. Korean program heads are constantly faced with situations that require them to make strategic decisions. Dealing with staff shortages is one such example. Given limited staff, some schools turned to Graduate Student Instructors (GSIs) or TAs, as UC-Berkeley and UCSD did, while other schools utilized part-time instructors (e.g., Rutgers). While not an ideal situation by any means, these schools are fortunate to be aided by TAs. A new TA support program proposed by the Korean Foundation, partnering with AATK, turned out to be an effective alternative until the Korea Foundation decided to discontinue the program as of 2015. The program awarded

28 Language requirement policies vary from school to school and usually consist of one to two years of study.

29 For detailed information on the Korean Flagship Program, readers are advised to visit their homepage at http://koreanflagship.manoa.hawaii.edu.

two to three schools each year on average, providing $10,000 to $12,000 in funds for each school. Renewal was also allowed when continued needs were justified and there was a satisfactory track record. Although this TA support program only provided temporary support for a year or two, it gave much-needed leverage to the recipients to build upon the goals of their program (either to add a new course, open a new section, or start a program completely from scratch). As a former recipient, OSU's testimonial is worth noting. Some schools also successfully applied to the AKS visiting lectureship (e.g., Indiana University) or the Fulbright foreign language TA program (e.g., Stanford). These are helpful in the absence of any permanent solutions but not problem-free either.

Using advanced graduate TAs for teaching content-oriented courses of their expertise would be a practical solution that can be implemented with less money and with minimal guidance from the program head. If implemented well, this option can be a win-win situation for both Korean programs and candidates. The TAs would gain some necessary teaching experience for their future careers while sharing their expertise and knowledge of a subject that they care about, unlike teaching the Korean language, a subject in which they are not trained. It would be easier for the program to locate candidates and get funding from graduate schools in the form of tuition aids rather than from external funding. State universities might be in a better position than small private colleges for utilizing such resources.

Empowerment of Korean program instructors is another important issue. According to Wang (2014), the general profiles of Korean teachers at colleges and universities show that a significant number of teachers are overqualified for the job (i.e., 66 percent of the survey respondents hold Ph. D. degrees and yet hired as lecturers), thus underappreciated for their contributions. Such a situation is prevalent in the language teaching field in general, as also acknowledged by other groups (e.g., Middle East Language Learning in Higher Education Report, p. 18), which claim that language faculty are hired as lecturers who "rarely have the clout to effectively advocate for what is needed to build and maintain first-rate programs." While this results from a lack of professorial positions in the field for the qualified teachers, the negative impact of this situation takes its toll on the field. Frequent turnover of faculty might jeopardize the stability of a language program because they can be easily tempted to leave the job for better positions (e.g., a tenure-track position), as seen in the stories of several schools. In addition, the attitudes and perceptions of language teaching, especially Korean language teaching within academia and within each institution, oftentimes cause discouragement and demoralization. A structural hierarchy between tenure-line faculty and non-tenure line faculty and between language faculty and literature and culture faculty — a Korean program often being part of a traditional language and literature, or language and culture (or civilization) departments in most schools — is a point of concern among many faculty members. This reflects the present working environment in many institutions, in which language lecturers are at the bottom of a multitier system and hold a minority status. There is still a long way to go, but it is nonetheless encouraging to see that more tenure-track faculty positions in the Korean language have been created (though still very few), and some of them have been promoted to tenured associate professors in recent years.

The survival of small programs is a serious issue, as they are very vulnerable, constantly threatened by many factors such as budget constraints, low enrollments, and changes in institutional focus or policy. Enrollment figures are significant in the fight for survival, as evidenced by the boom of Arabic and Chinese programs. Apparently, the idea that there is support where there is demand seems to hold true. Funding agencies tend to adopt a "select and focus" strategy because they hope to see the direct fruits of their investment within a short period of time. Bigger and more established programs are equipped with better tools to flourish and are thus more likely to receive support from funding agencies, whereas small, fledgling programs are faced with an array of difficulties. Even if such programs managed to start with one-time external funding, they may continue to struggle without strong university commitment and support, which is difficult to expect. A breakthrough needs to come at some point, and finding it may be key to program survival.

5. Closing Remarks

Through the stories presented in this book, we learn that Korean language (and Korean studies) programs in American higher institutions have gone through significant transformations in the past several decades. Much has been accomplished in terms of not only quantity but also quality, in spite of a wide array of challenges, both pedagogical (e.g., lack of learning conducive and instruction effective materials) and non-pedagogical alike (e.g., lack of student interest, lack of understanding and support of the each institution, budget constraints). Korea's strong economy and improved global image, generous and strategic funding support from Korean government agencies, and the recent "Hallyu" phenomenon have all worked favorably for the development of Korean programs. At the same time, enthusiastic support of many students, dedication of faculty in the Korean programs, vision of school administrators, and emphasis on foreign language education by the American government were other factors that contributed to the current state of Korean programs today.

While Korean programs will continue to develop and prosper in the years to come, there are factors that may affect them negatively as well. American language policy can change, Korea's economy can suffer from a long stagnation (as there are signs of low growth), funding from Korean government can diminish, and the "Hallyu" phenomenon can lose its impact and wither unless it sustains learners' interests. While the increase in student enrollments has been remarkable for the past decade, the Korean language is still not as competitive as other foreign languages in the top ten group listed by the MLA. Samsung and Hyundai have become household names in America, but many Americans remain unaware that they are Korean companies, and others have never heard of "Hallyu." There is a clear gap in the American public with respect to their perception of Korea, depending on how old they are and where they live. Despite rapidly growing interest in the country, many college students also do not perceive Korean language as valuable enough for years of commitment and thus turn to another field. For example, the work of Wang & Liu (2014) shows that "practicality" is one of the most compelling motivations for many college students to study the Korean language. Furthermore, the Korean language is transforming from a language of heritage learners (and thus taught more in a heritage language context) to a language of non-heritage learners (thus taught more in a foreign language context), gradually attaining the status of a true foreign language in American colleges and universities. Though this transformation surely was the ultimate goal of Korean language instruction from the beginning, responding to this new change while heeding the mission to educate heritage learners is the greatest challenge for the field, especially given limited resources.

The field of KFL has recently seen generational transition in its leadership as well. The first generation of teachers and scholars who were the backbone of the programs and leaders of the field began to retire in early 2000. Some have already retired (Yoo-Sang Rhee of DLI, Joe Ree of Florida State University, Dong-Jae Lee of the University of Hawaii, Clare You and Kay Richards of UCB), and some are about to retire (Ho-min Sohn at the University of Hawaii, Young-Key Kim-Renaud at George Washington University). Just as the programs have evolved over time, so have the people. A new generation of dedicated teachers and scholars will cherish their predecessors' legacy, learn from them, and follow in their footsteps.

What the future holds for Korea as a country and Korean (language) studies in American institutions of higher learning is uncertain. Programs will likely go through ups and downs, and twists and turns, but I remain optimistic, as most contributing authors of this book have envisioned. The future is bright as long as there are dedicated teachers and interested students. Time will go on, and another eighty-some years of Korean language instruction history in America will pass by.

REFERENCES

Bokamba, Eyamba G. (2002). *African language program development and administration: A history and guidelines for future programs*. Madison, WI: National African Languages Resource Center.

Cho, Hang-rok. (2005a). Developmental process and characteristics of overseas Korean language education I: Birth and leap, *Journal of Korean Language Education*, 16(1), 249-275.

______. (2005b). The history of Korean language education as a Korean as a foreign Language. In International Association of Korean Language Education (Ed.), *On Korean language education I* (pp. 29-68). Seoul: Hankookmunhwasa.

Gershenhorn, Jerry. "Not an academic affair": African American scholars and the development of African studies programs in the United States, 1942-1960. *The Journal of African American History*, 44-61.

Kang, Sahie. (2005). Korean language education in America. In International Association of Korean Language Education (Ed.), *On Korean language education III* (pp. 463-495). Seoul: Hankookmunhwasa.

Kim, Hi-Sun H. (2013). Globalization and process of transformation of language of Korean students in America. In S-O Sohn et. al. (Eds.). *Studies in Korean linguistics and language pedagogy: Festschrift for Ho-min Sohn* (pp. 267-285). Seoul: Korea University Press.

King, Ross. (2007). Current state of Korean language and Korean literature education in N. America. In The Korea Foundation (Ed.), *The whitepaper of overseas Korean studies* (pp. 282-299). Seoul: Eulyoomunhwasa.

Lee. Hyo Sang. (2008). Korean language textbooks used in colleges and universities in N. America. Retrieved from http://www.indiana.edu/~korean/textbooks.html.

Maloba, W. O. (2002). Challenges in sustaining small African studies programs. *African Issues*, 30(2), 37-41.

National Middle East Language Resource Center (2011). Middle East language learning in higher education report. (web publication)

Patrikis, Peter. (1995). The foreign language problem: The governance of foreign language teaching and learning. In C. Kramsch (Ed.), *Redefining the boundaries of language study*. Boston: Heinle & Heinle.

Silva, David. (2007). Issues in Korean language teaching in the United States: Recent facts and figures. *Korean Language in America*, 12, 106-125.

Sohn, Ho-min. (2011). Issues in overseas college-level Korean language education and Korean studies. *Korean studies education for intercultural communication* (pp. 11-52). Seongnam: The Academy of Korean Studies.

Wang, Hye-Sook. (2009). Left in the shade: 'Other' Koreans and non-Koreans in Korean language education. Paper presented at the 6th International Conference of the International Convention of Asia Scholars (ICAS),

Daejeon, S. Korea.
______. (2014). Korean language teachers in higher education in N. America: Profile, status and more. *Journal of Less Commonly Taught Languages*, 16, 147-187.
Wang, Hye-Sook & Liu, Christine. (2014). Biracial Koreans and their approaches to Korean language learning. *Teaching Korean as a Foreign Language*, 40, 171-206.

A History of the Korean Language Program at Harvard

Sang-suk Oh
Harvard University

1. Introduction

In 2011, the Korea Institute at Harvard celebrated its 30th anniversary with an eventful lecture by Professor Ezra F. Vogel, Henry Ford II Professor of the Social Sciences Emeritus, on 60 years of Korean Studies at Harvard. In his lecture, Professor Vogel capsulized the development of Korean Studies and highlighted how greatly it has transformed since the early fifties. As Vogel noted, some people claim that Harvard pioneered Korean Studies in the United States in 1952 with instruction in the Korean language and Korean history. Regardless of the accuracy of the claim, it is true that Harvard was one of the few institutions that introduced Korean Studies sixty years ago.

This article presents a narrative of the history of the Korean Language Program (KLP) at Harvard, focusing on the different Korean language classes and the instructors who taught them. The history of Harvard's KLP is segmented into four separate periods: the initial development (1952-1955), the Wagner period (1958-1995), the post-Wagner period (1995-1999), and the current period (2000-present). This narrative will be centered on describing the essential history of these four periods[1].

1 The historical data used in this narrative were obtained through Harvard courses of instruction catalogues and interviews with previous Korean instructors and professors from Korean Studies at Harvard, as well as administrative staff. Articles from Harvard's own newspapers, *The Harvard Crimson* and The *Harvard Gazette*, and from other newspapers, such as the *Los Angeles Times*, were used. Wikipedia and an article by Lee (2004) were still other sources of material. (See the References section for all details regarding sources used for this article.)

2. Initial Period (1952-1955)

The very first Korean language class at Harvard was offered in 1952 by Dr. Doo Soo Suh in the Department of Far Eastern Languages (currently East Asian Languages and Civilizations, or EALC). It was implemented about 40 years after the first Chinese class and about 20 years after the first Japanese class was offered on the Harvard campus. Asian studies in America was still in its infancy, and interest in it was only just beginning. The Harvard student newspaper, *The Crimson*, reported on Sep. 19, 1952:

> Prospective GIs who wish to be prepared can take a full course in Korean history this year. Korean 111, given by Dr. Doo Soo Suh, visiting lecturer in Far Eastern Languages, is one of three offered in this new and timely field. The others, two Korean language courses, will probably appeal less since they require a previous advanced knowledge of Chinese or Japanese. (Korean, Constant,1952)

As indicated in this Harvard newspaper, History of Korean Civilization (K111) was offered for both undergraduate and graduate students, whereas the Korean language classes K205a (fall) and K205b (spring) were designed primarily for graduate students who needed to do research on Korean history. Korean 205 could hardly be called a full-fledged Korean language course, as its prerequisite was "previous advanced knowledge of Chinese or Japanese." Its target students were primarily graduate students, but only one student took the Korean class in 1952 (see page 3).

At that time, Dr. Suh was a visiting lecturer. He had graduated from Kyungseong Cheguk Taehakkyo (currently Seoul National University), where he majored in Japanese language and literature, and he was a Japanese professor before he came to the United States in 1949 to study in a Ph.D. program at Columbia University. He was also a provost at Yonsei University and a dean at Kyungseong Cheguk Taehakkyo.[2]

2 Harvard EALC website and Wikipedia.

After obtaining his Ph.D. from Columbia, Dr. Suh was hired as a visiting scholar to teach Korean history and language for three years with the support of Professor Reischauer, acting director of the Harvard-Yenching Institute, and the help of Dr. Kwang-lim Koh, a one-time Korean consul and graduate of Harvard Law School.

World War II triggered some interest in the Chinese and Japanese languages, while the Korean War created strong interest in the Korean language. The EALC department website explains the situation during that time:

> America's involvement in the Korean War also added urgency to Professor Edwin O. Reischauer's ongoing efforts to create a Korean language program, which was finally inaugurated in 1952. For the first three years, the program was overseen on a temporary basis by Dr. Doo Soo Suh, a visiting professor and former Dean of Seoul National University. The first full-time tenure-track faculty position in Korean was filled by Edward Wagner in 1958.

There is no official record for student enrollment in Dr. Suh's classes, but an unofficial note, written by one of the department's administrative staff, indicates that there was just one student in Dr. Suh's Korean class in the first year. Interestingly enough, the single student was Edward Wagner, who was studying Korean history for his Ph.D. and became a pioneer of Korean Studies at Harvard a couple of years later. Mrs. Wagner also confirmed in an interview that Edward Wagner was Dr. Suh's only student during this period. Wagner faced challenges in the Korean class because Japanese was the only language they could use to communicate. Studies in Korean went into hiatus four years later, when Dr. Suh left Harvard in 1955 after his three-year contract was over[3].

According to the 1957 course catalogue, the Korean language (K301) was to be offered by Dr. Viglielmo "to specially qualified students with individual instruction provided after arrangements were made with

---

3 According to a Korean article from Wikipedia regarding Suh Doo Soo, Dr. Suh moved to the University of Washington in Seattle to teach Korean language and literature as a visiting instructor in 1955.

the instructor." However, no records exist that indicate an actual class took place. Moreover, no further information exists on Dr. Viglielmo, which indicates that he was probably a visiting scholar like Dr. Suh. The EALC website states that there was a three-year hiatus in Korean instruction between Dr. Suh's departure in 1955 and the beginning of new Korean instruction in 1958, and it does not refer to any activity in the program during 1957.

3. Wagner Period (1958-1995)

After a couple of years, the instruction of Korean resumed when Edward Wagner joined the faculty in the Department of Far Eastern Languages as a lecturer in 1958. Though Korean classes were offered six years earlier by Dr. Suh, Wagner was the first full-time instructor to offer genuine Korean classes at Harvard in the sense that the courses were targeted at undergraduates and taught by a regular faculty member. These courses included Korean Aa (fall) and Korean Ab (spring) for elementary-level students and Korean 102a (fall) and Korean 102b (spring) for intermediate-level students. For the same year, the course catalogue lists Korean 300, a reading and research course, but there was no record found regarding enrollment in this class. Moreover, no history course was offered to graduate students that year. According to an old photocopy[4] of the enrollment chart for 1958, the enrollment for Korean was six students (three students in the fall and three students in the spring).

It is interesting to note that Professor Wagner began his teaching career as a Korean language instructor even though his academic training was in Korean history. As mentioned earlier, Wagner was the first student in Dr. Suh's Korean language class in 1952. He entered Harvard University in 1943; he was then drafted and served as a civilian military

4 The photocopy was obtained from Ms. Rose Cortese, a former administrator in the East Asian Languages Program.

advisor, mostly in Japan and for a short time in Korea. Following his military service, he returned to resume his unfinished undergraduate studies at Harvard in 1948. After graduating in 1949, he continued as an M.A. student in Regional Studies until 1951, and then he began to study Korean history as a Ph.D. student in the Department of Far Eastern Languages in 1952. In 1953, in order to conduct research for his dissertation, which was entitled 'The Literati Purges: Case Studies in the Factionalism of the Early Yi Dynasty," Wagner visited Tenri University in Nara, Japan and stayed there until 1955. He also traveled to Korea during the following three years to conduct dissertation research and, in particular, to collect historical data on the Yi Dynasty by looking at *Chosun Wangjo Sillok*, the official dynastic history of the Chosun Dynasty kings (Lee, 2004). During this time, he met Ms. Namhi Kim, who later became his wife in his second marriage. Wagner started teaching Korean as a lecturer at Harvard for one year before he earned his doctoral degree in 1959.

In 1959, Wagner was appointed as assistant professor. Lee (2004) says the following about Wagner:

> In 1981, [Professor Wagner] became the first director of the Korea Institute. Wagner devoted his entire life to the development of Korean Studies at Harvard University. In seminars and lecture courses, he not only deepened knowledge of Korea's long history and culture but also helped to enlarge the Korea collection of the Harvard-Yenching Library. (Lee, 2004, p. 119-120)

Professor Wagner was later advanced to associate professor, then full professor, and dedicated thirty-five years to promoting Korean Studies at Harvard until he retired in 1993.

The only known official enrollment numbers in Wagner's early days were six students in 1958, ten in 1959, eight in 1960, twelve in 1961, and thirteen in 1962.[5] According to Mrs. Namhi Wagner, the only person available to relate the history of Korean instruction during this early period, instruction in both elementary Korean and intermediate Korean classes was based solely on the grammar-translation method. The majority of class time was used to help students learn formulaic expressions and sentence patterns. Mrs. Wagner stated that the purpose of Korean classes at that time was to help graduate students read academic materials for their research on Korean history and literature, and focus was solely on getting students to learn sentence patterns while improving their reading comprehension. Good teaching materials were not available, so Professor Wagner had to develop a teaching packet based on Professor Reischauer's Japanese language teaching materials, which had been developed using pattern building. In 1963, Professor Wagner compiled his teaching materials and published a Korean textbook, *Elementary Written Korean*, which was used in the program until 1995, according to Mrs. Wagner.

In 1964, Professor Wagner asked his wife, Mrs. Namhi Wagner, to help him teach Korean.[6] She had come to the United States to work as an assistant librarian at the Yenching Library in 1961, which was when Harvard began to collect Korean literature. It was during this time she and Professor Wagner were married.

In the beginning, Mrs. Wagner functioned as an assistant to Professor Wagner in his Korean classes. According to her, a typical lecture consisted of him explaining important Korean sentence patterns and grammar, while she provided actual sentences as examples. Conversational skills were not taught, as the presentation of grammar patterns and lexical expression sets was the focus. Mrs. Wagner remembers that she attended classes once or twice a week in a semester.

Mrs. Wagner also recalls that in the first year she taught with Profes-

5 Records of enrollment in Korean classes for other early years are not available. The photocopies of the enrollment for these three years mentioned here came from the former administrator, Rose Cortese.

6 Mrs. Wagner recalls that she was initially very hesitant when Professor Wagner asked her to help him teach Korean language classes because she felt she was not ready to teach. Having spent most of her life in Japan, she became very fluent in Japanese, but her Korean was not very strong. However, she studied Korean with diligence while teaching the language and eventually became a strong language teacher through her tireless endeavors.

sor Wagner, there were no students in Elementary Korean (KAa), and in the following years, there were only one or two students. In contrast, there were seven or eight students in Intermediate Korean (K102), most of them graduate students who had been members of the Peace Corps in Korea. The enrollment figures reveal a lack of strong interest in the Korean language and studies among undergraduate students in the sixties and seventies. In fact, only a few graduate students who had been exposed to Korean culture and society took Korean language classes.

In 1964 and 1965, Marshal Phil, a graduate of Seoul National University and a fluent Korean speaker, was at Harvard as a graduate student in Korean literature, and he helped Mrs. Wagner teach elementary Korean when enrollments rose. He later became a well-known Korean literature professor, working mostly at the University of Hawaii at Manoa until he passed away in the late 1990s.

In 1968, Vipan Chandra, the husband of Mrs. Myong-suk Chandra (who taught as a drill instructor at the KLP in the late nineties and later worked as an administrator at the Korea Institute at Harvard until 2014), taught one semester as a teaching assistant. He is originally from India and taught Hindi in Korea before he earned a Ph.D. in Korean History at Harvard. His Korean proficiency was excellent at the time, according to Mrs. Wagner. Professor Chandra is now a professor of Korean history at Wheaton College in Massachusetts.

From 1970 onward, Mrs. Wagner's name started to appear as a course head in the course catalogue. A course head for Harvard language courses is normally a preceptor, or a person in a higher position, but Mrs. Wagner did not become an official preceptor until 1976. Mrs. Wagner states that she was an instructor and then a lecturer before she became a preceptor. She became a Senior Preceptor in 1984, after completing her eight-year term limit as preceptor.

In the seventies, Mrs. Wagner taught mostly Korean B (Elementary Korean), a full-year course, while Professor Wagner taught semester-long courses in Korean 102a and 102b, and Korean 130a and 130b. According to the course catalogue, in 1972 and 1973, Mrs. Wagner taught Korean 102a and 102b, while Professor Wagner taught Korean

B. The class sizes ranged from a few students to a maximum of ten per semester; most of them were graduate students. Rarely were the students of Korean heritage, until the eighties, when enrollment of undergraduate heritage learners jumped. At this time, Korean classes started to include separate drill sections. Until then, elementary Korean and intermediate Korean classes were typically not much different from those held in the sixties. The central teaching methods involved explanations of basic grammar patterns, and students were expected to memorize sample sentences. Mrs. Wagner recalls bringing various reading materials into class for students to read. She also recalls using a voice recorder with Professor Wagner that she used for readings of texts.

Mrs. Wagner remembers that the seventies were "quiet days," when only a few students enrolled in Korean classes, but she recalls two renowned people who took Elementary Korean in this period: One is the well-known author and illustrator of children's books, Molley Bang. While pursuing Japanese studies for her master's degree, she took an interest in learning Korean. The other is Mr. Edward J. Baker who served as the Associate Director of the Harvard-Yenching Institute from 1981 to 2006, was a member of the Executive Committee of the Harvard Korea Institute from its beginning until 2012, and is now a member of the KI's Committee of Special Advisors.

This "quiet" period slowly changed in the eighties, when Korean heritage students started to appear in elementary Korean classes and formed the majority of the program until the nineties. They were mostly the children of Korean parents who were fearful that their children would not be able to adjust to the American education system, so many of them had prevented their children from learning their heritage language. For this reason, when their children entered university, most spoke little Korean and many could not speak Korean at all and became interested in learning the language. As will be discussed later, however, the majority of students in elementary Korean classes were gradually replaced by non-heritage students in the 2000s.

Sizes for the elementary class Korean Ba (by then, a semester-long course) grew from about twenty students in the early eighties, to forty students in the late nineties, to as many as fifty in the program's heyday. According to Mrs. Wagner, some MIT students also showed interest in learning Korean, but the program could not accept them due to a staff shortage caused by an insufficient department budget. Initially, the program started with one teaching assistant, and increased enrollment led to the addition of another, who was later replaced with a full-time drill instructor. The program relied on team-teaching: The professor or preceptor taught the lecture sections, and a teaching assistant or a drill instructor taught the drill sections.

The program developed significantly in the eighties. In 1985, the program offered one more course, totaling four courses from first-year to fourth-year Korean. The new course was a more advanced Korean course, Korean 104 (Readings in Contemporary Korean). The course catalogue shows that this class was assigned to Carter Eckert, who is currently a Korean history professor in EALC and the second director of the Korea Institute at Harvard. He was hired as a lecturer and was asked to teach the advanced Korean course. There is no official record for enrollment in this course, but internal enrollment charts indicate that there were nine students in Korean 104a in 1988, and enrollment varied from zero to seven students from 1989 to 1991. According to Professor Eckert, he taught this reading class until 1987, when he became an assistant professor. However, his name still appeared as the course head of K104 until 1993 in the course catalogue. It is most likely that he served as the course head until 1993, but an assigned teaching assistant covered the actual teaching of the course. Professor Eckert's major influence and contributions to the development of Korean Studies at Harvard took place during the post-Wagner era when he served as the director of the Korean Institute from 1993 to 2004.

In 1986, when Mrs. Wagner took a year off, Professor Young-Key Kim Renaud — currently a renowned Korean scholar and Professor of Korean at George Washington University — was invited to teach first-year Korean.

In 1987, Academic Written Korean (Korean 211) was offered by Professor Wagner, according to the course catalogue. Detailed information on this class was not available, but the catalogue says that it was offered mostly for graduate students who were pursuing Korean Studies.

In 1988, Korea hosted the Summer Olympic Games, after which enrollment for the entire program grew significantly, from 97 students in 1988 to 140 in 1989. This huge surge amounted to more than a 40 percent increase in just a single year. Though the sudden increase in enrollment could not be exclusively attributed to the Olympic Games in Seoul, the event was a major contributing factor. The possible internal factors are unknown due to insufficient data, and Mrs. Wagner also does not seem to recall them.

In the nineties, the trend of an increasing student population continued until it reached its peak with an enrollment of 159 in 1992. After that, this number dwindled very gradually down to 120 in 1999.

According to Mrs. Wagner, among several memorable students in the program from this period was an American Buddhist Reverend named Hyungak Sunim (Paul Muenzen). He was a graduate student at Harvard's Divinity School (1988-1992) and learned Korean in Mrs. Wagner's class around 1990. Inspired by a speech given by Zen Master Sung Sahn at Harvard, Hyungak Sunim became a disciple. Before he became famous in Korea, Mrs. Wagner came across him in Insa-dong, Seoul, while she was visiting Korea. At that time, it was Hyungak who recognized her first and said hello to her in Korean. Mrs. Wagner was pleasantly surprised to see how well her former student was functioning as a monk using Korean fluently. "It was profoundly rewarding," said Mrs. Wagner. Indeed, Hyungak successfully gave many public talks and lectures in Korean that were televised nationwide.

Professor Wagner taught Korean classes until 1991, and as his health worsened, he retired from the university in 1993. Throughout the seventies and eighties, he served as the course head of the intermediate (K102) and advanced Korean (K103) classes, while Mrs. Wagner taught the elementary Korean classes, which comprised the majority of the program's enrollment. Though Korean instruction during these decades was heavily dependent on Mrs. Wagner, the role Professor Wagner had in developing and advancing Korean language instruction at Harvard was undeniably important. He was the pioneer of both Korean language instruction and Korean Studies, not only at the university but also in the nation. His dedication, initiative, and influence were key in developing a flourishing Korean Studies program at Harvard. Professor Wagner passed away in December 2001.

In 1995, Mrs. Wagner also retired after teaching for 35 years. Unfortunately, before she retired, she was not able to finish publishing her own Korean textbooks, which she had been building diligently from her teaching materials over several years. However, she recalls that her materials were adopted by a few teachers in other programs such as the KLP at Columbia University.

Mrs. Wagner is a living witness of the history of the KLP at Harvard. Initially an assistant to Professor Wagner, she became a key figure who eventually managed the program and actively taught Korean classes for more than three decades. Due to her significant contributions to the expansion and progress of the program, she left a meaningful mark on the history of the KLP at Harvard. In 1995, Mrs. Wagner received a Culture Award and Medal from the Korean government for her long-term contributions to the advancement of Korean language studies in the U.S. In commemoration of Professor Wagner's significant contributions to the development of Korean Studies at Harvard and Mrs. Wagner's achievements in building the KLP, the Korea Institute (KI) at Harvard has been inviting Mrs. Wagner to attend major events, such as the annual KI reception, every year. The legacy left by Professor Wagner and Mrs. Wagner still remains strong in the Harvard community.

4. Post-Wagner Period (1995-1999)

In 1995, after Mrs. Wagner retired, Professor Kyung-Ja Chun was hired as preceptor to manage the KLP and to teach Korean. Professor Chun was from the English department of Sungshin Women's University in Korea, and she taught two courses: Elementary Korean (KBa) and Advanced Korean (K104). Meanwhile, Sook Lee, a linguistics graduate student, taught the two other courses (K102 and K103). Though enrollment was down somewhat from its peak of 159 in 1992, the number of students was still quite high, with 136 students registered.

In 1996, preceptor Hyun-Soon Kim was hired to teach Elementary Korean (KBa) and Advanced Korean (K104), while Professor Chun taught Korean 102 and Korean 103. The following year, preceptor Kim was replaced by Dr. Seok-Hoon You (currently a linguistics professor at Korea University in Korea), who taught Korean 102a and Korean 103a for one semester. Afterwards, Dr. Il-Sun Shin was hired. His stay in the KLP was also brief; he taught Korean 102 and Korean 103 for only three semesters.

According to Rose Cortese, a long-time administrator of the East Asian Languages Programs, this was a "turbulent" period with constant staff changes for a number of relational and professional reasons. Though the times may have been turbulent, enrollment was still high in the four courses. Two preceptors and two drill instructors were added to the teaching staff during this period. Mrs. Chandra, who was a long-time staff member at the Korea Institute at Harvard until the spring of 2014, began working as a drill instructor in the KLP in 1992 and continued working until the end of the post-Wagner period in 1999.

Professor Chun managed the KLP for four years until the spring of 1999, when she had to leave for Korea. A few teaching staff from this period recall that Professor Chun was a strict teacher and hard-working director, who demanded the teaching staff work diligently to create new teaching materials and held countless individual sessions for the students. Moreover, teachers were asked to work in the office from nine to five each day. Overall, the program maintained a good enrollment, though it was lower than that of the program's heyday in the early 1990s. Despite high enrollment rates and the strong work ethic of Professor Chun, this period was marked by constant changes in teaching staff, which undermined the stability of the program.

5. Current Period (1999-2014)

East Asian Languages Building

In the fall of 1999, Dr. Jiha Hwang was hired as a preceptor and the new director of the KLP. Dr. Hwang gradually stabilized the KLP by revamping its curriculum based on an up-to-date teaching methodology, increasing the number of courses offered, and developing a new heritage course track.

Dr. Hwang, who was the first genuine language pedagogue at Harvard KLP with extensive self-training and teaching experience in second language pedagogy, changed the teaching method used in the KLP from the traditional grammar-translation method to a combination of the communicative-language and proficiency-oriented teaching methods. Through his conscientious efforts and training of the teaching staff, most classes (both lecture and drill sections) were designed to fulfill more of the students' communication needs by providing more activity and task-based instruction. Recognizing the new needs of elementary level students, Dr. Hwang offered a heritage track at the beginner's level for the first time. He also added a fifth-year Korean course in order to meet the needs of high-advanced Korean learners, who were mostly Korean heritage students. As part of this curriculum innovation, he developed his own teaching materials for the third-year and fourth-year Korean classes. He was well-liked by most students, and his contribution to the program in terms of teaching and managing the program was significant.

Dr. Hwang served as director of the KLP for four years from 1999 to 2003, when he moved to the Department of East Asian Languages and Literatures (EALL) at the University of Hawaii as Assistant Professor in Korean. During this period, he taught Korean B and served as the course head of Korean 103, Korean 104, and Korean 105, while Dr. Sang-suk Oh taught Korean Bx and Korean 120.

Dr. Sang-suk Oh (the author of this article) came to Harvard in 2000 as a preceptor, and took over the KLP as acting director for two years starting in 2003. He was formally hired as the director of the program in 2005, following a formal search. In the same year, he was also promoted to senior preceptor.

Under Oh's management, Harvard's KLP maintained six courses, from beginner to high-advanced (fifth-year) Korean classes with just two course heads (one preceptor and one senior preceptor) and two drill instructors. The previous curriculum was updated with reinforcement of learning through media, technology, and more student-centered class instruction. Furthermore, a new unified placement test was developed to assess students at all levels of Korean, from beginner to high-advanced, with regard to their diverse skills. Considering the importance of learning classical Chinese for doing premodern and even modern Korean history and cultural studies at Harvard, the system for Chinese character instruction was revamped, and internal workshops for instructors' professional development began to be held every year. In addition, since Oh took over the directorship, enrollment has stabilized, and there has been steady growth for the past ten years. During the 2012-2013 academic year, 140 students enrolled in Korean classes. Considering there is just a one-year foreign language requirement at Harvard compared with the two-year requirement at several other Ivy League universities, such as Columbia and Cornell, it can be said that interest in Korean classes is strong at Harvard.

From 2003 to 2004, Ms. Sunghee Hong, once a drill instructor, joined the KLP as a preceptor, teaching elementary and third-year Korean. When Hong left the program in 2005, Dr. Mi-Hyun Kim joined the program in the fall of that year and worked in the program as a preceptor for seven years until 2012. During this period, she taught elementary Korean (for three years), intermediate Korean (for four years), third-year Korean (for five years), and advanced Korean (for one year). From 2000 to 2014, Oh taught elementary Korean (for six years), heritage elementary Korean (for four years), intermediate Korean (for seven years), advanced Korean (for eight years), and high-advanced Korean (K150a) (for ten years). He also taught independent reading and research. At times, his teaching load was four courses per semester, though, for several years he taught three courses. From 2003 to 2005, the program maintained two preceptors and two drill instructors, with preceptors functioning as course heads and teaching the lecture sections, while drill instructors taught the drill sections of the Korean classes. From 2005 until 2011, one preceptor and one senior preceptor taught the lecture sections of six courses as course heads, while two drill instructors taught the drill sections of lower-level classes. In addition, a graduate teaching assistant has occasionally been hired to assist with the teaching of the fifth-year Korean class.

6. Changes, Challenges, and Other Updates

Considering the ever-increasing enrollment and heavy teaching load, Oh submitted a petition with the approval of the department to the deans in 2011 to replace one of the existing drill instructors with a new preceptor so that there would be three course heads and one drill instructor (instead of two preceptors and two drill instructors). After a year of discussion, the petition was approved. In the fall of 2012, Harvard's KLP adopted a new curriculum with the revised staff system, in which two new preceptors, Dr. Hee-Jeong Jeong and Ms. Heeyoung Jung, were hired. Overall, changes included the following. First, two preceptors and one senior preceptor taught a total of six courses. Second, two preceptors taught two courses without separate drill sections, thus the preceptors integrated the lecture and drill portions into unified lessons in each Korean class. Within the East Asian language programs at Harvard, the KLP is the only program in which this integrated approach is applied. Third, only elementary Korean (KB) still maintained a team-teaching setting, offering separate lecture and drill sections, with one drill instructor devoting most of his or her time to the drill sections.

Over the period of the last seven years or so, a drastic change in the student composition of the lower-level classes has taken place. The gap left by the dwindling numbers of students of Korean heritage has slowly been filled by non-heritage students in a trend established by 2010. For example, in 2011, 98 percent of the elementary Korean class (Ba) was filled with non-heritage students, which is in stark contrast to the demographics of the 1990s, when the majority of students in KBa were heritage students. Furthermore, the ratio of heritage to non-heritage students among the total number of students enrolled in KLP classes was reversed for the first time in 2011. In other words, there were more non-heritage students than heritage students in the KLP. This transformation has had a significant implication: Our teaching staff needs to be more sensitive to the needs of non-heritage students and to strive to bridge the gaps of different needs among heritage and non-heritage students.

Though increased enrollment of non-heritage students and expansion of the program indicate a positive movement forward, the KLP still faces some challenges. One such challenge is the gap between heritage and non-heritage students in the upper-level courses, when the progress of non-heritage learners tends to slow in spite of their enthusiasm. At the third-year level, continuing non-heritage students start to realize the difficulty in achieving a similar level of proficiency as their heritage counterparts. In addition, the gap between continuing undergraduate and graduate students, particularly those studying Regional Studies on East Asia, creates another challenge due to different language-learning backgrounds and distinct linguistic needs. Instructors in the program are highly attuned to these challenges and are trying to bridge the gaps by creating more practical and helpful materials for separate groups of students. They also provide more scaffolding activities, differentiated instructions, and individualized support through individual teaching sessions.

Korean Studies at Harvard is now divided into two areas: (1) language and (2) history and literature. The Korean language is taught by the KLP staff, currently numbering four instructors (one senior preceptor, two preceptors, and one drill instructor). The KLP is contributing significantly to the field by serving the needs of undergraduate students, as well as some graduate students, who are interested in Korean language and culture. Another important contribution to the rising interest in Korean Studies at Harvard is Professor Carter Eckert's ever-popular course *Two Koreas*, which has attracted undergraduate students for many years. He is a Korean history professor in the EALC department and was once director of the Korea Institute (KI), which is the center for Korean Studies at Harvard. Another professor who teaches Korean history is Professor Sunjoo Kim, the current director of KI. Korean literature has been taught until this spring by Professor David McCann,[7] who also served as KI director for about ten years. Current KI committee members consist of the aforementioned faculty members, who are also faculty members of the EALC department, to which the KLP belongs. The role of KI in promoting Korean Studies at Harvard is significant. It hosts several visiting scholars from abroad and promotes various Korea-related activities and events, including colloquiums and talks by renowned politicians and dignitaries from Korea and the United States. Though they are affiliated, KI and KLP are run independently of each other, as EALC funds the KLP, and the South Korean government and other endowment funds support KI.

Since the summer of 2007, Harvard's KLP and KI began jointly hosting the Harvard Summer Program in Seoul. For the past eight years, it has taken place at Ewha Womans University. Hence, the summer program is called the Harvard-Ewha Summer Program. Equal num-

7 Professor McCann retired in the spring of 2014, and a new faculty member, Si Nae Park, joined in the fall of 2014.

bers of students from Ewha and Harvard jointly participate in content classes. Courses in Korean literature, history, anthropology, and film have been offered simultaneously with Korean language classes for Harvard students. Three to five different levels of language classes have been offered each summer, depending on participants' proficiencies. So far, two faculty members from KI have taught Korean history and literature courses, and other faculty members from the Anthropology Department and the Visual and Environmental Studies Department at Harvard have jointly taught content classes, along with professors from other universities. All different levels of Korean language courses have been coordinated and managed by the author of this article, the current KLP director. Harvard language faculty member Mi-hyun Kim and the author taught Korean language classes in the summer of 2007, after which local instructors from Ewha were hired to teach Korean classes, with supervision provided by the author. Thanks to the great teamwork among Harvard KI, KLP, and Ewha University — particularly the strong support and commitment from the Ewha side — the joint program has been very successful and fruitful every year, resulting in the prospect that it will last well into the future.

7. Concluding Remarks

As was stated, Harvard's KLP has gone through major transformations consisting of three major stages. The program started as a one-student program and grew into an approximately ten-student program in the sixties and seventies. Its size grew further, ranging from 40 to 70 students in the early eighties, with student enrollment leaping to 140 in the late eighties, and reaching 160 at its peak in the early nineties. After experiencing some decline in numbers in the late nineties and 2000s, it has nearly returned to its previous peak, with an enrollment of about 140.

Initially, the KLP started with the visiting scholar Dr. Suh Doo Soo in 1952, and from 1958, it was managed and taught by history professor Edward Wagner, who became the main figure in the development of

Korean Studies at Harvard. Edward Wagner and Mrs. Wagner taught Korean classes for over 30 years until 1991, when the program was led by Mrs. Wagner herself for an additional four years. After that, the staff system changed to a steady system of two preceptors and two drill instructors in a team-teaching setting for more than a decade. Beginning in 2005, the system changed to one senior preceptor and one preceptor together with two drill instructors, maintaining the same team teaching setting. Now, it has undergone another transformation, with one senior preceptor plus two preceptors and one drill instructor. With this change, team teaching has been abolished in all classes except for elementary Korean (KB). If the KLP wanted to restore the old team teaching setting[8] in the lower levels (KB and K120), it would need one more drill instructor. This is a goal for the future.

Though there have been positive aspects to the program, such as an increasing overall enrollment, a surge of non-heritage students in lower-level classes, and the success of summer study abroad program, there are still challenges. The term limits of eight years for a preceptor and six years for a drill instructor require frequent turnover of staff, undermining the stability of the program. The title "preceptor," which is equivalent to lecturer in other universities, is not desirable because it creates confusion for both insiders and outsiders of the university. The workload of each teacher at Harvard's KLP is also heavy.[9] Additionally, there is not enough funding from the department, and the funding from KI has been scarce, though this situation is expected to improve in the

---

8 There are advantages to a team-teaching setting in the lower-level classes since more personal attention can be paid to individual students, with smaller numbers of students in the drill sections and more opportunities to offer individual tutoring sessions. However, understaffing in multiple classes has led to the removal of drill sections in 2014.

9 Extensive care of individual students, in terms of having extensive individual sessions in addition to regular class teaching, is one of the unique features of Harvard's KLP. The care provided to one Harvard student can be equated to the care provided to two or more students at other universities, and in this sense, the meaning of enrollment numbers should be considered differently from that of other institutions.

near future.[10]

Harvard's KLP strives to create student-centered classes and multimedia-rich classrooms. Teaching staff members are provided training before each semester through internal workshops and program meetings, and they have opportunities to discuss and learn more about the topics covered. Harvard's KLP pioneered the multimedia-rich classroom starting in early 2000, among other East Asian Programs at Harvard, and it recently carried out a project for creating a multimedia database, which includes compilations of Korean songs, clips from Korean movies and Korean TV dramas, and videos of teachers acting out textbook dialogues. It also led a workshop, The Use of Multimedia for the Student-Centered Classroom, at an AATK (American Association of Teachers of Korean) conference at Yale in 2011. Harvard's KLP is now looking at developing new textbook material for upper-level classes and a new bridge course to connect language and content.

As it heads toward a new era, everyone at Harvard's KLP is looking forward to meeting the current challenges as well as the needs of Korean language learners in the future.

REFERENCES

Chong, Joseph. (1995). Faculty Profile: Namhi Kim Wagner. *Yisei Megazine*.

Doo Soo Suh, 87 began Harvard's Korean studies. (1994, October 25). *The Boston Globe*. Retrieved from http://www.highbeam.com/doc/1P2-8301276.html

East Asian Languages and Civilizations. (n.d.) In *Department of East Asian Languages and Civilizations*. Retrieved October 20, 2014, from http://ealc.fas.harvard.edu/

Eckert, Carter; Martina Deuchler; James B. Palais. (2007, March 22). *Memorial Minute*, "Edward Willett Wagner." Retrieved from http://news.harvard.edu/gazette/story/2007/03/edward-willett-wagner/

Edward Wagner, 77; Korea Scholar Taught at Harvard 35 years. (2011, Decem-

10 There has been little funding from KI until the past few years, when there were some isolated cases of meager support for programs.

ber 28). *The Los Angeles Times*. Retrieved from http://articles.latimes.com/2001/dec/28/local/me-18493

Harvard University. (1953-1999). *Harvard Courses of Instruction*. Cambridge: Harvard University.

Korean, Conant, More G.E. Head Fall Slate of Courses. (1952, September 19). *The Harvard Crimson*. Retrieved from http://www.thecrimson.com/article/1952/9/19/korean-conant-more-ge-head-fall/

Lee, Hoon-sang. (2004). Edward W. Wagner: The father of Korean studies in North America 119. *The Review of Korean Studies*, 7 (3), 117-132. Seongnam, Korea: The Academy of Korean Studies.

Suh Doo Soo. (n.d.) In *Wikipedia*. Retrieved October 20, 2014, from http://ko.wikipedia.org/wiki/%EC%84%9C%EB%91%90%EC%88%98_ (%EA%B5%90%EC%88%98)

APPENDIX. Interviews

Prof. Carter Eckert	Professor in Korean history at Harvard
Mrs. Namhi Kim Wagner	Former Director of the KLP
Mrs. Myong-suk Chandra	Former Drill Instructor; Current Korea Institute Administrative Staff Member
Mrs. Rose Cortese	Former EAL Administrator

The History of the Korean Language Program at Indiana University

Hyo Sang Lee
Indiana University

1. Introduction

The history of the Korean language program at Indiana University (IU) began in the early 1960s, when the newly created Department of East Asian Languages and Literatures (EALL) decided to offer Korean language courses, the first in the Midwest. It was a bold move on the part of the department because there was no sizeable Korean community in Indiana, let alone in Bloomington, except for the 50 or so Korean graduate students enrolled at the university.

From its inception, there were two notable characteristics of the Korean program at IU. One is that the department (in conjunction with the East Asian Studies Center), and not any other group of people or organizations associated with Korea, initiated the actions related to the Korean language or the Korean studies program at IU. The Korean program at IU began entirely from the will and vision of the department, which was then the EALL Department and is now the EALC (East Asian Languages and Cultures) Department. There was no initiation of, campaigning by, or pressure from the Korean government, Korean students, or the Korean community. This trend has continued for later developments in the Korean language and Korean studies program at IU.

The other characteristics of the Korean language program at IU are that from the beginning, non-heritage learners comprised most of the Korean language class enrollments, rather than heritage learners. This is different from most other American college-level Korean programs, in which Korean heritage students constituted the majority of Korean language class enrollments.

These two unique features of the Korean language and Korean studies program at IU proved to be both advantageous and disadvantageous to the program's development and expansion. On the one hand, the Korean language and Korean studies program had discipline-specific and cultural value, rather than being a demographically-motivated service program. On the other hand, the expansion of the program underwent hardships and even regressed a few times to reach the point where it is now, because of this very lack of influence from a demographic base made up of heritage learners and a Korean community.

The development of the Korean language program at IU can be divided into five periods: (i) 1962-1971 (ii) 1982-1986 (iii) 1986-1993 (iv) 1993-2014 and (v) 2014-present.

The first period covers the inception of the Korean language program to 1971, when the Korean program was canceled due to low enrollment. The second period began in 1982, when the Korean language program was reinstated after a 10-year hiatus. Tremendous efforts were made to build up the Korean language and Korean studies program in the next five years, and these efforts resulted in securing a tenure-track faculty position in Korean language and culture in 1986, which marked the turning point for the Korean language and Korean studies program. Kenneth Wells in Korean history was hired for that position, and he devoted himself to stabilizing a Korean language program that remained weak even after the restoration. The fourth period, during which the current program formed, began in 1993 when the department hired a tenure-track Korean language faculty member and coordinator, Hyo Sang Lee, who has since been running the Korean language program at IU. In 2014, the Korean language program added a second full-time faculty, a lecturer, to accommodate drastically large enrollments of recent years.

2. History

2.1. INCEPTION AND THE FIRST NINE YEARS: 1962-1971

Goodbody Hall

Korean language courses began to be offered at Indiana University in 1962, when the Department of East Asian Languages and Literatures (EALL) was created. The offering of Korean language courses was considered to be a key characteristic of the newly created department, as reported by many local and regional newspapers, such as *Indiana Daily News, Bloomington Harold-Times, Indianapolis News, Indianapolis Star, Louisville Courier Journal,* and *Cincinnati Post*:

> A new department of East Asian languages and literatures, the first in the [Midwest] to teach Korean, will come into being at I.U. this fall. (Indiana Daily News, July 10, 1962)
>
> Korean will also be taught, making I.U. the only Midwestern school to teach that language. (Indianapolis News, July 10, 1962)
>
> A new department of East Asian Languages to be established this fall will be the first in the [Midwest] to teach Korean. (Louisville Courier Journal, July 10, 1962)

John Y. Sohn, then the head of the Korean section of the Army Language School (currently the Defense Language Institute) in Monterey, California, joined the faculty of EALL as a lecturer to teach First and Second Year Korean. It was reported that the department envisioned expanding the Korean faculty to two members over the next few years. Sohn taught only the first three semesters, however, from the fall of 1962 to the fall of 1963, and another semester in the fall of 1966. Unfortunately, instructors changed almost every other year following Sohn's initial involvement. For example, Seok-Choong Song and W. E. Henthorn taught for a couple of years, followed by Joe Ree, who taught for three years. Edward Rockstein[1] and Helen Sang-ran Lee followed Ree. Many of these instructors were still graduate students at IU at the time of their hiring as lecturers, and as they moved on in their graduate careers, new instructors replaced them. Along with the low enrollments in the Korean language courses, this turnover worked against the stability of the Korean language program.

During the early years of the Korean language program, Fred Lukoff's *Spoken Korean* and Edward Wagner's *Elementary Korean* were used for First Year Korean, whereas the Defense Language Institute's *Intermediate Course* and *Glossary of Grammar Notes*, and Suk-In Chang's *An Intermediate Korean Reader* were used for Second Year Korean.

The enrollment was small. In the fall of 1962, in its very first semester, four students enrolled in First Year Korean 1 (K301) and two in Second Year Korean 1 (K401). In the spring of 1963, three enrolled in First Year Korean 2 (K302) and two in Second Year Korean 2 (K402). The enrollments in the following years would fluctuate. Seven enrolled in First Year Korean 2 (K302) during the spring of 1967 and six in Second Year Korean 1 (K401) in the fall of 1967. These numbers were the highest enrollments; usually there were only one or two students enrolled. During this period, almost all students were non-heritage learners. It

1 Edward Rockstein had received a B.A. from Indiana University in EALL with a Korean focus in 1966; according to Prof. Wu-chi Liu's Five-Year Report of the department, he was one of two students who received a B.A. in Korean in 1966. Rockstein came back to teach First Year Korean 1 (K301) in the fall of 1969.

was not until 1985-86 when heritage students began to take Korean language courses at IU.

To jumpstart the lackluster enrollments in Korean language courses, the department launched the Korean studies program in 1965, which had great potential with several Korean specialists already present on campus. The Korean specialists already present at IU were Ilpyong Kim in Government, Taiyul Kim in Comparative Literature, and W. E. Henthorn in the Uralic and Altaic studies program. Paul Kuznets, an expert in Korean economics, had also been hired in 1964 in the Department of Economics. Although these faculty members were not hired for Korean studies per se, they were valuable to the development of the Korean studies program at IU. It was the department's goal to "offer a full program, involving the humanities and social sciences, in which language training is applied in research activities" (*Program in Korean Studies* in C304.54 East Asian Language and Literature).

The 1969-70 College of Arts and Sciences (COAS) bulletin offers a glimpse into the courses offered in Korean studies: K422 Contrastive Grammar of Korean and Japanese, K493 Survey of Korean Culture, K494 History of Korean Literature, K421 Introduction to Korean Linguistics for Undergraduates, K511 Korean Bibliography, K531/532 Modern Korean Literature, and K651 Seminar in Korean Studies. Surprisingly, a fully recognized program did not materialize then. The EALL department's Five Year Report (1962-67) by Professor Wu-chi Liu, the chair of EALL, reports, "In Korean, a number of advanced courses listed in the catalogues have never been offered because there are no students." The low enrollments would eventually lead to the cancellation of Korean language course offerings after 1971, when there were no enrolled students in First Year Korean 2 (K302) and only one student in Second Year Korean 2 (K402). A memo of appeal by the department chair Y. J. Chi to the Dean of the College, Harrison Shull, was to no avail.

2.2. RESTORATION: 1982-1986

In February 1982, Robert Ramsey, an expert in Korean language and in Chinese and Japanese linguistics, then at Columbia University, gave his external review report on beginning-level instruction in Korean, Chinese, and Japanese at IU. Phillip West, the director of the newly established East Asian Studies Center (EASC), and Eugene Eoyang, the chair of the Department of East Asian Languages and Cultures (EALC), quickly collaborated on efforts to follow up on his recommendation. After a ten-year hiatus, the Korean language course offerings were reintroduced in 1982, with EASC's financial support.

Jae-ok Cho, then an IU graduate student in linguistics, was hired to teach First Year Korean in 1982, and she added Second Year Korean in 1983. After Cho taught for two years, Y. Choi taught for one year in 1984-85 and was followed by a Fulbright teaching fellow, Pong Ja Paik, in 1985-86. The enrollments in Korean language courses the second time around were still not huge, but they showed promise with seven to ten students in First Year Korean and one to six in Second Year Korean. Paik added Third Year Korean (K301) for the first time at IU, with five students enrolled in K301 and two in K302.

As for the textbooks used in these classes, Myongdo's Korean textbooks were used for a couple of years, but then the curricula were changed to use the Yonsei textbook series, because Myongdo's textbooks stopped being published.

The reinstated Korean language program would soon run into a crisis again, due to budget cuts from both the federal and the Indiana state governments in 1983. In order to overcome the crisis, fundraising efforts began with the collaborative work by the EASC director Phillip West and Dr. Heun Young Yune, a professor of radiology at the IU School of Medicine. Dr. Yune and a group of Korean-American medical doctors and businessmen formed a group called the Society of Friends of Korean Studies (SOFOKS) at IU in 1983, with Dr. Yune as the first president. SOFOKS raised $6,875 in its first fundraising campaign. Ever since then, SOFOKS has donated more than $200,000 over the past thirty years and has been important to supporters of the Korean studies program at IU through its instructional funds as well as graduate and undergraduate fellowships.

In addition, the tireless efforts of the Center's Director Phillip West yielded significant fundraising results for the Korean studies program at IU. The Korea Research Foundation gave $10,000 in 1984-85 and another $15,000 in 1987. Spencer H. Kim, the president of Kamex Construction, gave $2,100 for three students to attend the East Asian Summer Language Institute (EASLI), which was established in 1985 to offer intensive immersion programs in Chinese, Japanese, and Korean. To honor his father Dr. Lak-Geoon Paik (who was the president of Yonsei University), Mr. C. Charles Paik, an Indianapolis-based businessman, also established the L. Gregory Paik Scholarship in 1985 for students participating in the IU-Yonsei University exchange program.

Despite the active and significant fundraising, a fundamental problem in regularizing Korean language instruction at IU still remained: Instructional funding came only from outside sources drawn by the East Asian Studies Center and not regularly budgeted by the College. Therefore, the Center could hire only a graduate student for language instruction. On September 17, 1985, Phillip West proposed in his memo to the IU President John Ryan a strategic plan for 1986-88 that would "reduce the program's dependence on external and soft funding and build it into regular budgetary line." The newly elected EALC department chair Jurgis Elisonas also made a strong pitch to bolster the Korean studies program and drew positive support from College Dean John Lombardi.

The enthusiastic fundraising efforts by Phillip West and the SOFOKS members led to another fundraising campaign in 1985, this time to raise one million dollars for an endowed chair in Korean studies. As a result, Mr. C. Charles Paik was appointed as the President of the Board of Visitors for Korean Studies at Indiana University in 1986. The endowed chair fundraising campaign did not achieve its goal, but its efforts were not in vain. In response to the hard work of the East Asian Studies Center and the Department of EALC, Dean Lombardi of the College of Arts and Sciences announced a new tenure-track position in Korean language and culture at a banquet celebrating Korean Studies at IU on December 6, 1985. Accordingly, in 1986, Kenneth Wells, a New Zealand-born Korean historian, was hired as the first tenure-track assistant professor for Korean language and culture in the Department of EALC at IU.

Meanwhile, in 1985, the Indiana University East Asian Language Institute (EASLI), an intensive immersion summer language program, was established, thanks to the bold vision and leadership of Professor Eugene Eoyang. A model program had existed for Chinese and Japanese at Middlebury College, but IU was the first of its kind to include Korean. EASLI housed the Chinese, Japanese, and Korean Schools, and it became internationally known for its innovative teaching and unique learning environments. Nine students enrolled in the Korean School in the first year. EASLI lasted until 1999, and the following individuals served as its heads: Seok-Choong Song (1985-86), Joe Ree (1987-93), Hyo Sang Lee (1994-95), Young-mee Yu Cho (1996), Sungdai Cho (1997), and Jae-ok Cho (1998-99). Even though running the Korean School was hardly financially profitable due to its small size, the Korean School was always treated as an equal to its Chinese and Japanese counterparts. It is another example of how Korean was valued and considered important on its own merit.

Between 1982 and 1986, the Korean language and Korean studies program at IU achieved a great deal and laid a sound foundation for the program, as Korean language course offerings were reinstated in 1982. Other changes followed rapidly. As noted previously, the community-based support group Society of Friends of Korean Studies (SOFOKS) at IU, was established in 1983. An undergraduate exchange program with Yonsei University was established a year later. The East Asian Summer Language Institute (EASLI) was established in 1985, and it offered the only intensive summer immersion Korean language program located in the U.S. With all of these additions, along with the new hire of the tenure-track assistant professor of Korean language and culture Kenneth Wells, a new era of Korean language and Korean studies at IU began.

2.3. STABILIZING: 1986-1993

The Korean language and Korean studies program at IU reached a turning point in 1986, when Kenneth Wells was hired as a tenure-track assistant professor for the first time in Korean language and culture. The enrollment in First Year Korean quickly jumped from a single digit number in previous years to the high teens in the first three years of Professor Wells's hiring, and the number reached over twenty in his fourth year. Second Year Korean also received a boost in enrollment from low single digits to around ten on average. Third Year Korean, which was first offered in 1985, also consistently registered four to six students. Even though Professor Wells's specialty was in Korean history, he devoted himself almost entirely to Korean language teaching, often at the expense of teaching courses in his own specialty. He even developed Readings in Modern Korean Literature as a Fourth Year Korean course. With the help of native Korean graduate teaching assistants, he managed to teach two levels of Korean language courses every semester and offered his own courses as overload. During his first five years, he taught twenty-five courses. Thanks to his tireless efforts and hard work, the Korean language program not only became stabilized but also provided a full-fledged curriculum that regularly offered four levels of language courses.

While the Korean language program was firmly established after the arrival of Kenneth Wells, the Korean studies program had yet to develop in any substantial way, due to Professor Wells's commitment to developing the language program first. Still, even though he taught two language courses every semester, he managed to teach his own courses, such as Traditional Korea, Modern Korea, and a course on Korean Nationalism, but only as overload courses.

While Professor Wells could not offer courses in his own specialty to the fullest capacity during his tenure, he did organize a major international conference in 1989 on the Korean *Minjung* movement; its proceeding was published by the University of Hawaii Press in 1995 entitled "South Korea's *Minjung* Movement: the Culture and Politics of Dissidence." Meanwhile, he released a book entitled *New God, New Nation: Protestants and Self-Reconstruction Nationalism in Korea*, which was based on his dissertation and published by the University of Hawaii Press.

Another major achievement of his was a successful grant proposal for another faculty position in Korean studies. While the one million dollar endowed chair campaign was stalled, the East Asian Languages and Cultures Department (Professor Elisonas, Chair) and the East Asian Studies Center (Professor George Wilson, Director) did not shy away from developing the Korean studies program, which they saw as an integral part of East Asian studies. With Professor Wells's initiative, the department pursued another tenure-track faculty position in Korean culture. With the approval of Dean Mort Lowengrub, who was supportive of the East Asian studies program in the department, and the enthusiastic support of the East Asian Studies Center, Wells's proposal was integrated into the successful Title VI funding application of the East Asian Studies Center. After a failed initial search, the department hired Kyeong-Hee Choi, then a Ph.D. student in English literature at IU, in 1991. The Korean studies program at IU finally secured two tenure-track faculty members within the department in two key disciplines, Korean history and Korean literature.

Kyeong-Hee Choi taught advanced level Korean language courses as well as Korean literature courses she developed. She also arranged many visits and talks by famous Korean scholars of literature such as Young-Moo Kim (Seoul National University), Nak-Chung Paik (Seoul National University), U-Chang Kim (Korea University), and Sun-Young Lee (Yonsei University) to enrich the Korean studies program.

Another important component of the Korean studies program came from outside the EALC department. Roger Janelli, who was hired in 1975 in folklore, developed a course in 1981 entitled Korean Folklore and Elite Culture (E303), which started to draw a consistently large number of students. He also directed several dissertations on Korea and co-authored with Dawnhee Yim a book entitled *Ancestor Worship and Korean Society* in 1981 (Stanford University Press).

The interest in Korea at the IU campus grew steadily, and two big US-Korea Academic symposia were held, sponsored by Korea Economic Institute of America and East Asian Studies Center. The first symposium, entitled "United States-Korean Security Relations: Historical and

Economic Perspectives," was held on December 4-6, 1986. The second symposium, entitled "United States-Korean Economic Relations," was held on September 27-28, 1991.

With two tenure-track Korean studies faculty positions in history and literature within the department of East Asian Languages and Culture, and another faculty position in Korean folklore outside the department, IU was ready to develop a full-fledged Korean studies program, and it lacked only a Korean language expert. In 1991, the department (Richard Rubinger, chair) took the bold action of creating tenure-line language coordinator positions in all three East Asian languages. With another successful grant proposal for Title VI funding and the support of Dean Mort Lowengrub of the College of Arts and Sciences, the EALC department was able to hire three tenure-track language coordinators in Chinese, Japanese, and Korean in 1992. Hyo Sang Lee, a Ph.D. in linguistics from UCLA, was selected for the Korean language coordinator position; he deferred for one year in order to complete his University of California Presidential Postdoctoral Fellowship and then came to IU in 1993. At this point, all the necessary components had been filled, and the Korean language and Korean studies program at IU was ready to take off.

2.4. SOLIDIFYING: 1993-2014

Creating tenure-track language coordinator positions in all three East Asian languages had great implications for the field of language education and for Korean language education. First, it showed that the field was valued and respected as worthy of tenure positions, as in any other academic discipline. It is indeed rare, even now, that institutions of higher education grant tenure solely based on language education training. All three language coordinators hired at IU (in 1992 for Japanese and Chinese and in 1993 for Korean) have successfully been granted tenure. Many language educators at prestigious institutions, including the Ivy League schools, can serve only as lecturers, even those with Ph.D.s. Fortunate language educators who have been granted tenure by universities have been hired based on their distinctions in respective academic disciplines (which may include linguistics, second language studies, applied linguistics, etc.), not on their language teaching alone.

Second, the fact that hiring a Korean language coordinator was supported equally along with the additions of Chinese and Japanese coordinators was a clear indication that the EALC department and the East Asian Studies Center at IU valued Korean studies on its own merit and as an integral part of East Asian studies, not merely as an addition to the already existing Chinese and Japanese programs. At the time of Hyo Sang Lee's arrival as the Korean language program coordinator at IU, there were only a handful of universities that had tenure-track positions for those in charge of Korean language education: University of Hawaii, Ohio State University, Brown University, Brigham Young University, and University of Southern California. IU's bold action in fact might have influenced other institutions to consider creating tenure-track faculty positions for a Korean language program director or coordinator; UCLA, Rutgers University, and Arizona State University followed soon after IU helped set the precedent. Meanwhile, many Korean language programs, such as George Washington University and all SUNY programs (at Binghamton, Buffalo, and Albany), which created tenure-line faculty positions later, benefitted from the Korean government's initiative of globalizing Korean culture by obtaining funds from the Korea Foundation. The fact that none of the Korea-related faculty lines at IU were created with Korea Foundation funds — with the exception of the latest funding for an endowed chair (see section 3) — showed how much IU was committed to Korean studies. Considering the small size of the Korean language and Korean studies program, IU was commendable and pioneering in its approach, when many large and prominent Korean language programs, such as those at UC Berkeley, the University of Washington, University of Michigan, UC Irvine, Columbia University, Yale University, Stanford University, Harvard University, Princeton University, and the University of Pennsylvania, ignored the need for a tenure-track position for Korean language instructors. Even though it was still a small program, the Korean language program at IU decided to hire a tenure-track faculty member, putting the university on the map of Korean language education in the United States.

Hyo Sang Lee, the newly hired Korean language program coordinator, would play a prominent role on the national stage of Korean language education in the United States, co-authoring a major Korean language textbook series, creating widely used web-based material, becoming a key figure in the American Association of Teachers of Korean (a national organization of Korean language education), and helping to actively develop ACTFL National Standards for Korean.

Hyo Sang Lee inherited a quickly stabilizing Korean language program. The four-year language program had been firmly established; it included literature-reading courses and enjoyed decent enrollments. Lee would only have to solidify the curriculum and grow the program further. He first adopted new textbooks, the Korea University textbook series, for First through Third Year Korean. The series was new but was gaining popularity for its more colloquial dialogues and less mechanical drills than the well-known Yonsei University textbooks or the newly revised Myongo's Korean. The Korea University textbooks were used until the current textbooks, *Integrated Korean: Beginning 1* and *2* (University of Hawaii Press, 2000) and *Integrated Korean: Intermediate 1* and *2* (University of Hawaii Press, 2001) were published. *Integrated Korean: Beginning 1* and *2* were pilot-tested in 1999-2000 and adopted for First Year Korean in 2000. *Integrated Korean: Intermediate 1* and *2* were pilot-tested in 2000-2001 and adopted for Second Year Korean in 2001. Nam-Kil Kim's *Modern Korean: An Intermediate Reader* (University of Hawaii Press, 2000) was adopted for Third Year Korean. Fourth Year Korean courses had been literature-reading courses and were mostly taught by Kyeong-Hee Choi. After she left IU in 1997 to take a position at the University of Chicago, the Fourth Year Korean courses (Readings in Modern Korean Literature 1 and 2) could not be offered regularly and were last offered in 1997-98. When the Fourth Year Korean courses resumed in 2000-01 after a three-year hiatus, *Integrated Korean: Advanced Intermediate 1* and *2* were adopted as the textbooks in line with the new textbook series adopted for the lower-level courses.

Enrollment levels did not grow to an appreciable extent during the first ten years of Hyo Sang Lee's tenure but rather became solidified in the mid-twenties for First Year Korean, at about ten for Second Year Korean, and still around five for Third Year Korean. Notable changes in enrollment started to occur in 2002, incidentally coinciding with the change of textbooks. The Second Year enrollment marked consistently over ten, and the Third Year Korean enrollment also hovered around ten.

It is the last five years, however, that a more remarkable trend of increased enrollment began to emerge. The First Year Korean enrollment was 29 in the fall of 2009, thirty-six in fall 2010, 43 in fall 2011, and 51 in fall 2012. It jumped to 67 in fall 2013 and 81 in fall 2014, and it is expected to continue to grow in upcoming years. The ripple effect of the large enrollments in First Year Korean began to appear for Second Year Korean as well; 8 registered in the fall of 2009, 11 registered in fall 2010, and 18 in fall 2011. It passed 20 for the first time in fall 2012 with 21 students enrolled, then in fall 2013 with 24 students, and finally with 30 in fall 2014. The Third Year Korean enrollment also showed growth as well, as it has frequently enrolled over 10 students over the past eight years, particularly in 2013 and 2014. With the current enrollment of 30 in Second Year Korean, growth is expected in the upcoming years. Since the departure of Kyeong-Hee Choi, Fourth Year Korean courses (K401 and K402) were offered only sporadically until 2011; they were offered in 2000-01 and 2003-04. It was not until 2011-12 that Fourth Year Korean courses were offered again. Since then, they have been offered every semester for four years in a row, though enrollments have still been small and fluctuating. It was four and eight in K401 and K402 respectively in 2000-01, eleven and six in 2003-04, nine and ten in 2011-12, six and nine in 2012-13,[2] and four and four in 2013-2014. In the fall of 2014, there were five students enrolled in K401.

Since 2009, the total number of students enrolled in all Korean language courses in the fall semesters have increased from 48 in 2009 to

2 Fourth Year Korean courses in 2012-13 were taught as courses shared with University of Illinois. Three of the six students in K401 and four of the nine students in K402 were University of Illinois students.

57 in 2010, 76 in 2011, 85 in 2012, 107 in 2013, and 129 in 2014. The yearly total increased from 86 in 2010 to 99 in 2011, 131 in 2012, and 155 in 2013. It registered a huge jump to 184 in 2013-14. See the chart below.

Chart 1. Enrollments in Korean Language Courses 2009-2014

	F09	SP10	F10	SP11	F11	SP12	F12	SP13	F13	SP14	F14
K101/102	29	18	36	25	43	29	51	39	67	39	81
K201/202	8	8	11	9	18	13	21	16	24	23	30
K301/302	11	12	10	8	6	5	7	6	12	11	13
K401/402					9	8	6	9	4	4	5
Semester Total	48	38	57	42	76	55	85	70	107	77	129
Yearly Total	86		99		131		155		184		
AVE	43		49.5		65.5		77.5		92		

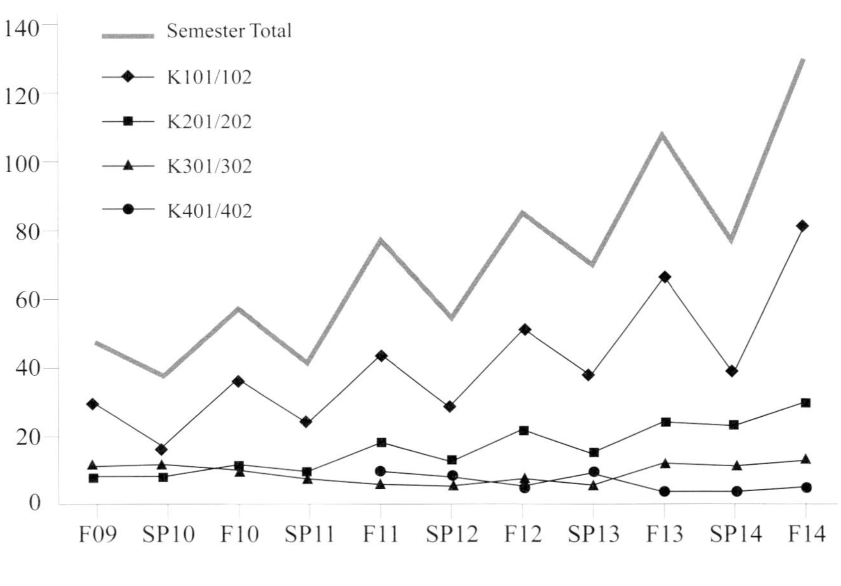

The increase in enrollments in Korean language courses seem to be attributed largely to three factors, which may be inter-related: (i) a strong South Korean economy, particularly represented by Samsung Electronics and Hyundai Motors, (ii) continued spread of the "Korean wave" in K-pop, K-drama, and K-movies, and (iii) a large influx of Chinese students into the United States. Notably, while it is definitely responsible for the large number of Chinese and other Asian students enrolled in Korean language courses due to the wide popularity of Korean popular culture, the "Korean Wave" is now widely spread among non-Asian students as well.

One of the most pressing issues for the Korean language program was how to best serve the needs of heritage learners. As mentioned earlier, heritage learners were scarce in Korean language courses at IU from the inception of course offerings in 1962. The number of heritage learners in Korean language courses began to increase in the mid-1980s, however, presumably due to the large influx of Korean immigrants in the 1970s. The increase in the enrollments of heritage learners was responsible for the overall increase in Korean language course enrollments in the late 1980s, and it helped stabilize the Korean program in terms of enrollment.

However, the presence of a large number of heritage learners caused formidable challenges for curriculum development. When possible, Hyo Sang Lee discouraged heritage learners from taking Korean language courses, particularly in lower-level courses. On the one hand, this decision helped to maintain a coherent curriculum from the beginning to advanced levels. On the other hand, it seemed to have worked against the Korean program's development in terms of enrollment. The heritage learners' presence reached the peak in the early 1990s at about 40 percent, but it fell back to 15 to 20 percent by the end of 1990s. Over the past few years, heritage learners have constituted only 10 to 12 percent.

With three tenure-track faculty members in all key disciplinary areas — language, literature, and history — along with another Korean specialist outside the department in folklore, Indiana University seemed poised to be a major center for Korean studies. Hyo Sang Lee, a Korean linguist, developed a full-fledged Korean language curriculum. Kenneth Wells, who had long been preoccupied with stabilizing the Korean language program, could now return to his own specialty, Korean history. Kyeong-Hee Choi, though still a lecturer without a Ph.D., was expected to draw national attention to the Korean literature program at IU. Roger Janelli continued to draw a large number of students to his popular course on Korean folklore and elite culture, and he also continued to produce Ph.D.s in Korean folklore.

The nineties brought unexpected changes to the program, as Kenneth Wells left IU in 1994, and Michael Robinson replaced him in 1995. Kyeong-Hee Choi, who was hired in 1991 while she was still a graduate student, finally received her Ph.D. in 1996. With the key components of Korean studies still intact, the department was about to submit a proposal for a Ph.D. program in Korean studies. However, Choi, who had been teaching courses on Korean literature and upper-level Korean language courses, left in 1997. No replacement was made, as the administration did not see signs of growth in the Korean literature program.

Meanwhile, the faculty productions in publication were stellar. In 1993, Roger Janelli published, with Dawnhee Yim, his second book entitled *Making Capitalism: The Social and Cultural Construction of a South Korean Conglomerate* from Stanford University Press. He also published, with Shima Mutsuhiko, an edited volume called *The Anthropology of Korea: East Asian Perspectives* (Senri Ethnological Series, No. 49, 1998). In addition, Michael Robinson co-authored with Gi-Wook Shin an edited volume entitled *Colonial Modernity in Korea, 1910-1945* (Harvard East Asia Council Publications, 1999), and he also published *Korea's Twentieth-Century Odyssey: A Short History* (University of Hawaii Press, 2007). Moreover, Hyo Sang Lee co-authored a series of major Korean language textbooks, *Integrated Korean: Beginning 1* and *2* (University of Hawaii Press, 2000), *Integrated Korean: Intermediate 1* and *2* (2001), and *Integrated Korean: High Advanced 1* and *2* (2005). The *Integrated Korean* textbooks have become the most popular Korean language textbooks, used by more than fifty colleges and universities in the United States.

With the tenure-track positions reduced to two in the department, however, the anticipated graduate program could not fully develop. The course offerings in Korean studies were limited to a few Korean history courses offered by Michael Robinson, the Korean Folklore and Elite Culture course taught by Roger Janelli in the folklore department, and a course in Korean language and culture, offered only sporadically by Hyo Sang Lee due to his primary focus on the language courses.

Kyeong-Hee Choi's leave and lack of replacement impacted not only the Korean studies program but also the language program. With no other faculty available to teach advanced level courses, Hyo Sang Lee could not cover even a three-year language program by himself, and he was forced to resort to having graduate students teach one of the three levels. The Korean language program was thus reduced to a three-year program from the four-year program it had once boasted.

In 2009, the EALC department finally added the third tenure-track position back into Korean studies. Still lacking demand for Korean studies, however, the department opened the search to all fields, and Heon Joo Jung in Political Science was hired freshly out of the University of Pennsylvania. He quickly boosted course offerings in Korean studies and drew a number of graduate students, particularly into the courses on security issues dealing with North Korea. Although the language program attracted a few graduate students in advanced language courses, it did not receive instructional benefits with the hiring of Heon Joo Jung, because as a social scientist, he could not contribute to teaching the upper-level language courses Kyeong-Hee Choi had taught.

Short on instructional staff, the Korean language program relied heavily on occasional outside resources. Hyunoo Lee, a Fulbright teaching fellow, taught a Fourth Year Korean in 2004. IU also gained from the visiting lecturer program of the Academy of Korean Studies on three occasions: the late Hyun-Gi Lee of Korea University taught various Korean language courses in 2000-2001, Sung-Hee Lee of Kyunghee University in 2007-2008, and Eunyoung Oh of Seoul National University in 2013-2014.

The rapid increase in enrolment in recent years made the need for an additional teaching staff more urgent. The EALC department began to pitch for a lecturer, and the search was approved in 2013. Starting from the fall of 2014, the Korean language program had two full-time language faculty members for the first time.

2.5. A NEW BEGINNING: 2014 AND BEYOND

With the recent drastic enrollment hike, the Korean language program at IU is flourishing. The fall semester of 2014 registered a record number of enrolled students, with 129 all together. There were 81 students in First Year Korean, which was offered for the first time as two lecture sections and five drill sections to accommodate the large enrollment.

Asian students still constitute a large body in First Year Korean courses, but non-Asian students outnumber Asian students in the current year, which is a positive trend for growth. The Second Year Korean enrollment has reached 30 for the first time. With the enrollment of Third Year Korean courses stabilized to over 10 students each semester, the courses will consist of 5 hours per week with 4 credit hours (they are currently 3 hour-per-week courses with 3 credit hours and no drill section), in parallel with their Chinese and Japanese counterparts.

Having anticipated the increased enrollment, the university had approved the department's request to add a full-time lecturer. Yuseong Cheon, who is finishing her Ph.D. degree in applied linguistics from the University of Minnesota, was hired in 2014, and the Korean language program at IU now has two full-time instructors. The addition of Ms. Cheon results in a number of positive effects: First, the IU Korean program is now a bona fide, full-fledged program, offering four levels of Korean language courses every semester. Before the hiring of the second full-time instructor, Fourth Year Korean had been offered only intermittently. Second, all Korean language courses are now taught by regular faculty members, not by a graduate student or a temporary visiting lecturer; previously a graduate student was hired to teach one of the Korean language courses, mostly Second Year Korean. Third, Hyo Sang Lee, a linguist, who had been teaching language courses, can now regularly offer content courses such as Korean language and culture and Korean linguistics, boosting Korean studies course offerings. Fourth, the addition of an expert in applied linguistics will help the Korean program develop a graduate Korean language pedagogy program.

Having to coordinate multiple lecture and drill sections and having to find suitable classrooms will be new but pleasant challenges for the future.

3. Prospects and New Challenges

While the Korean language program is flourishing, the Korean studies program at IU is undergoing changes and new challenges. Heon Joo Jung, the third tenure-track faculty in Korean studies, was hired in 2009 and left IU after the 2011-2012 academic year. Michael Robinson, the Korean history faculty, will retire after the 2014-2015 academic year. Having to fill these positions will be a formidable challenge, but fortunately, due to a generous grant from the Korea Foundation, a new faculty member for the Korea Foundation Endowed Chair in Korean studies is currently being sought. A social scientist faculty will be added to the Department of East Asian Languages and Cultures, just in time for the department's move into the newly established School of Global and International Studies, under the rubric of the College of Arts and Sciences. This position has been made possible with the efforts of three Korean IU alumni: Young-Jin Kim (CEO, Handok Pharmaceuticals Co.), Won-Suk Joo (chairman of Mediawill), and an anonymous third alumnus, who came up with a matching fund. It is our hope that Michael Robinson's position in Korean history will be filled promptly, and the loss of Heon Joo Jung's position will also be resolved sooner rather than later, preferably in cultural studies that cover literature, cinema, and popular culture. Although the Korean studies program at IU will be quite different in the future, the EALC department will have four tenure-track faculty members, which will not only boost both graduate and undergraduate course offerings in Korean studies but will also facilitate the long-overdue Ph.D. program in Korean studies. Additionally, stable numbers of graduate students will also be added to the advanced levels of Korean language courses, particularly in Fourth Year Korean.

IU President Michael McRobbie and the Office of International Studies are making efforts to expand ties and exchange programs with prominent Korean universities such as Sungkyunkwan University and Ewha Womans University, in addition to the currently existing exchange program with Yonsei University. With expanding programs in global and international studies and the newly established Korean chair, the outlook of Korean language and Korean studies program at IU is promising, especially if the vacant faculty positions are filled soon.

4. Summary

The Korean language program at Indiana University has a long history, dating back to 1962. Indiana University was the first institution in the Midwest to offer Korean language instruction. In 1965, the Korean studies program joined the then Department of East Asian Languages and Literatures (EALL). Despite the great vision and commitment of the department, Korean language course offerings came to a halt in 1971 due to insufficient enrollment. After a 10-year hiatus, Korean language course offerings were reestablished in 1982. Thanks to the tireless efforts of the East Asian Studies Center (EASC), the commitment and support of the department of East Asian Languages and Cultures (EALC), and the dedicated fundraising efforts of the Society of Friends of Korean Studies (SOFOKS), the first tenure-track faculty position for Korean Language and Culture was granted by the College of Arts and Sciences. As a result, Kenneth Wells, whose specialty is in Korean history, was hired in 1986. Wells devoted himself to establishing a viable Korean program, even at the expense of his own specialty, and worked to establish a firm four-year Korean language program. Thanks to Wells's hard work and devotion, another tenure-track faculty position was added in 1991, and Kyeong-Hee Choi was hired to teach Korean literature.

Hiring Hyo Sang Lee in 1993 as the tenure-track Korean Language Program coordinator helped to establish a full-fledged Korean language and Korean studies program, with three tenure-track faculty positions in key areas: language, literature, and history.

Unfortunately, when the Korean language and Korean studies program at IU was about to take off, Wells left in 1994. Even though Michael Robinson replaced him in 1995 for Korean history, Kyeong-Hee Choi left in 1997, and her Korean literature position was not replaced. Suddenly, the Korean studies program at IU was reduced to having only two tenure-track positions instead of three, and the Korean language program was reduced from a four-year program to a three-year program. The Korean studies program regained the third tenure-track faculty position when Heon Joo Jung in Political Science was hired in 2009 but lost it again when Jung left after the 2011-2012 academic year. With Michael Robinson retiring after the 2014-2015 academic year, the Korean studies program at IU will face a formidable challenge of having to fill these vacant positions. With the Korea Foundation grant and the three Korean IU alumni donors, however, the Korea Foundation endowed chair in Korean studies is currently being sought. We hope that the Korean studies program will be revitalized by the Korean chair and the addition of faculty members.

The enrollment in Korean language courses did not grow steadily and instead experienced a plateau for quite some time. It began to increase significantly starting in 2009, largely due to Asian students' interest in the "Korean Wave" but also due to the rise of the Korean economy on the international stage. In particular, the enrollment in First Year Korean has drastically increased and reached a record high of eighty-one students, which is nearly triple the figure from five years ago. To meet instructional needs, a full lecturer position has been added, and now there are two full-time instructors for the Korean language: one tenured faculty member and one full-time lecturer. The Korean language program at IU now is a full-fledged program that offers four levels of Korean every semester. We hope that the large enrollment in the lower level courses will solidify the enrollment in the advanced levels as well, particularly in Fourth Year Korean.

The unique characteristics of the Korean language and Korean studies program at IU are that (i) from the beginning, the Korean language and Korean studies program has been valued on its own merit and considered to be an integral part of East Asian studies, (ii) all the tenure-track faculty positions in Korean language and Korean studies were funded within the College of Arts and Sciences along with crucial help from the East Asian Studies Center, which subsidized the initial cost with the Title VI fund, and the SOFOKS (Society of Friends of Korean Studies), but not from any outside sources, except for the latest funding by the Korea Foundation for the Korean endowed chair, and (iii) from the program's inception in 1962, heritage learners were in the minority, and currently only about 10 percent of the students enrolled in Korean language courses are heritage learners.

There will be changes and new challenges in the near future, but with the continuing surge of the "Korean Wave," the current economic strength of Korea, and its strategic importance in the Northeast Asian region, the future of the Korean language and Korean studies program is bright at Indiana University.

ACKNOWLEDGEMENTS

Much of the information given here is based on material obtained from the Indiana University Office of University Archives and Records Management in Bloomington, Indiana. Some information is based on the documents about the Society of Friends of Korean Studies (SOFOKS) and the East Asian Summer Language Institute (EASLI) at the East Asian Studies Center.

I would like to thank Professors Jurgis Elisonas, George Wilson, Richard Rubinger, Bob Eno, Michael Robinson, Kenneth Wells, Kyeong-Hee Choi, and Sue Tuoy for providing me with valuable documents and information.

I am solely responsible for any errors or misrepresentations made in this article.

The Korean Program at Ohio State University

Danielle Ooyoung Pyun
Ohio State University

1. Introduction

Ohio State University (OSU) is one of the largest universities in the U.S. by enrollment, with a student population of over 51,000. The Korean program is housed in the Department of East Asian Languages and Literatures (EALL) in the College of Arts and Sciences. OSU's EALL Department is one of the largest East Asian programs in the U.S. and offers B.A. degrees in Korean, Chinese, and Japanese, as well as M.A. and Ph.D. degrees in Chinese and Japanese. Although graduate degrees in Korean are not yet offered in the Department (as of 2014), the East Asian Studies Center at OSU provides an interdisciplinary M.A. degree which includes Korea as a discipline of concentration.

The Korean program at OSU offers a wide array of language and literature courses as well as courses in culture, film, politics, and performance. Its faculty conduct research in the disciplines of literature, performance, and language pedagogy. Each year, the program has a vibrant community of over 350 students, who take Korean language, literature, and culture courses. Student organizations such as the Korean Student Association and the Korean International Student Organization are also active in collaborating with the Korean program to promote Korean language and culture. The program is committed to a high-quality undergraduate education that aims to train students in foreign language skills and to nurture their appreciation of cultural diversity so that they can cope with the challenges of globalization.

Figure 1. Hagerty Hall, where the Korean department is located

Figure 2. Cunz Hall, where the Korean department was housed until 2005

2. History

Ohio State University, which was founded in 1870, began its East Asian program in 1962 by establishing the Division of East Asian Languages and Literatures with three professors. The Division offered a B.A. in Chinese and Japanese, and soon added an M.A. in Chinese literature in 1967 and a Ph.D. program in Chinese in 1969. The Division later developed into the Department of East Asian Languages and Literatures in 1970. Afterwards, a Japanese graduate program was implemented by establishing a Japanese M.A. in 1971 and a Japanese Ph.D. in 1988.

Although Korean degree programs were not available at that time, the Department offered the first Korean language course (Elementary Modern Korean) in the autumn of 1981. It was taught by a graduate teaching associate, Youngman Kim, who is currently a Professor of Chinese at Pai Chai University in Korea but was then a graduate student in Chinese linguistics. The offering of the first Korean course was initiated and supported by the Department's then Chair, Timothy Light (1980-1986).[1] From 1981 to 1985, Elementary Modern Korean courses were offered and taught by Y. Kim, and the number of students enrolled was on average between 7 and 10 students per class. The Korean language program was supervised by Dr. Miles McElrath (Professor of Japanese)

1 The years in parenthesis indicate the duration of the professor's stay at the Ohio State University.

in 1981-1982 and then by Y. Kim from 1982 to 1985.

After Dr. Y. Kim left, Dr. Haeyon Kim (currently a Professor of English Language and Literature at Chung-Ang University in Korea) was hired as an instructor of Korean. During Dr. H. Kim's stay at OSU from 1985 to 1988, an intermediate-level Korean course and an advanced-level Korean course were offered. The move to add intermediate and advanced Korean courses was prompted by steady enrollments in beginner's level Korean as well as the students' wishes to continue their Korean language studies. When Dr. H. Kim left for Korea in 1988, the instructor position was succeeded by Professor SunAe Lee, who was at that time finishing her master's degree in Japanese at OSU. Professor S. Lee, who is currently an adjunct faculty at Santa Barbara City College, taught three levels of Korean (beginning, intermediate, and advanced) for three years from 1988 to 1991. During that time, enrollments ranged from 13 to 15 students for beginning Korean, 10 to 15 students for intermediate Korean, and around 10 students for advanced Korean. According to Professor S. Lee, the ratio of heritage versus non-heritage learners in the beginning and intermediate Korean classes was about 1 to 1 at the time. On the other hand, the majority of students in the advanced Korean course (about 80%) were heritage learners. Professor S. Lee recalls the challenge of teaching heritage and non-heritage learners in the same class, particularly in the beginning-level course. She remembers that she often had to provide different learning tasks for the two groups within the same classroom in order to cater to the distinct needs and abilities of two learner groups.

From 1983, the Korean program started to expand not only in language courses but also in non-language courses. That year, Professor Yung-Hee Kim (1983-1996) joined OSU as a Professor of Japanese Literature and took a leading role in forming the basis for the Korean program, especially its new non-language courses. The implementation of this initiative was made possible with Prof. Y.-H. Kim's passion to promote Korean studies at OSU as well as the department's plan to meet its vision of featuring all three languages and literatures of East Asia (Chinese, Japanese, and Korean), befitting the name of the department.

Several non-language courses were newly developed by Prof. Y.-H. Kim between late 80s and early 90s, including Elements of Korean Culture, Korean Literature in Translation, and Women Writers, Culture, and Society in East Asia. As a professor of Japanese literature, Prof. Y.-H. Kim's main teaching duty involved courses in Japanese literature, but she taught Korean courses occasionally. In 1990, with increasing interest in Korean language and literature and with the support of the Department's then Chair Shigeru Miyagawa, Professor Y.-H. Kim proposed a new faculty position for Korean. The position was supported by the department and filled by Professor Ik-sang Eom in 1991.

Professor Ik-sang Eom (1991-1993) was hired as Assistant Professor of East Asian Languages and was responsible for teaching Korean language, culture, and his area of specialty, Chinese linguistics. By this time, a more defined structure was achieved with the two professors, whose three levels of Korean language courses, a culture course, and a literature course have been the core components of the Korean curriculum through the present. Table 1 gives an idea of the scale of the program in its early days:

Table 1. Korean Courses and Enrollments in the Academic Years 1991-1993

Courses	Average enrollment per course
Level One Korean I, II, III	10-20
Level Two Korean I, II, III	5-10
Level Three Korean I, II, III	3-5
Korean Culture (Elements of Korean Culture)	15-17
Korean Literature (Korean Literature in Translation)	15-20

After serving two years at OSU, Professor Eom left OSU to assume a faculty position in Korea. After Professor Eom's departure, the program experienced a major crisis that nearly led to the program's closure. The proposal to close the Korean program was a cost-cutting measure as part of financial restructuring attempts made by the university at that time. The restructuring and budget constraints were affecting many programs and departments across the university, and Korean became one of the targeted eliminations. Professor Y.-H. Kim then stepped forward and fought to sustain the Korean program. She talked to the president and dean of the university in person, pleaded for support from students and the Korean community in Columbus, Ohio, and petitioned the university to keep the Korean program alive. In addition, she flew to Korea, met with government and academic authorities and OSU alumni to drive fundraising efforts, and called for financial support from the Korea Foundation. *The Korea Times* reports her desperate endeavors and resulting success as follows:

> To save Korean studies at the university, Kim made every possible effort that she could — from building awareness among university authorities of the university about the significance of Korean studies to organizing field trips to Korea which were accompanied by the president and dean of the university. ··· The department survived the tough times after the Korea Foundation (KF) committed to providing $100,000 to finance the university's hiring of a tenure track professor in 1994. (*The Korea Times*, September 13th, 2011)

Professor Y.-H. Kim's application to the Korea Foundation for the support of a new professorship in Korean studies was KF's first application of this kind, and as a recipient of the award, OSU was able to establish a new tenure-track position.[2] The position was offered to Professor Chan E. Park at the assistant professor level in 1995. After serving for 13 years, Professor Y.-H. Kim left OSU in 1996, when she was invited to the Department of East Asian Languages and Literatures

2 The Korea Foundation, which was established in 1991, is an organization intended to "promote better understanding of Korea within the international community and to increase friendship and goodwill between Korea and the rest of the world through various exchange programs" (Article 1, Korea Foundation Act). The Korea Foundation supports Korean studies at universities overseas, in part by funding the establishment and sustainment of tenure-track professorships for a period of three to five years.

at the University of Hawai'i at Manoa. Her position was filled by a new faculty member in Japanese literature. Professor Y.-H. Kim's initiatives and numerous contributions laid the firm foundation of the Korean studies program at OSU. In retrospect, Professor Y.-H. Kim recalls that awareness about Korea used to be very low, and this encouraged her to fight to make the university and administrative authorities aware of Korea's standing and leverage in the world.

Building upon the foundation formed by predecessors, Professor Chan E. Park continued to expand the program by launching various initiatives. Foremost, she pioneered degree programs in Korean. With her proposals and the persuasion of college authorities, a Korean minor was established in 1999 and Korean major in 2005, which gave the department a new structure as well as visibility within OSU and nationwide. As a result of these milestone achievements, the program started to become recognized as a solid academic discipline at OSU.

As a professor of Korean literature and expert in oral narratives and performance arts, Professor Park added new courses, including Performance Traditions of Korea and Interdisciplinary Courses in Korean Art, Music, Film, and Theatre. Her research, creative work, and hands-on performance arts workshops gained great popularity among students and significantly enhanced interdisciplinary relationships across departments such as dance, music, and comparative studies. The EALL Department views faculty research and teaching in East Asian traditional performance and oral texts as key elements of its distinct strength and reputation.

Under Professor Park's leadership and with the support of Professor Jim Unger, who was then the Chair of the EALL Department, a new faculty position was created in 2001, and it was funded by the Korea Foundation for 5 years. Thereby, having two tenure-track faculty members enabled the exponential growth of the program, making OSU one of the strongest undergraduate Korean studies programs in North America. In 2005, Professor Park was also recognized for her establishment and chairing of the Korean Studies Initiative (OSU's Korean Studies Center), which was the precursor of the present Institute for Korean Studies.

Professor Eun Joo Kim, appointed in 2001, was a specialist in Korean pedagogy and second language acquisition. She was given the responsibility of coordinating the growing Korean language program. Professor E. Kim was also active in research, the material development of Korean, and editing for the American Association of Teachers of Korean (AATK) newsletter. The Korean language program continued to gain national recognition during Professor E. Kim's prolific career at OSU.

After Professor Eun Joo Kim left for her new job in Oregon in 2005, the present author Danielle O. Pyun joined the Korean faculty in 2006 as an Assistant Professor. As a specialist in Korean language pedagogy and SLA (Second Language Acquisition), Professor Pyun assumed the responsibility of coordinating the Korean language program and developing materials for Korean Individualized Instruction (self-directed learning). During the first two years of her hire, she offered Individualized Instruction courses in Korean to keep stride with seven other foreign language programs that offered Individualized Instruction[3]. With the addition of the new Individualized Instruction track, coupled with the rising demand for Korean, the Korean language program grew to a substantial size, doubling enrollment from 60-65 per school term in 2002-2005 to 100-130 in 2010-2012.

In 2011, the department promoted one of the Korean lecturers to a senior lecturer in order to accommodate the increasing operational needs of the program. The position of senior lecturer was created to retain a Korean language professional with a doctorate degree and years of teaching experience, and this position thereby addressed increasing leadership and administrative responsibilities in coordinating the Korean language program. As the Chinese and Japanese programs both had non-tenure track academic program specialists who coordinated the Chinese and Japanese language programs, the department's decision to offer a senior lecturer appointment in Korean indicated one step forward

3 Individualized Instruction at OSU is an individually paced self-study program using programmed materials. As a mastery-based program, students are required to master each learning unit or module before proceeding to the following unit (see the section "*Two tracks of the language program*" in this paper).

towards achieving a greater balance among the three branches (Chinese, Japanese, and Korean) and securing more systematic management of Korean language courses.

3. Current Status

3.1. THE FACULTY, TEACHING STAFF, AND COURSE OFFERINGS

There are currently two faculty members (Professor Chan E. Park and Professor Danielle O. Pyun) in the Korean program. Professor Park teaches mainly non-language courses (e.g., literature, performance tradition, classical texts, Korean film/theatre), whereas Professor Pyun teaches language, culture, and language pedagogy courses. There are also a full-time senior lecturer and two full-time lecturers. In addition, part-time lecturers are hired at times on an as-needed, per-term basis to meet enrollment overloads.

Korean courses that are regularly offered directly in the Korean program are as follows:

- Level One Korean I, II (Classroom Track)
- Level One Korean I, II (Individualized Instruction Track)
- Level Two Korean I, II (Classroom Track)
- Level Two Korean I, II (Individualized Instruction Track)
- Level Three Korean I, II (Classroom Track)
- Level Three Korean I, II (Individualized Instruction Track)
- Level Four Korean I, II (Classroom Track)
- Elements of Korean Culture
- Korean Literature in Translation
- Korean Language: Structure, Culture, and Communication
- Performance Traditions of Korea
- Interdisciplinary Courses in Korean Art, Music, Film, and Theatre
- Interdisciplinary Topics in Korean Politics and Society
- Introduction to Korean Linguistics
- Readings in Korean Literary and Classical Texts

There are other courses on Korean topics (e.g., Korean politics, North Korea, Modern Korean history) offered by faculty members in other departments (e.g., Department of International Studies, Department of History) at OSU. In addition, OSU joined the Committee on Institutional Cooperation (CIC), a consortium of Midwestern universities, to create an e-class system of shared courses with Korea-focused content. Through the CIC program, students can take courses on Korean studies from professors at other institutions; courses include Korean 4194 (Cultures of the Cold War in Korea) and History 3194 (Controversies in Contemporary Korea).

The list of elective courses that are offered from departments other than Korean that are counted towards the Korean major and minor are as follows: Asian Philosophy; Introduction to Asian American Studies; History of Thoughts in East Asia; Asian American Film; East Asian Folklore; Women Writers, Culture, and Society in East Asia; Performance Tradition in Contemporary East Asia; Scripts of East Asia; and Buddhist Art of Korea.

3.2. KOREAN MAJOR AND MINOR

When the Korea Foundation funded two faculty positions for the OSU Korean program in 1995 and 2001, the department pledged to establish a Korean minor degree and a Korean major degree for each funding period. Accordingly, a Korean minor was created in 1999, and a Korean major was formed in 2005. Since the establishment of the Korean B.A. degree in 2005, the program started to attract students from other states. Many of the Korean majors reported that they chose or transferred to OSU to earn the degree in Korean.

Korean B.A. students at OSU are required to take a total of 80 credit hours of required and elective courses (prerequisites 25 credit hours and requirements 55 credit hours). Korean minors are required to complete 45 credit hours (25 credit hours of prerequisites and 20 credit hours of requirements). With the addition of a Korean major, Level Four Korean courses were implemented for the first time in 2006, and efforts have been made to maintain consistent course offerings to ensure that Korean major and minor students can fulfill required courses and graduate in a timely manner. On average, about five to seven students declare Korean as their major every year; thereby, there are about 20 to 25 Korean majors on campus. The total number of Korean minors ranges from 30 to 40. Although official data has not been collected, recent Korean B.A. graduates found employment in sectors such as federal/state government, international security, military, translation service, education (e.g., teaching in Korea), and graduate programs in Korea and the U.S.

3.3. STUDENT ENROLLMENTS

Unlike many colleges in the East and West coasts, the number of non-heritage Korean language students at OSU is considerably high, due to its location in the Midwest. On average, approximately 80 percent of the students are of non-heritage background. The proportion of heritage learners, however, increases as the class level increases. The recent ratio of non-heritage to heritage learners in the classroom track is about 85 to 15 percent in Level One Korean, about 80 to 20 percent in Level Two Korean, about 75 to 25 percent in Level Three Korean, and about 60 to 40 percent in Level Four Korean.

Currently, OSU provides five years of Korean language instruction. The four levels of language courses are offered every school term in sequence. The fifth-level course is offered once a year and involves readings of literary texts. The enrollments of Korean language courses have grown steadily over the past two decades. During 2002 to 2005, the total enrollment numbers for Korean language courses ranged from 53 to 64 students per quarter. With the implementation of Individualized Instruction in 2006, the program has seen a substantial increase in the number of Korean learners: The number of Korean language students from autumn 2002 (64 students) to autumn 2011 (121 students) doubled. Another notable achievement was maintaining Level Four Korean courses since 2006. In stabilizing fourth year Korean language courses, OSU has greatly benefited from the KF-AATK (Korea Foundation-American

Association of Teachers of Korean) fund for two years, in 2007 and 2008.[4] When this support ended, the department created an additional lecturer position to maintain Level Four Korean and to accommodate more students in Individualized Instruction courses. The enrollments for all Korean language courses (the combined number of students enrolled in the classroom track and Individualized Instruction) ranged from 84 to 96 per quarter between 2006 and 2009, 103 to 121 per quarter between 2010 and 2011, and 148 to 163 per semester between 2012 and 2014.[5]

In addition to language courses, non-language courses are popular with students from all disciplines. Among them, the two most popular ones are the Korean literature course and Korean culture course, which are undergraduate GEC (General Education Curriculum) courses. Each of the two courses is offered once a year and attracts on average 50 to 60 students.

With the strong undergraduate program in Korean studies, the Korean department has been committed to producing competent students who can work in Korea and the U.S. in various fields as well as producing potential scholars who will pursue graduate studies in Korea-related fields. In this endeavor, the Department of East Asian Languages and Literatures created the Korean Studies Award (with a monetary gift) for outstanding undergraduate students majoring in Korean, starting from the year 2007. The department also started offering summer Korean courses from 2007 in order to meet students' needs. In an effort to promote East Asian studies, the department also started to provide an annual undergraduate research forum for Korean, Chinese, and Japanese majors, who presented research projects on, for example, translations of pre-modern or modern Korean literature or in-depth research on other Korea-related issues.

---

4 KF-AATK (Korea Foundation-American Association of Teachers of Korean) fund is a graduate student teaching fellowship awarded by the American Association of Teachers of Korean with sponsorship from the Korea Foundation. The funding is awarded for one year but can be renewed for an additional year upon successful use of the fund and renewal application.

5 The Ohio State University converted its academic calendar from quarter terms to semester terms in 2012.

3.4. TWO TRACKS OF THE LANGUAGE PROGRAM

OSU provides Individualized Language Programs for 8 different languages (Chinese, French, German, Japanese, Korean, Portuguese, Russian and Spanish), which are innovative for their self-directed learning approaches. Individualized instruction offers "self-paced, mastery-based language learning programs designed to mirror the course offered in the classroom" (OSU Center for Languages, Literatures and Cultures, https://cllc.osu.edu/undergraduate/individualized).

While the Individualized Instruction (I.I.) program shares the same content and goals of regular Korean classes, students do not meet on a regular basis. Instead, I.I. students study programmed learning materials individually and have their self-learning checked by the I.I instructor through one-on-one meetings. Students can personally schedule the time of appointments with the instructor and can also decide or adjust the number of credit hours. An I.I. course equivalent to a classroom Korean course (e.g., a course with 4 semester credit hours) typically involves the completion of about 55 assignments. After self-studying each assignment, students are required to have a 15-minute check-up session with the I.I. instructor. During the appointment, the student's self-learning is evaluated by the instructor through various activities such as dialog performance, role play, or questions/answers. Ultimately, an I.I. course that is equivalent to a classroom Korean course will involve 55 individual sessions with the instructor (15 minutes × 55 sessions) in addition to one's self-study of the given materials. It is therefore critical for a student to engage in autonomous learning in a disciplined and responsible manner, by using the given material and following the guidelines specified in the course syllabus.

By implementing the individualized language track in addition to the traditional classroom track, the OSU Korean program was able to recruit more students including: (a) those who could not take a classroom Korean course due to time conflicts with other courses, (b) those who wanted to accelerate his/her learning pace (e.g., Korean heritage learners), as it is possible to take two language courses within a school term in the individualized language track, (c) those who had a much slower learning pace than others, (d) those who preferred one-on-one interactions between the instructor and the student. The advantage of Individualized Instruction was that "it can cater to the needs and abilities of the individual students" and "students are less affected by the time constraints which often prevent students from continuing their language study in a timely manner" (Pyun 2008, 356). This track was by no means considered a replacement for classroom instruction but rather regarded as complementary to it. As the content and goal of Individualized Instruction was the same as those of traditional classroom courses, a student who completed the individualized Level One Korean I class, for example, could proceed to either individualized Level One Korean II or classroom Level One Korean II. By providing both options of classroom and individualized courses, the OSU Korean department was able to improve the retention rate in language courses.

Currently, approximately 35 to 45 percent of the total number of Korean language students are enrolled in individualized courses. Individualized Instruction sessions are managed and taught by the regular Korean teaching staff (that is, Korean lecturers and teaching associates).

3.5. THE INSTITUTE FOR KOREAN STUDIES

The Korean program at OSU is operated under a very cooperative environment. The Korean program collaborates closely with OSU's East Asian Studies Center (EASC), which has been the recipient of the Title VI Grant from the U.S. Department of Education for years. In 2005, determined to strengthen OSU's high-ranking East Asian program, the Office of International Affairs created the Korean Studies Initiative under the East Asian Studies Center. The Korean Studies Initiative was directed by Professor Chan E. Park for six years. In 2010, the Korean Studies Initiative was promoted to the Institute for Korean Studies, for which Professor Park served as the inaugural chair. In 2011, Dr. Mitchell Lerner from the Department of History succeeded Professor Park as the Institute's director. Dr. Lerner's research focuses on modern American diplomatic/political history and U.S.-Korean relations during the Cold War.

The mission and vision of the Institute for Korean Studies (IKS) is "to provide leadership for Korean Studies at the Ohio State University and assist academic and administrative units of the Ohio State University to advance and disseminate knowledge about Korea" (the OSU Institute for Korean Studies website). The institute is devoted to enhancing OSU's Korean Studies program "in all areas of research, education, and professional service including outreach for K-12 education, business, the community, the state and the nation" (the OSU Institute for Korean Studies website). The IKS contributes to building a lively intellectual community, hosting lecture series in Korean Studies, and promoting student and faculty exchanges with Korea. A few examples of IKS-hosted Korean Studies lectures during 2011-2014 are as follows: *Korea and the United States in the 21st Century* by Ambassador Dr. Han Duk-soo, Korea Ambassador to the U.S; *Living on Air: The Art of Dae-Kyun Kim* by Dae-Kyun Kim, Preserver of the Tightrope Performance, Korea's Intangible CulturalAsset No. 58 and 2011 UNESCO designee as a World Intangible Cultural Heritage; *Korean Diaspora, Korean Christianity, and Cultural Challenge* by Young-chan Ro, Professor, Religious Studies, George Mason University; *Korean History Upside-Down: Why The Traditional Story Has It Wrong* by Mark Peterson, Professor, Brigham Young University; *Shamans, Ghosts and Healing the Community* by Michael J. Pettid, Professor, Binghamton University (SUNY).

3.6. THE NATIONAL EAST ASIAN LANGUAGES RESOURCE CENTER

The National East Asian Languages Resource Center (NEALRC) at OSU is another organization with which the OSU Korean program closely collaborates. The NEALRC was founded in 1993 with a mission to advance research and knowledge about East Asian languages; to develop Chinese, Japanese, and Korean language materials and assessment tools; and to train East Asian language program builders, educators, and pre-service teachers with proficiency-oriented and performance-based teaching methods. The center has particularly been striving to produce high-quality learning materials that will increase East Asian language learners' levels of language proficiency and cultural competence.

In 2006, NEALRC completed a project on Korean self-study materials, *Pathway to Korean: Beginning Spoken Korean From Zero*, consisting of five units and more than forty learning stages. The center published them in a print format with an audio CD program and also made them available online for the general public to access for free (https://pathwaytokorean.osu.edu/). It also published books on Korean language and literature through OSU's Foreign Language Publications (FLP), a nonprofit publisher of world language materials. Among them was a 2012 publication of research papers on Korean language acquisition, *Teaching and Learning Korean as a Foreign Language: A Collection of Empirical Studies*, which included contributions from leading scholars and teachers in the field of KFL (Korean as a Foreign Language); it was edited by Andrew Byon and Danielle Pyun. Another publication was a series of bilingual poetry books titled *Songs of Thorns and Flowers: Bilingual Performance and Discourse on Modern Korean Poetry*; this series was published between 2010 and 2013. The books were edited with an introduction, translation, and commentary by Chan E. Park. The titles are as follows: Volume 1, *The Tree*, selected poems by Kim Hyung-Young; Volume 2, *There Remain Words to Say*, selected poems by Yoo An-Jin; Volume 3, *Winter, 5 Minutes Past Midnight*, selected poems by Hwang Tong-gyu; and Volume 4, *Sunlight in a Distant Place*, selected poems by Hong Yunsook.

4. Future Prospects

OSU's increased enrollment in Korean language courses and offerings of new non-language courses are the direct outcomes of the Korean department's steadfast commitment to expansion. There is, however, much more to be accomplished in order to build a comprehensive, high caliber Korean program.

The current goal of the Korean faculty is to establish graduate degree programs (both M.A. and Ph.D.) in Korean. To realize this, the Korean faculty and the Institute for Korean Studies are making concerted efforts to secure one more tenure-track position in Korean studies. With the hiring of an additional faculty member, the faculty plans to offer graduate degrees with the following areas of specialization: Korean literature, Korean performance arts, and Korean pedagogy.

Another goal of the program is to hire one more Korean language instructor. At this point, due to instructor shortages, the program often cannot accommodate all wait-listed students in language courses. Furthermore, due to a lack of teaching staff, the Korean faculty at times has to teach language courses at the expense of some non-language courses. Having another Korean instructor will help the faculty to focus more on teaching, developing non-language courses, and supervising the language program.

The language program's overall goal is to produce competent students who are well-equipped with linguistic skills and cultural knowledge in Korean and who would further seek advanced professional or academic goals. A more specific goal is to increase students' proficiency levels in Korean and to provide more proficiency-oriented instruction and assessments. To this end, the program aims to conduct proficiency tests such as the ACTFL (American Council on the Teaching of Foreign Languages) OPI (Oral Proficiency Interview), given to students in Level Three or Four Korean as an exit exam so as to examine proficiency levels and to take their results as an evaluation of OSU's own Korean language program.

5. Closing Remarks

From its humble beginning in 1981 with fewer than ten students, the Korean program at OSU has expanded not only in size but also in scope and range of academic courses and activities. With a tradition of over 30 years, the Korean program at OSU has grown to be one of the few in the

U.S. offering a Korean B.A. The community of Korean Studies includes two core faculty members, three lecturers, and affiliated members in other departments including International Studies, History, History of Arts, and Comparative Studies.

Although the Korean program has made significant progress, it has not grown at a similar rate of development when compared to the Chinese and Japanese programs. A full-fledged graduate program for Chinese language and literature was established in 1969 and for Japanese language and literature in 1988, but there is not yet one for Korean. Among the twenty faculty members of the department, ten are specialists in Chinese language/literature, eight are in Japanese language/literature, and only two are in Korean language/literature. In order for the department to achieve a reputation as a truly leading East Asian program, a graduate program in Korean is essential. Under the financial pressure that many universities face, continuing challenges of the Korean program today are (1) securing financial resources to create more faculty positions and implement a graduate program and (2) maintaining a high level of instructional service (e.g., individualized attention to students) with a better ratio of instructors to students.

The Department of East Asian Languages and Literatures, the Institute for Korean Studies, the East Asian Studies Center, and the National East Asian Languages Resource Center are making collaborative efforts to offer or improve (1) new Korean courses (2) a Korean-library collection, and (3) degree programs in Korean. We envision that this collaborative endeavor will bring positive outcomes in the coming years.

ACKNOWLEDGMENTS

The author greatly appreciates the professors who provided valuable information regarding the history of the Korean program at the Ohio State University. Any errors or inaccuracies that remain are the sole responsibility of the author.

REFERENCES

AATK Korea Foundation Graduate TA Fellowship Grant. (n.d.) In *American Association of Teachers of Korean.* Retrieved October 20, 2014, from http://www.aatk.org/www/html/KF-AATK_Graduate_TA_Fellowship_Grant.html

About Us. (n.d.) In *The Department of East Asian Languages and Literatures.* Retrieved from October 20, 2014, from https://deall.osu.edu/about-us

AT&T Individualized Instruction. (n.d.) In *Center for Languages, Literatures and Cultures*, Retrieved from October 20, 2014, from https://cllc.osu.edu/undergraduate/individualized

Foundation Act. (n.d.) In *Korea Foundation*. Retrieved from October 20, 2014, from http://en.kf.or.kr/?menuno=524

IKS at a Glance. (n.d.) In *East Asian Studies Center.* Retrieved October 20, 2014, from http://iks.osu.edu/

Kang, Hyun-kyung. (2011). Scholar Fights for Korean Studies. *The Korea Times.* Retrieved from http://www.koreatimes.co.kr/www/news/art/2011/09/116_94655.html

Pyun, Danielle O. (2008). Curricular models for heritage Korean learners in U.S. Colleges. *Proceedings of the 18th International Conference on Korean Language Education*, (pp. 343-359).

[Untitled photograph of Hagerty Hall.] Retrieved October 20, 2014, from http://www.osu.edu/map/building.php?building=037

Welcome. (n.d.) In *The National East Asian Languages Resource Center*. Retrieved October 20, 2014, from http://nealrc.osu.edu/

Princeton Korean Language Program: Entering another 25 years and beyond

Joowon Suh
Princeton University

1. Introduction

It has been 25 years since a Korean language class was first offered at Princeton University. The Korean language program, housed in the Department of East Asian Studies (henceforth EAS), has since grown to offer five levels of Korean language instruction along with a specially-designed heritage-learner track and a total of four full-time lecturers of Korean. A program in Korean studies at the university came into existence much later; it was not until 2007 that the long-overdue Korean studies program was created with the hiring of two tenure-track professors in history and film studies. Despite the relatively small number of undergraduate and Korean-heritage students compared to peer institutions, the department has aimed to establish a small but robust Korean studies program within the field of East Asian studies. With the expansion of both Korean language program and Korean studies, many expectations as well as challenges lie ahead in the coming years at Princeton University, where diversity and globalization have been pursued and reinforced in recent years.

This chapter captures the past, present, and future of the Korean language program at Princeton University. First, the brief history of the EAS Department is reviewed. Next, the beginning of the Korean language program and its progress are examined and analyzed in detail, followed by the overview and development of its curriculum.The development of the Korean studies program is then examined. Finally, the challenges and future directions of the Korean language program are discussed.

2. Department of East Asian Studies

The Korean language program is centered in the well-established EAS Department, along with Chinese and Japanese language programs. Although its origin can be traced back to the Department of Oriental Languages and Literatures, founded in 1927, the EAS Department at Princeton truly began with Frederick Mote, a scholar of Chinese history. He came to the department in 1956 and started Chinese language instruction. Marius Jansen, the first Japan scholar, joined the Department in 1959 and started Japanese language instruction in 1960. The East Asian section of Oriental Studies grew steadily during the 1960s, mainly in Chinese and Japanese language, history, and literature. It was in 1969 that the Department of Oriental Studies was divided into East Asian Studies and Near Eastern Studies. These two departments, Princeton's only regional studies, still share Jones Hall and Frist Campus Center, which are adjacent to each other.

Picture 1. Jones Hall:
East Asian Studies Department

Picture 2. Frist Campus Center:
Chinese, Japanese &
Korean Language Programs

The EAS Department has long been deeply rooted in the humanities, primarily in literature and history. In the past few years, however, with several new hires in the social sciences and contemporary studies (i.e., anthropology, politics, cultural studies), the EAS curriculum has undergone substantial changes by integrating a wider range of new courses (e.g., *Contemporary East Asia, Contemporary Chinese Society and Culture, Japanese Pop Culture and Globalization, Sexuality and China, Gendered Identities in Contemporary Korea, East Asian Cinema, Korean Cinema, The Passionate Eye: Documentary Film in East Asia*) into the already-established undergraduate curriculum in languages, literature, and history. Although a relatively small department with 25 concentrators on average, the EAS has the second-largest language programs, following the Department of Spanish and Portuguese Languages and Cultures. Every year, more than 750 students enroll in all three East Asian language classes. In addition, the number of students obtaining the EAS Department and the EAS Program Certificates[1] has increased in recent years. In the academic year (henceforth AY)2013-2014, 30 students received the certificates, and among them 7 students pursued them in the Korean language, which is the highest number thus far for Korean.

As of AY2014-2015, the EAS Department includes 41full-time faculty members, including 23 language lecturers, 8 full-time staff members, 41 graduate students pursuing a doctoral degree, and 24 undergraduate majors. Table 1 is a summary of the EAS faculty in Chinese, Japanese, and Korean studies, including affiliated faculty members from the departments of art and archeology, comparative literature, politics, religion, sociology, and the Woodrow Wilson School of Public and International Affairs. In AY2014-2015, two searches for tenure-track faculty in Chinese literature and Korean studies have been conducted aiming at the appointment dates starting in September 2015.

Closely related to but financially separate from the EAS Department is the East Asian Studies Program, an umbrella organization for East Asian studies and related departments at Princeton such as art

1 A more detailed explanation on these two different certificates related to East Asian studies is provided in the next section, in which the Korean language program is reviewed.

Table 1. EAS Faculty as of AY2014-2015[2]

	Tenured/Tenure Track Faculty	Language Lecturers (including Senior Lecturers)	Affiliated Faculty	Total
Chinese	9	13	5	27
Japanese	8	6	6	20
Korean	1	4	0[2]	5
Total	18	23	11	52

and archeology, politics, religion, and sociology. With its independent financial resources, the EAS Program provides support to undergraduate concentrators as well as graduate students for their research and language studies, and it organizes various East Asia-related lectures, conferences, and events on campus throughout the year.

3. Korean Language Program

3.1. ITS BEGINNING AND EXPANSION

From the very beginning of East Asian studies at Princeton, language study has been viewed as the foundation of all further research at both undergraduate and graduate levels. The Chinese and Japanese language programs were created in 1956 and 1960, respectively. However, it was not until 1991 that Korean language courses were first offered at Princeton. This was possible partly due to the constant demand and support of Korean-American students, represented by the Korean American Student Association, one of the most active and dynamic student organizations on campus.

Having received her doctorate at Teachers College, Columbia University and having taught at Columbia University and Indiana University,

2 Gilbert Rozman, a professor of sociology, specialized in East Asian societies (including Korea), retired in 2013.

Gwee-Sook Kim joined the Department in 1991, first as a language lecturer. She started a Korean language program by offering *Elementary Korean I* in the fall of 1991 and *Elementary Korean II* in the spring of 1992, with a total of 33 students enrolled. With Kim's promotion to senior lecturer[3] of Korean language in the following year, a new half-time lecturer, Bonghee Choi (1992-1998), was hired to offer 2nd Year Korean. In AY1995-1996, within only four years since the first Korean language class on campus, the program grew to offer 3rd Year Korean.

Between 1996 and 2006, the Korean language program has stabilized with two full-time faculty members offering 1st through 3rd Year courses. Under the leadership of Gwee-Sook Kim as the director of the program, Eun Joo Kim (1999-2001), Chee-Hee Kim (2001-2003), as well as Joowon Suh (2003-2008), taught in the program as language lecturers. Until her retirement in 2008, Gwee-Sook Kim built and stabilized a strong foundation for Princeton's Korean language program. Despite the lack of steady courses in Korean studies, Kim implemented effective administrative visions and pedagogical strategies, which are great models for any language program director at the initial stage.

In 2006, the program expanded with a two-semester sequence in 4th Year Korean, initiated by a couple of students. The two students, who had completed 3rd Year Korean in the previous year, wrote a petition to the Department and had a meeting with the department chair to appeal for more advanced-level Korean classes. The course proposal was expeditiously processed and approved. After the three years of temporary-course status, a two-semester sequence of 4th Year Korean was permanently included in the course catalogue, with steady enrollment records. With the offering of 4th Year Korean, the EAS Department officially administered the *Language and Culture Certificate*, which requires a total of seven semesters of language instruction.

In the fall of 2008, after an extensive national search, Joowon Suh

3 In AY2014-2015 out of 22 foreign languages offered at Princeton, there are a total of 10 senior lecturers hired by foreign language programs to direct and coordinate the programs, including Arabic, Chinese, French, German, Italian, Japanese, Korean, Portuguese, Russian, and Spanish.

took over the director's responsibilities following Gwee-Sook Kim's retirement, and the Korean language program at Princeton has since started to expand to its full potential in terms of both student enrollment and number of teaching staff. For the past six years, enrollment numbers have clearly displayed continuous and steady growth, from a total of 43 students in AY2007-2008 to 149 in AY2013-2014 (see Graph 1). Such increased enrollment, which has more than tripled, is in line with a national trend in Korean language programs at other North American colleges and universities. The successful expansion of Princeton's Korean program has been possible thanks to the combination of the following internal and external factors: (1) the enhanced and stabilized curriculum offering 1st Year through 5th Year Korean; (2) individualized instruction that fosters the sense of community across all levels of Korean language courses; (3) the expanded and strengthened Korean studies at the university; (4) consistent support from the department and university; (5) carefully-devised short-term and long-term administrative plans and strategies; (6) the increasing popularity of Korean popular culture; and (7) the status of Korea as a nation, maintained via its economic power and geopolitical importance within the international community.

Graph 1. Korean Language Course Enrollment AY2003-2013[4]

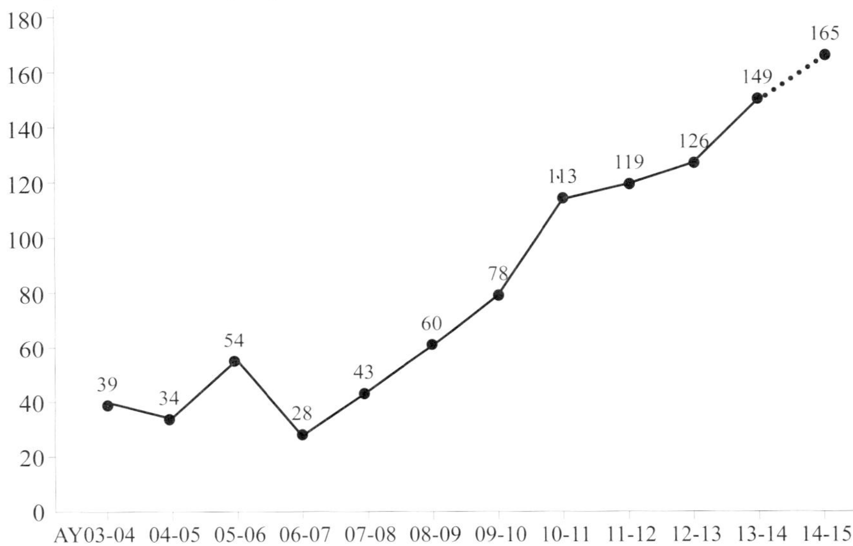

While the Korean language program is still the smallest within the EAS Department, with the rapid increase of student enrollment and growing demand in recent years, the number of Korean language faculty also expanded. For twenty years, the university maintained a two-full-time-lecturer structure but then developed to its current capacity of four full-time lecturers of Korean. Currently in AY2014-2015, Joowon Suh (Senior Lecturer and Director of the program), Ho Jung Choi, Eunjung Ji, and Yuseon Yun are the four lecturers of Korean.

The enrollment in 1st Year Korean increased sharply, in part due to the boost earned from the Global Seminar in Seoul in the summer of 2010, a funded seminar by the Princeton Institute of International and Regional Studies. A half-time position of Korean language lecturer was added in AY2010-2011, and Yuseon Yun was hired after receiving her master's degree in Korean language education at Ewha Womans University in Seoul and teaching at the Yonsei University Korean Language Institute. In the following year (AY2011-2012), this half-time position was expanded to a full-time position based on the results (i.e., enrollment) and prospects (i.e., plans for curriculum expansion). In the same year, with the sudden departure of Jini Noh (2008-2011), Ho Jung Choi, a Ph.D. candidate in the Department of Foreign Language Education at the University of Iowa, joined the faculty with his extensive teaching experience. Again in AY2012-2013, a quarter-appointment position was added to ease the workload of the current teaching staff.[5] In the following year (AY2013-2014), with the unexpected 25% increase in enrollment numbers (see Graph 1), this quarter-time position was modified to a half-time position, and again to a full-time position in AY2014-2015. Colleges and universities tend to be cautious about adding positions to current teaching staffs due to financial and institutional responsibilities,

4 As seen in the graph, the relatively sharp decrease in enrollment in AY2006-2007 is due mostly to the unusually low enrollment in 1st Year Korean (i.e., a total of six students). It may be related to the previous year's unusually high 1st Year enrollment (i.e., a total of 27 students).

5 At Princeton, 12 hours per week of classroom teaching are required for a language lecturer.

and in that sense, the Korean program at Princeton was truly fortunate to be able to make strong arguments for additional lecturer positions and to have the financial means to support these newly created positions.

This welcomed expansion of the teaching staff from two to four full-time lecturers made the creation of two new much-needed courses possible. In order to meet the needs of both undergraduate and graduate students with diverse language needs and levels of proficiency, particularly in upper-level classes, a year-long 5th Year Korean was officially offered in AY2011-2012. In the following year (AY2012-2013), a separate heritage-learner track was created in order to ease the varying needs of heritage and non-heritage learners in lower-level courses.

3.2. CURRICULUM OVERVIEW AND DEVELOPMENT

The Korean language program at Princeton currently offers five levels: *Elementary Korean* (KOR101/102), *Intermediate Korean* (KOR105/107), *Advanced Korean* (301/302), 4th Year Korean-*Contemporary Korean Language and Culture* (KOR401/402), and 5th Year Korean-*Readings in Modern Korean* (KOR405/407), along with a year-long heritage-learner track, *Intensive Korean* (KOR103/108).

All students in the Bachelor of Arts track[6] at Princeton are required to study two years of a foreign language unless they are placed out of 2nd Year-level language courses. Accordingly, completing two years of Korean, either up to 2nd Year Korean or the Intensive Korean I & II sequence, satisfies the university's foreign language requirement. Although a considerable number of students place out of the language requirement by taking placement tests at the beginning of an academic year, this two-year language requirement has helped to stabilize 1st and 2nd Year language courses, including Korean, at Princeton.

One of the advantages of learning Korean at Princeton is, first and foremost, small class sizes. With each class limited to 10 to 12 students,[7]

---

6 Students in the Bachelor of Science and Engineering track have no language requirement.

students can have ample opportunities to use the target language in classrooms. Particularly in 1st and 2nd Year courses, which meet five times per week in small groups, students develop a special sense of belonging to a community of learners, who share the same goal of becoming proficient in the language. In upper-level courses, an even smaller class is expected and, in fact, has become the norm. For instance, the smallest class that the author has taught at Princeton was one 4th Year Korean class with only three students. Currently, the maximum enrollment numbers for both 4th and 5th Year Korean classes are set at 12.

The Korean classes at Princeton are also known for individual care and attention. This is Princeton's overall atmosphere for undergraduate education, particularly in small departments such as the EAS. For instance, 1st Year and 2nd Year students have bi-weekly 15-minute individual speaking sessions with instructors. This is not officially implemented within the curriculum but has been welcomed by students as one of the most positive aspects of lower-level classes, in which students need more support and individualized care. In upper-level Korean courses, 30-minute individual writing conferences are held at least twice a semester. Since students' writing competences in upper-level courses vary significantly, individual attention to their weaknesses and difficulties is considered invaluable. It needs to be pointed out, however, that despite the rewards and benefits that can be earned from these sessions, these outside-class sessions tend to put additional pressure on the instructors.

Another characteristic of Princeton's Korean language classes is that there is no graduate teaching assistant system employed within the EAS Department. That is, all language classes are taught, homework assignments are reviewed, individual sessions are conducted, and quizzes and tests are administered and graded by language lecturers. This practice is deeply rooted in the belief that language courses must be taught by

7 The maximum number of students allowed to enroll in each language class varies from one foreign language to another. For instance, European languages set enrollment at around 14 to 16, whereas East Asian languages have 9 to 12 students per class.

professional instructors who have proper pedagogical training. This is unique to both the EAS and Near Eastern language programs. There are obviously different practices on campus; in other foreign language programs, such as French, German and Spanish, graduate student teaching assistants are employed and encouraged to teach classes, since these teaching opportunities are considered an integral part of graduate student training.

Over the past six years, since the author has taken over the program in 2008 as the director of the program, the Korean language curriculum at Princeton has undergone considerable changes in order to meet the varying needs of the diversified student population in Korean classes. For the last few years, several noticeable changes have been observed in the student population taking Korean language classes at Princeton: (1) the increasing number of non-heritage language learners enrolled in 1st and 2nd Year Korean; (2) the increasing number of heritage language learners who begin their Korean language instructions in upper-level classes; and (3) the diversifying heritage language learner population in terms of their backgrounds and proficiency levels in Korean. With ever-increasing diversity in students' proficiency levels and goals, it has become all the more necessary to reassess and reshape the Korean language curriculum. As part of the curriculum changes that reflect the varying needs of both heritage and non-heritage students, two new courses, 5th Year Korean and Intensive Korean, have been created.

First, in AY2010-2011, only after five years since the addition of 4th Year Korean, the two-semester sequence 5th Year Korean, *Readings in Modern Korean I* and *II*, was created. It was at first offered as a pilot program in the spring of 2011 with 11 students enrolled, close to the maximum enrollment number of 12. The 5th Year Korean course is aimed at four different student groups at Princeton: (1) students who wish to continue the Korean language study after having completed 4th Year Korean; (2) high-advanced heritage language learners; (3) graduate students who need professional and academic reading knowledge of Korean; and (4) native speakers of Korean with a few years of formal education in Korea. In particular, the course is designed to meet the needs of an increasing number of heritage learners, having come to the U.S. or other English-speaking countries after completing some formal education in Korea. It has been recognized that these particular students need to improve their literacy competencies as well as speaking abilities in formal settings.

The primary goal of the course is to raise levels of Korean competency to that of an educated native speaker of Korean by focusing on extensive reading, rapid vocabulary building, and employing a variety of authentic materials, which range from think pieces to literary short stories and historical texts. It should also be noted that Princeton's upper-level courses are designed for students to learn the language through lessons on Korean culture, society, and history. Based on these pedagogical goals, 5th Year Korean is conducted as a small seminar on Korean history and politics through literature and films, and it aims to promote a deeper understanding of Korea. Recognized by the department, all 5th Year courses in Chinese, Japanese as well as Korean are cross-listed with EAS departmental course numbers (e.g., KOR405/EAS405) and counted as an EAS-content course for EAS majors and certificates.

The creation of 4th and 5th Year courses has made it possible to earn official certificates in Korean, which are administered separately by the EAS Department (*Language and Culture Certificate*) and the EAS Program (*East Asian Studies Certificate*). The *Language and Culture Certificate* in Korean, offered by the EAS Department, stresses Korean language competence and proficiency, and it requires seven Korean language courses. The *East Asian Studies Program Certificate* is equivalent to a minor and is administered by the East Asian Studies Program. It requires four Korean language courses, including at least two courses beyond 2nd Year Korean. In AY2013-2014, six out of eighteen EAS Certificate recipients specialized in Korean, and this number represents a substantial increase from an annual average of one student earning the certificate in Korean. In this sense, steady growth in the number of students pursuing certificates is one of the forces that have vitalized upper-level Korean language courses.

Secondly, a much-needed separate heritage track, *Intensive Korean I* and *II*, was first offered in the AY2012-2013 with a total of 10 students enrolled. In the following year (AY2013-2014), a total of 14 students enrolled in this heritage track, showing a 40% increase. The need for lower-level intensive Korean courses for heritage language learners has long been an urgent issue for the growth of Princeton's Korean language program. The co-existence of heritage learners (i.e., those acquiring and using Korean at home) and non-heritage learners (i.e., those without any exposure to the Korean language prior to Korean classes at school) has always been one of the most pressing issues not only for the Princeton program but also for other Korean language programs in North America. The needs of heritage learners are quite different from those of non-heritage learners, even when their proficiency levels are similar. Heritage learners, growing up using Korean within a natural, input-rich setting (i.e., with their parents and relatives), tend to lack in reading and writing skills but are relatively competent in speaking and listening. On the other hand, non-heritage learners, comprising of more than 80% of the 1st and 2nd Year Korean classes in AY2014-2015, find speaking and listening the most challenging.

The presence of heritage learners in these lower-level classes, designed mainly for non-heritage learners, has presented the teaching staff with enormous pedagogical challenges due to their differing needs and variations in their knowledge of Korean. Offering a separate heritage-learner track eases these difficulties in that instructors are able to accommodate different needs of lower-level heritage learners, who would otherwise need to be placed in the second half of 1st Year and 2nd Year Korean in the spring, preventing these students from starting Korean in the fall. The creation of a separate heritage-learner track means fewer disruptions in 1st and 2nd Year Korean classes in the spring semester.

In addition, these accelerated courses for heritage learners are expected to strengthen 3rd Year Korean, since the students who have finished these year-long intensive courses would be able to make a smooth transition into upper-level classes. After only one year of offering the separate heritage track, the enrollment numbers of 3rd Year Korean have increased from 10 students in AY2012-2013 to 25 in AY2013-

2014. These numbers indicate the positive impact of offering year-long heritage-track courses.

4. Korean Studies

While Korean language instruction has been a featured part of the East Asian studies curriculum since 1991, opportunities for the study of Korean at Princeton were limited to language training and occasional coursework. A number of visiting scholars sporadically taught courses on Korean history, economy, and culture at the university over the years (i.e., five visiting scholars since 2001), but no regular tenure-track or tenured position in Korean studies existed until 2006.

In the grant proposal to the Korea Foundation, written by the then department chair, David Howell, a scholar of Japanese history who is currently at Harvard University, the institutional demand as well as an intellectual rationale for a program in Korean studies at Princeton was eloquently articulated as follows:

(1) No credible program in East Asian Studies can afford to dismiss Korea;

(2) The field of East Asian Studies has developed and matured to the point that it will soon be impossible to assert leadership in the area without a modest program in Korean studies;

(3) Within the East Asian context, Korea's history related to neighboring countries, geopolitical importance, and economic development as well as dynamic popular culture makes Korea a crucial location for the study of history, politics, international relations, and economy in the contemporary world.

Recognizing the growing importance of Korean studies, Joy S. Kim joined the EAS Department in 2006 as a tenure-track assistant professor of Korean history. Trained at Columbia University as a scholar of early modern Korean history, her specialization includes the social structure of the late Chosŏn period and the formation of modern cities in the context of Korea's modernization. She offered courses at both undergraduate and graduate levels: *Modern Korean History, Korea before 1875, Readings in Early Modern Korean History*, and *Gendered Identities in Contemporary Korea*.

In the following year (AY2007-2008), partially supported by the Korea Foundation, an additional tenure-track position in Korean studies was created and filled by hiring Steven Chung in Korean film and culture studies. Having earned his doctoral degree at the University of California, Irvine in film studies, Steven Chung's research interests are interdisciplinary, ranging from East Asian and Korean films to critical theories in literary and culture studies. He has offered undergraduate and graduate seminars such as *Introduction to Korean Cinema, Global Spectacle and East Asian Cinema, Cinematic Translation,* and *Critical Trespasses*.

A number of programs that aim to expand Korean studies' integration with scholarship across the Princeton campus have been initiated by these two assistant professors since their arrivals, such as annual invited lectures on campus. A Global Seminar organized by the Princeton Institute for International and Regional Studies is also a great example of their efforts. In the summer 2010, a six-week seminar titled *Dreaming, Mapping, Living: The City in the Korean Imagination* was co-taught by Professors Joy Kim and Steven Chung, who took 15 Princeton students to Seoul. As briefly mentioned in the previous section, the impact of the Seoul Global Seminar on the Korean language program as well as the Korean studies program was substantial in terms of raising the visibility of the programs at the university and increasing student enrollment in Korea-related courses.

In addition to the faculty appointments and growing language programs, the East Asian Library, which is a part of the Princeton library system, hired a full-time librarian, Hyoungbae Lee, through an initiative by the EAS Program in 2008. He now exclusively oversees the growing Korean language collection. It is clear that the seemingly fast development of Korean studies is the result of years in the making, with the support from the department and the EAS Program, which constantly seeks to secure financial resources inside and outside the university.

There were two more recent developments in the Korean studies program, one a disappointing one and the other encouraging one. Effective in AY2013-2014, Joy Kim, who had been an assistant professor of Korean history for seven years, left Princeton due to personal reasons. Her departure is undoubtedly a great loss for Korean studies, the department, the university, and the field of Korean studies in general. Losing 50% of the tenure-track faculty force, at first, seemed not only devastating but also regressive. In AY2013-2014, however, Steven Chung was promoted to an associate professor with tenure. In addition, in AY2014-2015, a search to fill Joy Kim's position for Korean studies has been conducted, chaired by newly-tenured Steven Chung, and the department expects a new faculty member in Korean studies to arrive at Princeton in the next academic year. In addition to this replacement in Korean studies, both the EAS department and the university are trying to create a third position in Korean studies within a few years to assure that the Korean studies at Princeton has a greater status within the field of Korean studies and East Asian Studies in the US.

Table 2. Korean Studies Faculty as of AY2014-2015 (in an alphabetical order)

Name	Position	Hired at Princeton	Area	Education
Choi, Ho Jung	Lecturer	2011	Korean language	M.A. University of Iowa Ph.D. Candidate, University of Iowa
Chung, Steven	Associate Professor	2007	Korean culture studies & cinema	Ph.D.,University of California, Irvine
Ji, Eunjung	Lecturer	2013	Korean language	Ed.M., Teachers College, Columbia University
Lee, Hyoungbae	Librarian, East Asian Library	2008	Library science	M.L.S., Syracuse University
Suh, Joowon	Senior Lecturer; Director, Korean Language Program	2003	Korean language	Ed.D., Teacher's College, Columbia University
Yun, Yuseon	Lecturer	2010	Korean language	M.A. Ewha Woman's University; Enrolled in Ph.D. Program, Rutgers University

As seen in Table 2, currently in AY2014-2015, excluding an unfilled tenure-track position, Princeton's program in Korean studies and language consists of one tenured professor, one senior lecturer as the director of the Korean language program, three full-time lecturers of the Korean language, and a librarian of Korean studies.

5. Korean Language Program: New Challenges and Future Directions

The main challenges that the Korean language program at Princeton faces, closely interconnected with one another, can be summarized in terms of the following three issues: enrollment, curriculum development, and the expansion of Korean studies.

5.1. ENROLLMENT

Most Korean language programs at private universities in the U.S. have been under pressure to maintain a certain level of enrollment numbers to make the program viable. This is clearly a different kind of pressure than that of large-scale state university programs, which may need to deal with more financial constraints.

The Princeton Korean language program is still the smallest language program in the department, following Chinese and Japanese, as in most U.S. colleges and universities. Although enrollment in Korean classes has increased in the last few years, the enrollment pressure is still the most imminent and pressing issue to which the Princeton program needs to attend. Princeton offers a total of 22 foreign languages, including Latin as well as classical and modern Greek. Korean maintains roughly the 9th largest enrollment at the university, closely following Portuguese and followed by Russian. It is crucial for the Princeton Korean language program to maintain its current size in order to grow further as a robust program that can be more visible not only at the university but also nationwide.

As briefly discussed in the previous section, the enrollment numbers in 1st and 2nd Year Korean have stabilized mainly because of increasing non-heritage students taking Korean. The 4th and 5th Year enrollment numbers have also stabilized due to the fact that a number of heritage students tend to start in upper-level Korean classes. As seen in Graph 2 below, the enrollment in 3rd Year Korean, however, is still relatively unstable and unsatisfactory. The rather weak enrollment records of 3rd Year Korean may be attributed to a number of factors. First, the foreign language requirement at Princeton is up to 2nd Year Korean; thus, most students stop taking language classes after 2nd Year. Second, there is a considerable leap from 2nd to 3rd Year in terms of the difficulty of vocabulary and reading materials, partially because the goal of instruction is refocused from speaking and listening to literacy development. Third, the instruction of Chinese characters starts from 3rd Year Korean and adds a new challenge for some students. Finally, 3rd Year Korean is when heritage and non-heritage learners, with varying proficiencies and needs, collide. Such mixed-level 3rd Year classes have presented new pedagogical challenges to the teaching faculty.

The issues regarding under-enrolled and mixed-level 3rd Year classes tend to become more complex, particularly within a 5-year curriculum, such as Princeton's. 3rd Year Korean, situated in the middle of the curriculum, may fail to identify its own distinctive pedagogical objectives and curricular roles. It may even turn into a mere stepping-stone course that is not necessary to stay within the overall curriculum. One way to deal with these issues is to develop a more flexible curriculum with various instructional materials. Its pedagogical goals should be concrete enough to be clearly presented to students but at the same time flexible enough to be adequately modified based on each year's student population. Administratively, creating hybrid courses such as the Intensive Korean sequences may also help to stabilize the enrollment of 3rd Year Korean.

Graph 2. Enrollment for 1st-5th Year Korean (AY2003-2013)

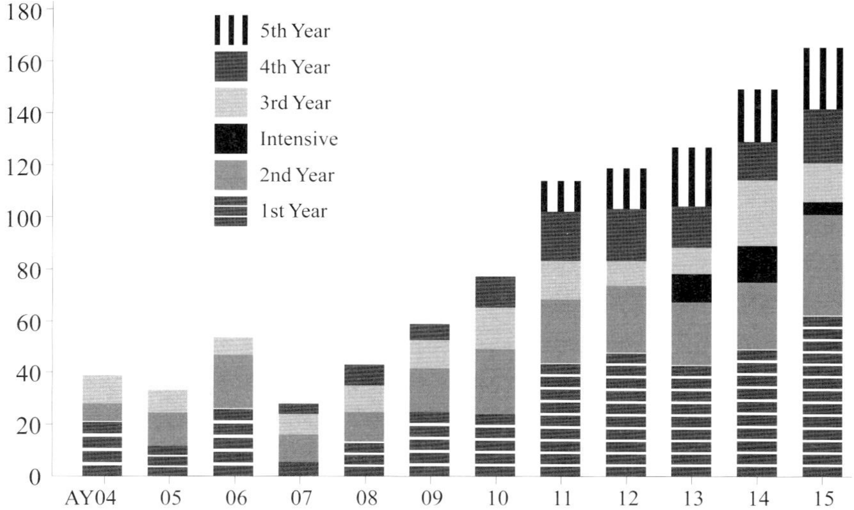

5.2. FURTHER CURRICULUM DEVELOPMENT

As previously examined in detail, the Korean language curriculum at Princeton has undergone substantial transformations in recent years in order to better serve the ever-changing student population and to prepare for further growth in the years to come. Considering a great range of practical issues (e.g., the size of both undergraduate and graduate student body, the number of Korean heritage students at the university, the curriculum of other foreign language programs on campus, the size of the Korean programs at other peer institutions), it may be a realistic and reasonable goal to sustain the existing structure of the Korean language program (i.e., five years of Korean instruction with a separate heritage learner track). I, as the director of the program, personally take great pride in the whole spectrum of courses that Princeton currently offers as well as its effective and successful development over a relatively short period of time. Still, it is vital to constantly revisit, modify, and refine the current curriculum, especially upper-level courses.

The increasing number of non-heritage students, who start in 1st Year

Korean and continue through 4th Year, makes it necessary to divide upper-level classes, particularly 3rd Year Korean, into separate heritage and non-heritage sections eventually. Presently, it is not plausible due to insufficient enrollment numbers and the small number of non-heritage students enrolled in upper-level courses. However pedagogically sound it may be, realistically this is possible only at a very small number of state universities with large-scale Korean programs. This issue indeed has become a dilemma for relatively small Korean language programs. There is a pressing need for separate heritage and non-heritage tracks, but practical difficulties make it challenging to execute such a plan due to the relatively small class sizes. Adopting a compromised and creative approach is one way to deal with the issue. For instance, because 3rd Year Korean at Princeton in AY2013-2014 shows unusually high numbers for both overall enrollment (25 students) and for non-heritage students (7 students), one out of three classes per week can be divided into two separate sections designed for heritage and non-heritage students.

Another challenge related to curriculum development is to establish an intensive summer language program in Korea. Princeton has long supported directly-run summer language programs. There are currently nine foreign language programs at Princeton that operate summer programs, ranging from 4 to 8 weeks of instruction in countries where the languages are spoken. Among these nine summer language programs, Chinese (*Princeton in Beijing, PIB*) and Japanese (*Princeton in Ishikawa, PII*) summer language programs, both of which started in 1993, are the oldest and the most established. Until recently, the Korean language program's relatively small size and the developmental stage of Korean studies program did not warrant a Korean summer language program on par with PIB and PII. In order to grow further as a robust program, however, there is strong need for a summer Korean language program run by Princeton faculty in cooperation with a major teaching university partner in Korea.

While a few undergraduate students attend summer language programs in Korea, such as those at Sŏgang University, Ewha Womans University, and Seoul National University, many more students hesitate enrolling in those programs since they do not automatically receive Princeton course credits for their 10-week coursework without taking examinations upon their return to Princeton. In addition, since these programs are outside the regular Princeton curriculum, it is not always easy for returning students to make seamless transitions into a next-level Korean course. Princeton-run summer programs would motivate more students to pursue Korean language learning during the summer and increase 3rd Year Korean enrollment numbers. Furthermore, this type of a summer program, functioning as a Korean counterpart to PIB and PII programs, would help the Korean language program to be better integrated into the EAS curriculum.

Despite all these potentially positive impacts, several constraints in launching a summer intensive program are also expected. Aside from logistical complexities of administering a US-based program in Korea, it would impose huge constraints on the current teaching staff of four. More importantly, there is a possibility that a summer language program may weaken 2nd Year Korean at Princeton instead of boosting 3rd Year Korean, since students can complete the Princeton language requirement within a year, through a sequence during the fall, spring, and summer terms.

It is still too early to say whether this type of summer program will come into existence in the near future, and if it does, whether it will be successfully implemented. It is necessary, however, to carefully consider the potential gains and losses of a summer language program before launching such a program. It may be helpful to conduct a one-time pilot program in order to gauge and assess students' needs more accurately.

5.3. FUTURE OF KOREAN STUDIES AT PRINCETON

The importance of a co-existing Korean studies program and a Korean language program at a research institution cannot be emphasized enough. In order to maintain a healthy and robust language program and to grow further, strong and steady support of a Korean studies program is unequivocally essential. In that sense, the Princeton Korean language program is fortunate to have a young and promising Korean studies program.

The back-to-back appointments of two junior professors marked an important step toward the creation of a strong program in Korean studies at Princeton. After eight years, however, the Korean studies program at Princeton has come to a crossroads. As mentioned in the previous section, the departure of Joy Kim (an assistant professor of Korea history) in AY2012-2013, the recent tenure of Steven Chung (a professor of Korean film and culture studies) in AY2013-2014, and the ongoing search for an assistant professor of Korean studies to replace Joy Kim in AY2014-2015 will play significant and decisive roles in the future of Princeton's Korean studies. A third tenure-track faculty position has now become even more essential for a competitive Korean studies program in order to produce both undergraduate and graduate students concentrating on Korea-related issues.

While the Korean studies program at Princeton stands on strong foundations with promising prospects, it also must make greater strides to become a leader in its own right. First, it needs the resources to raise its profile within Princeton to attract greater undergraduate student interest and more diverse faculty engagement. The Princeton Korean studies program also needs to increase its visibility within the field of East Asian studies, especially to prospective graduate students. These goals cannot be achieved without further expanding the Korean language program, sponsoring major research projects and events on campus, substantially augmenting the size of the Korean library collection, and advancing more cultural and language exchanges.

6. Conclusion

Thus far, I have reviewed the beginning and development of the Korean language program and Korean studies within the EAS Department at Princeton University. I have discussed in detail how Princeton's Korean language program and Korean studies program have developed over the years, what challenges both programs have encountered, and how we will deal with them together in the future.

In order to maintain a successful Korean language program, earning and sustaining departmental and university-wide support is crucial. The support needs to be practical, systematic, and durable. At Princeton, it is also essential to position the program within the established framework of the department, vis-à-vis the programs in the Chinese and Japanese language and studies. Maintaining a rigorous program with an outstanding reputation is the best way to earn respect from the department and to establish a good standing within it. In addition, it is important to have a long-term vision as well as short-term strategies for not only the program itself but also collaborations with other areas of East Asian studies. These may sound rather obvious and even trite, but I have learned as an administrator that these plans are never that simple to put into action.

It has been almost 25 years since the first Korean class was ever taught at Princeton University. Over those years, the program has developed into a robust curriculum consisting of five years of Korean instruction as well as a separate heritage-track. This was all possible thanks to consistent support from the EAS Department and Program, the devoted faculty of the Korean language program, and constant enthusiasm of both heritage and non-heritage students taking Korean classes. Issues remain and new challenges lie ahead for the program to further grow, but I, as the director of the Korean language program, hope that the Princeton program will become an ideal model of a small but robust language program at a private university. I remain cautiously but firmly positive and confident about its bright future in the coming years.

The Korean Language Program at Rutgers, the State University of New Jersey

Young-mee Yu Cho
Rutgers University

1. Rutgers University

Rutgers University is the largest institution for higher education in New Jersey and the eighth-oldest college in the United States, founded in 1766. Rutgers is the only public university in New Jersey in the Association of American Universities (AAU), a group comprising North America's 62 leading research universities. Rutgers and Princeton are currently New Jersey's only AAU members. Rutgers has three campuses across the State of New Jersey, with its largest campus located mainly in the City of New Brunswick and Piscataway Township, and two smaller campuses in the cities of Newark and Camden. These campuses comprise 27 degree-granting schools and colleges, which offer undergraduate, graduate, and professional levels of study.

Rutgers is a leading national research university with more than 54,600 students and 4,150 faculty members. Rutgers-New Brunswick is classified by the Carnegie Foundation as a "Research Intensive University." Eleven of Rutgers' graduate departments are ranked in the top 25 by the National Research Council among all universities. Rutgers is also home to the first and still top-ranked Women's Studies Department, and it is the only university in the United States to grant Ph.D.s in the interdisciplinary field of Childhood Studies. Rutgers' diversity — from age to sexual orientation to ethnic background — is one of its strengths, and it enables students to transcend boundaries to meet the challenges of a complex and interdependent world. Currently, about 23 percent of the entire student population consists of those of Asian ethnic backgrounds, including nine percent of Korean descent.

According to the 2010 U.S. Census, New Jersey has the third-largest Korean population in the U.S. states, following California and New York. As of 2010, there were approximately 1.7 million Korean Americans. Los Angeles, with its Koreatown district, is home to the largest population of ethnic Koreans outside of Asia. However, Palisades Park, New Jersey, which is only 40 miles from Rutgers-New Brunswick, has the highest concentration of people of Korean ancestry in the United States, at 51.5% of the city's population. A decade after Korean was included in SAT Subject Tests in 1997, the Korean community in New York and New Jersey came to recognize the need to establish permanent Korean language instruction on a broader scale throughout public school curriculum, in addition to university-level programs.

The Department of Asian Languages and Cultures at Rutgers was established in 1969 to cultivate, promote, and coordinate the study of East Asia. It is now home to three programs in East Asian Studies: Chinese, Japanese, and Korean; it offers a well-developed sequence of language programs from beginning courses to higher levels. Beginning courses are for students new to the study of East Asian languages, whereas upper-level courses offer more advanced students the opportunity for in-depth analysis of Asian cultures. Through courses on Chinese, Japanese, and Korean civilization and literature, more than 1,500 Rutgers students study the elements that formed these languages centuries ago and the forces that shape modern expressions today.

2. History of Korean Language Education at Rutgers

In response to the need for Korean courses at Rutgers, the Department of East Asian Languages and Cultures began preparations in spring 1992 for a Korean language program, in close cooperation with the Korean-American community. According to Professor Ching-I Tu, who served as Chair of the Department from 1969 to 2008, the Korean Student Association not only requested Korean language courses but also actively coordinated with both local community leaders as well as Korean professors at Rutgers to raise funding for the initial course offering in 1992. Most active among them were Dr. Youngbin Lee (a medical doctor who served as President of the New Jersey Korean-American Association in the 1980s and also co-founded the Asian American Heritage Council of New Jersey) and Professor Jong-Keun You of the Economics Department (who later served as Governor of North Jolla Province in Korea and as Economic Advisor to President Kim Dae-Jung).

The proposal for introducing Korean language study at Rutgers received approval from the Faculty of Arts and Sciences in May 1992, and an elementary Korean language course was offered for the first time at the university in September 1992. Ms. Insook Chung, a doctoral student in the Graduate School of Education at Rutgers, was the first instructor, and she continued to teach Elementary and Intermediate Korean courses as well as the summer intensive courses until 1997. She received her Ed.D. in Language Education in 2002 with a thesis titled "Korean-English Translation in the Context of Cross-Cultural Communication." Dr. Chung currently works at the Educational Testing Service in Princeton, New Jersey as an Assessment Specialist. Her responsibilities include developing the SAT Subject Test in Korean with Listening (1995-present).

The two-semester, eight-credit elementary Korean language course was designed for undergraduate students and met three times a week for 80 minutes per session. The course was received with great enthusiasm by the Rutgers community and enjoyed wide publicity. Due to the growing interest in Korea and Korean studies, this course had an excellent enrollment of 35 (with a long waiting list) and became a focal point for interested students. The strong response to elementary Korean and the enthusiasm generated by the introduction of Korean language study highlighted the need for further development in Korean studies. Consequently, a proposal for intermediate Korean was prepared and approved in spring 1993. The course was offered, along with elementary Korean, with an excellent enrollment in the 1993-1994 academic year.

In 1996, a long-term plan for the establishment and development of

Korean studies was inaugurated with the creation of the first tenure-track faculty position, funded by the Korea Foundation. This was made possible only because the Chair of the Department, Professor Ching-I Tu, communicated closely with Korean community leaders and applied for a three-year grant to the Korea Foundation in order to create a faculty position in Korean studies. Young-mee Yu Cho, who had started the Korean language program at Stanford University in 1984, was appointed as Assistant Professor in the fall of 1996. Within the first four years of her appointment, she developed a five-level program of language courses as well as other essential Korean studies courses. A second grant from the Korea Foundation allowed a tenure-track position starting in 2001. As was the case with the first grant, the university enthusiastically added faculty after the third year and continued with the appointments of Professor Ann Choi, who taught courses in Korean literature between 2001 and 2008, and of Professor Suzy Kim in 2010.

In sum, the university, the department, and the Korean community have been very enthusiastic and supportive of the introduction of Korean language courses, and this continuing support has been conducive for further development in Korean studies.

3. Current State of the Korean Language Program

Scott Hall

The Korean Studies program is currently housed in the Department of Asian Languages and Cultures in the School of Arts and Sciences, which is one of the 19 undergraduate, graduate, and professional schools located on the New Brunswick campus. The department offers an undergraduate minor and a graduate certificate in Korean Studies. The Korean Studies program not only shares a range of courses with the Chinese and Japanese programs but also has established close ties with Asian Studies, Global Studies, International Studies, the Program in Comparative Literature, and the Transliteratures Project within Rutgers University. In addition, there is an option for studying East Asian Literature within the Comparative Literature Ph.D. program and for studying Korean Linguistics within the Ph.D. program in Linguistics. Currently, Rutgers University provides study abroad and exchange programs with Ewha Womans University, Seoul National University, and Pohang University of Science and Technology. Since 2008, 50 students have participated in the Rutgers Study Abroad Program to Korea.

The overview of the program is illustrated under Appendix A. In the academic year 2011-2012, the department offered 28 courses in Korean studies, as listed in Appendix B. There are more than 400 students enrolled in these courses each year. In the academic year 2013-2014, the program implemented an accelerated curriculum for Korean heritage students with '103: Beginning Korean Reading and Writing for Heritage Students' and '203: Intermediate Korean Reading and Writing for Heritage Students,' which covered the first two years of non-heritage instruction in one year. These two courses alleviated the chaotic state of elementary level classes, which had been forced to accept a large number of receptive bilinguals in the past. By taking into account heritage learners' distinct linguistic profiles and a wider range of proficiencies, instructors could address the special needs of the heritage population.

As the number of Korean immigrants and students in the United States has increased, and with Korea's ever-growing interest in American culture, the demand for translations between Korean and English has risen steadily over the years. Korean culture is spreading fast, as seen with the "Korean Wave" in music and international television broadcasting.

Many official advertisements and documents published in the U.S. are now in both English and Korean, and the judicial system demands more qualified Korean interpreters and translators. Even though there are many bilingual Americans who understand and speak each language sufficiently, most feel inadequate when translating or interpreting from one language to the other. As a result, in the spring 2013 term, the department started offering 'Korean Translation: Introduction to Practical Translation and Translation Theories.'

This course is a survey of different kinds of translations, through which students gain both skills and confidence in translating. Each genre or subject area of translation requires a knowledge of certain terms or styles, which can be quickly referenced or learned. Based on their existing familiarity with both languages and cultures, students enhance their ability to translate efficiently and functionally. The Korean program has identified a qualified instructor in Ms. Flora Kim, a bilingual lawyer and librarian (with a J.D. degree from Rutgers Law School-Newark and a Masters in Library and Information Science from Rutgers). Born in New Jersey and educated in Seoul, Korea, she has always been fascinated by languages in general but especially by Korean and English literature, and she has continually offered her time as a translator and interpreter. She has recently helped develop the course description for the translation course as follows:

> *Korean Translation:*
> *Introduction to Practical Translation and Translation Theories*
>
> This practical translation class covers materials that have a high demand for translation (medical and legal forms, government and court documents, news articles and headlines, manuals and instructions, and short writings from diverse disciplines) as well as fundamentals of translation theory. Students will work on both Korean-to-English and English-to-Korean translations through weekly assignments, applying translation theories, methods, and techniques discussed in class, and will also learn to evaluate each other's work. While the primary language used for instruction will be English, and a heavier emphasis is on Korean-to-English translation, proficiency in both languages is expected.

Our Korean studies program has three full-time faculty members who hold a doctorate in Korean Linguistics, Korean History, or Language Education. Young-mee Yu Cho received a doctorate in linguistics from Stanford University in 1990 and continued to teach Korean language at the Asian Languages department at Stanford until she moved to Rutgers in the fall of 1996. She was granted tenure in 2000 and has continued to do research in linguistics and Korean language education. She also serves as a graduate faculty member in the Department of Linguistics at Rutgers University, Adjunct Associate Professor at The Center for Advanced Study of Language at the University of Maryland, and a member of the Korean Subject Test Committee for the SAT College Board.

Young-mee Yu Cho's research includes the following:

- *Parameters of Consonantal Assimilation* (1990) Doctoral dissertation, Stanford University
- *Integrated Korean. Beginning 1, 2, Intermediate 1, 2 (*2000-2012) (with H. Sohn, et. al.) Univ. of Hawaii Press
- "Laryngeal Contrast in Korean." (2011) *Companion to Phonology*. Eds. Marc van Oostendorp, et. al. Wiley-Blackwell
- "A Historical Perspective on Nonderived Environment Blocking: The Case of the Korean Palatalization" (2008) in *The Nature of Word.* Eds. S. Inkelas and K. Hanson. Boston, MA: MIT Press
- "Inalterability as Prespecification," (1993) (with S. lnkelas) *Language* 69.3

In addition to her research as a phonologist and language pedagogist, she has served as President (2006-2009) of the American Association of Teachers of Korean (AATK) and Co-Chair of the Task Force for establishing *The National Standards for Korean Language Learning*, the final version of which was published as a book (ACTFL, 2012, 3rd edition).

Professor Suzy Kim is an expert in Korean history. She is able to address a variety of issues related to contemporary social and cultural issues as well as Korean history. Professor Kim's research focus is on post-colonial North Korea, which has drawn increasing attention in the field of East Asian Studies. Her research is summarized below.

(1) Suzy Kim's research:

- *Politics of Empowerment: Everyday Life in Post-Liberation North Korea 1945-50 (2005)* Doctoral dissertation, University of Chicago
- "The Woman Question: The Making of North Korean Women as Revolutionary Mothers (1945-1950)," (forthcoming) *Comparative Studies in Society and History*
- "Everyday Life in the North Korean Revolution," *North Korea's Cold War* (forthcoming) Stanford University Press
- Review of *Famine in North Korea: Markets, Aid, and Reform* by Stephan Haggard & Marcus Noland (March 2010) *Journal of Asian Studies*, Volume 69, Issue 1: 286-288
- "Teaching North Korea with Visual & Online Resources" (Winter 2009) *Education About Asia*, Volume 14:3

Dr. Ji-Young Jung taught in the Korean program from 2009 to 2012. She holds a doctorate in Applied Linguistics from Columbia University. Her expertise in language pedagogy and second language acquisition was valuable in strengthening the language program and developing teacher training.

(2) Ji-Young Jung's research:

- "An Integrated Approach to the Teaching of Business Korean" (2011) (co-authored with Young-mee Yu Cho). *Korean Language in America, 16, 1-40.*
- "The Classroom Study on the Efficacy of Interactional Feedback for Korean Particles" (2010) *Journal of Korean Language Education, 21* (4), 255-282.
- *Discourse Markers in Contrast: 'But,' 'Actually' and 'Well' in Native-Nonnative English Conversations between Friends* (2009) Unpublished doctoral dissertation, Teachers College, Columbia University
- "Issues in Acquisitional Pragmatics" (2001) Teachers College, Columbia University Working Papers in TESOL & Applied Linguistics, 2 (can be retrieved from http://www.tc.columbia.edu/academic/tesol//Web-

journal/JungFinal.doc.pdf)

In July 2012, Dr. Jung left Rutgers University to join the University of Pennsylvania, and in September 2012, Ms. Hee Chung Chun joined the department as a full-time lecturer of Korean. Ms. Chun holds a master's degree in Teaching Korean as a Foreign Language from Ewha Womans University in Korea; her master's thesis was a study on the correlation between Korean-American youth learners' cultural identities and their Korean language proficiencies. She previously taught at the Language Education Institute of Seoul National University and volunteered at Korea Women Migrants Human Rights Center in Seoul. Her experience with students from diverse cultural and linguistic backgrounds is expected to enrich the Korean language program.

The Korean program also has a number of part-time instructors, some of whom hold advanced degrees in Foreign Language Education, Film Studies, Korean Literature, Library Science and Social Work. Many of our part-time instructors have been Ph.D. candidates in English, Political Science, Education, and Communication and Media Studies at Rutgers. In addition, there are collaborating faculty/staff members at Rutgers University: Mary Curran (Associate Professor, Language Education; Ph.D., University of Wisconsin-Madison), Yeon-soo Kim (Associate Professor of Spanish Literature; Ph.D., Yale University), Sukhee Lee (Assistant Professor of Chinese and East Asian History; Ph.D., Harvard University), Marion Yudow (Director, World Languages Institute), and Tao Yang (Librarian, the East Asian Library of Rutgers University).

In addition to fulfilling its regular teaching duties, the Rutgers Korean program strives to function as a national host for professionals in Korean language education. Its mission is to develop and maintain professional expertise in the field, via collaboration with Korean language education communities worldwide. Its primary goal is to compile past research on Korean pedagogy, teacher education, and curricular design in a systematic way, and to further interaction between research and reflective practices in order to promote educational improvement and professionalism in Korean language education. A taskforce of K-16 teachers collaborated to create *National Standards for Korean Language Learning,* which was published in the summer of 2012 as a chapter in *Standards for Foreign Language Learning in the 21st Century*.

The *Standards* documents were designed to secure foreign language learning as an integral part of K-16 education in the United States, and to connect the philosophy and goals of language learning with comprehensive views of cultures, larger academic pursuits, and communities both at home and abroad. The continued and coordinated efforts made by our faculty members in collaboration with major Korean studies-related organizations nationwide have contributed to improve and promote the Korean language and Korean cultural education throughout the U.S. In February 2012, based on the blueprint provided by *The Standards* documents, the Korean program initiated a college-level (13-16) curriculum development project, which joins together seventeen university instructors, including the AATK officers. The project will be carried out in close coordination with the AATK annual conferences.

The field of Korean language studies has been relatively underrepresented in foreign language education scholarship, despite its increasing importance in terms of demographic representation and its status as a critical language of the United States, after a half-century of close sociopolitical and economic ties to South Korea and tensions with North Korea. Within the past twenty years, programs in Korean studies have exhibited a strong institutional presence, especially at the college level. Recently, the nation has also witnessed a marked increase in Korean language and immersion programs at the K-12 level. The burgeoning of Korean language programs in classrooms, however, has yet to be connected to current research on language education in general and on Korean language education in particular. The Rutgers Korean studies program aims to address these crucial needs. An accelerated teacher certification program and a Master of Arts in Teaching (MAT) in Korean started in 2008 on a small, trial basis in collaboration with the Graduate School of Education (GSE) and the World Languages Institute (WLI) at Rutgers. The Certificate of Eligibility (CE) is a credential with lifetime validity, issued to an individual who has not completed a teacher preparation program per se, but who has met the basic requirements for certification, including academic study and applicable test requirements.

There are two options available at Rutgers for those wishing to pursue certification in East Asian languages (including Chinese and Korean) through the GSE's master's degree programs in foreign language education. One of these is a five-year master's degree and certification program for undergraduate students who are majoring in East Asian Languages and Area Studies, and the other is a two-year master's degree and certification program for those who already hold undergraduate degrees in the content area. Program participants study second language acquisition, teaching methodologies, linguistics, and general pedagogy, and they also engage in two semester-long practices and a teaching internship in public schools.

As a state university, Rutgers is uniquely positioned to respond to the challenges of establishing a long-term, qualified program to train K-12 Korean teachers. The Korean Language Association (KLA) was founded in 2007 by Dr. Sun Geun Lee and Dr. Youngduk Kim, two Korean-American community leaders, to promote the teaching of Korean as a foreign language at public schools in the tri-state area of Connecticut, New Jersey, and New York. It awarded five pre-service and in-service teachers full scholarships to complete the 30-credit requirement established by the New Jersey Department of Education at the GSE and the WLI of Rutgers University. As a result of a concerted effort, the program produced the first two certified teachers of Korean in New Jersey. The selection of qualified Korean teachers, as opposed to teachers with certifications in different subjects, is a significant milestone in the expansion of the K-12 Korean language program.

The Korean program encourages research, develops curricula, hosts visiting scholars, and sponsors lectures and cultural activities to enhance the understanding of Korea. Significant Korean studies-related lectures, cultural activities, and professional conferences in the past include the following:

(3) Korean Studies-related activities:

- Korea's 'Early Modern': Colonial Literature and the Constellation of History, November 5-6, 2004. First large-scale international conference in the U.S. that dealt with modernity in the colonial context of early twentieth-century Korea.
- 11th Annual Workshop and Conference of the American Association of Teachers of Korean (AATK), June 22-24, 2006. Workshops and panel discussion on any topic related to the enhancement of teaching Korean language, literature, and culture.
- Into the Disenchanted World: Korean Writing Today, April 17, 2003. Presentation by Kim Uchang.
- A Bilingual Reading of Korean Literature, November 10, 2003. Presentations by Ch'oruIm and Kwija Yang.
- 2004-2005 Global Futures Symposia: As East Asia Turns: Nationalism, Regionalization, and Cosmopolitanization, October 4, 2004. Lecture by Katharine H. S. Moon (Wellesley College).
- Progressive Religiosity: Minjung Christianity and Minjung Buddhism in Modern South Korea, September 25, 2007. Presentation by Vladimir Tikhonov.
- A History of Relief Efforts for Leprosy (Hansen's Disease) in Korea, March 13, 2008. Presentation by Keun-sik Jung (Seoul National University and University of Chicago).
- William Elliot Griffis Workshop, March 14, 2008. Workshop on the Korean materials of the William Elliot Griffis Collection at Rutgers University.
- A Teaching Asia Workshop: Teaching Asia Legacies organized by the Mid-Atlantic Region Association for Asian Studies (MAR/AAS) and Rutgers University, October 24, 2008. One-day workshop preceding the 2008 MAR/AAS conference that focused on the educational methods and approaches to teaching culture and language at the K-12 level.
- The 37th Annual MAR/AAS Conference: Competition in Asia, October 25-26, 2008.

4. Future Plans

The current MAT program offers a unique opportunity for prospective Korean teachers to obtain both a New Jersey Certificate of Korean Teacher and a master's degree for those who aspire to obtain a better credential.

When appropriate courses in second language acquisition, language policy, and sociolinguistics are developed, our programs will be aligned with the New Jersey Professional Teaching Standards, the national standards set by the American Council on the Teaching of Foreign Languages (ACTFL), and the New Jersey Core Curriculum Content Standards for World Languages. These programs are run through the WLI at Rutgers University, which has provided K-12 world language teachers with a graduate-level core program in pedagogy that reflects both state and national standards. In collaboration with the GSE, the curriculum will be customized to meet the needs of individual Korean language teachers.

Also, students enrolled in our Korean Teacher Certification Program (KTCP), the first in the northeastern U.S., will be given the opportunity to enhance their learning experience by completing a practicum that will allow for the actual teaching of students under the supervision of university faculty. The practicum course will be the result of a joint effort between Rutgers University and school districts in New Jersey that wish to offer Korean in their schools. As the first Korean teacher certification program recognized by the State of New Jersey, Rutgers' KTCP will play a pivotal role in securing permanent Korean instruction in secondary public schools and higher education, in addition to improving the quality of Korean language teachers nationwide. The KTCP will be able to meet the two serious challenges facing Korean language education in New York and New Jersey (the two states that have the biggest Korean communities in the east coast): (1) a lack of communication and collaboration between university researchers and school teachers, and (2) paucity of state-certified teachers of Korean in the public school system.

It is our goal to have Korean language teachers who are committed to offering innovative and practical training based on the most recent research. The eight Korean language classes already offered at Rutgers may be used by our pedagogues as an on-site laboratory, in which they can obtain data-driven knowledge and skills for teaching Korean. In Korean language education, as in foreign language education in general, there has been a gradual move away from a grammar-translation approach to a communicative approach, and from a cognitive approach to a socio-cultural approach. Adopting these recent trends, however, is a complex task that requires careful planning and implementation. A communicative approach values interactional competency and fluency in addition to linguistic accuracy, and in this context, foreign language learners' pragmatic/discourse competence has emerged as an essential component of communicative competence. Likewise, a socio-cultural approach assumes that language learning, as well as language use, should involve interactions that engage learners' social identities, cultural beliefs, and affective investments. Recent research emphasizes the importance of a learner-centered approach to language teaching, which must consider these aforementioned individual factors.

Separately from the MAT, the department began to offer a master's degree program in East Asian Studies in the fall of 2013. We plan to propose the following Korean studies courses that reflect the expertise of the Korean faculty:

(4) Graduate Courses for an MA in East Asian Studies:
   a. Advanced Topics in Korean Language and Linguistics
   b. History of Korean Writing and Literacy
   c. Language Change in Contemporary Korean
   d. Advanced Korean Translation: Practical Translation
   e. Advanced Korean Translation: Media Translation
   f. Contemporary Korean Culture and Society
   g. North Korea in the Socialist World
   h. Social Movements and Civil Society in South Korea

Korean Studies as an academic discipline has experienced remarkable progress during the past three decades, to the extent that more than 140 universities and colleges provide a regular language program, and an increasing number of institutions offer undergraduate and graduate degrees in Korean or a concentration on Korea within East Asian Language and Area Studies. These stages of development have reflected a growing recognition of Korea's cultural, economic, and strategic importance. Although in many universities, its marginal status is apparent when compared to Chinese and Japanese programs, a number of well-balanced Korean programs have emerged. The Korean program at Rutgers is one such example, particularly when comparing the first elementary course provisionally offered in 1992 with the 28 courses in the 2011-2012 academic year. We believe this positive gain is due to ever-increasing student enrollment and the commitment of the university, as well as the support of foundations in Korea, the U.S., and the Korean-American community. We aim to work towards the next step of development with a vision of pursuing a coherent language program, identifying resources to implement the vision, and contextualizing the language study within a strong Korean studies program.

APPENDIX A. Programs in the Department of Asian Languages and Cultures

Undergraduate Major Programs

Chinese:

Students majoring in Chinese take 24 credits in courses taught in Chinese beyond the intermediate (200) level, including courses in both modern and literary Chinese.

East Asian Languages and Area Studies:

Concentration in Chinese / Concentration in Japanese / Concentration in Korean. The interdisciplinary major in East Asian Languages and Area Studies requires a minimum of 12 credits in an Asian language (see above) beyond the intermediate (200) level, and 18 credits of appropriate courses related to Asia from more than two different disciplines. Half of the 18 credits should be in 300 and 400 level courses.

Undergraduate Minor Programs

Chinese:

The minor in Chinese consists of six courses of 3 or more credits beyond the elementary level, in both modern and literary Chinese. Of the six courses, at least three must be at the 300 level or above, and must be chosen from those acceptable for the major.

Japanese:

The Japanese minor requires six courses in Japanese beyond the elementary level. Of the six, at least three courses must be at the 300 level or above. Courses taught in English are generally not counted toward the minor requirements.

Korean:

The minor in Korean requires six Korean language courses beyond the elementary level, of which at least three courses must be at the 300 level or above.

Asian Studies:

· The interdisciplinary Minor in Asian Studies consists of nine courses: Four courses in one Asian language, normally two years of Chinese, Japanese, or Korean;

· Two courses in Asian Studies, specifically 01:098:322 and 444 (when these two specific courses in Asian Studies are not offered, other courses from the approved list of courses may be substituted);

· Three courses from the approved list, selected from two different discipline areas (e.g., humanities, social sciences, ecological sciences);

· A substantial paper written in Seminar on East Asian Societies or an approved equivalent.

APPENDIX B. The Korean Program

a. Overview

Language Courses:

Elementary Korean
Beginning Korean for Heritage Students
Intermediate Korean
Advanced Korean
Korea in Translations
Independent Study in Korean
Advanced Readings in Korean
Intermediate Korean for Heritage Students
Readings in Korean Literature
Advanced Korean for Business
Honors in Korean
Intensive Elementary Korean (Summer Session)

Related Courses in Korean Studies:

Introduction to Korean Culture

Gender and Social Change in Korea
North Korea in the Socialist and Post-Socialist Worlds
Korean Literature in Translation I and II
Modern East Asia
Global East Asia
Seminar on Asian Societies
Selected Interdisciplinary Topics in East Asia
East Asian Civilization: Traditional Era
East Asian Civilization: Modern Era
Korean Language in Culture and Society
Korean Cinema and Cinematic Language
Seminar on Modern Korean History
Classical Asia
Writing and Literacy in East Asia
Literature of the Asian Diaspora
Religious Themes in East Asian Literature
Women in Eastern Religion
Economics of Asia
The Sociology of Development

b. Courses Conducted in English

210 **Introduction to Korean Culture** (3)
Survey of Korean culture and society in a historical context. Exploration into the connection between language and culture. Examination of modern Korean novels and their social and historical relevance.

220 **Korean Literature in Translation I (**3)
Introduction to Korean literature in English translation from the early times to the 19th century; emphasis on historical and cultural contexts of major works.

221 **Korean Literature in Translation II** (3)
An overview of Korean literature of the 20th century. Explorations of historical backgrounds and cultural contexts of major works of various genres.

230 **Introduction to Korean Cinema and Cinematic Language** (3)
Cinematic development in Postcolonial Korea. Topics include depiction of traditional and contemporary Korea in films, reflecting political, social, and cultural changes.

250 **Korean Language in Culture and Society** (3)
Survey of Korean language in relation to its culture and society. Examination of language use (diglossia, language and gender, metaphors, and the writing system).

310 **Gender and Social Change in Korea** (3)
Exploration of the shifting categories of femininity and masculinity, women's roles and their experiences of social change in Korea from the late 19th century

into contemporary times.

350 **North Korea in the Socialist and Post-Socialist Worlds** (3)
Examination of social, political, economic, and cultural developments in North Korea by situating it within the context of regional and global developments.

470 **Seminar on Modern Korean History** (3)
Designed to introduce advanced undergraduate and graduate students to emerging scholarship and major debates in modern Korean history (since 1876). Topics vary by instructor and term offered.

c. Courses Conducted in Korean

101, 102 **Elementary Korean** (4,4)
Introduction to sound, grammar, and writing system of modern Korean; practice and exercises in speaking, reading, and writing.

103 **Beginning Korean Reading and Writing for Heritage Students** (3)
Development of foundation in Korean grammar and vocabulary. Practice in reading, writing, and oral skills.

203 **Intermediate Korean Reading and Writing for Heritage Students** (3)
Development of oral proficiency, practice in reading comprehension, composition, study of grammar, and vocabulary building.

201, 202 **Intermediate Korean** (4,4)
Development of oral proficiency, practice in reading comprehension, composition, study of grammar, and vocabulary building.

301, 302 **Advanced Korean** (3,3)
Study of advanced vocabulary and grammar through reading texts in various styles. Practice in composition and refinement of oral proficiency.

303, 304 **Advanced Korean for Business** (3,3)
Reading and discussion of business, culture, and society; specialized vocabulary, social skills, and practice in business correspondence.

401, 402 **Advanced Readings in Korean** (3,3)
Selected readings from modern Korean materials, including fiction, essays, newspapers, and journal articles. Discussion and some writing exercises.

410, 411 **Readings in Korean Literature** (3,3)
Selections from representative literary works from premodern times to the contemporary period. Exploration of major poetry, drama, and fictional narratives in the context of historical and cultural changes.

450 **Korea in Translations: Modern Literature and Film** (3)
Translation as a generative process. Korean literary fiction and poetry of the 20th century and their versions in English translations. Films as another mode of translation with its own language and grammar.

471 **Korea in Translations: Contemporary Media** (3)
Expository and journalistic writings with attention to contemporary language of the mass media. Broadcast news, documentary films, newspaper and maga-

zine articles studied and translated into English.

495, 496 **Independent Study** (3,3)
Independent reading under supervision of a member of the department.

497, 498 **Honors in Korean** (6,6)
Individualized honors projects for students who have fulfilled all requirements for the minor in Korean or the major in East Asian Languages and Area Studies. Both semesters must be completed to receive credit.

History of the Korean Language Program at Stanford

Hee-Sun Kim
Stanford University

1. Introduction

The Korean Language Program at Stanford University, part of the Stanford Language Center, has demonstrated a long-standing commitment to providing students the opportunity to develop Korean language competence and cultural knowledge. The Stanford Korean Language Program prepares students not only to communicate proficiently in Korean, but also to conduct research in their own academic fields by providing an excellent foundation in the language and culture of Korea. The program offers a wide variety of carefully developed courses, which range from general language classes for students of all levels to content courses designed specifically for upper-level students. There are also numerous language fellowships and internship programs available each year that are co-sponsored by the Center for East Asian Studies and the Korean Studies Program, which offer valuable opportunities for interested students to experience, study, and work in Korea. Today, the Korean Language Program is developing rapidly, as interest in Korea and Korean culture continues to grow.

2. The Beginning (1984-1995)

The history of the Korean Language Program began with the spring quarter of the academic year of 1984-85, when Young-mee Yu Cho was appointed as a Graduate Student Instructor of Korean. Before 1984,

Korean was taught intermittently as part of the Army Special Training Program. Korean language instruction was initiated at the request of five Stanford students, and in 1984, a beginning-level course was offered as part of the Special Language Program, the Stanford LCTL (Less Commonly Taught Languages) program. In the fall of 1985, the Korean Language Program moved to the Department of East Asian Languages and Cultures, whose chairman Dr. John Wang supported the Korean Language Program with help from a U.S. Department of Education Title VI National Resource Center grant in 1985. This grant enabled the Korean Language Program to expand Korean language instruction from one to two courses, Beginning Korean and Intermediate Korean, by hiring two additional graduate teaching assistants.

Dr. Cho received her Ph. D from the Stanford Linguistics Department in 1990. After earning her Ph.D. with a specialization in the area of Korean phonology and morphology, Cho became a full-time lecturer and the first coordinator of the Korean Language Program at Stanford. Cho added a third-year course to the program, Advanced Korean, with the help of one more teaching assistant assigned from the Department of East Asian Languages and Cultures. At the time, Korean language instruction was offered to a mixed group of heritage and non-heritage students. In addition to language courses, Cho also offered a linguistics course, Structure of Korean. She established a foundation for the Korean Language Program and continued to teach at Stanford until the spring quarter of 1996, when she left for a tenure-track position at Rutgers University.

3. Establishment of the Language Center and the Korean Studies Program (1995-2003)

The Stanford Language Center was formally established in the fall of 1995 with the appointment of Professor Elizabeth Bernhardt as its founding director. After a thorough analysis of the undergraduate curriculum, the university senate passed a strengthened language requirement, requiring all undergraduate students to complete one year of university-level language study. In 1995, the Stanford Language Center embarked on a round of curricular renewal and assessments in order to meet the university senate's serious commitment to language teaching and learning. All of the fourteen language programs, including the Korean Language Program, have been housed within the Language Center ever since.

Dr. Sungdai Cho was appointed as the second coordinator and lecturer of the Korean Language Program in 1996, and he served in this role until 1999, at which point he departed for a tenure-track position at Binghamton University. His area of specialization is Korean Syntax and Morphology. While he was at Stanford, the program continued to offer courses at three levels every year with continued support of graduate teaching assistants from the Department of East Asian Languages and Cultures.

During the same period, the Korean Studies Program was established in 2001 with an endowment from the Tong Yang Group, the Korea Foundation, and the Korea Stanford Alumni Chair of Korean Studies. Sociology Professor Gi-Wook Shin was appointed as the director of the Korean Studies Program. Since then, the Korean Studies Program has been offering a wide range of social science courses such as Asia-Pacific Transformation and Historical and Comparative Sociology. The Korean Studies Program has been conducting multidisciplinary research in collaboration with visiting scholars, in addition to hosting numerous seminars and conferences related to Korea. Since its establishment, the Korean Studies Program has worked closely with the Center for East Asian Studies and with other interdisciplinary departments and programs related to Korea.

Also in 2001, Dr. Eunjoo Lee joined the Korean Language Program as coordinator and lecturer. Due to a loss of funding for Korean teaching assistants before her arrival, Lee taught two courses herself during her first year, Beginning Korean and Intermediate Korean. In the following year, during her second (and last) fall quarter at Stanford, she offered three courses.

Picture 1: Knight Building, Home of Korean Language Program

In 2002, the Center for East Asian Studies initiated a new study abroad program, funded by a grant from the Freeman Foundation. In every year since, fifteen undergraduate students have received language study fellowships to enroll in accredited language programs in China, Japan, and Korea. The Korean Language Program has also been sending three to five students to Korea each summer. Through this fellowship, many students have had opportunities to combine classroom learning with real-world practice and knowledge gained through life and work experiences in Korea.

4. Curricular Reform, Professional Development, and Cultural Outreach (2003-2006)

In 2003, Dr. Hee-Sun Kim was appointed as coordinator and lecturer for the Korean Language Program. Following her appointment, the Korean Language Program began to work on reforming the Korean language curriculum and its assessment procedures in order to comply with the Stanford Language Center's educational goals and objectives.

The goal of foreign language education at Stanford is to foster the ability to function competently in the target language, i.e., students should be able to speak, write, and comprehend both spoken and written language in a real-world setting. Foreign language education at Stanford thus focuses not only on developing linguistic skills but also on making connections to other subject areas, cultures, and communities, with the goal of enabling students to live, study, work, and research successfully in the target language.

In order to accomplish this goal, the Stanford Language Center has adopted two frameworks for accountability: *The Standards on Foreign Language Learning in the 21st Century* (1996, 1999, 2006) and *ACTFL (the American Council on the Teaching of Foreign Languages) Proficiency Guidelines* (1986, 1999, 2012). The Language Center sees *The Standards* as a blueprint for language program development because the text provides well-articulated performance guidelines for K-16 students in all language competencies (interpersonal, interpretive, and presentational), acknowledging that language competencies are far more complex than mono-dimensional skills such as reading, writing, listening, and speaking. Since its first publication in 1996, *The Standards* have been widely adopted and endorsed by all major language-specific learned societies and educational agencies, such as the Modern Language Association and the American Association for Applied Linguistics. The *ACTFL Guidelines* serve as a benchmark for performance assessment because they provide a mechanism for language assessment based on a holistic concept of language development in function, content, and accuracy. Also, the ACTFL OPI (Oral Proficiency Interview) is a well-recognized measurement of proficiency with a long history of success.

In order for curricular renewal to be compliant with these goals, the Korean Language Program ultimately had to determine the concrete objectives for its curriculum on its own, with regard for Korean's status as a non-cognate language, and it had to provide a reliable measure of the objectives. To make these goals realistically achievable, instructors had to gain the knowledge of the standards and their uses through professional development.

The most urgent need of the Korean Language Program at that time was for a qualified tester who could assess students' performance with validity and reliability, as proper assessment would provide acceptable evidence of students' learning and hence lead to better instructional strategies and curriculum development in accordance with the program's objectives. Dr. Kim participated in ACTFL Oral Proficiency Interview (OPI) training workshops and the National Standard workshops with the support of the Stanford Language Center. Once she became a certified ACTFL OPI tester in 2006, meaningful curricular reform could at last be initiated.

During this period, the Korean Language Program created and added a series of fourth-year Korean courses to the existing three-year language curriculum. As more students became interested in Korea for career development and research purposes, they started to request higher-level courses. To meet the growing interest in Korean popular culture and international entrepreneurship, three content courses were developed in 2003-2006: Business Korean, Korean Language and Culture through Drama and Film, and Reading Korean. These courses were geared towards fourth-year, advanced level students. Since 2003, four sections (one for each level) and four-year level courses have been offered, all taught by Dr. Kim. In addition, throughout this time, the Korean Language Program has continued to seek and test new ways to enhance students' learning and expand their learning environments through innovative uses of technology, including Web 2.0 and the Course Management System.

In an effort for public outreach, the Korean Language Program hosted the first Korean Film Festival at Stanford in the spring of 2006, sponsored by the Korean Studies Program, to bring the Stanford community in contact with authentic cultural experiences related to Korea. The film festival was a joint project with San Francisco State University, Notre Dame University, University of Illinois at Urbana-Champaign, and KIMA (San Francisco Korean American Film Festival Association). As part of the festival, three South Korean feature films were screened on the Stanford campus, and invited panelists led a roundtable forum that included Korean filmmakers, media distributors, and distinguished film scholars in the U.S. The Korean Film Festival at Stanford was a great success; it drew a crowd of over 600 people and brought much attention to the program from not only the Stanford University community but also the general public in the Bay Area.

In 2005, the Stanford Library hired a Korean language librarian with funding from the Korea Foundation, and it started to build a strong research collection on Korean studies. Since its establishment, Stanford's

Korean-language library collection has now expanded to include at present 41,300 print volumes and 13 electronic databases. Also, in 2006, Dr. Yumi Moon joined the faculty of Stanford as an Assistant Professor of History. The Korea Foundation sponsored her professorship as well. Dr. Moon has been teaching a variety of Korean history courses, including a Modern Korea course that focuses on the colonial period.

5. Applying the Standards and Performance Assessment (2007-2009)

After obtaining certification as a Korean Oral Proficiency Interview (OPI) tester, Kim continued participating actively in other professional development opportunities, including Writing Proficiency Test (WPT) workshops, Stanford Coursework tutorial workshops, and annual ACTFL conferences. Between 2007 and 2009, the Korean OPI was added to the existing language placement tests for incoming students in the fall quarter. Advisory OPI tests were also given at the end of the academic year to diagnose proficiency levels of students in First-Year through Fourth-Year Korean classes. These three years of student performance data were then subjected to quantitative and qualitative analyses, and the results used to set realistic objectives for the program in accordance with the Standards and the ACTFL proficiency scale. Currently, the proficiency goals of Stanford's Korean Language Program are Novice-High for First-Year Korean and Intermediate-Mid for Second-Year Korean.[1] The proficiency goals for Third- and Fourth-Year Korean are a work in progress.[2]

1 All proficiency objectives stated above were set based on data from non-heritage learners who started learning Korean as true beginners.

2 There are two reasons for the ongoing determination of proficiency objectives for Third- and Fourth-Year Korean instruction. The first is that the number of student performance data was insufficient for stabilizing firm objectives. For over a decade, the students taking Third- and Fourth-Year Korean were predominantly heritage learners, with only one or two students who were non-heritage students. This trend has been changing recently, as more non-heritage students have been taking

With the broad map of proficiency goals established, the Korean Language Program launched three projects to ensure the highest quality of instruction. The first was the implementation of curriculum: classroom tasks and activities were created and organized to develop the three communicative modes (interpersonal, interpretive, and presentational) in a balanced manner. The second project was the revision of Korean placement exams, the SOPI (Simulated OPI) and WPA (Writing Proficiency Assessment) tests. Developed in collaboration with the Language Center, these tests were adopted in 2009 and have been used ever since. The third project was to integrate culturally authentic materials into the Korean language program. This has been accomplished by providing students with a technology-enhanced learning environment. One of the greatest challenges in aligning the program with *The Standards*' five goal areas (the 5 Cs: Communication, Cultures, Connections, Comparisons, and Communities) has been the task of linking classroom activities to the Connections and Communities standards. Successful achievement of these goals requires students' engagement with the target language community either locally or abroad. To overcome the physical and geographical limitations, various social networking and communication technologies have also been integrated into the curriculum to connect students to native speakers in virtual communities.

Although students welcomed the offering of a comprehensive Korean language program, enrollments did not increase significantly during this period, in large part because the Korean Language Program had enough teachers to offer only one class section per level. Also, although students demanded four years of Korean courses and hoped to continue their studies until graduation, they had to cope with serious time conflicts with other mandatory courses for their academic degrees.

In 2009, a Fulbright teaching assistant was added to the Korean Lan-

---

upper-level courses in Korean. Thus, we expect to be able to establish appropriate proficiency objectives in the near future after we have collected a statistically meaningful amount of data. The second reason is that Third- and Fourth-Year Korean courses meet for fewer class hours than third and fourth-year courses in other language programs at Stanford. Most of the other language courses at Stanford meet for four to five class hours per week.

guage Program with the support of the Language Center. Thanks to this addition, the Korean Language Program was able to offer two sections of First-Year Korean for the first time since 2000. The positive impact was not instantly noticeable during the first year, but enrollment in First-Year Korean doubled in the following year (2010) and has remained at this new higher-level enrollment since then.

In 2008, the Division of Literatures, Cultures, and Languages established a minor in Modern Languages, which opened up opportunities for students to pursue a minor degree specializing in Korean. Some students of Korean are making progress toward this minor now.

6. Curriculum Development and Outreach (2010-2012)

Spring 2010 marked the beginning of the program's commitment to a formal assessment of oral proficiency through the SOPI as an end-of-year exit test. In 2010, the SOPI was administered to evaluate students completing the first-year Korean sequence. That trial proved a success, and in 2011, both the SOPI and the WPA were administered to evaluate the oral and written proficiency of First-Year and Second-Year students' oral and written proficiency.

The majority of students indeed met or exceeded the proficiency goals. After analyzing the first official measurement of students' oral proficiencies in 2010, however, the Korean Language Program and the Language Center realized an urgent need for a separate class track for heritage learners. Most non-heritage students reached Novice High, but heritage students reached Intermediate Mid by the end of First-Year Korean instruction. This disparity could not be resolved by merely placing heritage students in the Second-Year Korean class because most heritage students had not reached the minimum proficiency in reading and writing required for Second-Year Korean. To remedy this problem, the Korean Language Program separated First Year Korean into two tracks starting in the fall of 2010. Both heritage and non-heritage students gave very positive feedback on the separate tracks, and non-heritage students in particular performed much better on both the SOPI and the WPA. Most of the students far exceeded their targeted objectives and reached the Intermediate Low level. We suspect that the separation of the First-Year class into two tracks reduced the anxiety level of non-heritage learners and led to an enhancement of their proficiency. Appendix 3 shows the oral proficiency ratings generated over the academic years of 2010-2011 and 2011-2012.

By the end of 2010, documentation of the Korean proficiency objectives and curriculum was officially completed and published on the Stanford Language Center webpage.[3] This open access made the standards more transparent for students and instructors, who could thereby set clear expectations for their learning and teaching at Stanford. The development of the documentation was inspired by the initial work in the Spanish program by Bernhardt, Valdes, and Miano in 2009, and the objectives reflected the uniqueness and specificity of the Korean language.

In an endeavor to embrace the Connections and Communities standards, the Korean Language Program established a partnership with Geochang County in Korea, and in 2011, they began a joint internship program called TELK (Teach English Learn Korean). This three-year contract program has brought immense benefits to Stanford students in the form of real-world experiences. Not only can students connect their Korean knowledge to other subject areas by teaching science, math, and English to Korean middle school students, they also gain valuable life experiences by working with Korean professionals in the field of education. The program also has offered participants a uniquely intimate and profound intercultural experience through home stays, Korean language training, educational excursions, and community service. The Stanford Language Program is currently investigating other opportunities for collaboration with Korean communities and universities that would encourage students to use the Korean language for their interests and academic goals.

---

3 https://www.stanford.edu/dept/lc/language/requirement/curriculum.html

In June 2012, the Korean Language Program hosted the 17th annual AATK (American Association of Teachers of Korean) conference. The theme of the conference was "Exploring the New Wave in Korean Teaching and Learning." This conference aimed to bring together people in the field of Korean language education to present their work and exchange ideas regarding the development of a Standards-based curriculum and innovative methods of teaching. The conference drew a record-breaking number of about 200 Korean educators and participants from K-12 schools and institutions of higher education.

After a long wait, Korean literature courses were introduced to Stanford in the fall of 2012 with the appointment of an Assistant Professor, Dr. Dafna Zur, in the Department of East Asian Languages and Cultures. She has been teaching a variety of courses on Korean literature, popular culture, visual culture, and Asian children's literature. We hope her appointment will lead to the establishment of a Korean minor for undergraduate and graduate students that will positively impact the enrollment in Korean language courses and other subject areas of Korean studies in general.

In the fall of 2013, a part-time lecturer position was added to the Korean Language Program temporarily in lieu of the Fulbright Teaching Assistantship (FLTA). Due to the nature of visiting instructors, little curricular consistency was observed in the courses taught by the FLTAs, because of frequent turnover. To meet university standards and objectives, we hope to secure this part-time position to guarantee a consistent curricular experience and quality education for our students.

7. Future Directions

The Stanford Korean Language Program strives to continue developing and expanding its comprehensive and balanced academic curriculum to assist students in fulfilling their educational needs and goals. The program maintains cordial ties with other programs including the Korean Studies Program, the Center for East Asian Studies, and the Department of East Asian Languages and Cultures. The Korean Language Program moves forward to provide future experts and leaders in the field with multicultural awareness and global competence.

Recently, Stanford has seen an increase in the number of Korean international students who are relatively fluent in Korean but still need rigorous language training to reach the proficiency level of an educated native speaker. For this group of students, we need to develop higher-level courses comparable to those they would have taken had they attended a Korean university. The establishment of an Overseas Study Program in Korea will also be necessary in the future. Through such a program, students could better prepare for careers in Korean affairs and related fields by enhancing their intercultural understanding and global leadership qualities.

REFERENCES

American Council on the Teaching of Foreign Languages. (2012). ACTFL Proficiency Guidelines: Speaking, Writing, Listening, and Reading. Retrieved from www.actfl.org.

Bernhardt, E., Valdes, G., & Miano, E. (2009). A chronicle of standards-based curricular reform in a research university. In V. Scott (Ed.) *Principles and Practices of the Standards in College Foreign Language Education* (pp. 54-85). Boston: Heinle & Heinle.

National Standards in Foreign Language Education Project. (2006). Standards for foreign language learning in the 21st Century.

Stanford Korean Studies Program. (2011). Ten Years of Korean Studies at Stanford.

Stanford Language Center. (2012). Annual Report to the Committee on Undergraduate Standards and Policy.

APPENDIX 1. Development of The Korean Language Program at Stanford

1984 Korean language instruction begins under the Special Language Program.

1985 The Korean Language Program is established as part of the Department of East Asian Languages and Cultures.

1990 Young-mee Yu Cho becomes the first coordinator and lecturer of the Korean Language Program. The Korean Language Program begins offering three levels of courses.

1995 The Stanford Language Center is established with the appointment of Professor Elizabeth Bernhardt. The Korean Language Program is housed within the Language Center.
1996 Sungdai Cho is hired as a Korean language coordinator and lecturer.
2001 The Korean Studies Program is created with the appointment of Professor Gi-Wook Shin. Eunjoo Lee is hired as a Korean language coordinator and lecturer.
2003 Hee-Sun Kim is hired as a Korean language coordinator and lecturer.
2004 The Korean Language Program begins offering fourth-year level courses by developing content courses: Business Korean, Korean Culture, and Reading Korean. The Stanford Coursework (course management system) is integrated into Korean language instruction and assessment.
2006 The Korean Language Program hosts the Korean Film Festival. Hee-Sun Kim becomes a certified ACTFL OPI (Oral Proficiency Interview) tester in Korean.
2006 Yumi Moon is hired as an Assistant Professor in the Department of History.
2007 The Korean Language Program adds the OPI and WPT to its annual placement test inaddition to the online written test.
2008 Hee-Sun Kim becomes a certified WPT (Written Proficiency Test) and OPIc (Computerized OPI) tester.
2009 The Korean SOPI is officially launched to measure students' performance at the end of the academic year.
2010 A heritage-track course is added to the first year Korean course, supported by a Title VI grant. National Standards-based curricular documents for First-Year Korean and Second-Year Korean are completed.
2011 Hee-Sun Kim becomes a Korean ILR (Interagency Language Roundtable) tester and begins ACTFL OPI trainer certification.
2012 The Korean Language Program hosts the AATK (American Association of Teachers of Korean) conference. Dafna Zur is hired as Assistant Professor in the Department of East Asian Languages and Cultures. Hee-Sun Kim becomes an official ACTFL OPI tester trainer.

APPENDIX 2. Courses in The Korean Language Program

KORLANG 1, 2, 3 First-Year Korean (5 units)

Basic communication skills, vocabulary, and grammar patterns. Culturally appropriate conduct relevant to contextual needs such as greetings, gestures, and body language. Prerequisite: None.

KORLANG 1H, 2H, 3H First-Year Korean for Heritage Learners (3 units)

For students with previous knowledge of Korean or a strong background in listening and speaking skills. Focus is on reading, writing, and spelling. Prerequisite: placement tests or consent of instructor.

KORLANG 21, 22, 23 Second-Year Korean for Heritage Learners (4-5 units)
More complex sentences and grammatical patterns. Goal is conversation in daily life situations such as making a polite request or a suggestion, and reading simple texts in addition to better knowledge of Korean culture. Prerequisite: 3 or consent of instructor.

KORLANG 101, 102, 103 Third-Year Korean (3-4 units)
Materials about Korean culture and society to help students achieve proficiency in interpersonal, interpretive, and presentational communication. Vocabulary, reading, and aural/oral skills. Prerequisite: 23 or consent of instructor.

KORLANG 120 Korean Language and Culture Through Drama and Film (2-3 units)
Korean culture and society through contemporary Korean drama and films. Advanced vocabulary, grammar, and idiomatic expressions. Prerequisite: 103 or consent of instructor.

KORLANG 130 Reading Korean (2-3 units)
Contemporary literature and academic texts. Prerequisite: 103 or consent of instructor. Prerequisite: 103 or consent of instructor

KORLANG 140 Business Korean (2-3 units)
For advanced students only. Business-related vocabulary, cultural etiquette and work ethics. Business letters, mock-interviews, and resume writing. Prerequisite: 103 or consent of instructor.

APPENDIX 3. First-Year Oral and Written Proficiency Assessments, 2010-2012

Figure 1

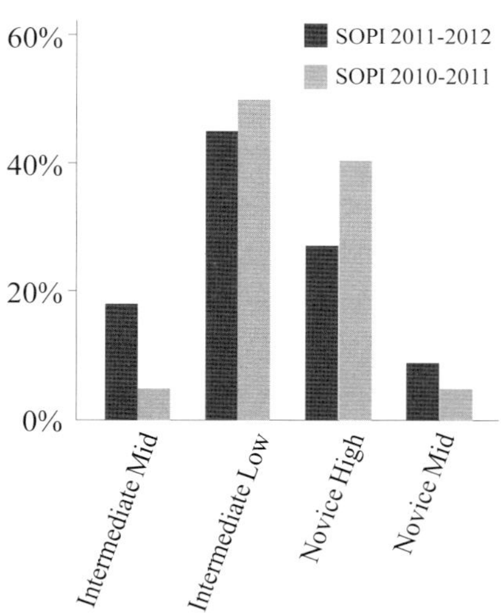

Figure 2

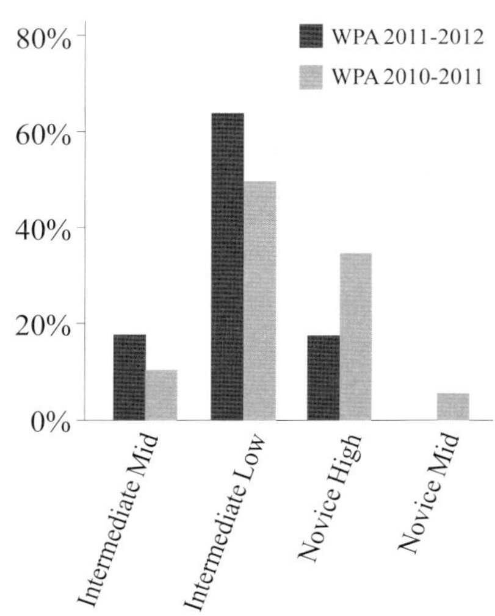

Korean Studies Program at Binghamton University

Sungdai Cho
State University of New York at Binghamton
(Binghamton University)

1. Outline of Korean Studies at Binghamton University

Binghamton University is one of four university centers in the 64-institution SUNY system (the largest comprehensive university system in the United States, with 459,550 students enrolled) and is widely considered to be the finest public university in the northeast. In a little over 60 years, Binghamton University has built a reputation as a world-class institution that combines a broadly interdisciplinary international education with one of the most vibrant research programs in the nation. Binghamton University is a highly selective institution with a student population of 16,077 (12,997 undergraduate and 3,080 graduate, 28.9% students of color, 15.9% international students) and 551 faculty members.

At Binghamton University, Korean Studies is offered through two academic units: as a major and minor in academic program. Established in 2008, Korean Studies is part of the Department of Asian and Asian American Studies (DAAAS) in the Harpur College of Arts and Science. As one of the university's research centers, the Center for Korean Studies (CKS), is affiliated with the Institute for Asian and Asian Diaporas (IAAD) and has been running independently under the supervision of the Division of Research at Binghamton University since 2010.

2. Past History of Korean Studies at Binghamton University

The history of Korean Studies at Binghamton University began as early as 1994, when Korean students and alumni in New York City donated seed money to offer the first Korean language course. A group of students, having organized their own non-credit Korean language and culture courses, advocated the offering of Korean language courses for credit.

The Korean Studies program at Binghamton University began with the combined efforts of students and faculty of the Department of German, Russian, and East Asian Languages. Between 1994 and 1999, Korean courses were offered in the Department of German, Russian, and East Asian Languages. Having grown from a modest beginning in 1994, the program now enjoys student demand beyond course capacity.

A formal Korean Studies program began in 2000, when a tenure-track position in Korean was established by the university, and Professor Sungdai Cho (Ph.D. in Linguistics, University of Hawaii at Manoa), a specialist in Korean linguistics and pedagogy, joined the faculty. The growth of the Korean program was bolstered by large-scale support from the Korea Foundation, which enabled the expansion of not only language courses but also content courses in linguistics, literature, and history. With the support of two grants from the Korea Foundation and the Freeman Foundation, the program established two tenure-track professorships in Korean Studies in 2001 and 2006.

Such growth allowed the program to offer a minor in Korean in the Department of German, Russian, and East Asian Languages beginning in the fall of 2006. The program continued to expand with the introduction of specialized fourth-year language courses and content courses in other disciplines.

In the fall of 2008, the Department of Asian and Asian American Studies was added to Harpur College of Arts and Sciences. It began with an emphasis on the studies of histories, languages, and cultures within Asia, and it has since expanded to include studies of Asian diasporas, with a particular focus on Asians of the Americas. Moreover, another two East Asian area studies, Japanese and Chinese Studies, were added as new academic programs in the department.

The Department of Asian and Asian American Studies has offered a Korean Studies as a minor since its inception in the fall of 2008. The department also offers Korean language courses up to the fourth-year level, in addition to other courses on Korean texts, including readings in modern Korean and literary Chinese. There are usually upwards of fourteen to sixteen courses on Korea every year in fields such as culture, history, political science, and sociology. In 2009, one more tenure-track Korea Foundation professorship was added in the faculty of Korean Studies.

Beginning in 2010, a Korean Studies major was launched under the Department of Asian and Asian American Studies. The Korean Studies major was somewhat different from the previous Korea Specialization major offered by the Department of Asian and Asian American Studies in that the language requirement was through the third year and the general focus of all courses was solely on Korea.

The Korean Studies major consists of 11 courses and includes the following language requirements:

Language Requirements: Students are required to successfully complete the following four language courses: KOR 203 Intermediate Korean I; KOR 204 Intermediate Korean II; KOR 305 Advanced Reading and Comprehension I; KOR 306 Advanced Reading and Comprehension II. (Note: KOR 101 Elementary Korean I and KOR 102 Elementary Korean II provide the basic linguistic knowledge and skills required to begin the major, but do not count towards the major.) After a proficiency test assessment and consultation with Korean Program faculty, students who already demonstrate competence in any of the required levels of the Korean language may waive part or all of the language requirements. Waived Korean language courses will not count toward the major and must be replaced with other Korean Studies courses to bring the total number of courses to eleven.

Elective Courses: Students choose six of the courses listed below (or other approved courses as they become available). Students are also required to successfully complete one course designated as Asian American and Diaspora Studies.

- AAAS 211 Korean Civilization
- AAAS 218 Structure of Korean
- AAAS 221 Korea Beyond the Peninsula
- AAAS 240 Korean Literature and Culture (Pre-20th Century.)
- AAAS 242 20th Century Korean Literature in Translation
- AAAS 311 Language, Culture and Society in Korea
- AAAS 313 Religions and Culture of Korea
- AAAS 340 Readings in Korean Literature
- AAAS 360 Korean History (Ancient-19th Century)
- AAAS 361 Korea in the Age of Empire, 1876-1945
- AAAS 363 Gender, Culture and Korean Society
- AAAS 385 Korean Politics through Cinema
- AAAS 414 Economic Development in East Asia
- AAAS 439 East Asian Linguistics
- AAAS 449 Pedagogy for East Asian Languages-Korean
- AAAS 431 Confucianism and Korea
- AAAS 432 Women in Korean History

In addition, students are also required to take two 400 level courses, at least one of which must be in their major. These courses must 1) be taught by DAAAS faculty members, 2) be non-language courses, and 3) be chosen in consultation with their primary advisor. At least six of the elective courses must be at the 300 or 400 level.

Since the fall of 2011, Binghamton University has offered an MA degree in Korean Studies under the Department of Asian and Asian American Studies. The MA in Korean Studies has two main branches: one is a combined five-year BA/MA program that caters to undergraduates at Binghamton, and the other is a stand-alone MA.

In the fall of 2012, one tenure-track professor and one full-time language lecturer in Korean Studies have been appointed with the support of the Academy of Korean Studies' Core University Program for Korean Studies (CUPKS). As of 2014, however, the Korean Studies program has 7 full-time tenure-track professors, 2 full-time language lecturers, and 2-3 adjunct instructors who teach depending on their teaching competencies and student demand.

Figure 1. Student Enrollments at Courses in Korean Studies, 1997-2013

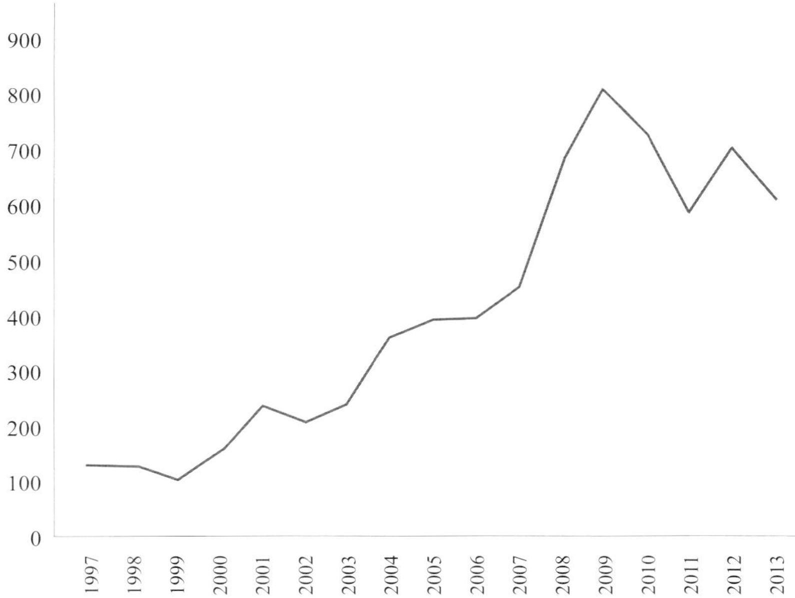

The Department of Asian and Asian American Studies currently offers five different tracks in both undergraduate and graduate programs: Chinese Studies, Japanese Studies, Korean Studies, South Asian Studies, and Asian and Asian-American Studies. Korean Studies is growing as one of the key majors among these tracks (see Figure 1).

3. Establishing the Center for Korean Studies

3.1. STRUCTURE OF THE CENTER FOR KOREAN STUDIES

On January 25, 2010, the Center for Korean Studies (CKS) was officially established at Binghamton University under the leadership of Professor Sungdai Cho, who served as the founding director. As described above, CKS is a single unit of the university's many organized research centers, and while it is affiliated with the Institute of Asian and Asian Diasporas, it runs independently under the supervision of the

Division of Research at Binghamton University. The structure of the CKS consists of the following three parts: 1) 4 full-time administrative lines (Director, Program Coordinator and International Program Korean Advisor, Research Coordinator, and Outreach Coordinator), 2) 6 core faculty and 3) 17 affiliated faculty as of the fall of 2014 (see Figure 2).

Figure 2. Structure of the Center for Korean Studies

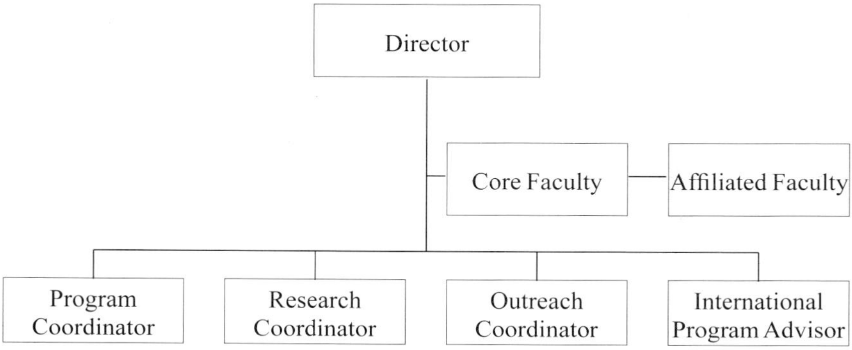

3.2. SUPPORTING THE KOREAN PROGRAM AND FACULTY'S RESEARCH IN KOREAN STUDIES

As a center devoted to the study of Korea, the primary mission of the CKS is to foster research across disciplines and to use the academic resources of Binghamton University to promote the understanding of Korea through interdisciplinary and intercultural approaches. Its faculty members specialize in disciplines as diverse as art history, Korean American diaspora, economics, history, language, linguistics, literature, political science, and sociology. CKS supports a Korean Studies program at the undergraduate level through the departments of art history, Asian and Asian American studies, economics, history, political science, and sociology.

To further develop Korean Studies, CKS has worked actively to expand faculty resources and initiate innovative projects. It provides funding for public programs (such as art exhibitions, film festivals, lectures, and conferences), individual faculty research, and the expansion of the library's Korea collection. It offers an active colloquium series, bringing eminent scholars from around the world to lecture on a diverse set of issues related to Korean Studies. The program also sponsors Korea-related events on campus, including undergraduate and graduate initiatives and cultural activities. To date, such activities and programs have raised awareness and appreciation of Korean culture across Binghamton University and in the surrounding community.

3.3. EXCHANGE PROGRAM

In addition, CKS supports Binghamton students who want the opportunity to enhance their language skills in Korean by participating in language programs overseas. Binghamton University currently offers four exchange programs to Korea University, Korea University's Business School, Korea Advanced Institute of Science and Technology, and Hanyang University's International Summer School. The exchange program at Korea University is open to students of all majors and features coursework taught in English as well as in Korean (for students who are sufficiently fluent). Second, the exchange program at the Business School at Korea University is open only to students in Binghamton University's School of Management. They take courses in accounting, management, finance, management information systems and international business. Third, the Korea Advanced Institute of Science and Technology (KAIST) exchange program began in spring 2013 for students in the Thomas J. Watson School of Engineering and Applied Science and Harpur College of Arts and Sciences students in the natural science fields. The program offers students an opportunity to study at one of the most elite science and technology research universities not only in Asia, but in the world. Fourth, a new opportunity for studying abroad in Korea through Hanyang University's International Summer School began in the summer of 2013. Outbound students are able to spend four weeks in the summer immersed in the culture and history of Korea, ultimately earning 6 credits toward graduation. Courses in

Korean Studies, Humanities/Cultural Studies, Business/Economics, International Relations, Media, Design/Fine Arts, Sciences and Engineering are available. All courses are taught in English, and Korean language courses are available at the beginning and intermediate levels. Students also have the opportunity to participate in field trips, excursions, and cultural programs. Faculty members also have the chance to access primary resources in Korea, extend their research, and to connect with scholars and institutions in Korea.

3.4. VISITING SCHOLAR PROGRAM

CKS also offers affiliations for scholars and fellows visiting Binghamton University for extended periods. Eligible affiliates include faculty holding appointments at other universities, researchers at research institutions, professionals from the media and civic organizations, government officials, and artists who seek to conduct research on topics related to Korea. During residencies, CKS provides scholars with access to the Binghamton University academic community and its renowned library system, and welcomes educational, intellectual, and artistic contributions to both the university and the larger Binghamton community.

The Center offers two types of affiliations:

- Visiting Scholar: Applicants must have earned a Ph.D. or other comparable terminal graduate or professional degree, and hold a faculty or other permanent research position at an accredited university, college, or research institution.
- Visiting Fellow: Eligible non-academic visiting fellows are senior government officials, researchers at research institutes or civic organizations, and prominent figures in business, politics, journalism, and activism.

3.5. FELLOWSHIPS AND GRANTS

CKS offers three kinds of student awards, which were made possible by the AKS grant. The BU-AKS scholarship is awarded to undergraduate and graduate students who have demonstrated scholastic excellence during their academic careers. The Research Fellowship is designed to advance graduate work that is in the developmental stages of Korea-related research, with the expectation that advanced graduate students will pursue a thesis or publication at Binghamton University. The Conference Travel Grant provides conference travel support for graduate students at Binghamton University who specialize in Korea-related topics and present papers at major scholarly conferences of professional academic associations/affiliations in the United States or overseas.

3.6. CORE UNIVERSITY PROGRAM FOR KOREAN STUDIES FROM THE ACADEMY OF KOREAN STUDIES

In 2011, CKS was selected for the Core University Program for Korean Studies Grant of the Academy of Korean Studies (AKS) for five years from 2011 to 2016 (PI: Director, Sungdai Cho). The grant provides CKS with nearly $1 million.

This multiple-year grant enables CKS to support a Korean Studies program at the undergraduate level through the departments of Art History, Asian and Asian American studies, Economics, History, Political Science, and Sociology. Activities of the Center for Korean Studies will also extend to host conferences and workshops, sponsor research projects, present lectures, support publications of significant research on Korea, and contribute to the enhancement of the university's library system and other research facilities. In the fall of 2012, the program also appointed a tenure-track professor and a full-time language lecturer, and the core CKS faculty is currently proceeding with 4 monographs and 2 edited volumes with the support of the grant. CKS has also been able to sponsor Korean events on campus, including cultural activities.

4. Outlook for the Future

The ultimate goal of Korean Studies at Binghamton University is to establish the most productive Korean Studies program in the northeastern United States. The program has outstanding faculty members, departments, and colleges within the university who are committed to expanding the Korean Studies program, and it also has a large student population that is interested in Korean Studies. Beyond that, CKS is uniquely placed in the northeastern United States as the only state school capable of enhancing and expanding Korean Studies in this region. Binghamton University now has a new Korean Studies major with growing enrollment, and the new MA program provides a place for those students who wish to pursue graduate degrees in Korean Studies.

Evolution of the Korean Program at the University of Hawaii at Manoa: A Narrative History

Ho-min Sohn
University of Hawaii at Manoa

1. Overview

The Korean Program at the University of Hawaii (UH) has 68 years (1946-present) of thorny history. Roughly speaking, the first 25 years (up to about 1970) was a long, tough struggle for the survival of both the program and faculty. During this Stage 1 period, the Korean program was shaky. Not many students wanted to take Korean classes and preferred Japanese, Chinese, Hawaiian, or European languages instead. After all, at that time, most Americans had a negative image of Korea as a former colonial territory of Japan, a poverty-stricken country, a country devastated by the Korean War, and (after the Korean War) a country that remained constantly vigilant against North Korea. As sociolinguists (e.g., Chaika 1982, Wardhaugh 2010) would say, the Korean language had no competitive power or market value. The Korean language was not particularly valued as part of Korean studies either, since Korean studies itself had not yet become an established field. This remained true even after the establishment of the Center for Korean Studies at UH in 1972. In their seminal book *East Asia: The Great Tradition* (1960), Reischauer and Fairbanks treated Korea as a variant of the Chinese cultural pattern, allotting only 9% of the entire book to the discussion of Korea, which was explored as topic only vis-à-vis China and Japan. In Academic Year (AY) 1960-61, the enrollments in Korean language classes at UH plunged to an all-time low of six (three in the fall of 1960 and three in the spring of 1961), threatening the very existence of the feeble program. UH's Korean language program, like many mainland universities at the time, was in a precarious situation.

Fortunately, the UH administration and the department endeavored to save the Korean program and position it alongside the thriving Japanese and Chinese programs. Two tenure-track faculty positions in Korean were created in 1962 and 1968. With the establishment of the Center for Korean Studies on campus, another tenure-track faculty position in Korean was added in 1972, resulting in a solid three-member faculty team.

Gradually, the Korean program saw a ray of hope during Stage 2, which took place over roughly seventeen years (1970-1987). Following the initial period of stagnation in Stage 1, Stage 2 saw a steadily growing increase in enrollments that paralleled the national trend in Korean enrollments (Goldberg, Looney & Lusin, 2015). This period reflected Korea's economic development, which began to change Americans' negative image of war-torn Korea into a positive one of economic and political progress. At the same time, due to the U.S. government's policy to open doors to Asian immigration in 1965, Korean immigrants flooded into the U.S., including Hawaii. Korean culture began to gain visibility in an increasingly multi-ethnic American society, and Korean heritage students began to register for Korean classes in record numbers. The enrollment peak of this period was AY 1985-86, when the annual enrollments reached 118 (57 in fall 1985 and 61 in spring 1986).

Stage 3, which lasted fifteen years (1987-2003), represents a stage of rapid growth due to Korea's distinct visibility worldwide, largely as a result of Korea's continued economic growth and hosting of the 1988 Summer Olympic Games. More American students, including heritage students, took Korean classes. Also, institutional changes started to take effect; in 1987, the department established both M.A. and Ph.D. programs in Korean, and it created the B.A. program in Korean in 1995, making its offerings parallel to the Japanese and Chinese programs for the first time. Annual enrollments rose as high as 343 in AY 2002-03 (187 in fall 2002 and 156 in spring 2003).

Finally, Stage 4, the current stage (2003-present), has seen a further great leap forward in the Korean program, especially with the introduction of the federally-funded Korean Flagship Program. Moreover, the so-called "Korean wave," which includes K-drama and K-pop music, has continued to attract a large number of students to Korean classes.

In AY 2011-12, for the first time in the history of the Korean program at UH, annual enrollments passed 1,000 (586 in fall 2011 and 465 in spring 2012). This number places Korean second to Japanese (2,459) and ahead of Chinese (855). Furthermore, the Ph.D. program in Korean language and linguistics attracts more students than either the Japanese or Chinese program does.

Korean Studies gradually became recognized as an established field worldwide. Ebrey, Walthall, and Palais's *East Asia: A Cultural, Social, and Political History* (2006), another seminal work on East Asia, allots 50 percent of the book to China, 30 percent to Japan, and 20 percent to Korea, which is described as being in an independent process of development.The Korean language is no longer a valueless, powerless language; it carries brand power with considerable market value worldwide.

As a reference point for discussion of the evolution of the Korean Program, a review of the major milestones is given in Table 1.

Table 1. Major Events Related to the Korean Program

Stage	Dates	Major Events	Remarks
Stage 1: 1946-70	Fall 1946	First instruction of Korean began in the Department of Asian and Pacific Languages, UH.	Kwandu Park began as a part-time lecturer.
	Fall 1962	The first regular tenure-track position in Korean was created. New litera.ture courses were added to the language curriculum, beginning in the fall of 1963.	Peter H. Lee was hired as assistant professor.
	Fall 1968	The second regular tenure-track position in Korean language was created.	Dong-Jae Lee was hired as an instructor.

Stage	Dates	Major Events	Remarks
Stage 2: 1970-87	Fall 1971	The Department of Asian and Pacific Languages was split into three departments: East Asian Languages, East Asian Literatures, and Hawaii and Indo-Pacific Languages and Literatures.	
	1972	The Center for Korean Studies was established as the first area center at UH and as the first of its kind in the U.S.	Dae Sook Suh was appointed as Director.
	Fall 1972	A third regular tenure-track faculty position in Korean language was created.	Ho-min Sohn was hired as assistant professor.
	Fall 1983	The Department of East Asian Languages and Department of East Asian Literatures merge into the current Department of East Asian Languages and Literatures (EALL)	
Stage 3: 1987-03	Fall 1987	New graduate programs for an MA & PhD in Korean language and an MA & PhD in Korean literature were established. Relevant curricula and required graduate courses in both language and literature were developed and introduced.	
	Fall 1995	The BA program in Korean was launched. Previously, only a minor program and Certificate in Korean had been in existence.	Ho-min Sohn was EALL department chair (1993-2000).
	Fall 2002	The federally-funded Korean Flagship program was established as a non-degree, post-baccalaureate program. The National Security Education Program (NSEP) was the federal sponsor.	Michael Long was appointed as Program Director.

Stage	Dates	Major Events	Remarks
Stage 4: 2003-	Fall 2003	A fourth regular tenure-track position in Korean language was created.	Ji-Ha Hwang was hired as assistant professor.
	Fall 2007	The Korean Flagship program was promoted to the Korean Language Flagship Center (KLFC). KLFC established an MA in Korean for Professionals in the Department of EALL as a third track of the Korean Program along with Language and Literature.	Ho-min Sohn was appointed as KLFC Director.
	Fall 2008	KLFC established new BA and Certificate programs in Korean for Professionals in the department of EALL as a second track along with the regular BA and Certificate program in Korean.	
	Fall 2010	A fifth regular tenure-track position in Korean language was created.	Sang Yee Cheon was hired as assistant professor.
	Fall 2012	Federal funding to the Flagship MA program was discontinued, resulting in complete institutionalization of the MA program.	The BA program is still funded by NSEP.
	Fall 2013	A sixth regular tenure-track position in Korean language was created to sustain the Flagship MA program.	Dong Kwan Kong was hired as assistant professor.
	Fall 2014	The King Sejong Institute Honolulu (KSIH) was launched by KLFC to teach Korean language and culture to high-school students and community adults.	Ho-min Sohn assumed the KSIH directorship.

Table 2 gives the years of the inceptions of Korean, Japanese, and Chinese instruction and degree programs.

Table 2. Years When Language Instruction and Degree Programs Were Launched

Languages	First language course offered in	BA program started in	MA program started in	PhD program started in
Japanese	1921	1942	Lang: 1968; Lit: 1968	Lit: 1969; Lang:1987
Chinese	1922	1942	Lang: 1968; Lit: 1968	Lang: 1987; Lit: 1987
Korean	1946	1995	Lang: 1987; Lit: 1987	Lang: 1987; Lit: 1987

2. Data and Information Sources

I can comfortably narrate the history of the past forty-four years of the Korean program because I have personally observed, experienced, and collaboratively led the program through both the initial dark period of struggle for survival and the bright period of growth. At first, I was simply an outside observer of the program as a Ph.D. student in linguistics in 1965-69 and as a linguistic researcher at the UH Pacific and Asian Linguistic Institute in 1971-72. Then in the fall of 1972, I joined the program as a tenure-track assistant professor of Korean in the Department of East Asian Languages. At the time of my hire, the Chair was John DeFrancis, a Chinese language specialist.

I am particularly in an excellent position to talk about the program development, as I served as Korean Section Head for many years, Interim Chair of the Department of East Asian Languages for two and a half years, Chair of the Department of East Asian Languages and Literatures for seven years (1993-2000), and Director of the Korean Language Flagship Center for six years (2007-present). I have also served as a faculty member of the Center for Korean Studies since its inception in 1972 and as its Director for six years (2004-2010), and thus, I am familiar with the close interaction between the Center and the Korean Program.

I am fortunate to be able to access the department's detailed records on enrollments, teaching faculty, and other relevant information. These records were carefully documented by office secretaries and Evelyn Nakanishi, a long-time student services specialist and graduate student advisor in the department. Ms. Nakanishi is also familiar with the history of the department, having served the department for more than forty years, including seven years as Assistant to the Chair when I was Chair of the department.

3. A Brief Narrative History

As in most other minority foreign language programs around the world, Korean language instruction at UH started in a poor state of affairs. Instruction first took place in the fall of 1946, one year after the end of World War II, which liberated Korea from thirty-five years of Japanese colonial rule. Instruction took place in the Department of Asian and Pacific Languages with Kwandu Park, an architect who had no training in language pedagogy but was employed as a part-time lecturer.[1] K. Park started with one basic-level general course, numbered KOR 100, with 10 enrollments in the fall of 1946 and 6 in the spring of 1947. Two years later, in the fall of 1948, the department added the first-year (elementary-level) course, numbered KOR 101, and in the fall of 1951, the second-year course, numbered KOR 200. K. Park taught these courses as a lecturer for five years until the spring of 1951. It is not clear who succeeded K. Park from 1952 to 1961, but the department record shows that a person named K. Kim taught in AY 1961-62, and then Peter H. Lee was hired in 1962 as a tenure-track assistant professor.

From 1960 to 1968, the department made a number of curricular changes: (a) Abolishment of KOR 100 and KOR 200: (b) Splitting of KOR 101 into 101 (fall) and 102 (spring); (c) Addition of KOR

1 In addition to Korean, the department also taught Chinese, Hawaiian, Hindi, Indonesian, Japanese, Sanskrit, Tagalog, Thai, and Vietnamese.

151-2 (Second-year Korean); (d) Addition of KOR 201-2 (Third-year Korean); (e) Addition of KOR 401-2 (Korean Literature in English); (f) Addition of KOR 415-6 (Korean Grammar); (g) Addition of KOR 417-8 (Fourth-year Korean); (h) Addition of KOR 491 (Contemporary Korean Literature); (i) Addition of KOR 499 (Advanced Study Essay) & KOR 699 (Directed Research); (j) Addition of KOR 750 (Research Seminar in Korean).

Table 3 shows enrollments in Korean courses for the academic years 1946 to 1968 in comparison with those of Japanese and Chinese. Summer sessions are not included.

Table 3. Course Enrollments from Fall 1946 to Spring 1968

AY total	46-47	47-48	48-49	49-50	50-51	51-52	52-53	53-54	54-55	55-56	56-57
KOR AY total	17	?	45	?	65	37	26	23	21	24	23
JPN AY total	583	762	815	602	1009	526	614	521	446	452	512
CHN AY total	135	143	98	90	101	54	37	63	37	50	40

AY total	57-58	58-59	59-60	60-61	61-62	62-63	63-64	64-65	65-66	66-67	67-68
KOR AY total	8	?	8	6	22	20	41	51	37	32	42
JPN AY total	466	538	836	965	1264	1677	1908	1911	2247	2427	2668
CHN AY total	47	56	96	172	323	371	416	426	438	608	547

Note: ? = no record is available.

Notice that the annual enrollments in Korean classes fluctuated from a low of 6 (in AY 1960-61) to a high of 65 (in AY 1950-51). In contrast, the Japanese academic year totals were between 446 and 2,668, while the Chinese totals were between 56 and 608.

In the fall of 1968, the language skill courses were renumbered based on the system still in place today: KOR 101-2 (Elementary), KOR 201-2 (Intermediate), KOR 301-2 (Third-level), and KOR 401-2 (Advanced).

In the fall of 1969, more literature courses were added to the curriculum: KOR 361-2 (Literature in translation-Poetry), KOR 461-2 (Contemporary literature), KOR 490 (Reference material-Korean studies), and KOR 495 (Advanced study senior essay). With the exception of KOR 361-2, these new courses failed to attract students until 1971.

In 1971, the department split into three separate ones: (a) the Department of East Asian Languages (EALA), (b) the Department of East Asian Literatures (EALI), and (c) the Department of Hawaiian and Indo-Pacific Languages and Literatures (HIPLL).[2] Thus, the Korean language program belonged to EALA and the Korean literature program to EALI. Due to this split, only the three East Asian languages (Japanese, Chinese, and Korean) constituted the Department of EALA, while the literatures of the three languages, along with the relevant faculty, curricula, and students, formed a separate department of EALI. As a result, the two full-time faculty members in Korean (Instructor Dong Jae Lee in language and Professor Peter Lee in literature), were separated, with two part-time language lecturers remaining in EALA. The Korean language skill courses (KOR 101-2, KOR 201-2, 301-2, 401-2) and the newly added KOR 431-2 (Selected readings in Korean) constituted the entire curriculum of the Korean language program at EALA, while all literature courses moved to EALI.

Table 4 reflects the above curriculum and program changes. Note that from the fall of 1971, the enrollments were only for the EALA courses.

Table 4. Course Enrollments from Fall 1968 to Spring 1977

AY total	68-69	69-70	70-71	71-72	72-73	73-74	74-75	75-76	76-77
KOR AY total	32	37	58	65	26	57	51	59	75
JPN AY total	2062	2344	2271	2524	2739	3152	3177	3162	2967
CHN AY total	860	611	627	617	774	854	663	539	525

2 HIPLL was recently disbanded with the creation of the current Department of Indo-Pacific Languages and Literatures (IPLL), and Hawaiian language and literature studies moved to the newly launched School of Hawaiian Knowledge in 2007.

As indicated earlier, I joined the EALA Department in the fall of 1972. As I was still committed to the UH Pacific and Asian Linguistics Institute, I had to split my time and worked for EALA on a half-time basis for a year. Due to my limited service, the annual enrollments were only 26. From the following year, I worked full-time for EALA, and enrollments gradually rose.

One conspicuous fact in Table 4 is that after the division of the languages and literatures in the three East Asian programs, student enrollments showed little change in EALA compared to the previously unified department. This means that enrollments were predominantly on the language side and that the separate literature department would not be able to sustain itself without the cooperation and the synergy of the language programs.

Indeed, twelve years later in the fall of 1983, university budgetary constraints and low enrollments in literature compelled the two East Asian departments to reunite into the single Department of East Asian Languages and Literatures (EALL), as it is now. Today, the Department of EALL is the largest of its kind in the world outside of East Asia, in terms of the number of faculty, curricular diversity, student enrollments, and degree programs. In particular, the Japanese program has always been predominant among all foreign language programs offered at UH, due partly to the large Japanese heritage population that occupies nearly 24 percent of the entire population of the multi-ethnic state of Hawaii.[3] In discussing the aspects of Korean language instruction at UH, I compare only these three East Asian languages, though other Asian and Pacific languages and European languages are taught at UH. With the merger of the East Asian languages and literatures departments, the literature side reintroduced KOR 261-2 (Literary Translation: Poetry), KOR 461-2 (Introduction to Korean Literature: Traditional-Modern), and KOR 610 (Korean Poetry) to the curriculum of the Korean Program. On the language side, existing KOR 431-2 (Selected Readings in Korean) was

3 The Korean heritage population is only about 4 percent of the entire population of Hawaii, and the Chinese heritage population is about 6 percent.

renumbered as KOR 481, which could be repeated once. New upper-division content courses KOR 470 (Korean Language and Culture), KOR 420 (Korean Composition), and KOR 451-2 (Structure of Korean: Sounds and Grammar) were added, which attracted advanced students, including linguistics graduate students. Note in Table 5 that the above curricular and program changes contributed to the enrollment increase.

Table 5. Course Enrollments from Fall 1977 to Spring 1987

AY total	77-78	78-79	79-80	80-81	81-82	82-83	83-84	84-85	85-86	86-87
KOR AY total	67	47	65	75	73	79	81	69	118	87
JPN AY total	2893	2490	2127	2007	2000	1971	2142	1901	1867	1833
CHN AY total	432	408	401	410	454	503	667	564	537	479

In the meantime, the UH system was reorganized, absorbing all seven community colleges and two four-year colleges spread across four islands within the state of Hawaii. The original UH was renamed as the University of Hawaii at Manoa (UHM), which is the flagship campus, where the Department of EALL and other language departments continued to be housed.[4]

In the fall of 1987, the Department of EALL launched the M.A. and Ph.D. degree programs in Korean language/linguistics and in Korean literature. For this purpose, a set of new graduate courses were developed and added to the curriculum. On the language/linguistics side, I developed courses such as KOR 631 (History and Dialects of Korean), 632 (Korean Phonology and Morphology), 633 (Korean Syntax and Semantics), 634 (Korean Sociolinguistics), 635 (Introduction to Korean

4 At present, Korean is taught at three community colleges of the UH system: Kapiolani Community College, Honolulu Community College, and Leeward Community College. Of these three, Kapiolani has the largest program with a tenured Korean language faculty member and two part-time lecturers. The Korean programs of Honolulu and Leeward are smaller in scale, each taught by a single part-time lecturer.

Language Pedagogy), and 730 (Seminar in Korean Language). More graduate courses have subsequently been added.

The graduate degree programs started to attract graduate students to the Korean Program, slowly at first but in larger numbers as years went by. Moreover, the 1988 Summer Olympic Games portrayed a brighter image of Korea and Korean people to the world. Thus, not only did the Korean course enrollments grow, but the rate of growth grew and even surpassed those of Japanese and Chinese, as shown in Table 6.

Table 6. Korean Course Enrollments from Fall 1987 to Spring 2003

AY total	87-88	88-89	89-90	90-91	91-92	92-93	93-94	94-95
KOR AY total	96	125	136	147	186	213	222	251
JPN AY total	2213	2361	2516	2828	2815	2594	2656	2728
CHN AY total	442	409	465	542	565	523	561	639
AY total	**95-96**	**96-97**	**97-98**	**98-99**	**99-00**	**00-01**	**01-02**	**02-03**
KOR AY total	228	268	234	260	227	257	225	343
JPN AY total	2740	2774	2570	2255	1994	2001	2028	2305
CHN AY total	635	521	584	583	553	497	553	580

During my time as EALL Department Chair (1993-2000), the department succeeded in establishing the B.A. in Korean program. Also in 1994, the American Association of Teachers of Korean (AATK) was launched in Washington, D.C., and I was elected as its inaugural president. Another major achievement during this period was the successful implementation of an international collaborative project for college-level language textbook development with a million-dollar grant from the Korea Foundation. This project, which joined more than thirty faculty members from English speaking countries and Korea, was initiated and implemented by the newly-established Korean Language Education & Research Center (KLEAR), incorporated with the State of Hawaii in 1994. Since its founding, I have been serving as President of KLEAR, and since 2000, a total of twenty KLEAR textbooks have been published, covering both language skills and cultural contents.

4. Recent Developments

The Korean Program has expanded and grown even more with the introduction of the Korean Flagship program in the fall of 2002. The Korean Flagship was implemented as an integral component of The Language Flagship initiative created by the National Security Education Program (NSEP) at the U.S. Department of Defense.[5] In 2002, NSEP awarded the first Flagship grants for Korean, Arabic, Russian, and Chinese; UHM was selected for Korean.[6] During a year of preparation, the Korean Flagship program recruited the first cohort of students for 2003-04. The two-year Flagship program was a non-degree, non-certificate program that included intensive one-year domestic training at UHM and one-year overseas training at Korea University in Seoul.

After four years of experience with post-baccalaureate training, NSEP transitioned all post-baccalaureate programs to undergraduate programs in 2007, with three exceptions: Korean at UHM, Chinese at Indiana University, and Arabic at the University of Maryland. UHM received an additional NSEP grant to implement an undergraduate Flagship program in Korean. At the same time, at NSEP's request, the Korean Language Flagship Center (KLFC) was established at UHM, with me as Director, and replaced the former Flagship program to operate all Korean-related Flagship education.[7] KFLC endeavors to fulfill

5 NSEP was established in 1991 to cultivate vital expertise in languages and cultures critical to U.S. national security and international competitiveness. Currently, nine languages are designated as critical: Arabic, Chinese, Hindi/Urdu, Korean, Persian, Portuguese, Russian, Swahili, and Turkish.

6 The grant proposal was prepared by Michael Long (at Department of Second Language Studies, SLA), Dong Jae Lee, and me. Michael Long assumed the directorship of the approved program.

7 Currently, a total of twenty-six such centers have been established, covering the

the Flagship mission to cultivate "global professionals commanding a superior-level of proficiency in a critical language." Flagship programs, including the KLFC programs, are unique in that they offer the following features:

- Intensive language and cultural instruction, including group training and individual tutoring, in a U.S. university setting
- Advanced language and long-term cultural immersion overseas, where students enroll in foreign universities
- Language immersion internships through public-private partnerships with international organizations and corporations
- The opportunity to attain professional-level language proficiency, including in a non-language academic major of the students' choosing

Upon its inception, KLFC established an M.A. in 2007 and a B.A. and Certificate in Korean for Professionals in 2008, as additional tracks to the existing M.A., B.A., and Certificate tracks in EALL. In 2009, we launched a pre-college program in an effort to encourage K-16 Korean language education. For a detailed account of the Flagship initiatives, see Sohn (2009).

Students in the regular tracks are more academically oriented, whereas those in Flagship programs are more professionally oriented. However, many undergraduate courses (such as Advanced Korean, Korean Language and Culture, Selected Readings in Korean, and Korean Proficiency through Film or Drama) are taken by both student groups.

Since 2003, one distinctive effect of Flagship education program is the enrollment increase, with another major jump in 2007, as indicated in Table 7. In addition, it is undeniable that the "Korean Wave" of K-drama and K-pop attracts many students to Korean classes, particularly non-heritage students. In a surprising finding, Korean enrollments have been surpassing Chinese enrollments since the fall of 2007. In AY 2011-12, Korean annual enrollments passed the 1,000 mark.

---

nine critical languages. UHM is the only center for Korean.

Table 7. Course Enrollment Trend Since 2003

AY total	03-04	04-05	05-06	06-07	07-08	08-09	09-10	10-11	11-12	12-13	13-14
KOR AY total	368	517	516	632	757	825	820	950	1051	1057	1060
JPN AY total	2531	2652	2813	2731	2687	2774	2535	2527	2459	2430	2333
CHN AY total	641	630	693	734	663	778	717	845	855	894	813

5. The Present State-of-the-Art of the UHM Korean Program

5.1. ORGANIZATIONAL STRUCTURE

Along with the Korean literature program, the Korean language and linguistics program constitutes the Korean Section of the Department of East Asian Languages and Literatures (EALL). The EALL Department, together with the Departments of English and History, is one of the three largest departments at UHM. The sister sections in EALL are those of Chinese and Japanese, each of which consists of language and literature programs. Only the Korean language/linguistics program is further sub-divided into the regular program and Flagship program. The Department of EALL, together with five other departments (English, European-American, Indo-Pacific, Linguistics, and Second Language Studies) constitutes the College of Languages, Linguistics, and Literature (LLL), the only college of its kind in American universities.

All three East Asian languages and literatures have B.A., M.A., and Ph.D. programs both in language/linguistics and in literature. Only Korean has additional tracks, specifically a B.A. and M.A. in Korean for Professionals (Flagship B.A. and M.A.). In addition, Korean has pre-college and adult programs, which are currently run by the King Sejong Institute Honolulu (as of 2014), an endeavor of the Korean Language Flagship Center. Thus, at present, the Korean Section of the Department of EALL consists of the academic programs presented in Table 8.

Table 8. Academic Programs of EALL Korean Section

Program	Regular Programs	Flagship Programs
Pre-college & adult	-	Pre-College and Adult Programs
BA	BA in Korean	BA in Korean for Professionals
Minor	Minor in Korean	-
Certificate	Certificate in Korean	Certificate in Korean for Professionals
MA	MA in Korean Language & Linguistics M.A. in Korean Literature	MA in Korean for Professionals
PhD	PhD in Korean Language & Linguistics PhD in Korean Literature	-

5.2. UNDERGRADUATE DEGREE PROGRAMS

As indicated earlier, unlike the Japanese and Chinese B.A. programs, both of which began in 1942, the Korean B.A. program was launched only in 1995, after many years of tireless petitions to university authorities. During the first thirteen years of the program, student enrollments fluctuated between 3 and 10 despite a considerable increase in course enrollments. Starting in 2008, however, the B.A. program attracted many students due to the initiation of the Korean Flagship B.A. program. At the same time, the regular B.A. program attracted many students as well.

At present (fall of 2014), the Korean Section of the Department of EALL has 58 Flagship-track B.A. students and 69 regular-track B.A. students.

Table 9. BA Degree Students in EALL Fall 2013-Fall 2014

Semesters	Japanese	Chinese	Korean	Total
Fall 2013	202	73	85 (37 regular; 48 flagship)	360
Spring 2014	222	97	91 (39 regular; 52 flagship)	410
Fall 2014	205	90	127 (69 regular; 58 flagship)	422

5.3. GRADUATE DEGREE PROGRAMS

Since their inception in 1987, the regular-track M.A. and Ph.D. programs in Korean have cultivated a number of MAs and PhDs. Many graduates and ABDs are currently working as full-time university faculty. Thus far, three PhDs and six MAs in literature have graduated. The three PhDs are professorial faculty at Ohio State University, SUNY-Binghamton, and the University of Auckland in New Zealand.

On the other hand, as of fall 2014, 25 PhDs in language and linguistics have been produced. Out of 18 current Ph.D. candidates in language and linguistics, 13 are ABDs. A total of 14 MAs in language and linguistics have also graduated.

As of fall 2014, a total of 30 PhDs, ABDs, and MAs in language and linguistics are working at the following institutions of higher education as full-time faculty: Harvard (2), Georgetown (1), Virginia (1), Notre Dame (1), Emory (1), Pittsburgh (1), Penn State (2), SUNY-Albany (1), SUNY-Binghamton (1), Iowa (1), Rice (1), Arizona State (1), UC Berkeley (2), UCLA (1), UC San Diego (1), Defense Language Institute (5), Chicago (1), UHM (2), UH-Kapiolani (1), Auckland, New Zealand (1), Kyushu, Japan (1), and Hankuk University of Foreign Studies, Korea (1).

Since its inception in 2002, the Flagship graduate program has graduated a total of 100 students. Under a non-degree post-baccalaureate program (2002-2007), a total of 44 graduated from the program. Under the MA program (2007-present), a total of 56 students with an MA in Korean for Professionals have graduated. Our former graduates are working in various honorable positions in the public or private sectors. At present, more than 30 of our graduates are holding public or government positions in Washington, D.C. alone.

The statistics of the current graduate students are given in Table 10, in comparison with the Chinese and Japanese programs. Of the 15 MA students in Korean language and linguistics, 14 are Flagship MA students, while only 1 is in the regular program.

Table 10. Graduate Students Enrolled in EALL as of Fall 2014

Degree	Japanese		Chinese		Korean		Total
	Lang/Ling	Literature	Lang/Ling	Literature	Lang/Ling	Literature	
MA	17	3	4	4	15	2	45
PhD	13	7	9	3	18	2	52
Total	30	10	13	7	33	4	97

5.4. FACULTY

As indicated in Section 3, Korean language instruction started in 1946 with one part-time lecturer, who taught for five years. A large number of temporary part-time lecturers have been employed as needs arose on a semester basis. Some UH faculty members in other programs were occasionally assigned to teach Korean language classes (e.g., W. Henthorn, Z. Song, Y.S. Kubota). A number of visiting professors and scholars have been invited from Korea: Park Chang Hae, Kim Sun Jae, Seo Sang Kyu (Yonsei University); Lee Young Sook, Yang Hye Soon, Suh Sook (Ewha Womans University); Cho Choon Hak (Seoul National University); Han In Kwon (Korea University); Koo Sang (Catholic University of Korea); Kim Taeok (Sogang University); Park Jae Doo (Kyung Hee University); Eom Jeong-ho (Dong-A University); and Shin Hyun Sook (Sangmyung University). Some stayed only one semester while others stayed for multiple years.

Thus far, the Korean Program has been allotted six regular tenure-track positions, one in literature and five in language/linguistics. The six positions have been maintained as follows:

Table 11. Hiring of Tenure-track Positions

Faculty	Disciplinary area	Year hired	Remarks
Peter H. Lee	Korean literature	1962	Moved to UCLA in 1987. Retired.
Dong Jae Lee	Korean language & linguistics	1968	Retired in 2010.

Faculty	Disciplinary area	Year hired	Remarks
Ho-min Sohn	Korean language & linguistics	1972	Current professor
Marshall Phil	Korean literature	1989	Passed away in 1996.
Yung-Hee Kim	Korean literature	1997	Current professor
Ji-Ha Hwang	Korean language & linguistics	2003	Passed away in 2005.
Mee-Jeong Park	Korean language & linguistics	2006	Current associate professor
Sang Yee Cheon	Korean language & linguistics	2010	Current assistant professor
Mary S. Kim	Korean language & linguistics	2010	Current assistant professor
Dong Kwan Kong	Korean language & linguistics	2013	Current assistant professor

Thus, the six regular positions have been filled as follows. Italicized faculty members are current occupants of the positions:

(1) Peter H. Lee → Marshall Phil → *Yung-Hee Kim*
(2) Dong Jae Lee → *Mary S. Kim*
(3) *Ho-min Sohn*
(4) Ji-Ha Hwang → *Mee-Jeong Park*
(5) *Sang Yee Cheon*
(6) *Dong Kwan Kong*

From the program's inception until 2009, Flagship faculty members have been hired with federal funding. For example, in 2009, three faculty members in the M.A. program, two in the B.A. program, and one program officer were fully supported by federal funds provided by NSEP. Due to the gradual reduction in federal funding in subsequent years, UHM has absorbed two faculty lines as tenure-tracks (one in 2010 and the other in 2013), while integrating certain language and cultural courses offered by the regular and Flagship programs. The two tenure-track positions have been filled by Flagship faculty Sang Yee Cheon and Dong Kwan Kong, respectively. At present, only two Flagship faculty members (full-time instructor Sumi Chang and program officer Lydia Chung) are fully funded by NSEP.

In the fall of 1993, a full-time instructor position was created, and Seok-Hoon You (currently professor of linguistics at Korea University) was hired to fill the position. When he moved to Harvard in 1996, the position was closed, and two Graduate Assistant positions were created instead. As of fall 2014, the Korean Section of EALL has been provided with a total of seven Graduate Assistants (GAs), who teach independently in mainly lower-level language courses. At present, five of these GA positions are in the language/linguistics program, one in the literature program, and one in the Flagship (Korean for Professionals) program.

In addition, usually a half a dozen part-time lecturers are employed every semester to teach undergraduate language and literature courses. These lecturers are hired mostly from among current Ph.D. students in Korean language/linguistics and literature.

5.5. COURSE OFFERINGS

A wide variety of undergraduate and graduate courses in Korean language/linguistics and literature are offered every semester. While most language courses are offered every year, most of the graduate courses (600 level and above) are offered once every two years. The Korean courses offered at present by the Korean Section of the department are presented in Table 12.

Table 12. Current Course Offerings (as of AY 2013-14)

Course number	Course title	#of credits	# of sections	Frequency of offering
KOR 101	Elementary Korean 1	4	6	fall & spring
KOR 102	Elementary Korean 2	4	3	fall & spring
KOR 105	Accelerated Elementary Korean	8	1	fall
KOR 111	Elementary Conversational Korean 1	3	1	fall
KOR 112	Elementary Conversational Korean 2	3	1	spring
KOR 201	Intermediate Korean 1	4	4	fall & spring
KOR 202	Intermediate Korean 2	4	2	fall & spring
KOR 205	Accelerated Intermediate Korean	8	1	spring
KOR 301	Advanced Intermediate Korean 1	3	2	fall
KOR 302	Advanced Intermediate Korean 2	3	2	spring
KOR 307	Readings in Chinese Characters 1	3	1	fall
KOR 308	Readings in Chinese Characters 2	3	1	spring
KOR 380	Korean Proficiency through TV Drama	3	1	fall&/or spring
KOR 399	Directed Reading in Advanced Intermediate Korean	variable	1	spring& fall
KOR 401	Advanced Korean 1	3	1	fall
KOR 402	Advanced Korean 2	3	1	spring
KOR 403	High-Advanced Korean 1	3	2	fall
KOR 404	High-Advanced Korean 2	3	2	spring
KOR 420	Korean Composition	3	1	spring &/or fall
KOR 421	Media Analysis in Korean 1	3	2	fall
KOR 422	Media Analysis in Korean 2	3	2	spring
KOR 425	Selected Readings in Korean	3	2 (regular/ flagship)	fall & spring
KOR 451	Structure of Korean 1	3	1	Fall

Course number	Course title	#of credits	# of sections	Frequency of offering
KOR 452	Structure of Korean 2	3	1	spring
KOR 470	Language and Culture of Korea	3	1	fall &/or spring
KOR 480	Korean Proficiency through Film	3	1	fall &/or spring
KOR 485K	Korean for Career Professionals	3	1	fall
KOR 486K	Korean for Academic Purposes	3	1	spring
KOR 493	Introduction to Traditional Korean Literature	3	1	fall
KOR 494	Introduction to Modern Korean Literature	3	1	spring
KOR 496	Korean Abroad	variable	1	fall & spring
KOR 499	Directed Reading in Advanced Korean	variable	2	fall & spring
KOR 613	Korean Verse	3	1	as needed
KOR 614	Korean Narrative	3	1	as needed
KOR 615	Korean Drama	3	1	as needed
KOR 621	Media Research in Korean	3	1	fall
KOR 622	Comparative Studies of Contemporary South and North Korea	3	1	spring
KOR 623	Interdisciplinary Research in Korean	3	1	fall
KOR 624	Analysis of Korean Academic Discourse	3	1	spring
KOR 631	History and Dialects of Korean Language	3	1	as needed
KOR 632	Korean Phonology and Morphology	3	1	as needed
KOR 633	Korean Syntax and Semantics	3	1	as needed
KOR 634	Korean Sociolinguistics	3	1	as needed
KOR 635	Pedagogy of Teaching Korean as a Second language	3	1	as needed

Course number	Course title	#of credits	# of sections	Frequency of offering
KOR 636	Korean Conversation Analysis	3	1	as needed
KOR 640	Literary Translation of Korean	3	1	as needed
KOR 645	Research in Korean Languages Acquisition	3	1	as needed
KOR 652	Major Authors in Modern Korean Literature	3	1	as needed
KOR 655	Practicum: Teaching Korean as a Second Language	3	1	as needed
KOR 664	Topics and Issues in Modern Korean Literature	3	1	as needed
KOR 699	Directed Research	variable	1	as needed
KOR 720	Research Seminar in Korean literature	3	1	as needed
KOR 730	Research Seminar in Korean language	3	2 (regular /flagship)	fall & spring
EALL 281	Korean literature in Translation: Traditional	3	1	fall
EALL 282	Korean literature in Translation: Modern	3	1	spring
EALL 360	Literary Traditions of East Asia	3	1	as needed
EALL 472	East-West Cultural Encounters	3	1	as needed
EALL 601	Current Issues in East Asian Languages	3	1	as needed
EALL 602	Introduction to East Asian Linguistics	3	1	as needed
EALL 603K	Bibliographical and Research Methodology	3	1	as needed
EALL 700	Thesis Research	variable	1	as needed
EALL 800	Dissertation Research	1	1	as needed

5.6. THE CENTER FOR KOREAN STUDIES (CKS)

Established in 1972, the Center for Korean Studies (CKS) coordinates and develops resources for the study of Korea at the University of Hawaii. The Center seeks to promote interdisciplinary and intercultural approaches to Korean studies by drawing on its faculty members in disciplines as diverse as anthropology, architecture, art, Asian studies, communication, creative writing, economics, ethnomusicology, education, geography, history, language, linguistics, literature, management, political science, sociology, and urban and regional planning.

The Center was created by the University of Hawaii's Board of Regents as the first of its kind in the nation and the first area center at the university. Before 1972, a group of several UH faculty in areas such as Korean history, literature, and political science initiated and developed the idea of establishing the CKS on campus. To my recollection, the main argument for creating a center for Korean studies at the UH was that at least one U.S. campus of higher education should have a center to study Korea (a) as a historical and cultural bridge between China and Japan and (b) as a politically, ideologically, and physically divided country. Additionally, the University of Hawaii was the most suitable and ideal venue for such a center because (a) it was equipped with a concentration of the most Korea specialists among U.S. institutions, (b) Hawaii was the first settlement for many Korean immigrants, (c) Hawaii was a geographical center connecting Korea and the U.S. mainland, and (d) Hawaii was a typical multicultural society.

The Center's aim is to promote Korean studies worldwide as well as within the UH system through instruction, research, publication, support for faculty and students, and community outreach. It interacts closely with the Korean language and literature programs, and all the faculty members in Korean language and literature are regular faculty members of the CKS. Student scholarships, faculty research, and conference management are also generously supported by the CKS. Finally, many academic, cultural, and community-related events and activities are implemented jointly by CKS and the Korean Section of the Department of East Asian Languages and Literatures.

The CKS started in 1972 with ten Korea-related faculty, including myself. In the past forty years, it has evolved to comprise some forty faculty members at present, covering many colleges and departments. The first Director was Dae Sook Suh (1972-95), during whose term the CKS building was completed in 1980, with funds contributed by the Korean government, the State of Hawaii, and the Korean-American community in Hawaii. The succeeding directors were Chung H. Lee (Economics, 1995-98), Edward Shultz (History, 1998-04), Ho-min Sohn (Language/Linguistics, 2004-10), Yung-Hee Kim (Literature, 2010-13), and Sang-Hyop Lee (Economics, 2013-). Up until now, the CKS has received about six million dollars in endowed funds for Korea-related activities, including a two-million dollar endowment for faculty recruitment from the Korea Foundation and other sources.[8]

6. Prospects and Conclusions

At present, the Korean language and linguistics program at UHM is recognized as one of the largest and most well-established academic programs of its kind in the world outside of Korea. The Korean program has made enormous progress from its faltering inception to its productive place today, especially in language instruction and linguistics research. As I have mentioned above, the underlying external and internal factors that jointly motivated and propelled such a rapid development may be summarized as follows, roughly in order of importance:

External factors:

(a) Korea's rapid economic growth and effect on the global economy

(b) Rapid increase in Korean immigrant population (more than two million Koreans in the U.S. at present)

8 I was instrumental in establishing this endowment when I was CKS Director, receiving a one-million dollar grant from the Korea Foundation and raising a significant portion of the required matching funds.

(c) The "Korean Wave" (especially K-drama and K-pop)
(d) Introduction of SAT II Korean
(e) Korean-American community's efforts to promote Korean among heritage children
(f) Korean government's globalization policy and investment to promote Korean language education and Korean studies overseas (e.g., Korea Foundation and Academy of Korean Studies)
(g) Increase in close interactions between Korea and the U.S. in all areas
(h) Presence of Korean businesses and government agencies in the U.S.
(i) U.S. government's critical language policy
(j) U.S. government's policy to promote foreign languages and area studies
(k) National-level Korean language associations' initiatives and activities

Institutional factors:
(a) UH's strategic, financial, and moral support to promote Korean language and Korean studies
(b) Korean Program faculty's vision, initiative, leadership, and dedication
(c) Institutionalization of the foreign language requirement (UHM has long established two years of foreign language study as a graduation requirement for most majors)
(d) Academic diffusion of Korean studies

All the above factors have favorably interacted in the creation of the Korean program as it is today. As long as these factors sustain synergic interaction, the Korean Program at UHM will continue to grow and flourish.

Needless to say, there are many areas yet to be improved, such as curriculum innovation, development of innovative instructional methods, improvement of assessment tools, and online distance learning.

While instruction and research in Korean language and linguistics have made a great leap forward, Korean literature has long suffered from a shortage of degree students. This trend generally applies to other languages as well. Cooperation between Korean language and Korean studies is essential, but unfortunately, this has not been satisfactorily implemented, as not many Korean studies courses are offered to interested American students. Strengthening this link is important to pursue (for a detailed discussion of this issue, see Sohn 2011).

ACKNOWLEDGEMENTS

This paper was written at the Research Center of Korean Studies (RCKS) of Kyushu University in Fukuoka, Japan in the summer of 2012, when I was invited as a visiting scholar for one month. I am grateful to Professor Takatoshi Matsubara, the RCKS Director, for giving me the opportunity to work at RCKS. Special thanks go to the RCKS staff members (especially Fujita Hanae) for taking care of all procedural matters and logistics prior to and during my stay with the Center. I am grateful to Haejin E. Koh for her meticulous editing of this paper.

The various statistical data in this paper are culled from old hand-written records and printed documents stored in the Department of East Asian Languages and Literatures facilities. I am indebted to Evelyn Nakanishi, who assisted me in uncovering the relevant data for this study.

REFERENCES

Chaika, E. (1982). *Language the Social Mirror.* Rowley, Mass: Newbury House Publishers, Inc.

Center for Korean Studies. (n.d.) Mission Statement. In *University of Hawaii at Manoa Center for Korean Studies*. Retrieved from http://www.hawaii.edu/korea/pages/about/mission.html

Ebrey, P.B., Walthall, A., & Palais, J.B. (2006). *East Asia: A Cultural, Social, and Political History.* Boston: Houghton Mifflin Co.

Goldberg, D., Looney, D., & Lusin, N. (2015). Enrollments in languages other than English in United States institutions of higher education, Fall 2013. *Modern Language Association Web publication,* February 2015.

Reischauer, E.O. & Fairbanks, J.K. (1960). *East Asia: The Great Tradition.* Boston: Houghton Mifflin Co.

Sohn, Ho-min. (2009). Han'gugŏ kyoyuk ui sae p'aradaim (A new paradigm of Korean language education). *Kugŏ Kyoyuk Yŏn'gu* 24, 7-36.

Sohn, Ho-min. (2011). Haeoe taehak ui han'gugŏ kyoyuk kwa han'gukhak ui hyŏnan (Issues in overseas college-level Korean language education and Korean studies). In *Korean Studies Education for Intercultural Communication.* (pp. 11-52). Academy of Korean Studies, Korea.

Wardhaugh, R. (2010). *Introduction to Sociolinguistics, Sixth Edition.* West Sussex, England: Wiley-Blackwell.

History of the Korean Language Program at UC Berkeley: From a Mere Appendage to a Prestigious Program

Kijoo Ko
The University of California, Berkeley

1. Introduction

UC Berkeley's Korean Language Program has become one of the largest and most esteemed Korean teaching programs in the United States. Though it is still threatened by challenges, budget cuts, and job losses for the very people who have made the program great, the program's birth amidst a war, struggles through financial crises, and cultivation from the ground up has earned it a place in both American and Korean histories. Inspired by a spark of inspiration from a patriotic educator, the program has grown due to the tireless sacrifices of passionate and dedicated teachers; here stands proof that education and scholarship can and will prevail.

2. Past: An Early Pioneer

In 1942, the late Professor Bong-Youn Choy, having completed M.A. and Ph.D. courses in political science at UC Berkeley, was hired as a lecturer for the Department of Oriental Languages (currently the Department of East Asian Languages and Cultures) to teach Japanese. He did regret, however, that while the department offered Chinese, Japanese, and even Mongolian language courses, it did not also offer classes in Korean, his native language. Out of patriotism and conscience, he asked Professor Peter Boodberg, then the department chair, to offer Korean, but his proposal was rejected due to the department's insufficient budget. Rather than abandon his goal, he instead volunteered to teach Korean gratis. Professor Boodberg was concerned about Professor Choy's teaching overload, but this young patriot said, "Others are risking their lives to fight for the independence of our country. I don't think this is the time to worry about how many hours I teach" (Richards, 2009). The chair agreed, and the wheels for UC Berkeley's Korean Language Program were set in motion.

In the spring of 1943, Professor Choy's Korean language class made its debut on the Berkeley campus. In fact, it was the first time that the Korean language was offered in any college or university in the United States presumably other than Columbia University. It indeed was a momentous occasion in Korean education. The department's benevolent trailblazer, Professor Choy was concerned that he would be unable to fulfill the student quota to sustain his class; he needed at least thirteen students to enroll. Fortunately, the inaugural Korean class ended up with a total of eighteen students, none of whom had Korean ethnic backgrounds, though half were also taking Japanese, and two-thirds of whom were women, which was not surprising, as many male students had been enlisted in the war effort.

Though this new class had an eager, capable professor and enough willing students to begin, it still met challenges. One was the complete absence of ready-made Korean language instruction books. Professor Choy had to write his own materials, *Korean Reader: A Textbook for*

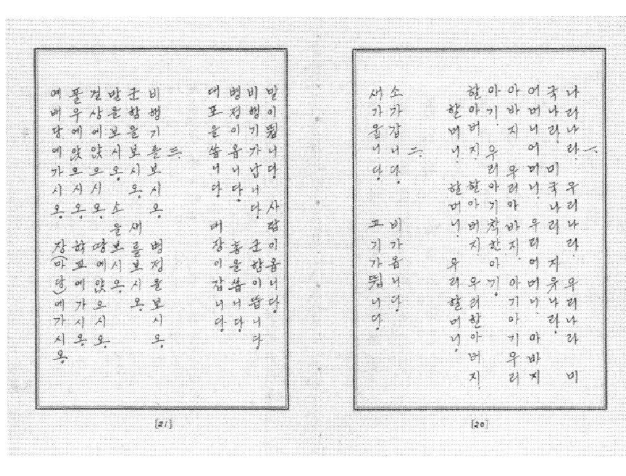

Beginner, by hand; this text was published in 1943 by UC Press.

After three years of teaching beginner-level Korean, Professor Choy eventually left Berkeley in 1946 to teach his original major, political science, at Seoul National University in Korea. His successor was the late Professor Ha-Tae Kim, President of the Methodist Theological Seminary in Seoul, and he was followed by the late Professor Michael Rogers, who had studied Latin and French at San Diego State University, then Mongolian at UC Berkeley, and, after serving in the military as a language officer, he returned to Berkeley to study Chinese and Tibetan. Finally, he received his Ph.D. in Oriental Languages in 1953 and joined the department as a professor to teach Chinese, Japanese, and Korean, and he eventually became chair of the Department of East Asian Studies. With the pioneering efforts of his predecessors during the program's nascent stages, Professor Rogers' dedication and hard work built a solid foundation for UC Berkeley's Korean Language Program. Tireless and pragmatically creative, "Rogers was a meticulous scholar and linguist," said Jeffrey Riegel, a professor of the East Asian Languages and Cultures (Maclay, 2005). Professor Rogers authored two influential Korean textbooks, *Outline of Korean Grammar* and *College Korean*, which became integral to Berkeley's Korean classes. In addition, he was a historian in his own right, having a profound knowledge of Chinese and the Classics; he wrote many articles about the Koryo Period as well as the historical relations between Korea and China.

Andrew Barshay, a current professor of history at UC Berkeley, recalls of Professor Rogers, "I think I remember him saying that he didn't speak colloquial Korean fluently, but he seemed to pronounce it with ease and had a good ear for correcting my pronunciation and getting the intonation of sentences right" (Maclay, 2005). If Professor Rogers lacked anything in Korean conversation and colloquialism, he received plenty of help from native Korean speaking graduate students as his Graduate Student Instructors (henceforth GSI), who served not as mere drill instructors but as independent teachers. Sung-Mee Lee, Kyung-Nyun Kim Richards, and Clare Chung-bin You led the first three levels of Korean courses. When Kyung-Nyun Kim Richards began to teach as a 25% GSI in 1968 while studying Linguistics, she did not expect that she would be engaged in Korean language education for the next thirty-two years (1968-1973, 1980-2008). During a personal interview (2012), Kyung-Nyun Kim Richards recalls that "Professor Rogers would teach two days a week, mostly grammar and reading, and I would teach three days a week, covering grammar, speaking, listening and conversation." While Kyung-Nyun Kim Richards was on maternity leave in 1973, Mrs. John Jameson stepped in to teach for a couple of years, as did Clare You, who joined the program as a graduate student in 1976.

In these early years, mostly non-Korean students with East Asian majors made up the Korean classes, and their approach was serious and scholarly. They were especially interested in reading and writing, rather than speaking. Although the students were eager to learn the language, limited resources and teaching methods were significant obstacles for the professors. In the 1950s, Professor Rogers used a mimeographed version of his own material, *Outline of Korean Grammar*, for the elementary level, and it has been used each year since the class' inception in 1943. The intermediate and advanced levels, which were offered every other year, used collected materials that he selected and used as readers. By the 1960s, two more books were made available, but these still had their own limitations. *Beginning Korean* (Samuel Martin), used for the elementary level, was written in Romanized Korean. Kyung-Nyun Kim Richards said in an interview, "I remember writing all of the text and exercises of the book in Hangul on ditto-masters so that the students could learn to read and write Hangul." Machines that were outfitted to print Hangul, which is the Korean alphabet composed of characters and symbols, were not made available in the United States until years later, and having the texts printed in Korea and then sent to the States was not only expensive but also a huge feat considering that Korea's top priority was to recover from war. *Elementary Written Korean* (Wagner & Kim), used in the 1970s, had extensive but unwieldy grammar, which was not helpful to students. These old textbooks today are almost enchanting and endearing, with its oversimplified cultural and social allusions, faded ink, yellowed pages, and seemingly archaic font type. These texts make better history books than language books. Yet another concern at that time was enrollment. "I even taught a single student for an entire semester!" smiles Richards. Luckily, the program was allowed to continue to offer classes, perhaps so that the university could continue to offer a balanced language program or because of both the program's projected success for the future.

And indeed, the future brought much success for UC Berkeley's Korean Language Program. In the 1980s, as family sponsorships within the United States increased, so too did Korean immigration, and with the thriving Korean population in the United States at the time, Berkeley's Korean Language Program burgeoned. For example, enrollment in the elementary level Korean class doubled that of the previous year. In order to accommodate the sudden increase in enrollment, most of which included 1.5th and 2nd generation Korean-Americans, the department grew to offer more classes. Clare You, needing another skilled Korean language instructor to further fortify the program, asked Kyung-Nyun Kim Richards to return and teach as a 50% GSI. Richards did return to help the program in 1980 and ended up staying for the next 28 years.

Supply met the demand, and intermediate and advanced classes began to be offered every year. In 1986, a total of six classes (three elementary, two intermediate, one advanced) were offered, and the number of students exceeded one hundred. Clare You and Kyung-Nyun Kim Richards eventually became lecturers (part-time for some years and full-time later) alongside Professor Rogers, thus strengthening the Korean teaching staff. Since then, the number of Korean language classes at UC Berkeley has steadily increased.

Although Rogers was not a native Korean speaker, his passion for Korean language was obvious. In honor of his devotion and scholarly achievement, the Korean government awarded him the Korean National Bogwan Medal of Culture in 1985. Shortly thereafter, he also set up the Education Abroad Program, a study abroad program between UC Berkeley and Yonsei University, and he served as the first director of the program for two years in Korea. Participating UC students could have the opportunity to have a first-hand cultural experience and full immersion in the Korean language. He returned to Berkeley and retired in 1987, having served at Berkeley for thirty-four years.

After Professor Rogers' retirement, the program's welfare lay in the hands of two lecturers, Clare You and Kyung-Nyun Kim Richards, co-coordinators and lifelong colleagues who shared the same office. Their immediate concern was to develop a way to accommodate the increasing number of students who had various backgrounds, abilities, and needs. A placement test, which included an oral interview and a proficiency test, were administered to assess students' ability levels. In order to accommodate those students with higher proficiencies (i.e., the 1.5th generation Korean-Americans), the fourth-year reading course (Korean 101/102) was also added in the early 1990s and covered broader content such as literature, culture, history, and social sciences.

In order to teach contemporary Korean in a more systematic way to a broad range of students, new materials had to be developed. For the elementary level, *College Korean* (Rogers, You, & Richards) was written in the 1980s and supplemented with corresponding audiotapes, but it wasn't until much later in 1993 that the book was published by UC Press. One of the authors, Clare You, recalled the process in an interview:

> It was the pre-computer age; everything was hand-written and manually-typed. There were few reference materials or curriculum guides to get help from — and all from scratch, which seemed to take forever. Publication from the UC Press is another long process; many rounds of outsider and insider reviews, editing, proofreading, finding the printer who can handle both English and Korean, etc. *College Korean*, being the first of its kind for UCP, had a quite long incubation period before it was published.

Since You and Richards felt that many textbooks available in Korea could not engage most American collegians, *College Korean* was specifically designed to reflect college life in the United States. It is no wonder that the protagonist of the text is Hyunbae, a Korean-American college student at UC Berkeley. The text was designed to cover one lesson per week, focusing on reading, writing, and speaking. In the fall of 1989, the sequel to *College Korean*, *Intermediate College Korean* (Clare You & Eunsu Cho), began to be used in class. Online companion materials were also developed to accommodate new technologies in language teaching. The textbook, which received outside funding from the Korea Foundation and University of Michigan (where Eunsu Cho was teaching), was published in 2002, also by UC Press. These textbooks are still in use at Berkeley for beginning and intermediate classes, and revisions for *College Korean* began in 2008.

At the height of UC Berkeley's Korean program, a number of GSIs (graduate student instructors) supported You and Richards, and upon completing their degrees, they accepted positions both in Korea and in the United States. To name a few, GSIs included Eunsu Cho (Seoul National University), Kyung Hwan Mo (Seoul National University), Sunyoung Oh (Seoul National University), Seung-ju Han (Yonsei University), Sung-taek Cho (Korea University), Intaek Han (Ewha Womans University), Min-kyo Koo (University of Southern California), Yoon-suk Chung (Smith College), Hun-Joo Park (Korea Development Institute), and Chung-woon Park (Hankuk University of Foreign Studies). The structure of team-teaching was firmly established during this period, with two or more instructors for each level and one (mostly a lecturer) supervising other GSIs. This structure was the most effective system, allowing the program to offer many sections for a growing number of students, despite having limited full-time lecturers and GSIs.

The team-teaching structure, however, was not without its shortcomings. Although these young, ambitious teaching assistants were a boon to the program, they still had their own majors to pursue and, upon finishing their degrees, would ultimately leave UC Berkeley and the program. For example, most of the GSIs studied non-linguistics majors and had bigger learning curves when it came to the craft of teaching languages. These GSIs often needed more time and resources to train properly. For GSIs who did major in a language-related field, teaching positions in Korea seemed more appealing than teaching Korean in the United States. Consequently, many of them moved to Korea soon after graduation. And, of course, some GSIs never intended to have a career as language educators but had taken the position on as a source of income during their graduate stints, so they left the program as soon as they received their degrees. Therefore, new GSIs had to be recruited and trained every one to five years. The high attrition rate amongst the GSIs began to take a toll on the program, its lecturers, and its students.

As a solution, the department decided to replace the GSIs with full-time lecturers who could devote their professional time and energy solely to teaching the language. Kijoo Ko joined UC Berkeley as a full-time lecturer in the spring of 2002, marking the beginning of this new phase. Additions to the full-time teaching staff continued over the next several years with Meehyei Lee in 2003, Soojin Lee in 2004, Junghee Park in 2005, Minsook Kim in 2007, Seung-Eun Chang in 2008, Shinyoung Park in 2012, and Jiyoung Kim in 2014. Luckily, the department and university, no doubt recognizing the importance of the Korean Language Program and seeing its dire need for change, gave full financial and moral support during the hiring process. Although nationwide budget cuts made funding the program and its lecturers difficult in 2008, the hired lecturers had linguistics backgrounds and actively sought to pursue their Korean language teaching careers in the United States. The program was able to hone in on its exact needs and find individuals who met those needs and were willing and able to fortify the program further. The transition has since proven to be positive for the program, lecturers, and students. Currently, full-time lecturers are able to accommodate many students and run the program self-sufficiently, occasionally hiring a GSI or two only when necessary. Much of the program's stability is due in large part to the dedicated, skilled full-time staff.

Harmonizing the seasoned and the new teachers, as well as the traditional and the novel teaching methods, the program became a well-oiled machine. More sections were added, new courses were developed, and many innovative teaching methods were designed to include and address each generation's new technological resources and its limitations. In 2005, a course on translation was offered, and the fifth-year Korean course was added in 2006 with the support of the Title VI fund. These two courses offered great opportunities for Korean émigrés to refine their high level of Korean. Finally, an American university had a comprehensive series of Korean curricula for college students, from the very basic to the most advanced levels.

However, in typical UC Berkeley fashion, the program refused to stop there. Thanks to the faculty's strength and creativity, separate tracks were developed for heritage and non-heritage students (Korean 1 in 2004, Korean 10 in 2005, and Korean 100 in 2012), which more appropriately addressed the distinct needs and learning styles of the two groups. Also, in the fall of 2004, Korean was finally made available as a minor in the undergraduate program. As of fall 2014, a total of 22 students have Korean as a minor; that number has steadily grown since the program's inception.

With all the phenomenal successes since the beginning of the millennium, 2005 marked the saddest year for all involved in UC Berkeley's Korean language program, as we lost both Professor Bong-Youn Choy, the program founder, who died on April 15th and Professor Michael Rogers, who died on June 6th. Whether their tenures at UC Berkeley were planned or not, these individuals worked tirelessly to build the Korean language program into what it is today. It's clear that the program's success is due in large part to their inspired vision and unwavering dedication.

Moreover, much heartache was also felt in losing some of the program's most integral leaders: Clare You left the Korean program in 2007 to serve as a director at the Center for Korean Studies. A year later, Kyung-Nyun Kim Richards retired in May 2008. Both were recognized with many awards in and outside the United States, including the Medal of Merit by the Korean government: You received the Korean National Silver Medal of Culture in 2003, and Richards received the Korean National Dongbaek Medal of Culture in 2008.

Clare You and Kyung-Nyun Kim Richards taught Korean at Berkeley for 31 years (1976-2007) and 33 years (1968-1973, 1980-2008), respectively. Their lives paralleled each other's in many ways: both attended Ewha Womans University in Korea; both came to the United States and studied linguistics at Berkeley, where they started to teach Korean as graduate students; and they both wholeheartedly and unflinchingly invested their lives into the Berkeley Korean Program. During those periods, they developed teaching materials, wrote textbooks, and taught their culture and language to their beloved students together. In addition to teaching the language, their interests in Korean literature, translations, and education in general led each to publish numerous articles and books. Also, both were deeply involved in the Korean community and participated in activities such as literary associations. They will be warmly remembered as life-long colleagues who gave their expertise and passion openly to the development of the Korean Language Program at Berkeley.

Recollecting her days of teaching at UC Berkeley, Clare You said in an interview in 2012, "It was an unexpected, unplanned career, but now, in retrospect, I feel it was a very rewarding experience." Similarly, Kyung-Nyun Kim Richards also said modestly, "I enjoyed what I did."

3. Present: Picking Up the Pace

As aforementioned, 2002 to 2014 marked attempts to stabilize and fortify the Korean program by replacing most teaching positions with full-time lecturers. Full-time lecturers have been hired almost every year since 2002, and this increase in faculty members has contributed greatly to making an even stronger program with quality, cohesive teaching. After Clare You and Kyung-Nyun Kim Richards left the program, Kijoo Ko, who joined as a lecturer in 2002, has been serving as the Program Coordinator since 2008. As of fall 2014, the program has a total of eight lecturers (six continuing lecturers who passed the 6-year review and two pre-review lecturers), making the UC Berkeley Korean Language Program's staff one of the largest in the United States.

In addition to its size, though, the quality and enthusiasm of the teaching staff provide students with stability and variety. All the current lecturers studied language-related majors: Kijoo Ko (Ph.D. in Linguistics, University of Illinois at Urbana-Champaign), Meehyei Lee (M.A. in Linguistics, Cornell University & M.A. in ESL, SUNY Stony Brook), Soojin Lee (M.A. in TEFL, University of Illinois at Urbana-Champaign), Junghee Park (Ph.D. in Applied Linguistics, UCLA), Minsook Kim (Ph.D. in English, University of Wisconsin-Milwaukee), Seung-Eun Chang (Ph.D. in Linguistics, University of Texas at Austin), Shinyoung Park (M.Ed. in Korean Language Education as a Foreign Language, Yonsei University), Jiyoung Kim (Ph.D. in Korean, University of Hawaii at Manoa). Their solid linguistic backgrounds, coupled with strong commitments to the field of Korean language education, have been integral to the program's own teaching materials and unique pedagogy. Skill and knowledge, however, are incomplete without efficiency and cohesion, which were finally achieved once the full-time lecturers filled the staff.

Currently, to further its efficacy and efficiency, the program adopts both team- and solo-teaching methodologies. Two, sometimes three instructors teach the lower-level classes together as a team. One instructor is in charge of the level's schedule planning, coordination of activities, and course management. The primary instructor facilitates the overall classroom planning and should be accountable, dependable, and extraordinarily organized. Instructors on each team communicate with one another as often as needed, alongside a more formal weekly meeting to discuss each day's lesson plans. In contrast, only one instructor is assigned to each upper-level class (Advanced Korean, 4th year Korean, 5th year Korean) and is responsible for developing curricula and managing the course accordingly.

Having different teaching methodologies has been effective for the program so far, allowing the instructors plenty of opportunities to complement one another's style while also giving each time to work independently and feel ownership of her classes and projects. For the lower levels, team-teaching works better because many sections with the same curricula can be made available to the students, who benefit from the feedback that co-teaching team members provide. For the upper levels, solo teaching allows the accommodation of different proficiency levels, as it is easier to offer individualized attention in this system. Curricula can also be adjusted to reflect rapid cultural changes in the upper levels. The Program Coordinator is in charge of overseeing the courses and making necessary guidelines for both overall and specific formats.

The various and unique methodologies seem to work well for the students. Every year, the enrollment rate for Korean language classes reaches almost 350 students for the fall semester and 300 for the spring semester, and student demand continues to grow. Overall enrollment figures have steadily increased over the past 10 years: 404 (2003-2004) to 635 (2013-2014). Unfortunately, however, state and federal budget cuts in the latter part of the decade have mandated the reduction of classes, forcing many students to remain on waiting lists for Korean classes. Ideally, the program should be able to embrace all students who want to learn. We hope to offer enough sections not only to accommodate the students' needs and desires to learn Korean but also to allow our program and school to continue to thrive. Statistics show that our program's popularity will only intensify since its provenance will evolve over time.

The students' ethnic backgrounds and their motivations for taking Korean classes have greatly shifted. Prior to 2000, heritage students took Korean language classes either because their parents advised them to do so in solidarity with their ethnic identity, or just simply to get an easy grade. Non-heritage students, mostly American or Asian, claimed to want to learn the language because their close friends were Korean. Since 2000, however, an unofficial poll shows that not only are more students from different ethnic backgrounds enrolling in Korean language classes, but the motivations to learn the language have strayed from purely parental or social pursuits. More students seem to want to learn Korean out of cultural interest in Korean pop culture (e.g., television dramas and music) or, pragmatically, to broaden job opportunities after graduation. Therefore, in order to better serve the students' various interests, it has been essential for the staff to revise its teaching methodology (e.g., having separate tracks for non-heritage students) and adjust the curriculum accordingly. As a result, effort has been made to offer a separate track for non-heritage students in the upper levels, just as is available in the lower-level classes.

Another unique example of the program's evolution can be seen in its heritage and non-heritage populations. Since the 1980s, more heritage students were enrolled in Korean classes at all levels, but an exciting transition occurred in 2008, when a growing number of non-heritage students enrolled, particularly in the elementary levels: 85 non-heritage students and 137 heritage students enrolled in the 2004-2005 academic year, 102 non-heritage students and 91 heritage students in 2008-2009, and 183 non-heritage students and 86 heritage students in 2011-2012. In the fall of 2010, the program initially scheduled two sections of Elementary Korean, which could hold only up to 22 students in each class. On the first day of class, however, a remarkable total of 77 students showed up. As a result, more sections had to be added for non-heritage students. Drawing from the Korean program's reserve fund, the faculty made room for one more section to accommodate the overwhelming demand from new students. A new section of elementary Korean for non-heritage students has been added every year since.

Similarly, upper-level classes (Advanced Korean, 4th year Korean, 5th year Korean) typically had many more heritage students than non-heritage students (70-80% for Advanced Korean and 90-100% for the 4th and 5th years), but that figure, too, is shifting. Compared to previous years, nowadays it is not uncommon to see non-heritage students in upper level classes. Even for the heritage students, there are some changes. Unlike in the 1980s, when most students in the Korean classes were 1.5 generation Korean-Americans, more students are 2nd generation Korean-Americans who were born in the United States. The non-heritage student population growth indicates that the program's student body cannot be measured by the general Korean population in the state or country, because students from all backgrounds and interests are enrolling in classes.

Federal budget cuts have had a huge impact on the UC Berkeley Korean Language Program, sometimes stymieing growth, but sometimes encouraging innovation to work with what that program does have. As of 2014, the Korean Language Program at Berkeley regularly offers five levels of modern Korean. The lower-level classes (Elementary Korean, Intermediate Korean) meet five times each week, while the upper-level classes (Advanced Korean, 4th year Korean, 5th year Korean) meet three times each week. Intensive 10-week courses for the lower levels are offered over the summer and meet every weekday for three hours. But some classes (e.g., Translation: Theory and Practice) that were once offered on an irregular basis are no longer offered due to budget constraints. To better serve students' different interests, it will also be necessary to offer various content classes (e.g., Business Korean). With limited funding, however, the program is focusing on improving the language classes with given resources for now.

Similarly, much thought goes into the program's materials and curricula, which were created specifically for UC Berkeley students by Berkeley's Korean Language Program instructors. The lower-level classes use the *College Korean* series. Elementary Korean has been using *College Korean* (Rogers, You & Richards) since the 1980s. Intermediate Korean has used its sequel, *Intermediate College Korean* (You & Cho), since 1989. To update the vocabulary and recent cultural changes, a major revision of its content and organization began circa 2008. In 2012, a total of 24 lessons were completed for *College Korean* and are now being tested in classes on a trial run. Originally, the curriculum was designed to be taught over the course of one year, but it has since been modified and extended to cover one and a half years of coursework to accommodate for the levels of non-heritage students. Hopefully, the revised text will be perfected and published in the near future. Accompanying workbook and homework packets as well as supplementary teaching materials for the new edition are also in development, with heavy utilization of information technology for maximum relevance and efficiency.

The same textbooks are used for both heritage and non-heritage classes, but they are utilized differently; certain sections of each book are emphasized, omitted, and/or supplemented with worksheets, lessons, and activities created by the instructors specifically for their students. The program's instructors work hard to ensure that, though each student's proficiency level may vary greatly from another's at the beginning, the end result is that all of our students achieve the same level of comprehension at the final stage, especially at the end of Advanced Korean. The goal is to make the transition as seamless as possible for students advancing to the 4th-Year Korean level and beyond, which do not have separate tracks for heritage and non-heritage students as of fall 2014.

The upper-level classes (Advanced Korean, 4th year Korean, 5th year Korean) use selected materials instead of a pre-set textbook. Not only does an appropriate text simply not exist, but also there have been continuous changes in our students' backgrounds, needs, and goals. Furthermore, there is wide variation in regards to the students' language levels, so it is difficult to choose one textbook that would be effective and efficient for all learners. For example, until several years ago, most students who took Advanced Korean had some experience in Korean schools as young children. However, as previously mentioned, there are a growing number of students who either move up from Intermediate Korean at UC Berkeley or were born in the United States and obtained their proficiency level through Korean classes at the university. As a result, the materials must be adjusted each semester to accommodate different needs. For now, the instructors thereby choose readings from various genres and sources depending on students' varying levels and interests. The faculty intends to continue experimenting with several options before it decides either to invest in one existing textbook or develop its own text entirely.

In addition to the main textbooks, supplemental teaching materials are used, including movies, drama clips, books, and other items to teach Korean culture and lifestyles. Currently, the program has about 100 DVDs and 800 books that students can freely borrow to improve their Korean. It will keep updating the materials and incorporating them more

Dwinelle Hall

systematically in the teaching curricula.

Supplementary to the textbooks are other contemporary methods, which make lessons more engaging and relevant. Several options include ANVILL (A National Virtual Language Lab), which is used for speaking practice; LFLFC (Library of Foreign Language Film Clips), which was developed by Berkeley Language Center and is used for listening practice; and podcasts or digital storytelling. Recently, social networking services such as Facebook or Twitter are creatively integrated as class activities to incorporate the digital generation further.

In addition to in-class activities, students are encouraged to get involved in extracurricular activities to enhance their language proficiency. This includes tutoring sessions, a Korean language conversation club, and a language exchange program in which students in a UC Berkeley Korean class are partnered with visiting scholars from the Center for Korean Studies (CKS) or native Korean students from an ESL institution to engage in colloquial Korean conversation. Also, a collaborative teleconferencing program with college students in Korea has been developed and is open to intermediate-level students. Such expansions will continue so that students can have more opportunities to meet Korean speakers and improve their oral proficiencies. These activities will be incorporated into the syllabus at each level so that more systematic curricula can be developed.

Furthermore, because of the program's close relationship with the Center for Korean Studies (CKS), which is directed by UC Berkeley's own Clare You, students in Korean classes also have several opportunities to experience Korean culture via the CKS's events, which include traditional music/dance performances, film festivals, and seminars featuring topics in politics, economics, literature, and society. Established in 1979, the CKS receives grants from sources like the Korea Foundation and the Academy of Korean Studies, which help promote Korean studies by sponsoring colloquia, seminars, conferences, and visiting lectures for both students as well as the program's lecturers, who are able to continue their professional education by attending conferences or doing research alongside the CKS. In addition, visiting CKS scholars sometimes offer special lectures in the upper-level Korean classes. It also supports the Korean Language Program financially by donating small but regular funds that can be used for Korean collections, teaching materials, and program projects. Clearly, the CKS plays an integral role in the program's efficacy, efficiency, and success.

Every year, the program offers various events and activities to give first-hand cultural experiences that include, but are not limited to, field trips to Korean markets and restaurants, singing Korean karaoke, writing calligraphy, and making Korean origami. In particular, special celebrations are coordinated for traditional holidays such as New Year's Day (e.g., making Jegi, playing the Yoot game) and Korean Thanksgiving (e.g., making Songpyun, special rice cake). Special guests in literature, academics, journalism, science, et cetera are invited to give a lecture to upper-level students. For students who are interested in literature, the Korean Literature Essay Contest has been hosted since 2011, with the support of the Literature Translation Institute of Korea. Also launched in 2011, Korean Day is held annually at the end of the spring so that students in all the Korean classes gather and enjoy each other's performances, which reflect what they have learned during the academic year. Korean Day is a fun opportunity for students to preview the curricula in the next levels and to see and hear how their Korean proficiency will evolve.

4. Future: Challenges and Future Plans

Despite its achievements so far, UC Berkeley's Korean Language Program still faces several challenges to improve the program. The first and most urgent challenges are budget limitations. Especially recently, the nationwide economic crisis has left the Korean program highly vulnerable and susceptible to cuts. When the nation's budget cuts devastated the country's schools in 2009, the Korean Language Program had no choice but to cut staff members, leaving only one continuing lecturer at the time. At the height of the program's crisis, two thirds of the lecturers' contracts were about to be discontinued, but as a testament to the program's positive influence and importance to both the university and the public, UC Berkeley students and faculty initiated the "Save East Asian Languages and Korean Studies at Berkeley" campaign, which spread from campus to the greater Korean community in the Bay Area. The campaign held a series of campus-wide demonstrations, several open forums arguing the importance of language teaching at Berkeley, and various events, such as a fundraising dinner in April 2009 hosted by the East Asian Languages and Cultures department. The program survived the academic year, keeping the same number of classes and instructors as in previous years. Leftover funds from the campaign are now reserved for the Korean Language Program and have been used as a helpful subsidy for emergency cases, such as last-minute class additions or tutoring sessions.

Although the program persevered through the most trying time to date, the fundamental problem of funding remains unsolved. Still six out of eight lecturers in the Korean Language Program have 'continuing employment status' as of fall 2014, but other lecturers' positions remain insecure, especially considering the nation's and the university's dire financial situations. Unfortunately, year after year, the program cannot guarantee all course offerings, and, thus, employment for lecturers is left uncertain until the very last minute. This insecurity remains the program's biggest stressor, forcing many teachers to worry about their jobs while simultaneously trying to focus on their classes and students. Although the program has the faculty, bandwidth, willingness, and demand to offer the same amount of classes each semester and then some, it must still cut classes and lecturer's percentages according to the budget.

As mentioned earlier, the financial shortage stymies attempts for separate heritage and non-heritage tracks for the upper level courses. Likewise, without the proper funds, the program cannot develop wider varieties of classes (e.g., Business Korean, Korean Film/Drama, Language and Culture) to improve, enrich, and enhance Korean language levels. There is growing interest from all both heritage and non-heritage students, and these types of genre-specific classes will nurture a deeper understanding of, respect for, and comprehension of the Korean language. In fact, many Korean programs in the United States already offer these classes; it is a shame that UC Berkeley's Korean Language Program, one of the most prestigious in the nation, should fall behind in this way.

In a slight but important turn of events in 2011, the university decided to set aside half a million dollars every year for the Foreign Language Common Good Funding so that some critical languages could continue to add more classes to avoid overenrolled sections. With its proven long waiting list every semester, Korean was selected as one of the critical languages to benefit from this funding, and it has earned security for a number of classes, at least for a while. Even with this funding, the program depends on the financial health of the nation and state, and it hopes that the situation improves before more cuts are made, jobs are lost, and students are lost in the shuffle.

Another challenge is to develop a higher degree level in the Korean program. There is an undergraduate minor program in Korean, but a Korean major has not been established, despite overwhelming demand. A Korean graduate program is not available either. It is regrettable that neither an undergraduate major nor a graduate program exists, considering the long history and the relative large size of the program. In order to achieve this goal, more faculty members must be hired, and additional courses should be added.

Also, tenured professors in Korean literature and culture would further fortify the program. Professor Jiwon Shin was teaching Korean literature for several years before she left in 2011, after which Professor Jinsoo An (whose major is Korean Cinema and Culture) took the role in spring 2012, but the program needs to recruit more professors with specific research interests. Of course, the lack of funding worsens the situation. So far, much of the program's assistance comes from professors in other departments, Korea-related institutes at Berkeley, and the Center for Korean Studies, which has been a great companion with both its academic and financial support. The CKS receives funds from Korean government-related institutions (e.g., the Korea Foundation, Academy of Korean Studies), private organizations (e.g., the Koret Foundation), and companies (e.g., Samsung) that support visiting scholars and potentially tenured positions in the program. With their continued support, we hope to establish a Korean major and a graduate program in the very near future.

5. Conclusion

To borrow a phrase, Rome was not built in a day. The same goes for the Korean language program at UC Berkeley. Thanks to the help of limitless students, instructors, the department, and the school, the Korean Language Program has grown and evolved much over the years. Despite recent financial crises, it has not only survived but thrived beyond Professor Bong-Youn Choy's wildest hopes in a relatively short amount of time. With a substantial number of students who are interested in learning Korean (both heritage and non-heritage populations alike), our future is more than bright. It began as an appendage to the Japanese program, taught for free by a generous and willing patriot, and has since become one of the nation's oldest, largest, and most esteemed Korean programs in the United States. Yet, we still have a long way to go. As Clare You advises, "Korean should be taught as a legitimate foreign language," and we will do our best to maintain a high-quality program now and into the future.

REFERENCES

Ko, Kijoo. (2011). Korean Language Program at UC Berkeley. Report at Program Review, UC Berkeley.

Maclay, Kathleen. (2005, May 24). Michael Rogers, UC Berkeley professor emeritus who helped with first Mongolian-to-English dictionary, dies. *UC Berkeley News*.

Richards, Kathleen. (2004). Cultural pioneers 101: The origins of teaching Hangukmal in America. *KoreAm*, 76-78.

Richards, Kay. (2002). 미국 대학에서의 한국어 교육 현황. http://www.iic.edu/Main/AboutUs/publications/KoreanLangEdUS_kr.htm

Richards, Kay. (2009). Korean Studies at Berkeley. Manuscript presented at the Department of EALC fundraising event.

You, Clare Chung-bin. (1989). U.C. Berkeley 한국어 프로그램의 소개와 전망, *이중언어학, 5,* 61-68.

You, Clare Chung-bin. (2011). Developing Korean Studies at Berkeley. CKS report, UC Berkeley.

The Korean Program at the University of California, Los Angeles (UCLA)

Sung-Ock Sohn
The University of California, Los Angeles (UCLA)

1. General Overview

1.1. PROGRAM HISTORY

The University of California, Los Angeles (UCLA) is located in the heart of a large and diverse Asian community. There are at least 14,000 Asian Americans, including both undergraduate and graduate students, on UCLA's campus (as of 2014). In addition, UCLA has approximately 3,300 Korean-American students on campus. It is located Los Angeles, which has the largest Korean community in North America, but the Korean program at UCLA started relatively late, mainly due to limited human resources and funding for Korean Studies. Funded by the university, it began to offer Korean language classes in September 1985 in the Department of Asian Languages and Cultures. The department (formerly East Asian Languages and Cultures) offered elementary and intermediate levels of Korean classes during the first two years. They were taught by Professor Chungmin Lee, a visiting scholar from Seoul National University. Professor Lee taught Korean language classes at UCLA from 1985 to 1988. In 1987, Professor Peter H. Lee, a renowned scholar in comparative and Korean literature, was appointed to be the first ladder faculty member in Korean Studies at UCLA. The position was created by the university in an effort to expand Korean Studies beyond mere language instruction at UCLA. Professor Lee served as Chair of the Department of East Asian Languages and Cultures (1988-1995) and established the Korean division in the department, which had been comprised of mostly Chinese and Japanese studies courses until then. Professor Lee has been internationally recognized as one of the foremost, pioneering scholars in the field of Korean literature in the English-speaking world[1].

Picture 1. Korean Language Program in Royce Hall, UCLA

With a strong demand for Korean language classes, the department added a new full-time Korean language instructor position, which was funded by the university. Sung-Ock Sohn arrived at UCLA as the first full-time language instructor and coordinator of the Korean language program just one week after her hooding ceremony (Ph.D. in Linguistics) at the University of Hawaii at Manoa in August 1988. With the historical event of the Seoul Olympics in 1988, enrollment in Korean language classes at UCLA exploded. During her first quarter of teaching, as the sole full-time instructor of the Korean language program, Sohn taught over 120 students in one elementary Korean classroom. During that time, the Department of East Asian Languages and Cultures at UCLA adopted a combination of lecture (two days a week) and discussion sections (three days a week) for all Asian languages including Chinese, Japanese, and Korean. Students attended a large lecture in a big auditorium on Tuesdays and Thursdays, and went to small discussion sections (15 students on average) on Mondays, Wednesdays, and Fridays. The full-time lecturer was in charge of large lectures, while graduate teaching assistants conducted discussion sections. Although this system is generally useful for departments with limited resources, a large lecture size of over 120 students would be a challenge for even the most qualified instructor, let alone a young instructor who had only recently graduated. Until she arrived at UCLA, the largest class Sohn

---

1 For more details about Professor Peter H. Lee, see http://muse.jhu.edu/journals/azalea/v001/1.hong.html#img01

had taught consisted of 17 students at the University of Hawaii.

1.2. PAST CHALLENGES

In addition to large class sizes, there were many challenges during the early years of the Korean language program at UCLA. First of all, due to the large numbers of Korean heritage students on campus, there were two distinct groups of students within the same classroom: heritage and non-heritage students.[2] While non-heritage students begin with little knowledge of the target language, Korean heritage students typically had high oral and aural proficiency, with more limited written literacy. Sohn's survey, conducted in the early 1990s, indicated that nearly 80% of heritage students enrolled in Korean classes had not received any formal instruction in the language prior to taking Korean classes at the university (Sohn, 1995). Placing heritage students into higher-level classes did not work well because the classes did not meet the unique needs of heritage students.

A mixed group of students within the same classroom poses a challenge not only for instructors but also for students. Non-heritage students frequently feel left out and intimidated when their heritage classmates appear to have almost native-like fluency in the target language. Heritage students often feel unchallenged and are misunderstood by their peers, who assume that their heritage classmates take language classes just to earn an easy grade (Sohn & Shin, 2007).

Sohn initiated a two-track curriculum in 1994 in order to provide both heritage and non-heritage students with optimal opportunities to develop their language skills. Under this dual system, heritage and non-heritage learners were placed in separate classes during the first two years of Korean.[3] The dual-track system was very effective for the

---

2 Korean heritage students comprised 70%-80% of the enrollment in Korean language courses in American colleges and universities during the 1990s. For details, see Sohn (1995).

3 Traditional foreign language instruction is provided for non-heritage learners, whereas literacy skills and cultural enhancement have been emphasized for

UCLA Korean program and resolved the problem of how to deal with the presence of large numbers of heritage learners in the beginning and intermediate language classes.

Due to the relatively short history of teaching Korean as foreign language in the United States, there were very few instructional materials available for English-speaking Korean learners during the program's early years at UCLA. Like most other universities, the UCLA Korean program tried to adapt textbooks published in Korea to American programs, but these textbooks did not meet the academic as well as cross-linguistic standards of American universities. Students often complained about the awkward and inadequate English descriptions in these textbooks. In order to resolve these ongoing problems, shared among most American universities in the early 1990s, a group of Korean language specialists in North America initiated a five-year Korean textbook project (Korean Language Education and Research Center: KLEAR) under the leadership of Professor Ho-min Sohn at the University of Hawaii in January 1994. The project, funded by the Korea Foundation, produced a series of textbooks (a total of 21 volumes) entitled *Integrated Korean* (University of Hawaii Press). The beginning level was first published in 2000 (second edition in 2010) and the intermediate level in 2001 (second edition in 2011). The new textbooks, which were accompanied by workbooks, were very helpful and eased the burden of instructors who constantly struggled to develop supplementary materials and handouts for Korean studies.

In spite of its short history and challenges, the UCLA Korean program has continued to grow. With increasing enrollment and a strong demand for Korean history from undergraduate and graduate students, a new ladder faculty position was added and funded by the university in 1989. Professor John Duncan, an internationally renowned scholar in premodern Korean history joined the Department of East Asian Languages and Cultures in the fall of 1989. Recognized for his mastery of Korean

---

heritage speakers. However, all students are merged in the advanced classes (3rd year Korean) because of the lack of sufficient enrollment in the non-heritage track.

and classical Chinese, Professor Duncan taught Korean civilization and advanced Korean language classes during the early years of his appointment at UCLA.[4] As one of very few Western scholars of Korean Studies who demonstrated a superior level of proficiency in the language, Professor Duncan has been a role model for non-Korean American students who aspire to achieve a high level of proficiency in Korean.

With a growing demand for modern Korean history from both undergraduate and graduates students, the Department of East Asian Languages and Cultures added another position in Korean history. Until then, there had been only four faculty members of Korean studies in the department — Peter H. Lee, Sung-Ock Sohn, John Duncan, and Robert Buswell. Professor Henry Em joined the department as an Assistant Professor of modern Korean history in 1995 (funded by the Korea Foundation) and taught Korean history until he left for another university in 1999. Currently, the department maintains two historians of Korea: Professor John Duncan for pre-modern Korea and Associate Professor Namhee Lee for modern Korea. Professor N. Lee was hired in 2002 to fill the position vacated by the departure of Professor Henry Em. Professor Duncan's research interests are in the cultural and intellectual history of the late Koryô and Chosôn eras, whereas Professor Lee's research interests are in the cultural history of contemporary Korea.

2. Current Status

2.1. FACULTY STRUCTURE AND DEVELOPMENT

The UCLA Korean program has grown rapidly since its inception in 1985. The Korean division of the Department of Asian Languages and Cultures (henceforth ALC) has added four full-time Korean language lecturer positions (mostly funded by the university and partly by the

4 As Professor Duncan has become busy due to other administrative responsibilities (e.g. Chair of the ALC Dept. and Director of the UCLA Center for Korean Studies), all advanced language classes are now taught by language professionals (e.g. full-time lecturers) in the department.

Freeman Foundation) since 1996, and the language coordinator's (Sung-Ock Sohn) position was converted into a ladder faculty position. In addition, a new ladder faculty position in Korean Studies (Professor Sung-Deuck Oak in Korean Christianity in 2007) was created. The new position in Korean Christianity was made possible by the generous donation of one million dollars in 2006 from a married couple in Los Angeles, Dongsoon and Mija Im, who dedicated funds to establish a chair in Korean Christianity Studies at UCLA in their names.[5]

Currently, over 2,000 students every year take classes with an emphasis on Korea at UCLA. The enrollments in Korean language courses alone exceed 1,000 students annually, and the numbers of students taking content courses (e.g., Korean civilization, literature, etc.) range from 1,000 to 1,200 annually.

2.2. THE UCLA CENTER FOR KOREAN STUDIES

The Center for Korean Studies was established in 1993 to coordinate the development of UCLA's rapidly growing programs in Korean Studies. Like other multidisciplinary centers and programs focusing on world regions and global issues at UCLA, the Center for Korean Studies is housed in the UCLA International Institute, which is comprised of close to 30 interdisciplinary centers. Professor Robert Buswell (Distinguished Professor of Buddhist Studies in the UCLA Department of Asian Languages and Cultures) was instrumental in the establishment of the Center for Korean Studies, for which he served as the director from 1993 to 2002.[6] Since 2002, Professor Duncan has been serving as director of the Center for Korean Studies. Professor Duncan says the following:

I hope to continue the work of my predecessor, Robert Buswell, in

5 The coverage of the Ims' generous gift has appeared in the *Korea Central Daily*, *The Korea Times*, and the South Korean daily newspaper *Chosun Ilbo* (January 28, 2006).

6 Professor Buswell is the founding director of the university's Center for Buddhist Studies.

maintaining UCLA as the premier institution for the study of Korea in the West, and at the same time, I also hope to build strong cooperative relations with my colleagues in the centers for Chinese, Japanese and Southeast Asian studies in order to integrate Korea more effectively into research and teaching about Asia and to promote a more comprehensive vision of the region as a whole. (John B. Duncan, Director, UCLA Center for Korean Studies)[7]

The UCLA Center for Korean Studies now presides over one of the biggest Korean Studies programs on the mainland of the United States in terms of faculty members and the range of courses offered; the program has the most specialists dedicated to Korea on its faculty (10 tenured professors of Korean Studies and 5 full-time lecturers) and the largest number of students studying Korean subjects. There are about 40 undergraduate majors and 50-55 graduate students in Korean Studies. The program has produced about 50 Ph.D.s over the past 12 years, most of whom work at top U.S. universities and proudly refer to themselves as products of the "Westwood School," named after the area in which UCLA is situated.

The Center also maintains exchange agreements with 11 major Korean universities: Seoul National University, Sungkyunkwan University, Pusan National University, Kyungbuk National University, Yonsei University, Korea University, Dongguk University, Won-Kwang University, Ewha Womans University, Yeungnam University, and the Academy of Korean Studies. The University of California Education Abroad Program also maintains an office in Korea at Yonsei University and offers UCLA students an opportunity for intensive study abroad.[8]

The UCLA Center for Korean Studies hosts scholars from universi-

---

7 See UCLA International Institute. (n.d.) Center Mission. In *UCLA Center for Korean Studies*. Retrieved from http://www.international.ucla.edu/korea/mission.asp

8 For more information, see UCLA International Institute. (n.d.) Center Mission. In *UCLA Center for Korean Studies*. Retrieved from http://www.international.ucla.edu/korea/mission.asp

ties and institutions around the world, who are drawn to UCLA for its dynamic research environment. These visitors include academics, scholars, and senior government officials, representing every subdiscipline of Korean Studies. These visitors provide valuable resources for the Center's faculty and graduate students, as well as for the Los Angeles community as a whole.[9]

The UCLA Center for Korean Studies has also played an active role in organizing a worldwide consortium of Korean Studies centers, which includes about dozen universities such as Seoul National University, Yonsei University, and Korea University in Seoul, UCLA in the U.S., and the University of British Columbia in Canada.

In addition, the UCLA Center for Korean Studies was selected by the Korea Foundation to lead a five-year project entitled "Korean Studies in the Americas" to support Korean Studies in Latin America (2006-2011). Because of the growing interest in Korean language and culture and the limited number of experts specializing in Korean Studies in Latin America, the Center created a series of online courses for undergraduate and graduate students living in Latin America. Professor John Duncan has led this innovative program. Furthermore, the Center offered e-classes through video conferencing technology such as Skype for students in Mexico and Argentina during the 2011-2012 academic year. The Korea Foundation gave UCLA more than $200,000 to pioneer and host the e-school.[10]

Another major project for the UCLA Center for Korean Studies is the establishment of the Religious Studies Program. The Center long has probed religion's powerful impact on Korean society through leading research on Buddhism, Confucianism, Shamanism, and Christianity. In 2000, UCLA received a four-year grant of $504,000 from the Henry Luce

---

9 UCLA International Institute. (n.d.) Program. In *UCLA Center for Korean Studies*. Retrieved from http://www.international.ucla.edu/korea/programs/visitingscholars.asp

10 UCLA was chosen to pioneer the program because the campus had prior experience conducting Korean Studies classes and researching with Latin American universities.

Foundation to establish the nation's first scholarly program in Korean Christianity Studies. The grant allowed the Center to probe into topics such as Koreans' conversion from Buddhism to Christianity.[11] In addition, with a generous donation from Dongsoon and Mija Im in 2006, the Center has been organizing regular conferences entitled the "Im Conference of Korean Christianity." The 2013 conference investigated the growth and decline of Christian churches in the post-Korean War period.

3. Undergraduate Korean Program

The Department of Asian Languages and Cultures at UCLA has grown rapidly in recent years to become the second largest department in the Division of Humanities, with 23 ladder faculty members, 20 language professionals (lecturers), and 7 staff members. Of the linguistic faculty, 2 ladder faculty members (Sohn and Tao) and 13 language specialists hold Ph.D.s in linguistics or language pedagogy.[12] In terms of the breadth of its coverage, the research productivity of its faculty, and the success it has enjoyed in placing its Ph.D.s into post-doctoral work, the ALC Department ranks among the best of such programs in the country.

3.1. THE KOREAN DIVISION OF THE ASIAN LANGUAGES AND CULTURES DEPARTMENT

The Korean division of the Department of Asian Languages and Cultures offers the widest range of undergraduate course offerings of any university in North America, with 40 regularly scheduled courses on Korea. These include not only lower-division courses (e.g., Korean

---

11 In Los Angeles alone, as many as three-fourths of all Korean Americans are Christians, according to the UCLA Center for Korean Studies. They have established more than 800 immigrant churches in Los Angeles, compared to about 20 Buddhist temples.

12 The ALC Dept. is now comprised of 6 major divisions: Buddhist Studies, Chinese, East Asian Linguistics, Japanese, Korean, and South & Southeast Asian Languages and Cultures.

language, Korean civilization, literature, and introduction to Korean religions courses) but also upper-division courses.[13] The Korean division currently offers seven upper-division courses in Korean history and thought, five upper-division courses in Korean literature and film, four upper-division courses in Korean religions (Buddhism, Christianity, and folk religion), seven upper-division courses in the Korean language, three upper-division courses in Korean linguistics, one upper-division course in folklore, and two upper-division undergraduate seminars on pre-modern or modern Korea.

The ALC Department has an undergraduate major and minor in Korean, offers an M.A. in Korean language and culture, and provides Ph.D. training in several fields related to Korean language and culture. The department has seven ladder faculty members offering courses on Korean history, religions (Buddhism and Christianity), folklore, and Korean language and linguistics.

The Korean division has one linguist (Professor Sung-Ock Sohn), two historians of Korea (Professor John Duncan for pre-modern and Associate Professor Namhee Lee for modern Korea), one specialist in Korean Christianity (Associate Professor Sung-Deuk Oak), one scholar in Korean Buddhism (Professor Robert Buswell), one specialist in Korean folklore (Professor Timothy Tangherlini), and one faculty in modern Korean literature (Associate Professor Christopher P. Hanscom). Professor Timothy Tangherlini holds a joint appointment in Korean and Scandinavian programs. Professor Hanscom took over the position of Professor Peter Lee, who retired from UCLA in 2007. As the majority of faculty members in Korean Studies are tenured senior faculty, this ensures the stability of the program.

3.2. THE KOREAN LANGUAGE PROGRAM

The Korean program offers the largest number of language courses

13 Lower-division classes at UCLA are basically general education courses and pre-requisites (numbered 1 through 99). Upper-division classes are major-related and are more specialized classes (numbered 100 through 199).

among all Asian languages offered in the ALC department at UCLA. In particular, it provides the widest range of upper-division language courses in the United States. Currently, the department offers a total of nine Asian languages: Chinese, Hindi, Indonesian, Japanese, Korean, Tagalog/Filipino, Thai, and Vietnamese. The Korean language program provides separate tracks for heritage and non-heritage learners for the first two years of language coursework. It also offers a broad range of courses, including Advanced Reading, Advanced Conversation, Readings in Sino-Korean Characters, Korean Composition, and Readings in Academic Korean,[14] at the fourth-year level to meet the specialized needs of both advanced undergraduate and graduate students. These courses are handled largely by four full-time lecturers (Jae-Eun Yoon, Jane Choi, Jae-Eun Im, and Seon-Kyung Jeon), who display strong teamwork and excellence in teaching. To give an example, one instructor in charge of the third-year Korean class, in which both heritage and non-heritage students are merged, developed an innovative instructional methodology to accommodate these two distinct groups of students. A graduate student in the advanced Korean class stated in a course evaluation, "I found her courses and teaching methods exceptional not only for effectively exercising and building language skills but also in how she balanced challenging and encouraging students, even graduate students." Students in a large elementary Korean class (over 100 students) commented on the instructor, "She is patient, and gives good guidance to the students" and "She is a highly skilled and experienced instructor who organizes her classes very well."

In addition to the language courses, there are three upper-division courses in Korean linguistics, such as "The Structure of Korean", "Korean with Service Learning", and "Contrastive Analysis of Japanese and Korean". The numbers of students taking these upper-division linguistic courses range from 35 to 40.

---

14 See the appendix for descriptions of these courses.

4. Graduate Program

The Department of Asian Languages and Cultures at UCLA established a graduate program in Korean Studies in the late 1980s with the arrival of Professor Peter H. Lee in Korean literature. The department offers an M.A. in Korean language and culture, and provides Ph.D. training in a wide range of fields, including Buddhism, history, linguistics, and literature. The Korean division offers a total of 22 graduate courses on Korea. There are four courses in linguistics: Korean 220, on the structure of Korean; Korean 224A-B, selected topics in Korean linguistics; Korean 225, on corpus linguistics and language pedagogy; and CM227, a contrastive analysis of Korean and Japanese. In addition, a research methodology course is required for all graduate students.

The Korean program has enjoyed extraordinary success in training and placing its graduate students into postgraduate positions. There are currently more than 30 graduate students in the Korean division of the ALC department: 15 in history, 5 in literature, 8 in Korean linguistics, and 5 in Buddhism. We have admitted 14 graduate students to the Ph.D. program in Korean linguistics since 1996. Within the ALC department, 7 graduates of the Ph.D. program in Korean linguistics have landed jobs as coordinators and/or instructors of Korean language programs: Minju Kim (Associate Professor, Claremont-McKenna College), Mary Kim (Assistant Professor, University of Hawaii at Manoa), Jane Choi (Lecturer, UCLA), Soojeong Kim (Lecturer, Arizona State University), Jieun Kim (Lecturer, University of Chicago), Sangbok Kim (Lecturer, University of Colorado at Boulder), and Hee Ju (Lecturer, University of Southern California). In addition, three have advanced to candidacy and are working on their dissertations on Korean language and linguistics (Craig Merrill, Jihyeon Cha, and Heeju Lee) in the ALC Department. Lastly, 4 new Ph.D. students are currently completing coursework on Korean language and linguistics under the supervision of Sung-Ock Sohn.

Finally, a number of graduate students from the Department of Linguistics or Applied Linguistics at UCLA who worked as teaching assistants in the Korean program of the ALC Department have received tenure-track faculty positions at major universities in Korea. They include Professors Seung-Ho Nam, Yong-Yae Park, and Jongho Jun at Seoul National University, Eunjoo Lee at Ewha Womans University, Kyu-Hyun Kim at Kyunghee University, and Kyung-Hee Suh at Hankuk University of Foreign Studies.

The graduate program increases the competitive power of the UCLA Korean Studies program by offering teaching assistantships for graduate students. Ph.D. students in Korean linguistics receive financial support as well as rigorous training in language pedagogy while serving as teaching assistants.

5. New Challenges and Prospects

The UCLA Korean Language Program has continued to grow rapidly since its inception in 1985, adding 4 new full-time lecturer positions, creating a ladder faculty position in Korean language and linguistics, and offering a comprehensive and innovative curriculum in the Korean language. However, it still anticipates a number of new challenges.

The most urgent issue is the university's financial crisis in recent years. Due to budget constraints, most language classes at UCLA are forced to maximize the caps on enrollment at 20 to 25 per discussion section. (The enrollment cap used to be 15 students per section in the 1990s.) The increased enrollment is not effective for language classes, and instructors of upper-division language courses such as composition and conversation classes struggle to accommodate the needs of as many as 28 students in one class. Furthermore, a lack of funds for teaching assistants has forced the program to place caps on lower-level Korean courses and content courses such as Korean Civilization. Due to the enforced cap, the program has to turn away many students and may be unable to meet the needs of undergraduate students who major or minor in Korean language and cultures or students who concentrate in East Asian Humanities and East Asian Studies. The aforementioned issues affect not only the merit of the Korean language program but also the overall quality of the Korean studies program at UCLA. Due to severe budget cuts in California, the department is unable to offer enough scholarships for the recruitment of top graduate students.

A second major problem is the assessment method and placement of students into Korean language classes. Currently, the UCLA Korean placement test is offered three times a year (fall, winter, and spring). Students take the placement test to determine their placements in one of the Korean language classes or to receive a waiver from the foreign language requirement. Students who place out of the first-year level can fulfill the university's one year foreign language requirement. However, there are many transfer students from other universities or junior colleges who take the placement test. Due to the differences in Korean language standards among colleges and universities, it has been very difficult to place transfer students into appropriate levels. Some are unable to pass the one-year competency exam administered at UCLA, even though they have already completed one year of elementary Korean at a previous institution. Since most universities and colleges (and some high schools) now use the same textbook (*Integrated Korean*), these students feel bored when they are placed into an elementary Korean class with the same textbook.

In addition, we receive many requests from other universities and high schools for their students to take the UCLA Korean competency test in order to fulfill the foreign language requirement at their home campuses. However, it is an extremely resource-intensive process to prepare, administer, and assess the Korean language proficiency test, which involves speaking, writing, reading, and grammar/usage sections. Moreover, there are considerable nationwide discrepancies in the proficiencies and needs of heritage and non-heritage learners in foreign language classes. Standard placement exams for foreign language students often do not discriminate among aspects of proficiency that are relevant to many heritage language speakers. In order to resolve this problem, the UCLA Korean program has been developing a series of Korean tests for both placement and exemption purposes. In 2014, we also implemented a new online Korean placement test; a total of 150 students took it and received their test results, including the writing section, on the following day.

A third problem, which is also related to language assessment, is the issue of the language instructors' workload. In recent years, there has been increasing demand for the acquisition of advanced language proficiency across all languages. The UCLA Korean program has a number of graduate students every year who receive the federally funded Foreign Language and Area Studies (FLAS) fellowship. The fellowship program supports graduate training in modern foreign languages and related area studies. The recipients of the FLAS fellowship must take at least three advanced language courses during the one-year fellowship period.[15] The FLAS awardees must take oral proficiency tests in the target language at the beginning and end of their FLAS award periods. Consequently, the language instructors spend substantial time and effort measuring and submitting reports on these students' proficiencies. Language instructors are implicitly expected to play a role in placement and exit examinations as well as FLAS evaluations, but these expectations need to be stated clearly, and they should also be compensated for this work.

A fourth problem is the high attrition rate among students in intermediate and advanced Korean classes. Although overall enrollment in beginning Korean has been increasing dramatically in recent years, only less than one-third of students who complete elementary Korean continue onto the intermediate level. The high attrition rate from elementary to intermediate level Korean seems to be partly due to the fact that the foreign language requirement at UCLA requires only one year at the elementary level. High attrition beyond the first year is very common across foreign language programs at UCLA and at other universities

15 Since the purpose of the program is to enrich the nation's pool of area and international specialists, applicants must be planning to use their training to teach, serve in government or international agencies, or engage in other work that advances American understanding of other countries. For more information, visit the following URL: http://www.gdnet.ucla.edu/asis/entsup/titlevi.htm

in America. It is imperative to promote advanced language learning, however, because society is in great need of global professionals with high-level proficiency in Korean language and culture. Recently, the Division of Humanities at UCLA (led by Dean David Schaberg) initiated a new project, the Language Alliance, which will receive a total of $750,000 from 2012 to 2015 from the Andrew W. Mellon Foundation. The project will greatly enhance UCLA's excellence in the areas of language instruction, assessment, and proficiency. Its top priorities are to create web-based placement tests and to provide students with internationally recognized proficiency scores that reflect measurable achievements in language study.

In addition, there has been a major change in student demographics in Korean language classes at UCLA. Traditionally, the majority of students enrolled in Korean were heritage students (i.e., 1.5 and 2nd generation Korean immigrants) who were exploring their ethnic roots. But in recent years, the number of non-heritage students has mushroomed. During the academic year 2012-2013, out of a total of 548 students enrolled in elementary Korean at UCLA, the number of non-heritage students was more than twice that of heritage students (70% vs. 30%). The sharp increase in non-heritage students in Korean language classes appears to be a nationwide trend in the United States. (The University of California at Berkeley shows a similar pattern.) In order to accommodate the increasing number of non-heritage students, we have been offering three different levels of elementary Korean every quarter (Korean 1, 2, and 3). The true beginners' class (Korean 1) has been by far the most popular. Although we offer it three times a year, the course is consistently at full enrollment.

Finally, it should be noted that enrollments in Korean language have drastically increased nationwide since 2006. The Modern Language Association Report, published in the fall of 2009, showed that course enrollments in languages other than English have reached new highs. Enrollments in Asian languages in particular have dramatically increased since 2006: Japanese by 10.3%, Chinese by 18.2%, and Korean by 19.1%. This increase in interest is undoubtedly a reflection of the growing importance of Korea in the modern world. With the Korean language rapidly gaining global importance, there is stronger demand for fluency in the language.

In order to meet the increasing demand for Asian language professionals, UCLA plans to implement a master's degree program in Teaching Asian Languages, which will include Chinese, Japanese, and Korean. The new M.A. program will offer diverse courses on the sociocultural and linguistic foundations of Asian languages; best practices for teaching, learning, and using Asian languages (e.g., writing systems, sound systems, grammar, discourse, etc.); heritage language acquisition; articulation of K-16 standards and assessment methods; and emerging trends in Asian language teaching.

Our goal is to prepare the next generation of Asian language professionals by providing a curriculum of graduate-level courses on the aforementioned topics and by offering advanced professionals an adequate foundation in language teaching and research. UCLA will be the first to offer a master's degree in Asian language pedagogy among the University of California campuses. M.A. graduates of the programs will be equipped to obtain positions as instructors in private schools, colleges, and universities. In addition, they will be qualified to work as translators and in various other capacities, such as in private firms and government services.

In summary, the UCLA Korean program has had great success since its inception in the late 1980s. There was only one Korean Studies professor in the Department of Asian Languages and Cultures in 1987, but today, the program has expanded to include seven Korean Studies professors and sixty Korean Studies courses. Furthermore, there has been a major change in student demographics in Korean classes at UCLA. While the vast majority of students in the courses were Korean heritage students twenty years ago, today non-Korean U.S. students account for more than two-thirds of enrollments in elementary Korean classes. Moreover, there is a strong demand for upper-level Korean language and content courses. During the 1980s, there was not a single upper-division language course in Korean. Now, the ALC department offers at least 8 upper-division Korean language courses (see Appendix) and 23 upper-division content courses in Korean Studies.

With the widest range of undergraduate Korean course offerings of any university in North America, UCLA has over 2,000 students who take classes with an emphasis on Korea annually. The graduate program also has continued to grow, adding new ladder faculty positions and enjoying extraordinary success in training and placing its graduate students in postgraduate work.

In recent years, many of the UCLA Korean division's accomplishments have been threatened by the financial crisis in California. Like other University of California campuses, UCLA is heavily dependent on the state budget. We have been forced to place caps on enrollments in many of our courses because of the lack of funds to hire TAs for discussion sections, and we are also facing the prospect of being unable to offer sufficient scholarships for graduate students.

In addition, we face challenges due to the administrative burdens of large enrollments and a wide range of course offerings in Korean Studies. It is extremely difficult to coordinate all Korean courses and to meet student demand, since faculty members in Korean Studies are overburdened with heavy administrative responsibilities due to the large size of the program. In order to maintain the excellence of the UCLA Korean program, we need a new ladder position in language pedagogy. A pedagogy specialist with strong theoretical training and management skills would be able to coordinate a large program with many language faculty and lecturers in the ALC Department.

REFERENCES

Sohn, Sung-Ock. (1995). The design of curriculum for teaching Korean as a heritage language vs. as a foreign language. In Ho-min Sohn (Ed.), *The Korean Language in America 1: Proceedings of the First National Conference on Korean Language Education* (pp.19-35).

Sohn, Sung-Ock & Shin, Sang-geun. (2007). True beginners, false beginners, and fake beginners: Placement challenges for Korean heritage speakers. *Foreign Language Annals*, 40 (3), 353-364.

UCLA International Institute. (n.d.) Center Mission. In *UCLA Center for Korean Studies*. Retrieved from http://www.international.ucla.edu/korea/mission.asp

APPENDIX

The following Korean language courses (from beginning to the fifth year level) are currently offered at UCLA. (Each lower-division course is 5 units; each upper-division course is 4 units).

Lower Division Courses

Elementary Modern Korean 123 (5 units):

Lecture, two hours; discussion, three hours. Not open to students who have learned, from whatever source, enough Korean to qualify for more advanced courses. Introduction to standard spoken Korean and Korean writing, with emphasis on conversation. P/NP or letter grading.

Elementary Korean for Korean-Heritage Speakers: Korean 1A2A3A (5 units):

Lecture, two hours; discussion, three hours. Not open to students who have learned, from whatever source, enough Korean to qualify for more advanced courses. Designed for Korean-heritage learners who have very limited knowledge in Korean language or have had no formal instruction in it. Emphasis on spelling, basic grammar, reading, writing, and daily conversation. P/NP or letter grading.

Intermediate Modern Korean 456 (5 units):

Lecture, five hours. Enforced requisite: course 3 with grade of C or better or Korean placement test. Not open to students who have learned, from whatever source, enough Korean to qualify for more advanced courses. Continuation of course 3. Conversation, composition, and readings with structural analysis in modern Korean. P/NP or letter grading.

Intermediate Korean for Korean Speakers: Korean 4A5A6A (5 units):

Lecture, five hours. Enforced requisite: course 3A with grade of C or better or Korean placement test. Not open to students who attended elementary school in Korea for more than one year or who have learned, from whatever source, enough Korean to qualify for more advanced courses. Designed for students who seek training in written components of standard Korean (spelling, reading, writing, and grammar) at intermediate level. Continuation of course 3A. P/NP or letter grading.

Elementary Korean: Intensive Korean 8 (15 units):
Lecture, 10 hours; discussion, 10 hours. Not open to students who have learned, from whatever source, enough Korean to qualify for more advanced courses. Intensive course equivalent to courses 1, 2, and 3. Introduction to fundamentals of standard Korean, including pronunciation, grammar, and Korean characters, with emphasis on all four basic language skills-speaking, listening comprehension, reading, and writing. Offered in the summer only. P/NP or letter grading.

Intermediate Modern Korean: Intensive Korean 10 (15 units):
Lecture, 10 hours; discussion, 10 hours. Enforced requisite: course 3 or 8 with grade of C or better or Korean placement test. Not open to students who have learned, from whatever source, enough Korean to qualify for more advanced courses. Intensive course equivalent to courses 4, 5, and 6. Conversation, composition, and readings with structural analysis in modern Korean. Offered in the summer only. P/NP or letter grading.

Upper Division Courses

100ABC. Advanced Modern Korean (4 units):
Lecture, five hours. Enforced requisite: course 6, 6A, or 10 with grade of C or better or Korean placement test. Course 100A with grade of C or better or Korean placement test is enforced requisite to 100B; course 100B with grade of C or better or Korean placement test is enforced requisite to 100C. Not open to students who have learned, from whatever source, enough Korean to qualify for more advanced courses. Continuation of courses 6/6A. Readings of modern prose and poetry, with emphasis on grammar and Sino-Korean. P/NP (undergraduates), S/U (graduates), or letter grading.

101ABC. Advanced Readings in Modern Korean (4 units):
Lecture, three hours. Enforced requisite: course 100C or Korean placement test. Course 101A or Korean placement test is enforced requisite to 101B; course 101B or Korean placement test is enforced requisite to 101C. Advanced readings and discussion for students planning to do advanced coursework or research on Korea. Topics selected from magazines, journals, and books related to humanities and social sciences. P/NP (undergraduates), S/U (graduates), or letter grading.

102ABC. Advanced Korean Conversation (4 units):
Lecture, three hours. Enforced requisite: course 100C or Korean placement test. Course 102A or Korean placement test is enforced requisite to 102B; course 102B or Korean placement test is enforced requisite to 102C. Not open

to students who attended elementary school in Korea for more than two years or who have learned, from whatever source, enough Korean to qualify for more advanced courses. Reading and discussion of modern Korean authors, designed to further improve spoken proficiency. P/NP or letter grading.

103ABC. Readings in Sino-Korean Characters (4 units):
Lecture, three hours. Requisite: course 100C or Korean placement test. Course 103A or Korean placement test is requisite to 103B; course 103B or Korean placement test is requisite to 103C. Sino-Korean vocabulary and characters necessary for advanced and superior level of knowledge in Korean. Sino-Korean characters are used differently from the same Chinese characters used in contemporary China in terms of pronunciation, meaning, and word formation. Professional-level Korean speakers need to be able to read at least 1,800 Sino-Korean characters. Reinforcement of collocation patterns and semantic association of Sino-Korean vocabulary. P/NP or letter grading.

104ABC. Korean Writing for Advanced Learners (4 units):
Lecture, three hours; discussion, one hour. Enforced requisite: course 100C or Korean placement test. Emphasis on academic writing in Korean, including rhetorical conventions, argument construction and coherence, and development of prose style. Readings include representative examples of diverse genres selected from magazines, journals, and books. May be taken independently for credit. P/NP (undergraduates), S/U (graduates), or letter grading.

C105ABC. Reading Korean Academic Texts (4 units):
Lecture, three hours. Enforced requisite: course 101C or Korean placement test. Intended to improve reading skills for students who have studied Korean to an advanced level, with coverage in Korean of materials on Korean history, culture, and society. May be taken independently for credit. Concurrently scheduled with course C205A. P/NP or letter grading.

106ABC. Superior Korean (4 units):
Lecture, three hours. Recommended preparation: course 101C. May not be taken concurrently with course 102A, 102B, or 102C. Use of speaking, listening, reading, and writing skills to participate effectively, or understand without difficulty any practical, social, and professional topics, whether those topics are familiar or not. May be taken independently for credit. P/NP or letter grading.

107ABC. Professional/Academic Korean (4 units):
Lecture, three hours. Requisite: course 101C or Korean placement test. Course 107A or Korean placement test is requisite to 107B; course 107B or Korean placement test is requisite to 107C. May not be taken concurrently with course 102A, 102B, or 102C. Development of professional and academic proficiency in oral and written Korean to understand many sociolinguistic and cultural references as well as variety of styles and forms pertinent to professional needs, meet demands of professional interactions, and carry out professional-

level tasks in student specialization areas. Special attention to vocabulary development on the professional level. Development of both interactive and noninteractive listening. Research projects to be assigned according to student interests. P/NP or letter grading.

History of the Korean Program at the University of California, San Diego: Celebrating Its First Twenty Five Years

Jeyseon Lee
The University of California, San Diego

1. Introduction

Year 2014 marks the 25th anniversary for the Korean Language Program at the University of California, San Diego (hereafter UCSD), which was established in 1989 at the Graduate School of International Relation and Pacific Studies (hereafter IRPS). During the past 25 years, the Korean Language Program has been continuously growing and, with an average of 240 students enrolled per quarter in the 2013-2014 academic year,[1] it ranks as the fifth most-studied foreign language on campus after Spanish, Japanese, Chinese, and French.

The Korean Language Program has been housed in the Literature Department since 1997 and offers a curriculum in the Korean language covering three years (Beginning, Intermediate, and Advanced) and nine courses of Korean language instruction (three courses per each level). Besides these language courses, the Literature Department offers a class called Readings in Korean Literature and Culture, which is instructed in Korean; the Linguistics Department has also been offering two Korean heritage language courses since 2003.

As of the 2014 spring quarter, an associate professor of Korean literature, a full-time Korean language lecturer, and nine Korean language teaching assistants have been serving approximately 270 students in the

1 This number is equivalent to approximately 220 students in the Literature Department and 20 students in the Linguistics Department.

Literature Department.[2] The majority of the student body (over 90%) in the Third-Year Korean language class and the Korean literature class is comprised of heritage students; over 80% of the student body in the First-Year Korean classes and about 50% of the Second-Year classes are non-heritage students. The Linguistics Department has no Korean faculty member in it yet, but two graduate student teaching assistants are instructing 20-25 heritage Korean students.

The purpose of this article is to review the history of the Korean Language Program at UCSD, from its beginning to its expansion into a full program today, and to offer future prospects of the program. In addition, this article will review the background history of the Transnational Korean Studies Program at UCSD, which was launched in January 2014.

2. Beginning (1989-2000)

Korean language was first taught at UCSD in September 1989, two years after the IRPS was established. Dr. Yasu-Hiko Tohsaku, founding IRPS Language Program Director, included the Korean language as a language requirement for students majoring in Regional Studies with a focus on Korea.

Dr. Tohsaku is a specialist in second language acquisition theory and language pedagogy. He is studying the effects of explicit grammar instruction on the development of language skills, the acceleration of language acquisition through process-oriented vocabulary and grammar activities, and higher-level cognitive skills in the development of reading abilities. He wrote the first communicative-oriented Japanese language textbooks published in the United States: *Yookoso!: An Invitation to Contemporary Japanese* and *Yookoso!: Continuing with Contemporary Japanese*. He received his Ph.D. from the Linguistics Department at UCSD and has been serving as IRPS Language Program

---

2 This number is equivalent to approximately 220 students in the Korean language classes and 50 students in the Korean literature class.

Director for over 25 years.[3] According to an email interview with Dr. Tohsaku, Dr. Larry Krause (founding Dean of the IRPS) played a key role in the decision, and the IRPS used its own graduate school fund to establish the Korean language classes.

The first Korean language course at the IRPS was taught by Dr. Steven K. Lee, who received his Ph.D. from the University of Southern California (hereafter USC). His research specialty is in bilingual and multicultural education, international education, comparative linguistics, educational policy, and leadership studies. Dr. Lee moved to California State University at Dominguez Hills as an Assistant Professor, after his last quarter at UCSD in the spring of 1996. After expanding his career as chair or director at a few other universities, he is serving as Adjunct Professor of East Asian Language and Culture Department at USC and Director of the USC Korea International Office.[4]

According to him, Korean language classes were popular when they were first offered at the IRPS in 1989. New courses were added each year for the first three years: First-Year Korean (IR/Lang 1AX, 1BX, 1CX) from 1989, Second-Year Korean (IR/Lang 2AX, 2BX, 2CX) from 1990, and Third-Year Korean (IR/Lang 100A, 100B, 100C) from 1991. Dr. Lee remembered nearly 150 undergraduate and graduate students were enrolled in the IRPS Korean language courses in the spring 1996 quarter, and he taught three courses per quarter with 5-6 teaching assistants. From the fall 1997 quarter, however, the IRPS changed the Korean language class from lower-division to upper-division, offered only one course per quarter under the title of Korean language for Professional Proficiency, and focused on teaching its own graduate students.[5]

3 Yasu-Hiko Tohsaku. (n.d.) In *UC San Diego School of International Relations and Pacific Studies*. Retrieved from http://irps.ucsd.edu/faculty/faculty-directory/yasuhiko-tohsaku.htm

4 New Director prepares to launch Educational Doctorate program. (2007, November). *California State University Stanislaus Digest*. Retrieved from http://archive.csustan.edu/digest/archive/November2007/faculty_staff_notes/story_2.html. Steven Lee. (n.d.) In *USC Korean Studies Institute*. Retrieved from http://dornsife.usc.edu/ksi/steven-lee/

5 Record from the UCSD Registrar's office.

Beyond Korean language classes, the Korean Film Festival was first held in 1990, and from 1991 onward, the IRPS expanded it into the Korean Cultural Festival of San Diego. In the 1993-1994 academic year, the IRPS invited distinguished scholars, a traditional Korean dance company, a modern dance company, pop-singers, and orchestra members to the festival, and it also hosted a month-long art exhibition. All of these events were supported by donations from the UCSD Events Office, Korea Culture Center, Korea Film Councils, Korea Foundation, Korea Research Foundation, Asia Society, Korea Society, San Diego Mayor's office, Korea Times, Radio Korea, Korean Association, and various local supporters. These events were covered by the Korean Broadcasting System (KBS) as well as the American Public Broadcasting Service (PBS) several times.[6]

Since no Korean language course was offered for undergraduate students at UCSD until the spring 1997 quarter, many undergraduate students who wanted to learn the Korean language had no choice but to enroll in IRPS Korean language classes. However, the number of undergraduate students who wanted to enroll in IRPS Korean classes exceeded the limit that the IRPS could hold, so the Literature Department decided to offer Korean language classes to undergraduate students from the fall 1997 quarter.

The second Korean language lecturer, Dr. Sunny Jung, began to teach Korean language courses in both the IRPS and the Literature Departments from the fall 1997 quarter.[7] Dr. Jung received her M.Ed. from Ewha Womans University and an Ed.D. from the U.S. International University. She researches Korean Zen poetry, classical poetic views and indigenous thoughts in modern poetry, multicultural education, and teaching pedagogy. Before joining UCSD, she taught at USC, the University of California at Irvine, the U.S. International University at Osaka, and the Defense Language Institute, and after the spring 2000

6 From an email interview with Dr. Steven Lee.

7 Record from the UCSD Registrar's office shows Dr. Jung taught LTGN 173: Contemporary Lit./Korean Lit. in the 1996 spring quarter, before she began to teach Korean language courses in the Literature Department in 1997.

quarter, she moved to the University of California at Santa Barbara.[8]

According to an email interview with Ms. Lucinda Rubio-Barrick, former Literature Department Management Service Officer (hereafter MSO), Dr. Lisa Lowe, Professor of Literature at the time, played a key role in housing the Korean Language Program in the Literature Department to assist undergraduate students. Dr. Lowe studied European intellectual history at Stanford University and French literature and critical theory at UC Santa Cruz. She was a member of the Literature Department for more than two decades and served as department chair from 1998 to 2001. She taught European and American studies and was an affiliated faculty in the Department of Ethnic Studies and the Program in Critical Gender Studies. She is now a Professor of English at Tufts University.[9]

Ms. Rubio-Barrick also noted that the Korean Language Program in the Literature Department was established in 1997 solely with the department fund, which sustained it until the spring 2000 quarter. The Literature Department first received financial support from the Dean's office to run the Korean Language Program in the 2000-2001 academic year. The record from the Registrar's Office shows that the Literature Department has been offering First-Year Korean (LTKO 1A, 1B, 1C) since 1997 and Second-Year Korean (LTKO 2A, 2B) since 1998.

Literature Building

8 Faculty. (n.d.) In *East Asian Languages & Cultural Studies*. Retrieved from http://www.eastasian.ucsb.edu/faculty/jung.htm.

9 Lisa Lowe. (n.d.) In *UC San Diego*. Retrieved from http://literature.ucsd.edu/people/faculty/emeriti/llowe.html

3. Expansion (2000-2012)

In the 2000-2001 academic year, when the third Korean language lecturer Jeyseon Lee (the author of this article) took over the Korean Language Program at UCSD as Faculty Supervisor, the Literature Department began to offer the third quarter of Second-Year Korean (LTKO 2C) for the first time: LTKO 1A and LTKO 2A were offered in the fall, LTKO 1B and LTKO 2B in the winter, and LTKO 1C and LTKO 2C in the spring. As of the fall 2000 quarter, approximately 60 students were enrolled in the First-Year Korean class (LTKO 1A) and almost 40 students in the Second-Year class (LTKO 2A).

Among the five class hours per week, lecture classes were taught by a lecturer on Tuesdays and Thursdays to all students enrolled in each level, while discussion classes were run by graduate teaching assistants on Mondays, Wednesdays, and Fridays with about 20 students per section. There were three discussion sections in the First-Year course and two discussion sections in the Second-Year course.

The Korean language for Professional Proficiency (IR/Lang 420A) class was offered solely to IRPS students, and only 5 students enrolled. Considering that the maximum enrollment capacity for the IRPS language classes was 15 and average enrollments for other IRPS language classes (such as Spanish, Chinese and Japanese) were between 10 and 15, the Korean language class was comparatively too small.

Starting from the 2001-2002 academic year, the Third-Year Advanced Korean class (LTKO 3) was offered for the first time at UCSD. Since the IRPS stopped teaching Third-Year Korean (IR/Lang 100A, 100B, 100C) after the spring 1996 quarter, Advanced Korean class was not offered at UCSD until the fall 2001 quarter. During these years, therefore, high-advanced students with Korean language abilities were unable to take a Korean class, and low-advanced students were mixed with intermediate students in the Second-Year Korean class.

The upper-division Korean literature course Readings in Korean Literature and Culture (LTKO 100) was first offered in the fall 2000 quarter by Dr. Jin-kyung Lee when she joined UCSD and covered materials appropriate for superior or above-level students with Korean language abilities; thus, no class was available for students who had advanced proficiency (i.e., students who were too advanced for the LTKO 2 series but not ready for LTKO 100). Jeyseon Lee brought up this issue to Dr. Lisa Lowe, the Literature Department Chair at the time, and the department approved her proposal to offer a Third-Year Advanced Korean class without any hesitation. Students with advanced proficiency in Korean could then have the option of taking the class and being placed at the right level.

Student enrollment in Korean language courses increased slightly from 2001 to 2003; there were about 70 students in the First-Year class, about 50 students in the Second-Year, and about 15 students in the Third-Year class. During this period, lecture classes on Tuesdays and Thursdays were given to about 50 or 70 students in each level. The quality of teaching in the lecture-discussion system could not be as effective as the section system, since an instructor could not closely monitor each student's learning progress during the lecture session. Moreover, the Korean Language Program could not expand further under the lecture-discussion system, because 50-70 students were already too many for one class.

From the spring 2003 quarter, the IRPS decided to stop offering Korean language classes for their graduate students separately, so all IRPS students who wanted to learn Korean language were advised to enroll in the Literature Department based on their levels in Korean-language proficiency. This was because all the students in the IRPS Korean language class passed their language proficiency exams during or before the winter 2003 quarter, and they were no longer required to take another Korean language class.

The IRPS considers knowledge of a foreign language an indispensable skill for international relations professionals. Hence, students must demonstrate a level of proficiency in a foreign language in order to be admitted to the Master of Advanced Studies in International Affairs (MAS-IA) program. They are required to pass a proficiency exam equivalent to the Foreign Service Institute (FSI) scale. The minimum required level of proficiency is equivalent to a FSI Scale 2+ for Spanish, 2 for Portuguese, and 2- for most other languages, including Korean.[10]

Before the 2002-2003 academic year, all IRPS students were mandated to pass this proficiency exam to fulfill their language requirement. From the 2002-2003 academic year, however, the language requirement for the Master of Pacific International Affairs (MPIA) program changed, so successful completion of an approved, college-level sixth-quarter (or fourth semester) course, including courses completed during undergraduate or graduate degree studies, could satisfy the language requirement. Due to this change and to budget problems, the IRPS decided to close its own Korean language class and send students to the Literature Department from the spring 2003 quarter.

The 2003-2004 academic year brought a profound change to the UCSD Korean Language Program in many ways. First, the lecture-discussion system was changed into a section system with a maximum capacity of 22 students per section. This change relieved the inefficiency of having over 50-70 students in one classroom for a lecture, and it brought remarkable improvements in terms of teaching effectiveness. Also, all First-Year and Second-Year courses began to be offered twice a year, as shown below:

Chart 1.1. Literature Department Korean Language Courses Offered from the Fall 2003 Quarter to the Spring 2012 Quarter

Fall	Winter	Spring
LTKO 1A: Beginning Korean I	LTKO 1B: Beginning Korean II	LTKO 1A: Beginning Korean I
LTKO 1B: Beginning Korean II	LTKO 1C: Beginning Korean III	LTKO 1C: Beginning Korean III

10 Applying to the MAS-IA Program. (n.d.) In *UC San Diego School of International Relations and Pacific Studies*. Retrieved from http://irps.ucsd.edu/programs/master-of-advanced-studies-in-international-affairs-masia/admissions-information. The IRPS offers two different master programs; 1) Master of Advanced Studies in International Affairs (MAS-IA) program and 2) Master of Pacific International Affairs (MPIA) program.

LTKO 2A: Intermediate Korean I	LTKO 2B: Intermediate Korean II	LTKO 2A: Intermediate Korean I
LTKO 2B: Intermediate Korean II	LTKO 2C: Intermediate Korean III	LTKO 2C: Intermediate Korean III
LTKO 3: Advanced Korean I	LTKO 3: Advanced Korean II	LTKO 3: Advanced Korean III

Second, the two-track system, which offered separate classes for students depending on their linguistic background and proficiency, was first adopted in the First-Year level (LTKO 1A), allowing non-heritage students and heritage students to register in different sections. This system benefited students by offering more effective learning opportunities; moreover, it benefited instructors by providing them with students of similar proficiency levels.

The two-track system was expanded to the Second-Year level over the next year; consequently, the number of non-heritage students dramatically increased, especially in the First-Year classes. Fewer than ten non-heritage students were enrolled in LTKO courses before the two-track system was adopted, but thanks to the two-track system (and to the "Korean Wave" *hallyu*), there was a notable increase in the enrollment of non-heritage students. The number of non-heritage students in LTKO 1A in the fall 2012 quarter (approximately 60 students) exceeded the number of heritage students (approximately 40 students).

Many non-heritage students are Asian-Americans or Asians from China or Southeast Asia, but an increasing number of students are from other ethnic backgrounds. They are interested in learning the Korean language mainly because of the "Korean Wave" and the nation's rapid economic growth. The Korean Language Program grew rapidly from 2003 to 2012, during which the enrollment and number of section offerings almost doubled.

This dramatic change was due to the Literature Department's strong financial support and commitment to the Korean Language Program students. Jeyseon Lee explained the inefficiency of the lecture-discussion system and need for two-track system to Ms. Rubio-Barrick (MSO at the time); she and Dr. Kontje (the Literature Department Chair at the time) happily accepted her proposal. By adopting both the section system and two-track system, the Literature Department hired more teaching assistants (from 3-4 in the previous system to 6-8 in the new system) and spent additional funds on the Korean Language Program. Because of the system change, many more interactions between students and instructors took place, and the instructor was able to monitor the students more closely and give effective feedback to each student.

From the fall 2003 quarter, the Linguistics Department was interested in heritage language teaching and learning, and it began offering Korean for Korean Speakers (LIHL 115). For this decision, Dr. Maria Polinsky, who was Chair of the Linguistics Department at the time and now Professor of Linguistics at Harvard University, played a key role. Dr. Polinsky's research is at the intersection of theoretical syntax and the study of cross-linguistic variations in sentence structures. She is interested in the ways linguistic theory can be used as a roadmap for understanding how people process language and for obtaining meaningful results that feed back into theory. She also has a particular interest in understanding why heritage languages share so many grammatical similarities with each other.[11]

In the fall 2006 quarter, the Linguistics Department added one more heritage Korean language course, Advanced Korean for Korean Speakers (LIHL 135), and offered two heritage Korean language courses per quarter. These two courses were offered to help heritage Korean students improve their language skills, help professors and graduate students conduct heritage language research, and to financially support Korean graduate students who were studying in the Linguistics Department.[12]

Admittedly, there were some concerns in the beginning about how to coordinate these two different Korean Language Programs in separate departments, but these two Korean Language Programs have been

11 Maria Polinsky. (n.d.) In *Scholars at Harvard*. Retrieved from http://scholar.harvard.edu/mpolinsky

12 From Dr. Polinsky's presentation during the UC Consortium Conference, which was held at UCLA in the spring of 2003.

positively influencing each other and maintaining cordial relations. These two heritage Korean language courses were established with department funds and have been taught by graduate student teaching assistants in the Linguistics Department under the supervision of their Heritage Language Program Director. These two courses steadily have 10-15 students per class in each quarter.

4. Current (2012-Present)

The Korean Language Program at UCSD has been growing steadily over the past two decades, and as of the spring 2014 quarter, Korean ranks among the top five most studied foreign languages on campus after Spanish, Japanese, Chinese, and French. Currently, the overall number of students in these lower-division Korean language classes averages about 220 students each quarter. Among them, approximately over 80% of the First-Year class students and over 50% of the Second-Year class students are non-heritage. Despite the dramatic increase in non-heritage students' enrollment, the total number of enrollment has not changed drastically. This is because the number of the heritage Korean students has significantly decreased from the 2012-2013 academic year, probably because of the UCSD language requirement waiver policy change.

From the fall 2012 quarter onward, students could receive a language requirement waiver by earning a qualifying AP or IB score or earning a score of 700 or higher on SAT II Language exam. Consequently, many heritage Korean students are no longer required to take any language classes. Due to this policy change, all the major language programs at UCSD except Japanese (Spanish, Chinese, and French) lost more than 15% of their enrollment over the past two years; Korean language program also lost approximately 3% of the enrollment overall (about 15 students a year average), despite the dramatic increase of non-heritage student enrollment.[13]

Currently the Literature Department employs two Korean faculty members (one associate professor who is in charge of the Korean literature courses and a lecturer who is in charge of Korean language courses) and nine Korean language teaching assistants. As of now, the Linguistics Department has no Korean faculty member, but there are two graduate teaching assistants. Korean language courses offered by the Literature Department are shown in Chart 1.2 below, and Korean literature courses listed on the Literature Department course catalogue are shown in Chart 2 below. To accommodate more non-heritage students, the Literature Department decided to offer LTKO 1ABC and LTKO 2A every quarter, from the fall 2012 quarter onward.

Chart 1.2. Literature Department Korean Language Courses Offered from the Fall 2012 Quarter to the Present

Fall	Winter	Spring
LTKO 1A: Beginning Korean I	LTKO 1A: Beginning Korean I	LTKO 1A: Beginning Korean I
LTKO 1B: Beginning Korean II	LTKO 1B: Beginning Korean II	LTKO 1B: Beginning Korean II
LTKO 1C: Beginning Korean III	LTKO 1C: Beginning Korean III	LTKO 1C: Beginning Korean III
LTKO 2A: Intermediate Korean I	LTKO 2A: Intermediate Korean I	LTKO 2A: Intermediate Korean I
LTKO 2B: Intermediate Korean II	LTKO 2B: Intermediate Korean II	LTKO 2C: Intermediate Korean III
LTKO 3: Advanced Korean I	LTKO 3: Advanced Korean II	LTKO 3: Advanced Korean III

---

13 LTKO Language Class Enrollment History

	Fall	Winter	Spring	Average
2013-2014	233	215	208	219
2012-2013	207	179	204	197
2011-2012	259	165	180	201
2010-2011	233	191	250	225
2009-2010	230	184	194	203
2008-2009	248	187	248	228
2007-2008	235	166	222	208

The average enrollment per quarter from fall 2007 to spring 2012 was 213, and the average enrollment per quarter from fall 2012 to spring 2014 was 208.

Chart 2. Korean Literature Courses Offered by the Literature Department[14]

LTKO 50	Intermediate Readings and Composition
LTKO 100	Readings in Korean Literature and Culture
LTKO 192	Senior Seminar in Literatures in Korean
LTEA 140	Modern Korean Literature in Translation from Colonial Period
LTEA 141	Modern Korean Literature in Translation from 1945 to Present
LTEA 142	Korean Film, Literature, and Popular Culture
LTEA 143	Gender and Sexuality in Korean Literature and Culture
LTEA 144	Korean American Literature and Other Literatures of Korean Diaspora
LTEA 145	Literature, History, and Colonial and Postcolonial Modernity in Korea

Chart 3.1. LTKO Language Class Enrollment
from the Fall 2009 Quarter to the Spring 2014 Quarter[15]

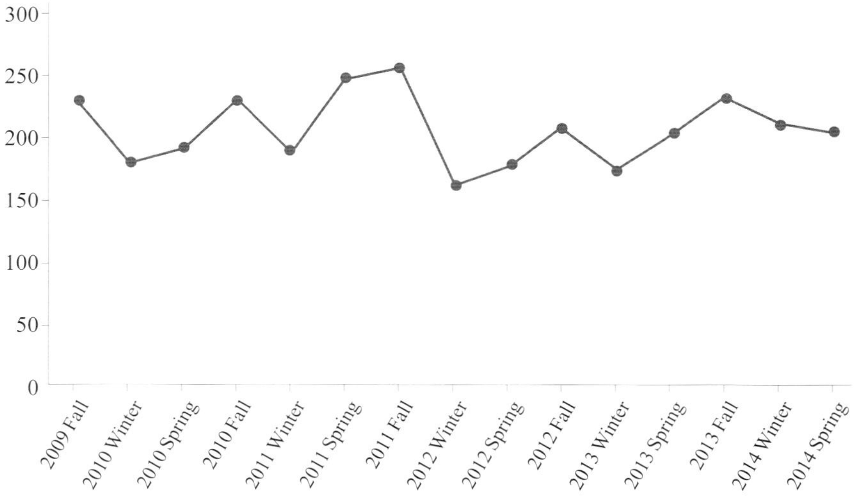

14 Instructional language for LTKO courses is Korean and for LTEA courses is in English. Although LTKO 50 is listed in the general catalogue, it was never offered.

15 Record provided by Ms. Alyssa Simon, a current Literature Department staff member.

Chart 3.2. LTKO Literature Class Enrollment from the Fall 2009 Quarter to the Spring 2014 Quarter[16]

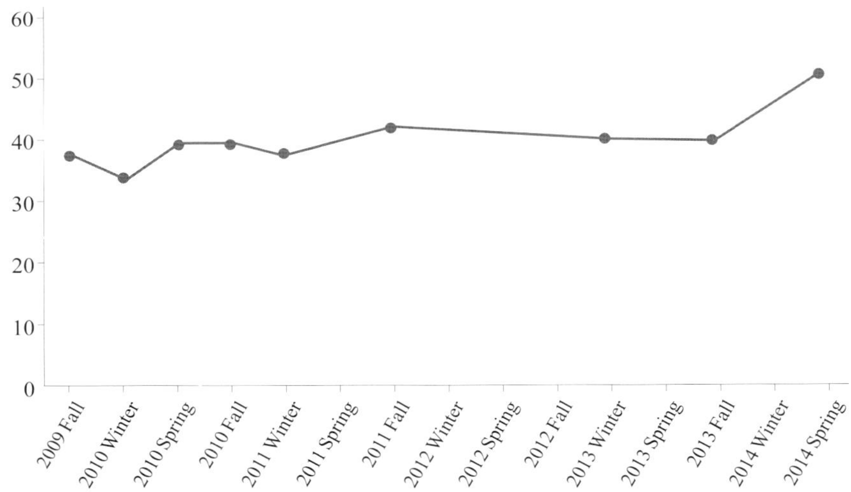

Considering that the spring 2014 quarter enrollment for the Linguistics Department's Korean language courses (LIHL 115 and LIHL 135) was 25 and Korean literature class (LTKO 100) enrollment was 51, the estimated number of students who took either the Korean literature or Korean language courses in the spring 2014 quarter was approximately 285. The estimated enrollment for only the Korean language course (combining the Literature and the Linguistics Departments) was about 235. Charts 4.1 and 4.2 below show the LIHL enrollments from the fall 2012 quarter to the spring 2014 quarter.

16 Ibid.

Chart 4.1. LIHL 115 Enrollment
from the Fall 2012 Quarter to the Spring 2014 Quarter[17]

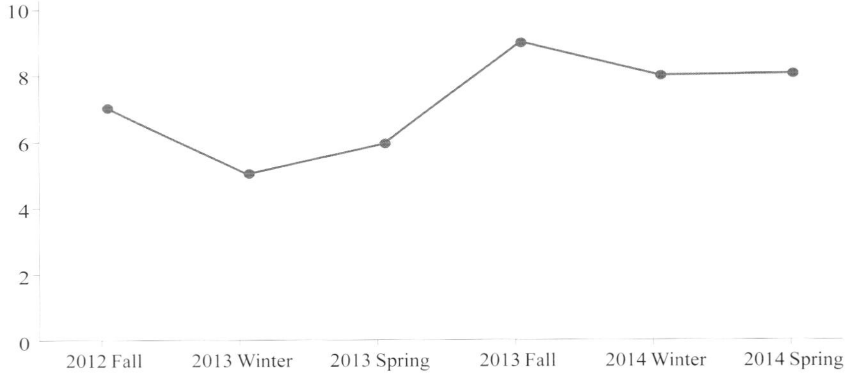

Chart 4.2. LIHL 135 Enrollment
from the Fall 2012 Quarter to the Spring 2014 Quarter[18]

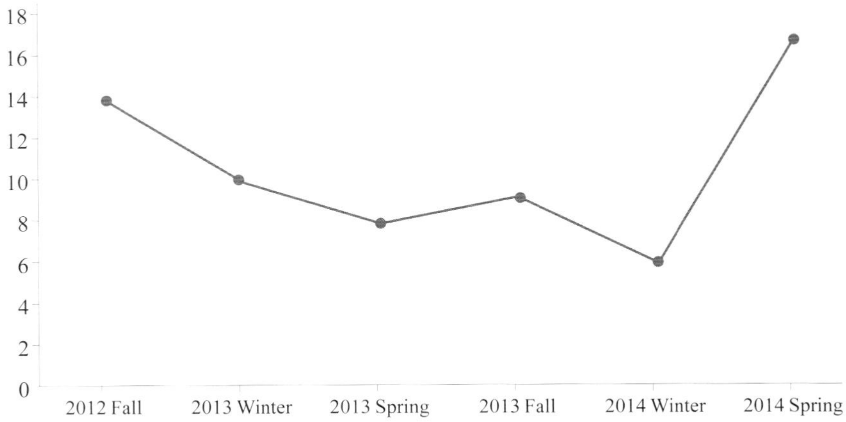

17 Schedule of Classes. (n.d.) In *UC San Diego Instruction Tools*. Retrieved from https://act.ucsd.edu/scheduleOfClasses/scheduleOfClassesFaculty.htm

18 Ibid.

5. Korean Studies Program

UCSD does not have a Center for Korean Studies yet. For several years, both the faculty members and many students have been looking forward to establishing the Korean Studies Program so that students can have the opportunity to take Korean Studies as a major or minor. In 2010, the Korean Studies Initiative was housed in the History Department, and the faculty members worked hard to establish a Korean Studies Program. In December 2013, the Transnational Korean Studies Program was officially approved by the university, and from the fall 2014 quarter onward, the Transnational Korean Studies Program can offer a minor degree for interested undergraduate students.

The names of the Korean Studies Program faculty members and their affiliations, as of 2014 spring quarter, are shown in Chart 5. Before the 2000-2001 academic year, there were only two faculty members (Dr. Stephan Haggard and a Korean language lecturer). In the 2000-2001 academic year, Dr. Jin-kyung Lee (now an Associate Professor) joined the Literature Department, Dr. Jong-Sung You joined the IRPS in the 2006-2007 academic year as an Assistant Professor, and Professor Kyo-ng Park joined the Visual Arts Department in the 2007-2008 academic year as a Professor. In 2009, the History and the Music Departments hired one assistant professor each (Dr. Todd A. Henry and Dr. Eun-Young Jung), and as a result there are now seven core faculty members and seven affiliated faculty members in the Korean Studies Program. The faculty positions in the Literature and Music Departments were funded solely by each department, and the positions in the IRPS and the History Department were funded by each department with partial support from the Korea Foundation.[19]

---

19 Information about funding for the faculty position was provided by Dr. Jin-kyung Lee and Dr. Jong-Sung You. According to Dr. You, his position was funded by the IRPS, and Dr. Haggard's position was funded by the Korea Foundation. According to Dr. Jin-kyung Lee, his position in History was funded by the department, with partial support from the Korea Foundation. Information about the funding for the Visual Arts Department position was not available.

Chart 5. Faculty Members of the Korean Studies Program

Core Faculty

Stephan M. Haggard

Graduate School of International Relations and Pacific Studies

Dr. Haggard is a Professor and the Director of the Korea-Pacific Program at the IRPS, where he specializes in the Korean economy. He received his Ph.D. in political science in the University of California, Berkeley. His research interests center on international relations and political economy, with a focus on East Asia and Latin America. He has been serving in the IRPS from 1992.[20]

Todd A. Henry

Department of History

Dr. Henry is an Assistant Professor and a specialist of modern Korea with a focus on the period of Japanese rule (1910-45). He is also interested in social and cultural formations linking post-Asia-Pacific War South Korea, North Korea, and Japan (1945-present) within the geo-political contexts of American militarism and the Cold War. He received his Ph.D. from UCLA and joined the History Department at UCSD in 2009.[21]

Eun-Young Jung

Department of Music

Dr. Jung is an Assistant Professor and a classically trained pianist who earned her Ph.D. in Ethnomusicology along with an Advanced Certificate in Asian Studies in 2007, followed by a postdoctoral fellowship in Japanese and Korean Studies, all at the University of Pittsburgh. Her research focuses on exploring transnational popular cultural dynamics in East Asia and examining postcolonial cultural politics and cultural industries. She joined the Music Department at UCSD in 2009.[22]

---

20 Stephan M. Haggard. (n.d.) In *UC San Diego School of International Relations and Pacific Studies*. Retrieved from http://irps.ucsd.edu/faculty/faculty-directory/stephan-m-haggard.htm

21 Todd Henry. (n.d.) In *UC San Diego Department of History*. Retrieved from http://history.ucsd.edu/people/faculty/henry.html

22 Eun-Young Jung. (n.d.) In *UCSD Department of Music*. Retrieved from http://musicweb.ucsd.edu/people/people.php?cmd=fm_music_directory_detail&query_Full_Name=%20Eun-Young%20Jung&query_Active_Status=Faculty

Jeyseon Lee

Department of Literature

Dr. Lee is a Lecturer and Korean Language Program Faculty Supervisor. She received her Ph.D. from the Department of East Asian Languages and Literature in the University of Hawaii at Manoa. Her research interest is in Korean linguistics, second-language acquisition, curriculum development of second/foreign language courses, language pedagogy and instruction. She has been serving in the Literature Department at UCSD since the fall 2000 quarter.[23]

Jin-kyung Lee

Department of Literature

Dr. Lee is currently an Associate Professor in Korean and Comparative Literature. She received her Ph.D. from UCLA in Comparative Literature and joined UCSD in the fall of 2000. Her research interests include nationalist culture and politics of the colonial era, militarism and development in post-colonial South Korea, representations of gender and ethnicity, Asian labor migration in South Korea, and the Korean Diaspora.[24]

Kyong D. Park

Department of Visual Arts

Professor Park joined UCSD from the fall 2007 quarter, and he is currently a Professor in the Visual Arts Department. He is involved in a wide range of works on Public Culture, including research, documentation, and representations focused on the urban landscapes that delineate the economic, political, and cultural borders and territories of the contemporary social geography.[25]

23 Jeyseon Lee. (n.d.) In *UC San Diego Literature*. Retrieved from http://literature.ucsd.edu/people/lec-affiliated-associn/jlee.html

24 Jin-kyung Lee. (n.d.) In *UC San Diego Literature*. Retrieved from http://literature.ucsd.edu/people/faculty/jlee.html

25 Kyong Dong Park. (n.d.) In *UC San Diego Department of Visual Arts*. Retrieved from http://visarts.ucsd.edu/gallery/Kyong-Dong-Park

Jong-Sung You

Graduate School of International Relations and Pacific Studies

Dr. You received his Ph.D. from Harvard University in public policy and joined the IRPS in 2006 as an Assistant Professor. His area of specialization is comparative politics, political economy, corruption, social trust, inequality and social policy, and Korean politics.[26]

Affiliated Faculty

Joseph D. Hankins	*Department of Anthropology*
Lawrence B. Kraus	*Professor Emeritus, Graduate School of International Relations and Pacific Studies*
Nancy Kwak	*Department of History*
Ping-Hui Liao	*Department of Literature*
Susan Shirk	*Graduate School of International Relations and Pacific Studies*
John Skrentny	*Department of Sociology*
Daniel Widener	*Department of History*

The IRPS and the Korean Studies Initiative (now the Korean Studies Program) have been hosting numerous events every year. The IRPS hosts eight to ten Korea-focused events each school year and invites Korean government and academic experts to the campus. Sometimes, sponsors from the community provide grants, but mostly the professors have university funds to bring in speakers; IRPS staff members take care of the coordination to prepare for these events.[27]

A film festival and symposium titled "Korea, North and South: A Cinematic Perspective" was held in January 2008, and it was the biggest event ever held by IPRS. Notable media outlets such as *KPBS/NPR*, *Radio Free Asia*, *KBS News*, *The Joong-Ang Daily*, and *Korea Policy Review* covered the event. More than 2,000 people attended the screening of five North Korean films, five South Korean films, and one

26 Dr. You moved to the Australian National University after the 2013-2014 academic year.

27 From an email interview with Ms. Portia Bibb, Special Events Manager in the IRPS.

U.S. documentary film. The festival included seven lectures and one open panel by internationally-renowned film directors and scholars. It was the first North American film festival dedicated to contemporary films from both the Republic of Korea and the Democratic People's Republic of Korea.For this event, grants totaling $39,715 were given by the Korea Foundation, Institute on Global Conflict and Cooperation, California Institute for Telecommunications and Information Technology, and others.[28]

A significant event that the IRPS recently hosted was a public lecture in October 2012. Mr. Sung Kim, Ambassador of the United States to the Republic of Korea at that time, and Mr. Choi Young-jin, Ambassador of the Republic of Korea to the United States at the time, spoke about important changes taking place on the Korean peninsula, including elections in the South and the succession and possible reforms in the North. The U.S. Ambassador to the Republic of Korea and the Republic of Korea's Ambassador to the U.S. reflected on recent developments and the current state of the alliance, including blocked progress on the denuclearization of the peninsula and the Six Party Talks.[29]

The Speaker/Performer Series in the Arts and Humanities first started in the 2010-2011 academic year by the Korean Studies Initiative and embodies an inter-departmental effort among three specialists of Korea in the Division of Arts and Humanities: Dr. Jin-kyung Lee, Dr. Todd A. Henry, and Dr. Eun-Young Jung. One of the purposes of this series is to bring greater awareness and visibility to the fast-growing presence of the Korean Studies Initiative (now the Korean Studies Program) at UCSD and to a program already established as social sciences in the IRPS. By offering humanistic and artistic re-conceptualizations of modern Korean history and culture, they hope that this particular series will build conceptual bridges to a variety of disciplines. They also anticipate that such a program will allow scholars and students at UCSD to engage in much-needed intellectual exchanges with academic

28 Ibid.

29 Information provided by Ms. Portia Bibb, Special Events Manager in the IRPS.

communities throughout the U.S.[30]

One example of this Speaker/Performer Series was a *p'ansori performance* (traditional Korean narrative for solo vocalist) and a workshop in May 2012 by Dr. Chan E. Park, an associate professor of the Department of Korean Language & Literature at Ohio State University. Dr. Park is renowned as both a performer and scholar of *P'ansori*, and she has published extensively on the theory and practice of oral narrative, addressing the musical, literary, and theatrical dimensions of *p'ansori* and related genres. She has also presented many lectures, seminars, workshops and *p'ansori* performances throughout the world. By inviting the local Korean community to her public performance, organizers intended to advance the community outreach of the Korean studies series.[31] According to Dr. Jin-kyung Lee, this Speaker/Performer Series was available thanks to the grant from the Korea Foundation and a matching fund from the Division of Arts and Humanities Dean's office.

In October 2013, the Korean Studies Initiative at UCSD was selected as the recipient of a five-year (2013-2018) $600,000 grant from the Academy of Korean Studies (hereafter AKS) as a Core University Program for Korean Studies. Consequently, the Transnational Korean Studies Program was launched at UCSD in January 2014. It intends to accomplish the following projects: 1) build an integrated, campus-wide program in Transnational Korean Studies, 2) institutionalize a minor degree in Korean Studies, 3) establish internships in Korea, 4) develop new courses, 5) create AKS postdoctoral fellows in Transnational Korean Studies, 6) increase the number of visiting scholars, 7) enhance the Speaker Series and host events, 8) organize and host four topical conferences, 9) consolidate, enhance, and manage the Korean film and library collections, etc.[32]

---

30 Cited from the Speaker/Performer Series in the Arts and Humanities Proposal by Dr. Jin-kyung Lee.

31 Cited from Dr. Jin-kyung Lee's Speaker/Performer Series in the Arts and Humanities proposal.

32 Cited from the 2013 Overseas Leading University Program for Korean Studies-A Project Proposal from UCSD: Program in Transnational Korean Studies, submit-

Thanks to this grant, $18,000 has been allocated to the Korean Language Program to develop 6 new courses. Course requests for LTKO 2D and LTKO 2E (lower-division intermediate-advanced level language courses) and LTKO 149: Readings in Korean Language History and Structure I, II, III (upper-division content courses) have been submitted and approved during the 2013-2014 academic year, and the classes will be offered starting in the 2015-2016 academic year.

6. Future Prospects of The Program

Over the past two decades, the Korean Language Program at UCSD has been steadily growing without experiencing many obstacles, thanks to the strong support of three home departments: Literature, the IRPS, and Linguistics. However, there are still some issues to be considered.

The most urgent problem the Korean Language Program faces is the hesitance of students to learn Korean language past the First-Year level if it is not required. Since UCSD did not have the Korean Studies minor program before the 2014-2015 academic year and does not yet have a major or minor program in Korean Language, Linguistics, or Literature, most students who take First-Year Korean classes do not feel it is necessary to continue Korean. Since most students take Korean language courses to fulfill their language requirement (up to the fourth quarter) or general education requirement (three quarters), or just for their general interest, it is understandable that students would rather take lower-level classes, in which good grades are obtainable with less effort.

A solution to this problem is to establish the Korean Studies major program and the Korean Language and Literature major/minor program for undergraduate students. Currently, UCSD's Korean Studies Program has six ladder-rank faculty members and is one of the largest faculties in North America. UCSD offers a wide variety of Korea-related courses in several departments, including Literature, History, Music, Visual Arts,

ted to the AKS in June 2013.

and the IRPS.[33] To establish the Korean Studies major and the Korean Language and Literature major/minor programs, strong support from the related departments and the university is necessary.

The second issue has to do with course offerings. Recently, there has been a rapid increase in the number of non-heritage students interested in learning Korean, so all sections in the First-Year level were over-enrolled for many years. To solve this problem, the Literature Department approved opening all three parts of First-Year classes (LTKO 1A, LTKO 1B, LTKO 1C) every quarter, starting from fall 2012. Second- and Third-Year classes, however, remain the same as before, except for some minor changes, shown in Chart 1.2 above. This is because of the University of California regulation that one lecturer can be in charge of a maximum of six courses per quarter; hence, there is no possibility of opening all three classes for both First- and Second-Year levels each quarter. Considering that the Second-Year Korean classes are not as popular as the First-Year courses, this is not a significant issue yet, but this system is inconvenient for the students who take LTKO 2A in the winter quarter, for example, because they must wait a quarter to take LTKO 2B after taking LTKO 2A, and then have to wait yet another quarter to take LTKO 2C.

The third issue is coordination. Many people ask why UCSD's Korean language courses are scattered between the Literature and Linguistic Departments. UCSD's language programs are unique in certain respects. For instance, while First-Year European language courses (such as Spanish, French, German and Italian) are under the Linguistics Department, whereas Second- and Third-Year levels of these language classes are under the Literature Department. Many people are surprised to learn that Chinese and Japanese Language Programs are housed in the History Department. For Korean, most of major courses are under the Literature Department, and only two sections for the superior or above-level heritage students are under the Linguistics Department.

---

33 Cited from Dr. Jin-kyung Lee's Speaker/Performer Series in the Arts and Humanities proposal.

Under the current one-lecturer system, the Korean Language Program could not offer classes beyond the Third-Year level in the Literature Department. Therefore, it was a credible decision to offer Korean for Korean Speakers (LIHL 115) and Advanced Korean for Korean Speakers (LIHL 135) under the Linguistics Department for the entire UCSD Korean Language Program and for the future UCSD Korean Studies Program. However, to avoid any problems and to maintain complementary relations, an intimate cooperation is necessary between the lecturer of the Literature Department and the graduate student teaching assistants who are in charge of Korean language courses in the Linguistics Department.

The final issue is student density in classes. While Korean Language Programs in many other universities have 10-12 students per class, the UCSD Korean Language Program has 25 students per section, and this poses a challenge for both students and instructors. Nevertheless, students in Southern California have the advantage of having a prominent Korean community nearby; the students can practice Korean on and off campus. Although they may have less time to practice in class due to large class sizes, they can actively practice outside of the classroom. However, it is surely advantageous for the students if the class sizes were to decrease to fewer than 15 students per section.

The UCSD Korean Language Program's highest priority is to build upon the strong program and to improve its curriculum to accommodate students' needs. Admittedly, most Korean language students at UCSD in the past were heritage students who wanted to take the courses to fulfill their language or general education requirements, to enjoy Korean pop culture, or to learn their parents' native language for better communication with them. Currently, however, as Korea gains more power and voice in the international community and global economy, Korean studies becomes increasingly important. Thanks to this change, more non-heritage students are becoming interested in learning Korean at UCSD. Therefore, it is time to prepare for the upcoming decade by restructuring the Korean Language Program not simply as a means to fulfill a language requirement, a general education requisite, or general interest, but to help students prepare for their careers. The Korean Language Program will continue to explore better ways to provide quality instruction for students and to strengthen the Korean Language Program at UCSD.

REFERENCES

Applying to the MAS-IA Program. (n.d.) In *UC San Diego School of International Relations and Pacific Studies*. Retrieved from http://irps.ucsd.edu/programs/master-of-advanced-studies-in-international-affairs-masia/admissions-information/

Faculty. (n.d.) In *East Asian Languages & Cultural Studies*. Retrieved from http://www.eastasian.ucsb.edu/faculty/jung.htm

Haggard, Stephan M. (n.d.) In *UC San Diego School of International Relations and Pacific Studies*. Retrieved from http://irps.ucsd.edu/faculty/faculty-directory/stephan-m-haggard.htm

Henry, Todd. (n.d.) In *UC San Diego Department of History*. Retrieved from http://history.ucsd.edu/people/faculty/henry.html

Jung, Eun-Young. (n.d.) In *UCSD Department of Music*. Retrieved from http://musicweb.ucsd.edu/people/people.php?cmd=fm_music_directory_detail&query_Full_Name=%20Eun-Young%20Jung&query_Active_Status=Faculty

Lee, Jeyseon. (n.d.) In *UC San Diego Literature*. Retrieved from http://literature.ucsd.edu/people/lec-affiliated-associn/jlee.html

Lee, Jin-kyung. (n.d.) In *UC San Diego Literature*. Retrieved from http://literature. ucsd.edu/people/faculty/jlee.html

Lee, Steven. (n.d.) In *USC Korean Studies Institute*. Retrieved from http://dornsife.usc.edu/ksi/steven-lee/

Lowe, Lisa. (n.d.) In *UC San Diego Literature*. Retrieved from http://literature.ucsd.edu/people/faculty/emeriti/llowe.html

New Director prepares to launch Educational Doctorate program. (2007, November). *California State University Stanislaus Digest*. Retrieved from http://archive.csustan.edu/digest/archive/November2007/faculty_staff_notes/story_2.html

Park, Kyong Dong. (n.d.) In *UC San Diego Department of Visual Arts*. Retrieved from http://visarts.ucsd.edu/gallery/Kyong-Dong-Park

Polinsky, Maria. (n.d.) In *Scholars at Harvard*. Retrieved from http://scholar.harvard.edu/mpolinsky

Schedule of Classes. (n.d.) In *UC San Diego Instruction Tools*. Retrieved from https://act.ucsd.edu/scheduleOfClasses/scheduleOfClassesFaculty.htm
Tohsaku, Yasu-Hiko. (n.d.) In *UC San Diego School of International Relations and Pacific Studies*. Retrieved from http://irps.ucsd.edu/faculty/faculty-directory/yasuhiko-tohsaku.htm

The Korean Language Program at the University of Chicago

Hi-Sun Kim
The University of Chicago

1. Introduction

As a part of the 2010 lecture series on the history of East Asian Studies at the University of Chicago (arranged by Ed Shaughnessy, Professor of Early China and Department Chair at the time), Kyeong-Hee Choi, an Associate Professor of Modern Korean Literature in the Department of East Asian Languages and Civilizations (EALC), was asked to give a talk on Korean studies. She opened her talk with a scene from the final chapter of the famous first modern Korean novel, *The Heartless* (무정), published in 1917 and written by Yi Kwang-su. Its protagonists, Hyeong-sik and Seon-hyeong, are anticipating college graduation and their return to Korea after graduating from the University of Chicago:

> 형식과 선형은 지금 미국 시카고대학 사학년생인데 내내 몸이 건강하였으며 금년 구월에 졸업하고는 전후의 구라파를 한번 돌아 본국에 돌아올 예정이며 김장로 부부는 날마다 사랑하는 딸이 돌아오기를 기다려 벌써부터 돌아온 후에 할 일과 해 먹일 것을 궁리하는 중 (Ch. 126)
>
> Hyŏng-sik and Sŏn-hyŏng are now fourth year students at the University of Chicago. They have been well, and plan to travel through post-war Europe after graduating in September. Then they will return to Korea. Elder Kim and Mrs. Kim eagerly await their dear daughter's return, and are already thinking about things to do and what to feed their daughter when she returns." (Translation from *Yi Kwang-su and Modern Korean Literature: Mujŏng* by Ann Sung-hi Lee, 2005)

About ninety years after this novel's publication, the reality has far outstripped the imagination of Yi Kwang-su, in that now the University of Chicago not only has a long history of Korean alumni from various fields, but also a distinguished program in Korean language, literature, and history.

Within the university's long-held intellectual tradition, the Korean language program began in 1985 with the late William Sibley, Professor of Japanese and the Department Chair (1984-90) at the time. He was one of the driving forces behind the establishment of Korean Studies at the University of Chicago, as documented in the funding proposal to the Department of Education. It was submitted by the Center for East Asian Studies (CEAS) for the academic year of 1984-85 and states,

> In the initial years of its new effort in Korean studies, the University will emphasize the building of a basic research collection of written materials for graduate students, an introductory language program, as well as visiting lectures and speakers. (p. 55)

It is not clear if they received funding for Korean from the Department of Education that year, but in the following years, the CEAS did receive funding from the Korea Research Foundation (also known as Korea Foundation for Advanced Studies), which was founded by the late Chairman of Sunkyong Textiles Ltd, Jong-Hyon Chey (A.M. '61 University of Chicago). In the progress report to the Korea Research Foundation for 1986-87, it is stated that partial to full funding was provided for a Senior Lecturer in Korean Language, an Assistant Professor in the Department of Economics, visiting faculty in Korean Civilization, a post-doctoral fellow, and library staff for the Korean section. Consequently, in 1985, the first Korean language courses were offered by the Department of Far Eastern Languages and Civilizations (FALC), which is now known as the Department of East Asian Languages and Civilization (EALC).

2. Building the Foundation: 1985-1989

Wieboldt Hall

Suk-In Chang, one of the co-authors of *Korean Grammar for International Learners*, published by Yonsei University, was hired as the first Director of the Korean Language Program. In the autumn quarter of 1985, a beginning level Korean class-Introduction to Korean Language (K111-112-113)-was offered with an enrollment of 20 students. In the second year of the program (1986-87), with 22 new students beginning first-year classes, an Intermediate Korean (K211-212-213) course was added for 10 enrolled students in the autumn quarter. By the fall of 1987, the program showed stable enrollment for first-year (36 students) and second-year Korean (11 students), and it expanded the program by adding third-year Korean-Advanced Korean (K311-312-313)-with 4 students registered. The academic year of 1988-89 marked the fourth year of the program and saw courses offered in beginning, intermediate, and advanced levels of Korean. The enrollments for autumn 1988 in Korean 111, Korean 211, and Korean 311 were 37, 15, and 5 respectively, reflecting a steady increase of students every year since 1985. In addition, it was noted in the 1988-89 progress report to the Korea Research Foundation that the percentage of heritage learners had decreased in four years, while the number of non-heritage learners increased; this change was interpreted as a sign of growth in student motivation and interest in Korean studies rather than just in language acquisition. It is not clear what textbooks were used during the first few years of Korean language teaching at Chicago, but on several occasions, it was noted that Suk-In Chang had been developing textbook materials for the intermediate and advanced level classes. Considering that she was the co-author of several textbooks published in Korea prior to her directorship at the University of Chicago (e.g. *Korean Grammar for Foreigners I*, 1982, Yonsei University Press; *Modern Conversational Korean I*, 1982, Seoul Computer Press; *Second Level Reader*, 1977, Yonsei University Press, etc.), it can be conjectured that one of these was used for first-year Korean instruction.

With the motivation of developing a multi-faceted Korean studies program, the University of Chicago hired historian Bruce Cummings as a Professor of Korean history in 1987, two years after the Korean language program's launch. Hence, in the course catalogue for 1988-89, a history course entitled Korean Civilization (K307, cross listed with Hist 307) was taught by Cummings and appeared under the listing for Korean courses in EALC. One year later, the Korean Studies Committee of CEAS and the Department of EALC decided that it was time to build on the foundation of the newly established Korean language program by further expanding Korean studies. This was documented in the 1989-90 funding proposal submitted to the Korea Research Foundation:

> Now that the foundation program is in place, the Korean Studies Committee, the East Asian Languages and Civilizations Department and various graduate programs in other departments, are committed to finding ways to help advanced students bridge the often difficult gap between basic language learning and using a language — particularly complex languages like modern and premodern Korean — for research purposes. In the long run, the fulfillment of this need will depend on the appointment of a fulltime scholar-teacher with a specialization in some aspect of traditional Korean society and culture, someone who also has the ability and the interest to teach the language at an advanced level, with emphasis on reading. (p. 3-4)

As the University of Chicago is known for its rigor in research and higher education, it is apparent that the ultimate motivation for establishing the Korean language program was in order to pave the way for advanced scholarship and research in Korean studies.

3. 1990-1998

In the years between 1990 and 1998, several significant developments occurred within Korean studies at the University of Chicago. First, in 1990, Jae-Ohk Cho, who had received her Ph.D. from the University of Illinois in Linguistics, became the second Director of the Korean Language Program at the Department of EALC. Not long after this, however, in the spring of 1991, Chicago's Joseph Regenstein Library made the decision to dismiss the Korean librarian, On-sook Lee. The first five years of the Korean language program was supported by a $1 million endowment from Korea's Sunkyong Group (Korea Research Foundation), which also went into establishing the Korean library collection at the university, but the end of this funding resulted in Lee's dismissal. This turn of events prompted a protest by the students on campus, and accordingly "the U of C Korean Society, the Korean Undergraduates of the U of C, and the Korean Studies Group signed a petition asking the library to continue Korean librarian services and maintain its commitment to Korean Studies" (*The Chicago Maroon*, March 5, 1991). According to the university's student newspaper, the forty or so graduate students in Korean Studies expressed how the termination of the Korean librarian had put a halt to their research. The chair of the Korean Studies Group at the time and current Professor of Korean History at Columbia University, Charles Armstrong, was quoted as stating, "It's more than just the issue of the librarian per se. We think this issue reflects the general lack of commitment to Korean Studies at the Library."

Similar sentiments were expressed by undergraduate students in an article entitled "Asian students speak on minority issues," published in a later issue of *The Chicago Maroon* (May 31, 1991). In a discussion of the academic life of Asian students at the University of Chicago, minority students pointed out that although the core courses at the university heavily emphasized Western thinking, the university was also sensitive to Asian students by offering courses on East Asian and South Asian Civilization. In this vein, the article added, "Korean students said they would like the Korean curator back at the Regenstein Library and would also like to see the library's Korean section expanded," indicating that the issue had gained prominence on campus and that the development of Korean Studies at the University of Chicago had become a campus-wide priority.

Subsequently, in the early 1990s, the university received a challenge grant of $2.5 million from the Korea Foundation towards establishing a professorship in the field of Korean Studies. As a result, the University of Chicago raised $1.5 million to match the challenge grant to bring the endowment to nearly $5 million in its commitment to developing a leading center for Korean Studies. Hence, a Korean search committee was formed by the Humanities and Social Sciences Divisions and chaired by Norma Field, a Professor of Modern Japanese Literature (EALC), who had been studying and teaching the history of Korean-Japanese relations and of Koreans living in Japan. This committee opened three professorial positions in the fields of Korean history, sociology, and literature with the goal of having three tenured professors by the year 2000. This plan prompted *The University of Chicago Chronicle*, the school's official bulletin, to run an article announcing in its August 17, 1995 issue, "U of C to become leading center for Korean studies." Unfortunately, out of the three proposed professorships, only the position of Assistant Professor of modern Korean Literature in the Department of EALC was ever filled, awarded to Kyeong-Hee Choi in 1998.

As efforts were being made to expand Korean studies, the language program was also growing. Jae-Hoon Shim (currently a Professor in Early China at Dangook University in South Korea), a graduate student in EALC's Early China Studies Program who previously worked as a teaching assistant for Jae-Ohk Cho, was hired as a full-time lecturer in 1993. Two sections of first-year Korean were taught by Cho, while second- and third-year Korean was taught by Shim. The textbook series used was *Speaking Korean, I & II* by Francis Park. In 1995, Jae-Ohk Cho requested a leave of one year, and Kijoo Ko, a graduate student in Linguistics from the University of Illinois, became her replacement for the academic year of 1995-96. In that same year, despite the absence of the program's director, an advanced level course called Fourth-Year

Rapid Reading (designed and taught by Shim) was added to the Korean language program for the winter and spring quarters of 1996. The reading material was compiled from various sources, including advanced-level textbooks from Korea University and Yonsei University.

In 1997, Jae-Ohk Cho left the program, resulting in the cancellation of first-year and fourth-year Korean language courses during the academic year of 1998-99, leaving Jae-Hoon Shim as the sole instructor and acting director of the Korean Language Program. In that year, the EALC department organized a search committee for a new Korean language program director, chaired by the brand-new Assistant Professor in Korean literature, Kyeong-Hee Choi. These efforts resulted in the hiring of Kijoo Ko as the third director of the Korean Language Program at Chicago.

4. 1999-2007

The academic year of 1999-2000 began under the new directorship of Kijoo Ko; the Korean language program was fully back on track and offered all four levels of Korean language, with roughly 30 students in the first-year class and 10 students in each of the second- and third-year classes. Along with the language courses, two content courses were offered on Korean literature: K255 Literature of War and Division and K256 Gender and Modernity in Colonial Korea, taught by Kyeong-Hee Choi. Another class was offered on Korean history, K410 Seminar course on Modern Korean History, which was taught by Bruce Cumings. Additionally, several other courses that covered topics related to Korea were also cross-listed under the heading for Korean courses in the university catalog, including K520 Empire and Nation in East Asia, taught by Prasenjit Duara (Professor of History of East Asia), and K275 Premodern East Asia, taught by Norma Field (Professor of Japanese) & Ed Shaughnessy (Professor of Early China). This momentum continued into the year 2000, in which the first intensive summer Korean language courses (Intermediate level) were offered, co-taught by Kijoo

Ko and Jung-Hyuck Lee (who had been a teaching assistant the previous academic year).

However, the Korean Language Program underwent yet another transition when Kijoo Ko decided to leave the program in 2001, after two years as director. As a result, Jung-Hyuck Lee, by now a full-time lecturer, became the Acting Director of the Korean Language Program from 2001-2008. During her leadership, the department hired Ooyoung Pyun from Ohio State University to join the program starting in the fall of 2001. With a teaching faculty of two full-time lecturers, a graduate-student part-time lecturer, and a TA, the university offered two sections of first-year Korean, one each of second-year and third-year Korean, and a fourth-year course entitled Reading Course on Korean Culture, Politics, and Society. After three years of teaching, however, Ooyoung Pyun (now an Associate Professor of Korean at Ohio State University) resigned, resulting in the hiring of Hi-Sun Kim, a Ph.D. student from the University of Hawaii, to fill the position as Visiting Lecturer in the fall of 2004. The following year, upon receiving her Ph.D. degree in Korean linguistics, Kim became a full time lecturer of Korean.

However, despite positive gains in the hiring of teaching faculty and curriculum development during these years, changes in the university's undergraduate foreign language requirements affected the growth of Korean language teaching around the turn of the century. Prior to 2000, students were required to take at least one full year of a language at the level in which they were placed. For instance, if a student's placement was in third-year Korean, then he or she would fulfill their requirement by taking a full year of the language, or three quarters of Korean, in this case K301, K302, K303. However, when the university's language competency requirement was changed to require that students demonstrate reading, writing, listening, and speaking skills equivalent to only one year of college-level foreign language study, enrollment in Korean language courses began to show yearly decreases. Furthermore, with a sudden surge of interest in China, many students, even Korean heritage learners, began choosing Chinese classes over Korean ones. Nevertheless, the Korean Language Program at Chicago gained an increasingly sound professional footing in the field by hosting the 2007 annual conference and workshop of the American Association of Teachers of Korean (AATK), co-chaired by Jung-Hyuck Lee and Hae-Young Kim (Professor of the Practice in Korean Language at Duke University). The University of Chicago showed its support for the conference by providing funding from the Humanities Division, the Center for the Study of Languages, and the Center for East Asian Studies. The conference was a noted success, with a record-breaking attendance of 129 participants, and ended up setting a precedent for AATK conferences to come.

5. 2008-Present

In the winter of 2008, the Department of EALC finally launched a search for the fourth director of the Korean Language Program, with the committee again chaired by Kyeong-Hee Choi, who had received tenure as an Associate Professor of Korean literature in 2005. Acting Director Jung-Hyuck Lee had accepted an offer from the University of Notre Dame to serve as Associate Teaching Professor and Coordinator of the Korean Language Program and decided to leave the University of Chicago at the end of the spring quarter. From among three candidates, Hi-Sun Kim was selected as the next director and was appointed to Senior Lecturer of the Korean Language Program in the fall of 2008. To make up for the loss of faculty, a search for another full-time lecturer was conducted that year, resulting in the hiring of Hye-Sook Lee, a recent Ph.D. graduate in Linguistics from Cornell University. However, in 2010, Hye-Sook Lee (now currently at Georgetown University) resigned and was replaced by Jieun Kim, a Ph.D. in Linguistics from UCLA.

With the rising popularity of Chinese language learning on campus, student enrollment and retention in the Korean Language Program had become a critical priority since the beginning of the 2000s. The assessment of potential Korean language student demographics at the University of Chicago identified the following groups: (a) Non-heritage learners, including both undergraduate and graduate students; (b) Heritage language (HL) learners with either both parents speaking primarily English at home and/or having only one Korean parent, thus resulting in minimal or limited exposure to Korean language and culture; (c) HL learners with both parents primarily speaking Korean at home and/or having frequent visits and exposure to Korea and Korean culture. Consequently, this group of HL students had good receptive skills but poor productive skills and no metalinguistic knowledge; (d) International students (*joki yuhaksaeng*) who had studied in English-speaking countries (US, Canada, Australia) since middle or late primary school. These students had native or near-native listening and speaking skills, but lacked in academic writing and reading skills, and possessed no deep knowledge of Korean literature or history.

Based on the identification of these linguistic groups, the Korean program has experimented with increasing enrollment by designing innovative courses that would address the needs and engage the strengths of each type of potential student. One issue that all Korean language programs face is catering to the vastly different needs of HL learners. Hence, some of the larger programs have employed a two-track system, separating HL and non-HL learners. Even though the two-track system appears to be an ideal solution, it is only possible if there are large numbers of students and instructors. Hence, when a two-track system is not possible, Korean programs often arbitrarily place HL learners in beginning, intermediate, and advanced levels. When HL learners start from the introductory level, although they may benefit from the metalinguistic instruction of Korean grammar, due to their advanced listening and speaking skills they tend to lose the motivation to continue studying and ultimately do not improve their language skills. On the other hand, when HL learners are placed in upper levels, due to a severe gap in their metalinguistic knowledge, their errors (or stabilized/fossilized forms) are not properly addressed, and in turn these students may find themselves lost, confused, and ultimately fail to improve as well. In order to attend to this problem, in 2008, the U of C Korean language program began offering a one–or-two quarter course titled Accelerated Korean for Bilingual Speakers to fast-track the HL learners into upper-level courses after solidifying their language foundations. This research-based curriculum specifically addressed the linguistic needs unique to HL learners and provided them with important metalinguistic knowledge to go beyond their colloquial level efficiently.

Despite the program's efforts, the course for HL learners did not reach stable enrollment levels, and the program continued to face challenges with the consistency of language proficiency among HL learners. Also, with the lack of teachers, the accelerated course could not be offered as a three-quartered series, but only in one or two quarters. This inconsistency of course offering resulted in HL students opting to take the regular track over the fast track designed for them. In addition, due to processes of globalization and the appeal of Korean popular culture, Korean-Americans today tend to be more balanced bilinguals than in the past. That is, as multilingualism becomes an important asset in the global economy, more Korean-Americans (as well as international Korean students) are raised in a much more balanced bilingual and bicultural context, whereas in the past, assimilation to the dominant society was often enforced by their immigrant parents. Accordingly, with more truly bilingual HL learners, fewer end up needing to take the accelerated course in the first place.

Also, intending to increase the appeal of Korean language study to a larger group of students and to promote better enrollment at the University of Chicago, the language program began collaborating with the Korean literature professor and graduate students in Korean Studies in the development of a new content-based fourth year language course series on Korean society through media, literature, and film. This course was designed for advanced students as well as international students who had attended schools in the United States from an early age. The course had two main goals for its students: The first objective was to foster speed, accuracy, and comprehension in the reading of authentic contemporary texts, as well as to refine writing skills in various styles; The second objective was for the students to acquire a deeper, analytical knowledge of cultural and historical issues in modern Korea. The uniqueness of this curriculum design came from the collaborative effort fostered between the language instructors, who provided the linguistic framework for attaining advanced-level proficiency, and graduate students in Korean Studies, who helped to customize the content with expert contributions from areas such as literature, history, film, and sociology. In the academic year of 2013-2014, rather than a typical in-class final presentation, which would be given in front of the instructor and the class, a mini-conference component was added in which each student presented his or her final research paper to a larger, invited audience that included professors and graduate students in the fields of literature, history, and film. Through this opportunity, students gained the experience of not only giving a formal presentation in a conference context but also encountering spontaneous questions from native experts in the field.

The first course of this 400 series entitled Korean Contemporary TV and Language (K421) was a sociolinguistics course, in which students read academic papers on issues such as language and gender, honorific and address terms, language and nationalism, dialects, etc. and analyzed different genres of Korean TV programs, such as dramas, entertainment talk shows, game or variety shows, and news segments, based on their readings. The second course designed in the 400 series was called Family, Society, and History in Korea through Film and Fiction (K422), in which students learned and discussed modern and contemporary Korean history through literary works, movies, and documentary films. Lastly, Korean 423, entitled Changing Identity of Korea in Contemporary Korea through Film and Essays, looked into how contemporary Korean society was re-imagined by the diverse perspectives of emergent minority groups. The issues addressed included language and identity, gender and sexuality, and Korea as a multi-ethnic society.

What differentiated this new series of courses from regular fourth-year language classes was that rather than putting a sole emphasis on language development, these courses were designed by experts in the field to foster critical thinking and discussion about Korean society in order to acquire advanced proficiency. In other words, the Korean program at the University of Chicago decided to follow a model similar to that of the Romance and Germanic language departments, in which literature and content courses were taught to language students not only by the professors in the field but also entirely in the target language.

Unlike most other East Asian language programs, in which instruction in language and literature often work separately, the Korean literature and language program at the University of Chicago is now working through mutual collaboration, using University of Chicago graduate students of Korean Studies as an asset for Korean language curriculum development. As a result, the responses of students who have taken fourth-year level courses have been extremely positive, as they express satisfaction with the acquisition of a deeper understanding of both the language and Korean society.

With a healthy increase in the enrollment and popularity of advanced Korean in recent years, in the summer of 2014, the Korean language program and a Ph.D. student from the Department of Economics developed a new fifth-year level course using the same type of content-rich, theme-based model at the University of Chicago. By applying the same collaborative method between language and economics, the program will pilot a fifth year course with the title Microeconomics and Its Application to Korean Economy in the spring quarter of 2015, before launching a three-quarter, fifth-year series.

Since 2008, the enrollment has stabilized and continued to show slight increases, both at the lower levels (Beginning and Intermediate) and advanced level (4th Year). Although there have been some fluctuations in numbers, overall there have been healthy signs of retention. In the fall of 2011, while the director was on leave for one quarter, the program was asked to collapse the two sections of first-year Korean, which resulted in an enrollment of twelve students. A year later, in the fall of 2012, thirty-two students enrolled in first-year Korean, which has resulted in the re-opening of a second section of Korean 101. Out of thirty-two students, only four students were Korean-Americans, and the rest were non-heritage students from various ethnic backgrounds, such as Chinese-American, Mexican-American, Vietnamese, French,

Belgian, etc. In recent years, one of the explanations for the increase in enrollment of the Korean language program was the rise in popularity of K-pop music and Korean drama, known has the Korean Wave (*hallyu*). However, a second wave of Korean popular culture, initiated by the unexpected popularity of the K-pop artist Psy in September 2012, suggested that the Korean program at the University of Chicago, and possibly all over the U.S., should anticipate an overall increase. Furthermore, during the academic year of 2013-2014, there was a significant increase of students enrolled in content-based fourth-year courses (total=28), which revealed how students today are interested in achieving a very high level of language proficiency as well as cultural competency. Hence, as more students show genuine interest in multilingual and multicultural studies, the Korean language program must take this opportunity to develop innovative courses with the goal of cultivating students and majors of Korean Studies, especially at the undergraduate level.

6. Conclusion: "U of C to become the leading center for Korean Studies"

While the university is known for its intellectual rigor and solid grounding in academic traditions within the study of East Asia at Chicago, scholarship has been at the forefront of interdisciplinary and intra-regional perspectives and has distinguished it from other universities. Despite the somewhat late beginning for Korean Studies at the University of Chicago in 1985, thanks to the high-minded scholarship at the Department of EALC, Korean Studies was not merely an additive to fill the roster of East Asian countries but an area of knowledge whose inclusion was deemed necessary by scholars of Japanese and Chinese already present. Ultimately, the launching of Korean Studies at Chicago, and by extension the establishment of Korean language instruction, has been the result of the department's desire to foster the critical study of shared historical legacies of interaction between Japan,

Korea, and China, especially through the lens of modern experiences such as colonialism, imperialism, and nationalism. For instance, in the early 90s, Norma Field, Professor of Modern Japanese Literature, conducted pioneering research on writing by Koreans living in Japan. Also, the scholarship of Prasenjit Duara, Professor Emeritus of History in East Asia (currently a Professor of Humanities in National University of Singapore), researched Koreans' fates in the transnational, Japanese-sponsored wartime in the northeast Asian border-state of Manchukuo. The university's Korean Studies faculty, such as Bruce Cumings and his ground-breaking work on the history of the Korean Conflict as well as Kyeong-Hee Choi and her research on censorship and the shaping of Korean literature in the colonial period, point to the distinction of academic inquiry at Chicago on the most intellectually challenging topics in Korean history.

Consequently, the distinction of the faculty has also been reflected in the studies of the Ph.D. students in EALC, many of whom have pursued cross-cultural or comparative research on the historical and literary ties binding Korea and Japan or Korea and China. Some of the University of Chicago graduates who have produced scholarship in this vein have included Sam Perry (Assistant Professor, Brown University) on Japanese and Korean literature, Hyun-Jeong Lee (Assistant Professor, University of Seoul) on Chinese and Korean literature, Hee-kyoung Cho (Assistant Professor, University of Washington) on Russian and Korean literature, Yoon-Sun Yang on Modern Korean literature (Assistant Professor, Boston University), and Hyun-ho Joo (Assistant Professor, Yonsei University) on Korea in19th century Chinese journalism. The Korean Language Program has contributed to and grown alongside the general development of Korean Studies at the University of Chicago by providing over twenty years of language instruction to undergraduates and graduate students. Now more than ever, the Korean Language Program at Chicago is well-positioned to make even more direct contributions to the training of future scholars of Korean Studies, as well as continuing to help enrich the language and cultural education of students from other disciplines as well. Although the title of the 1995

The University of Chicago Chronicle article promising the school's ascendance to "leading center for Korean Studies" has yet to become the truth, the program has never lost sight of that goal and continues to make steadfast progress towards it.

* The information provided in this paper is based on the materials obtained from Special Collections Research Center, The University of Chicago Library, Department of East Asian Languages and Civilizations, Center for East Asian Studies, and *The Chicago Maroon* (student newspaper of the University of Chicago).

ACKNOWLEDGEMENTS

I would like to express my gratitude to Professor Ed Shaughnessy, Professor Norma Field, Professor Kyeong-Hee Choi, Professor Jae-Hoon Shim, Dr. Theodore Foss, and Dr. Kijoo Ko for their valuable time and information.

I am solely responsible for any error or misrepresentation made in this article.

APPENDIX

Table 1. Yearly Enrollment of Korean Language Students at the University of Chicago (total of 3 quarters) : 1985-2013

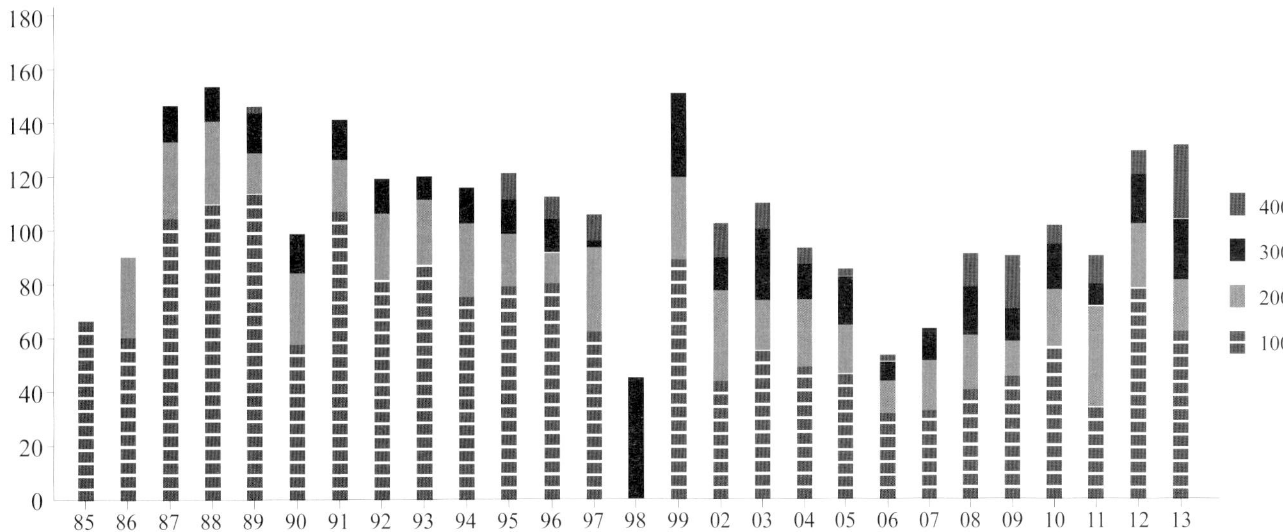

*The enrollment for the academic year 1999-2000 is an approximate number (30 in first year, 10 in second year, 10 in third year x 3 quarters), based on a report of the Korean Language Program made by Kijoo Ko.

*The enrollment for 2000-01, 2001-02, and 2002-03 are missing.

The Korean Language Program at the University of Minnesota: Focus on Non-heritage Learners

Hangtae Cho
The University of Minnesota

1. Introduction

This narrative seeks to chronicle the rise and growth of the University of Minnesota Korean Language Program (UMKLP) and to set forth its intended future direction. The UMKLP boasts one of the largest Korean as a Foreign Language (KFL) programs geared toward non-heritage learner populations in the nation. In its infancy, the program offered Korean courses as one or two extension night classes, with enrollment averaging around 10 students each quarter in 1993. By the year 2000, the UMKLP joined the Department of Asian Languages and Literatures (ALL) as an academic program, and enrollment rose to 46 students in the beginning sections and 24 in the intermediate sections. As of 2014, with 400 students (90% non-heritage) per year (excluding the students in the Korean culture and literature courses), four full-time instructors and two graduate instructors, the UMKLP offers a complete Korean language curriculum that covers five full years of instruction. The program's rapid growth is attributed to an increased focus on non-heritage learners, attention to sound pedagogical practices, and generous support that has enabled the addition of key faculty members.

2. Korean Heritage Learners

Most university-level Korean programs in the U.S. have been established to serve ethnic Korean descendants, such as second or third-generation Korean Americans who constitute upwards of 70-80% of enrollment in Korean language classes.[1] By and large, the focus of these programs centers around the heritage learners' linguistic needs and then expands outward to accommodate non-heritage learners, who are true beginners. While these percentages are in flux nationwide and slowly gravitating toward non-heritage learners of Korean, the majority of well-established university-level Korean language programs throughout the U.S. are built on the foundation of Korean heritage learner education. This observation is corroborated by U.S. census data that shows high populations of Korean Americans situated in proximity to universities that have traditional Korean language programs (see Appendix A). Generally speaking, the initial growth of KFL in the U.S. began as a response to demands from concentrated Korean-American student populations.

3. History of Asian Languages and Literatures at The University of Minnesota

The UMKLP can be considered to be quite different from traditional programs, as it is currently comprised mostly of non-heritage speakers and has grown very rapidly over the past decade. It was not always this way, however. Beginning in 1993, the Korean language was offered as an extension class on a quarterly basis through the School of Continuing Education. Prior to this, Japanese and Chinese were the only East Asian languages taught at the University of Minnesota. Japanese was first introduced in the late 1940s and joined with Russian language instruction to form the Department of Linguistics and Comparative Philology. Chinese was added later when the now-renowned Richard Mather joined the department in 1949; he remained at the university until he retired in 1997. In 1950, Mather was joined by Robert Brower, a celebrated professor of Japanese. Throughout the first few decades, the

1 Cited from the UMKLP external review (Sohn 2008).

emphasis of the different departments remained on language, literature, and linguistics/philology training. In the 1960s, this focus was expanded to include Ph.D. programs, which continued up to the end of the century and centered primarily on language, linguistics, and classical literature. It was during this time of expansion that the East Asian Library was established under the directorship of Qiu Kaiming (Chiu K'ai-ming), formerly of the Harvard Yenching Library. The library now holds more than 154,000 volumes in Chinese, Japanese, and more recently Korean.

Over the years, the programs grew, and the department went through a series of changes and expansions. It first became the Department of Slavic and Oriental Languages, and then, when Hindi-Urdu was added to the department in 1963, it became the Department of East and South Asian Languages. Five years later, the Department of East Asian Languages separated into its own division. In the 1970s, the department went through an expansion when it was asked to offer more undergraduate East Asian humanities courses. Then in the 1980s, the Department of East Asian Studies merged with area studies faculty; however, the core faculty remained in distinct language and literature fields. During this decade, a number of faculty members were added to the programs, both in permanent and visiting positions. In the 1990s, further reorganization created more focused language and literature programs in Chinese, Japanese, and South Asian studies — each with its own director. It was during this phase that the Korean language was first offered through the School of Continuing Education since there was no East Asian entity with which to affiliate. Late in the 1990s, the College of Liberal Arts (CLA) decided to form a new department that gathered these various language, linguistics, and literature programs into one, called the Department of Asian Languages and Literatures. Joseph R. Allen arrived at the university in 2000 and was appointed as the founding chair of this new department.

4. Korean Language Courses in The School of Continuing Education

Beginning in 1993, Korean was taught sporadically in the after-hours extension program in the School of Continuing Education. There was an average of around 10 students per quarter at that time, and classes were taught by several different graduate students and part-time instructors including Jihyun Jeon (1993-1995), Sang Cheol Lee (1995), and In-Ah Ha (1995-1997). Hangtae Cho also began teaching extension classes as a graduate-student instructor in 1997. His main concern at that time was not about teaching, but rather about marketing: Who would be interested in learning Korean, and how could the program find those students?

Initially, Cho faced a variety of challenges. One problem was the program's low visibility at the university compared to larger Asian language programs. Another challenge was the dual nature of the students in the program. In 1997, about half of the students were Korean adoptees (those of Korean heritage who were adopted into the U. S. at a young age and grew up without any cultural or linguistic influences from Korea), and the other half were Korean heritage learners. Heritage learners, as briefly mentioned previously, were students who typically acquired Korean at home and had high oral/aural proficiency but were more limited in written literacy. The primary dilemma facing the fledgling Korean program was how to cater to two very different student populations in one classroom. It was impractical to split the class due to minimum enrollment requirements, yet neither group was getting the attention they deserved. The response from the heritage learners was that the class pace was too slow, whereas the non-heritage learners (including the adopted Korean students) struggled to keep pace with the accelerated heritage learners. The Korean language courses thus did not meet either of the two groups' needs, frustrating students and instructors alike. This struggle continued until the turn of the century.

5. Korean Language Courses in The Department of Asian Languages and Literatures

When the Department of Asian Languages and Literatures (ALL) was formed in 2000, it incorporated the programs of Chinese, Japanese, and South Asian languages. Although up to that point, Korean was still being taught as part of the School of Continuing Education and thus outside of the departmental structure, ALL decided to invite the small Korean language program to join the department as an equal partner, alongside the older and bigger programs. After establishing Korean within ALL, a nation-wide search for a director of the program was conducted, and the selection committee decided to retain Hangtae Cho for that position.

Upon joining ALL, Cho and department chair Allen decided to tackle issues facing the budding program. After a few years, Cho had observed stunted growth in enrollment, in addition to a variety of administrative difficulties relating to identifying an appropriate curriculum for a mixed population. Together, Allen and Cho set long-term goals and envisioned the creation of a true KFL program by placing students with prior Korean language experience in an accelerated class and focusing on teaching Korean to true beginners separately. This decision bucked the national trend of Korean language programs. However, Cho perceived that such a program would be right for Minnesota because of the high percentage of motivated beginner students, about 30% of whom were

Folwell Hall

Korean adoptees at the time. Thus, the division between true beginners and heritage learners was finally established without sacrificing either student population. Interestingly, the accelerated class was later canceled due to low enrollment, whereas the enrollment of non-heritage learners has maintained or increased its numbers annually since 2000 (see Appendix B). In retrospect, the vision shared by professors Allen and Cho was very insightful. Restructuring the program was a good decision, considering the lack of a major source of Korean-American heritage learners due to the relatively small size of the Korean immigrant community in Minnesota and the surrounding states that fed into the university's student population.

Another issue facing the developing program was locating appropriate textbooks and other materials for both heritage and non-heritage learners. In 1997, most Korean language classes were taught to heritage learners who had varying levels of background in the language, resulting in the use of textbooks that were inappropriate for non-heritage learners. The available and popular texts at that time did not begin with the basics, thus leaving true beginners at a disadvantage from the start. Over the last ten years, however, there have been improvements and revisions of various textbooks, and Cho was involved in the revision of the KLEAR textbook series and their corresponding workbooks, which are more accessible to non-heritage true beginners. This textbook series is currently used by about 70% of college-level Korean language programs nationwide and has contributed to the growth and development of the UMKLP. Following its inclusion in ALL, the explosive growth of the program led to the hiring of a second full-time instructor, Sang-Seok Yoon (2004), who contributed immensely to the establishment of the second-year curriculum and deserves special credit for the success of the program. Later, other teaching specialists were also hired, including Sugyung Kim (2011), who had extensive Korean teaching experience in Korea; Bryce Johnson (2012), a non-heritage teacher hired to replace Yoon, who took a position at the University of Iowa as the Director of the Korean Language Program; and Inhye Lee (2014), who was hired with 'Brain Korea' funding from Korea University. Additionally, many graduate-student instructors were hired over the years including Eun-Chung Chung (2000-2001), Haesook Koo (2001-2005), Hyunjoo Jung (2004), Jinbong Choi (2005-2007), Changhee Kim (2005, 2008), Kim Nelson (2006-2007), Sook-Jin Kim (2006), Yunseong Cheon (2006-2011), Eunjoo Kim (2009), Hunjin Jung (2009-2011), Sejung Ahn (2009-2011), Saena Ryu (2011-present), Minhwa Ahn (2013-present), and Soo Hyun Lee (2014-present).

A major portion of the true beginner population enrolling in Korean courses initially consisted of Korean adoptees. Minnesota is home to the largest Korean adoptee population in the United States.[2] These students demonstrated a deep commitment to the study of Korean, having largely been adopted into white, middle class families as infants and small children. These students flocked to Korean language classes in order to explore the culture of their birth country. Therefore, in spite of an absence of exposure to Korean culture while growing up, their strong desire to discover their heritage drove them to study the language. Although language learning is the most basic part of the UMKLP, the depth and breadth of Korean-related topics offered is also important in establishing a top-quality program; this development was the next challenge at the University of Minnesota.

6. Program Development[3]

Joining ALL allowed the Korean program to add courses in Korean literature and culture, making it possible for students to obtain a Korean Studies minor. Since 2001, the UMKLP has offered Korean literature or culture courses. One or two courses were offered every semester through temporary arrangements with graduate students majoring in areas like literature (Yoonkyoung Kim, Changhee Kim and Eunjoo

2 Kim Park Nelson (2009).

3 The story of Korean program and Korean adoptees in Minnesota was covered by *Korean Quarterly* (2007), and the article has greatly contributed to this narrative history.

Kim) and speech communication (Jinbong Choi), and with visiting professors in foreign policy (Professor Daeyeol Koo, Ewha Womans University) and geography (Professor Jaehun Choi, Konkuk University). In rounding out its offerings, the UMKLP has also put energy into offering topics that are both Korean and Minnesotan, including a history of Korean adoption course offered in 2006 and 2007, the first of its kind in the country. Ph.D. candidate Kim Park Nelson (currently a professor at Minnesota State University) taught the course. At the time, Nelson was earning her Ph.D. in American Studies at the University of Minnesota, and her thesis was entitled "Korean Looks, American Eyes: Korean American Adoptees, Culture, Race, and Nation." Her course was built on the Asian American Studies model and was designed to suit the needs of adopted Koreans, many of whom had never heard their own history before. Overall, the class was a success in contributing to the development of Korean Studies at the University of Minnesota.

During the fall 2007 and spring 2008 semesters, post-doctoral fellow Jieun Lee (currently Professor of Korean literature, Washington University in St. Louis) taught a course on women in literature and film. Lee said there was a lot of interest in the course "Making Women in Korean Literature and Film: Representations of Women, Men, and Gender Issues." She attributed the interest, in part, to the general interest in Korean popular culture (particularly films and TV dramas), which was a primary driving force for enrollment in the language courses as well. The course included readings that depicted women and men in both ancient and modern Korean society. This course further supported the growth of the UMKLP from a language-focused program to a budding Korean Studies program.

In the infancy of the UMKLP (1993-2000), about 30-50% of students were Korean adoptees. As the overall size of the program grew between the years 2000-2008, the percentage of Korean adoptees dropped to 5-20%, and since 2008, that figure has drastically dropped to less than 5%. Tighter adoption regulations and the rise of domestic adoption in Korea resulted in the sharp drop of international adoption numbers, particularly after the 1988 Seoul Summer Olympics. Currently, the

Korean adoptee student population is less than 5% of the student body in the program. Contrary to expectations, however, the number of overall students in the program has not decreased, a fact that indicates there are more students from a variety of backgrounds who are interested in Korean Studies. Following the national trend, the UMKLP student population now includes more African American, non-Korean Asian American, as well as Euro American students. The contribution from Korean heritage speakers in the UMKLP is also highly valued, as strong enrollment from this sector of students continues. Placement tests are now being utilized to expand the program and reach out to students who have previous exposure to the Korean language (such as Korean heritage students or those with substantial study abroad experience in Korea). Another aim is to add advanced level classes. For example, in 2007 discussions of Sino-Korean texts were added to the Korean course offerings.

The next breakthrough in the UMKLP came through generous funding from the Korea Foundation. Cho felt that the program could not continue to grow as it had over the past ten years without additional funding. The focus would no longer be about increasing enrollment but rather about offering quality courses. Throughout the first decade of the program, Cho had worked to build a solid foundation, but he also wanted to build a durable and valuable program with more Korean culture and literature courses. The key to offering solid coursework for a Korean Studies major was the addition of at least one new faculty member with a broad knowledge of Korean literature, history, and culture. During the summers of 2003 and 2005, Cho met with the officers of the Korea Foundation to discuss funding in order to add a tenure-track position in Korean cultural studies at the University of Minnesota. Then in the winter of 2005, Cho and Allen (ALL Department Chair at that time) visited the Korea Foundation's Washington D.C. office to brief them on the UMKLP's need. This was followed by a visit in the summer of 2006 by Cho to the Korea Foundation headquarters in Seoul, South Korea. Finally, in 2008 the funding application was submitted and accepted, resulting in a grant to open a tenure-track position. ALL completed the search for a new assistant professor in Korean literature and culture, and the department offered the position to Dr. Travis Workman (Ph.D. Cornell University 2008), who had just completed a postdoctoral fellowship at the University of California at Los Angeles and became the first professor of Korean Studies to have a full-time position at the University of Minnesota. Beginning in 2010, Dr. Workman began teaching classes in Korean culture, modern Korean literature, and Korean cinema. Dr. Workman has worked extensively on the cultural and literary history of Korea's colonial period and during the 1950s and 1960s, and his current project is a book-length manuscript based on his dissertation entitled "Living for History: Culture, Time and Form in Imperial Japan and Colonial Korea (1919-1945)." His work with leading scholars of cultural studies at Cornell University puts him at the vanguard of work in Korean Studies in the United States and in the field of cultural studies as a whole.

7. The UMKLP's Current State and Future Growth[4]

With the addition of Korean culture and literature courses, ALL now offers a major with a concentration in Korea in addition to a Korean minor. Dr. Workman's appointment came at a time when interest in Korea had expanded tremendously in Minnesota. Professor Workman's arrival ushered in an exciting new phase of Korean Studies at the university. Demand for courses on Korean subjects increased greatly in the past several years, and the university had hitherto been able to offer only temporary postdoctoral positions (often supported by the Korea Foundation) to fulfill student interest. With the arrival of Professor Workman, the department could offer a full specialization in the study of Korea for the first time as a major, which accompanied the language courses already present. Moreover, Professor Workman's interest in the

4 This summary of the current state and future direction of the Korean program was contributed by Professor Paul Rouzer (Chair of the Department of Asian Languages and Literatures 2008-present).

history of Korean cinema allowed him to work cooperatively with an extensive humanities faculty with specializations in the study of film; three of the professors in ALL now work with cinema studies and are equipped to train both undergraduate and graduate students in the study of East Asian cinema. The department is thus looking forward to the considerable contributions that Professor Workman will bring to the Minnesota scholarly community in the coming years.

As of the 2014-2015 academic year, barely 14 years after joining ALL, the UMKLP now offers a complete curriculum with five full years of Korean language instruction. Four full-time instructors and two graduate-student instructors oversee 400 students, of whom approximately 90% are non-heritage learners. Through an external review of the program, the UMKLP language instruction and curriculum was found to follow the National Standards for Foreign Language Education, as it incorporates the five Cs: Communication, Cultures, Connections, Comparisons, and Communities.

Ross King, professor of Korean Studies at the University of British Columbia in Vancouver and former dean of the Korean Language Program at the Minnesota-based Concordia Language Village, said Cho and the UMKLP have "pulled off something close to a miracle." The program demonstrates that Korean language programs can succeed without heritage learners, which is a step in the right direction in marketing Korean as a "global language." King said, "A well-equipped Korean Studies program should be able to attract the same students who would also be interested in Chinese Studies, Japanese Studies, or studies in any other important language." The fact that Cho built the language program "from the bottom up" means he is doing it "the right way," King said, by building language proficiency first with the beginning learners, and then adding culture and literature courses after the language program was established. "Slowly, Korean Studies is building legitimacy as a university field in North America," King added, "but it has been a long struggle." Although the UMKLP made a risky decision in 2000 by focusing on non-heritage students, in retrospect, it was on the leading edge of a trend. In some ways, the UMKLP has contributed to Korean Studies and Korean language education in the U.S. by setting a precedent for education focused on non-heritage speakers.

8. Conclusion

From humble beginnings, the UMKLP has grown rapidly in its 20-year history. The crucial decision to shift the focus of the program to non-heritage beginners marked the transition of the program from a modest few Korean language classes to a major KFL program. As the program continues its quest to offer quality Korean language, literature, and culture courses, it hopes to become a leader in the field of Korean studies.

APPENDIX A. Distribution of Korean Speakers in U.S.A

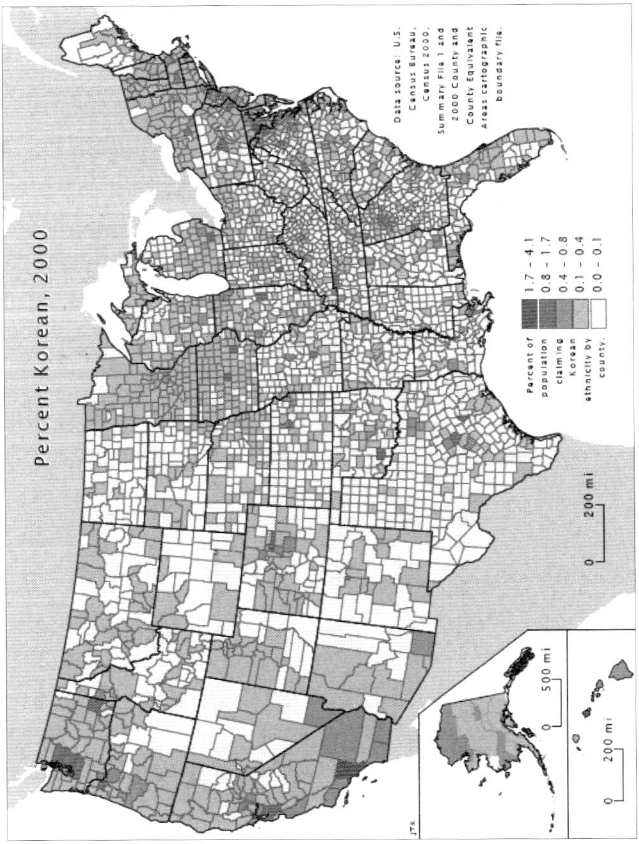

(Source: Modern Language Association)

APPENDIX B. Enrollment Trend for Korean Language (1999-2011)[5]

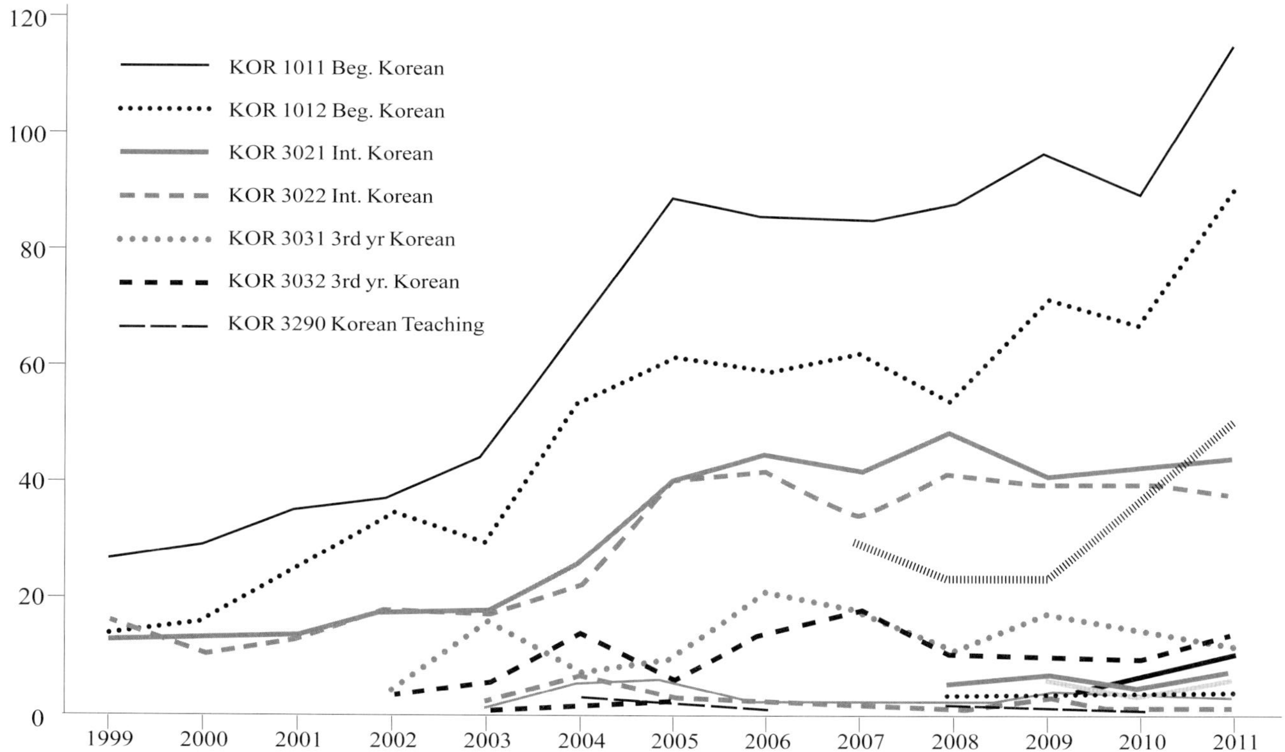

5 The statistics of the enrollment number for Korean language was contributed by Ms. Jennifer Wilson (Office Specialist of the Department of Asian Languages and Literatures).

The Korean Language Program at the University of Pennsylvania: Walking Through 35 Years of Its History and Highlights

Haewon Cho
The University of Pennsylvania

1. Introduction

Envisioned in 1980 and officially established in 1984, the Korean Language Program (KLP) at the University of Pennsylvania (Penn) has developed remarkably over the past three decades and has become one of the largest Korean language programs within the Ivy League and other private universities. Korean stands as one of the over 50 foreign language tracks offered by the School of Arts and Sciences language departments and the Penn Language Center at the University of Pennsylvania[1]. As of 2014, the KLP at Penn offers a complete curriculum in the Korean language, covering five full years and seventeen courses of Korean language instruction. Each year, three full-time and one part-time lecturers work with about 200-220 students. The initial establishment and subsequent development of the Korean Language Program at Penn are greatly indebted to the commitment and selfless dedication of the department's outstanding instructors,[2] as well as the strong support of the Korean studies and East Asian studies faculty members, and generous contributions from local communities and Penn alumni in both the U. S. and South Korea. The aim of this paper is to tell the story of the Korean Language Program at Penn, from its humble

---

1 Languages Offered. (n.d.) In *Penn Arts & Sciences*. Foreign Language Study. Retrieved from https://www.college.upenn.edu/language-study

2 Please see the acknowledgements at the end of this essay.

beginning to its expansion into a fully-fledged program, and to offer preliminary speculations about the future of the KLP, as the program faces its next transition.

2. Dawn (1963-1983)

In order to better understand the history of Penn's Korean Language Program, it is imperative to examine the development of the Korean studies program at Penn since the KLP and Korean studies have been closely tied together. Dr. F. Hilary Conroy, Professor of Far Eastern History at the time, joined Penn's History faculty in 1951 and was the first to teach Asian American History and Korean History courses, such as the History of Colonial and Modern Korea.[3] Following Conroy, Korean studies at Penn officially began in 1963 when Professor Chong-Sik Lee, an internationally-renowned scholar and one of the founders of Korean studies in the United States, joined the university's Department of Political Science.[4] Lee was a professor of Political Science and International Relations, focusing on contemporary East Asian politics and modern Korea. During his career, Lee wrote several books dedicated to Korean and East Asian politics. His landmark book *Communism in Korea*, which was co-authored with UC Berkley's Political Science Professor Dr. Robert A. Scalapino, was published in 1972 by the University of California Press and received the prestigious American Political Science Association's Woodrow Wilson Foundation Award in 1974.[5]

Chong-Sik Lee was the first Penn professor who focused mainly on Korean studies and was the only Korean studies professor until Dr.

---

3 Eugene Park, personal interview. March 15, 2012.

4 Korean Studies: $5 Million for Chairs. (1997, February 11). *University of Pennsylvania Almanac,* Vol. 43, No. 21. Retrieved from http://www.upenn.edu/almanac/v43/n21/korean.html

5 East Asia Scholar Robert A. Scalapino dies at 92. (2011, November 4). *UC Berkeley News Center*. Retrieved from http://newscenter.berkeley.edu/2011/11/04/east-asia-scholar-robert-a-scalapino-dies-at-92/

Milan Hejtmanek joined the department much later in 1995 as a professor of Korean History. This long interval was due partly to the fact that neither the university nor Professor Lee actively sought support from the Korean government for Penn's Korean studies program until the late 1990s, due to complicated political situations in Korea at the time. In an email interview, Professor Lee stated that his decision to abstain from seeking support from the Korean government in 1970s was deliberate; in 1971, because of his discomfort with the dictatorship, Lee cancelled his meeting with President Park Chung Hee in Seoul at the last minute. Nonetheless, Professor Lee continued his tireless efforts to promote Korean studies until his retirement in 1990.

Professor Lee was also the first to launch a pilot effort towards establishing Korean language courses at Penn. In response to growing demand for a Korean language course from Penn students, Lee invited Dr. Kijoong Song, who received a Ph.D. in Linguistics at Harvard University, to Penn around 1980.[6] Song offered First Year Korean as an evening course through the College of General Studies. However, enrollment was low, and as an evening course, the class could not count for official university credit. Lee worked hard to create a permanent position for Song but was unfortunately unsuccessful due to the lack of support from the university.[7] After two years of arduous trials, Song left Penn in 1982 for a faculty position at Seoul National University, and the Korean language course stopped being offered until 1984.

3. The Beginning (1984-1989)

After Song left Penn, the demand for Korean classes continued to rise. Around 1984, a group of undergraduate students filed a petition to the

6 Professor Victor Mair, personal interview. February 24, 2012.

7 Bill Hannas, quoted by Professor Victor Mair, Email to Haewon Cho on February 25, 2012. He stated that "the university rejected funding for the position even though he acquired enough funding for a permanent position" in his email to Professor Mair.

Provost to request Korean courses at Penn. The School of Arts and Sciences (SAS) acknowledged the pressing need for coursework in Korean topics and decided to provide a special fund to support a trial Korean course. This time, the course was officially offered for credit through the Department of Oriental Studies, the former name of the Department of East Asian Languages and Civilizations. Upon the request of Professor Victor Mair (Professor of Chinese Language and Literature and the Head of the East Asian section of the department at that time), Dr.William Hannas (then a Ph.D. student and Chinese language instructor) helped set up the Korean course within the department.[8] Next, Professor Labov from the Linguistics department was asked to recommend a capable Korean instructor.[9] Fortunately for the Penn KLP and the entire department, the outstanding and dedicated teacher Dr. Yunsook Hong was hired to teach First Year Korean again. Hong was pursuing a Ph.D. degree in Linguistics while taking a leave from her appointment as Professor of English Language and Literature at Hanyang University in Seoul, Korea.

Finally, in the fall of 1984, one class of First Year Korean with Hong was offered on an experimental basis with a strong enrollment of 24 students. Upon the successful launch of the first Korean language course, the department decided to keep Korean language courses and attempted to attract outside funding to stabilize the program in terms of staffing and course offerings, making sure to avoid possible competition for limited university funding with Japanese and Chinese language programs. With the backing of Professor Conroy in the History Department, Chong-Sik Lee continued to mobilize support from the local community for the Korean language courses, while Allyn Rickett, the Chairman of the Oriental Studies Department, sought extra support from the school.[10] From these early fundraising efforts until today, Mr. James Joo-Jin Kim,

8 Dr. Hannas established the Korean Language Program at Georgetown University in 1990.

9 Professor Victor Mair, personal interview. February 24, 2012. Yunsook Hong, phone interview. April 14, 2012.

10 Yunsook Hong, phone interview. April 14, 2012.

a Penn alumnus, has been the most important source of external funding for the founding and progress of both the Korean Language Program and Korean studies at Penn. After providing $7,500 to support the Korean Language Program for the academic year of 1985-1986, Kim pledged to continue his support over the next two years[11]. Additional donations from the local community continued to support the programs as well. Thanks to the generous gifts from Kim, the local community's support, as well as special university funding for Korean language courses, the department was able to continue offering Korean language courses at Penn.

Appointed as a Visiting Lecturer, Hong started from scratch and used excellent instructional skills and good judgment to organize the course efficiently. She successfully overcame difficulties and setbacks, such as the lack of teaching materials or pre-established pedagogy. Despite the unstable future of the program, Hong developed two different sections of First Year Korean in 1985 to meet the pedagogical challenge of teaching students with a wide range of linguistic backgrounds. While a majority of the enrolled students were of Korean-American descent, there were also students who had minimal knowledge of Korean. Hong taught these students in a separate section. Hence, following Hong's proposal, by the spring of 1985 the department offered two sections of First Year Korean II: one for heritage and one for non-heritage students, in order to meet growing demand. Within only one year, the program grew quickly and proved its academic viability, and two sections of First Year Korean and one section of Second Year Korean were offered in the fall of 1985. Dr. Sunhae Hwang, a Ph.D. student in Educational Linguistics at the Graduate School of Education at Penn at the time, was hired as a second instructor to teach Korean. In 1986, when Hong returned to her appointment at Hanyang University, Dr. Hwang was repositioned as a full-time lecturer and taught Korean language courses until she returned to Korea in 1989 to accept a faculty position at Sookmyung Women's University. By 1989, thanks to Hong and Hwang's excellent

11 W. Allyn Ricket, Acting Chairman of the Department of Oriental Studies, Letter to the Dean of School of Arts and Science. February 15, 1985.

leadership and teaching, the Korean Language Program expanded to two sections for both the first- and second-year students. The enrollment was over 60[12] with about 15% of the student population being non-heritage learners.[13] Furthermore, this language level and experience-based system lasted until 1990, when the program was moved to the College of General Studies.

In the early 1990s, two important changes took place within the Department of Oriental Studies and the Korean Language Program. Firstly, there was a change in naming: The department, which dates back to 1910, was one of the first in the United States to offer courses in Asian topics and languages.[14] Over the years, the department developed an exceptionally wide reach, housing Asian and Middle Eastern languages such as Persian, Hindi, Turkish, Chinese, and Japanese as well as relevant discipline courses in the area of Middle Eastern and Asian languages and civilizations. However, as the term "Orient" originated in Western colonialism, by the late 1980s the department's official name had spurred a nationwide debate. After two years of heated discussions, the name "Orient" was finally changed to "Asian and Middle Eastern Studies" in the fall of 1991. The decision to change the department name was reported in *The New York Times*:

> The University of Pennsylvania's Oriental Studies Department will change its name this fall after a yearlong dispute over whether it is offensive to Asians, as some students have contended… Some students, largely members of the university's Asian community, assert that the current name is racist, connoting an exotic society whose people are submissive. (Campus Life: Pennsylvania; Oriental Studies To Be Renamed After Criticism, June 16, 1991)

---

12 Spring 1989 class enrollment data, *SAS Planning and Administrative Information System*.

13 Sunhye Hwang, email interview. April 14, 2012.

14 Penn to Rename "Oriental" Studies Dept. (1991, December 18). *Philadelphia Inquirer.* Retrieved from http://articles.philly.com/1991-12-18/news/25811476_1_asian-american-students-penn-faculty-asians-and-asian-americans

As for the Korean Language Program, Korean courses were removed from the Oriental Studies Department and alternatively housed in the Penn Language Center with other small language programs such as Persian, Arabic, Vietnamese, Turkish, and Cantonese in the fall of 1990.[15] The Penn Language Center (PLC) was established in 1989 as an administrative unit of the College of General Studies (CGS), which is the former name of the College of Liberal and Professional Studies (LPS). Over the years, the PLC has supported and housed lower-level courses for less commonly taught languages as well as content-based courses, such as business language courses for more commonly taught languages.[16] That is, while the Korean language courses were listed as "Oriental Studies" and then "Asian and then Middle Eastern Studies," until 2002 the Korean Language Program was housed in and funded by the PLC, which offered a Korean course as one of the CGS evening courses through the Language Center.[17]

Dr. Chang Bong Lee, who is currently Professor of English Language and Culture at Catholic University in Korea and was a Ph.D. student in Linguistics at Penn at the time, succeeded Mr. Jaehyun Lee, a graduate student at Penn, in 1991 and coordinated the Korean Language Program and several graduate student instructors until 1994. The program grew rapidly in terms of enrollment and class offerings. According to a review of the KLP conducted by Professor Kim-Renaud, the total enrollment in the spring of 1993 was an impressive 124 spread across a four-year curriculum, including courses in Business Korean.[18] The number of sections also increased to three sections of Elementary Korean and Intermediate Korean courses respectively. The program enjoyed a tremendous increase in enrollment in just four years; however, a key issue was that the program lacked a full-time specialist in language pedagogy,

15 Hiroko Sherry, personal interview. April 12, 2012.; *Penn University Course Catalog* spring 1991 & fall 2000.

16 Lada Vassilieva, personal interview. April 12, 2012.

17 Milan Hejtmanek. *Center for Korean Studies Annual Report*. AY 2002-03.

18 Young-Key Kim-Renaud (1993). *Review of the Korean Language Program at the University of Pennsylvania: March 16-18, 1993.*

a position vital for the development of a solid curriculum. Moreover, as non-heritage student rates had dropped from 15% to less than 5% of enrollment, the administration was concerned that the curriculum was designed mainly for heritage students.[19]

4. The Development of The Korean Language Program and The Rise of The Korean Studies (1994-2000)

In response to the pressing need for strong leadership, Ms. Youngro Yoon Song was appointed as Coordinator of the Korean Language Program around 1994.[20] She was the first officially-appointed full-time coordinator of the KLP who specialized in language teaching, and in 2000, she became the first Korean language lecturer who was promoted to a Lecturer in Foreign Language, a senior-level lectureship at Penn.[21] Song made a significant contribution not only to the improvement in the quality of teaching but also to the overall growth of the Korean Language Program at Penn. Under Dr. Song's directorship, the KLP curriculum was restructured and stabilized. The enrollment in Korean courses increased steadily, peaking at a total enrollment of about 250 students during the 1995-1996 and 1996-1997 academic years, making Korean one of the largest "less commonly taught" language courses in the Penn Language Center.[22]

Additionally, more sections were added to the first- and second-year Korean courses. In 1995, the Korean Language Program offered four sections of Elementary Korean, three sections of Intermediate Korean, and one section of Advanced Korean, as well as one section of Business Korean. Advanced Reading Modern Korea, which was a fifth-year level

19 Ibid.

20 *Report of Faculty Appointments and Promotions*. University of Pennsylvania Archives. June 1997.

21 *Report of Faculty Appointments and Promotions*. University of Pennsylvania Archives. June 2000.

22 Lada Vassileva, personal interview. April 12, 2012.

course, was added in the fall of 1997. New part-time instructors who specialized in language teaching were hired from relevant fields, such as the Department of Educational Linguistics and the Teaching English to Speakers of Other Language (TESOL) Program from the Graduate School of Education at Penn, as well as the TESOL Program at Temple University. By the fall of 2000, the program had maintained an enrollment of around 240 students and expanded Advanced Korean lectures to two sections. Within the PLC, the Korean Language Program stood as one of the strongest programs in terms of enrollment and curriculum, until the Korean Language Program was moved back to the Department of Asian and Middle Eastern Studies in 2002.

In addition to restructuring and standardizing the academic curriculum, Song was deeply involved in various cultural activities at Penn. She initiated and led several cultural events, such as Kimbap-making sessions,[23] and gave speeches on Korean language and culture, such as "The Interrelationship Between Korean Language and Culture (1994)."[24] Although there were minor increases in the enrollment of non-heritage students throughout the 1990s, the majority of language students were heritage students who gradually established stronger ties to Korea through the Korean language courses, and they formed an informal Korean cultural club within the program.[25] Song left Penn right after her promotion to the Lecturer in Foreign Language in 2000 due to personal reasons, and her sincere dedication to language teaching and to the KLP is still fondly remembered by many of her colleagues at Penn.

In the meantime, important events began to gain momentum in the mid-1990s and marked the beginning of a new chapter of the Korean studies and East Asian studies departments at Penn. First, Professor G. Cameron Hurst III (B.A. from Stanford in 1963, M.A. from the University of Hawaii in 1966, and Ph.D. from Columbia in 1972) joined Penn after working as a Professor of History and East Asian Studies as well as

---

23 Lada Vassilieva, personal interview. April 12, 2012.

24 *University of Pennsylvania Almanac,* Vol. 42 No. 25. (1996, March 26).

25 Seyung-gyu Jo, email interview. April 15, 2012.

being the Co-Director and Director of the Center for East Asian Studies at the University of Kansas from 1969 to 1995.[26] In September 1995, Dr. Hurst, Professor of Japanese and Korean Studies at the time, established the Center for East Asian Studies (CEAS) for the first time in Penn's history. The purpose of the center was to coordinate teaching methods and research efforts across different disciplines of East Asian studies and to promote the umbrella discipline at Penn. Hurst was appointed as the Director of the newly-launched CEAS at Penn and remained as the head of the Center until he resigned due to health problems in 2007. The subsequent expansion of the Center was enthusiastically welcomed by East Asian Studies professors and students alike. On February 28, 1996, *The Daily Pennsylvanian* cited several professors' comments and responses to the opening of the CEAS. For example, Dr. Nancy Steinhardt, Professor of East Asian Art History, was quoted as saying, "[T]he East Asian Center is the most exciting initiative in East Asian Studies at Penn since I have been here."[27]

It is necessary to give credit to both Professor Chong-Sik Lee and Professor Hurst for paving the way for Korean studies at the university. Although Lee was a Political Science professor, his work in pioneering the field at Penn was instrumental to launching the Korean studies program. Hurst, who officially founded the Program, was also critical to the expansion of Korean studies at Penn. Because Penn did not have enough faculty members to build the Korean studies program at that time, both Lee and Hurst actively sought external funding for endowed professorships of Korean studies. However, by the time Hurst came on board, Hilary Conroy of History Department, who taught East Asian history and Asian-American history, had already retired five years before, and Chong-Sik Lee, who taught East Asian politics for years, was about to retire soon. Furthermore, Cameron Hurst of the Asian and Middle

26 Profile of G. Cameron Hurst, III. (n.d.) In *Senior Fellow, Foreign Language Research Institute*. Retrieved October 20, 2014, from http://www.fpri.org/about/people/hurst.html . ; Paula Roberts, personal interview. April 9, 2012.

27 "Center offers East Asian resources." (February 28, 1996). Daily Pennsylvanian.

Eastern Studies Department mostly specialized in the pre-modern history of Japan, although he later expanded his research to include Korean history and eventually offered Korean history courses. Hence, by the close of the decade, an impending hiatus of faculty members in all areas of Korean studies was evident.

This urgent need to fill in these pending gaps in the Korean studies staff at Penn was understood by Penn alumni in Korea. The Penn Alumni Association of Korea worked hard to seek support and to raise funds from the Korea Foundation (KF). The alumni members who cooperated with the campaign included renowned scholars such as Professor Yun-sook Hong of Hanyang University, Professor Sunhae Hwang of Sookmyung Women's University, and Professor Kwanbong Kim of Kyunghee University as well as philanthropic entrepreneurs such as Mr. Byungchan Park, the president of Hwashin Co., and Mr. James Joojin Kim, the founder of Amkor Technology.[28]

In 1997, Mr. Jungwon Kim, Korea Foundation President, and Dr. Judith Rodin, President of the University of Pennsylvania, signed a historical agreement to commit five million dollars to finance the promotion of Korean studies at Penn.[29] *The University Almanac* on February 11, 1997 reported as follows:

> The Korea Foundation of Seoul and the University of Pennsylvania signed an agreement last week to commit $2.5 million each to create an endowment of Korea Foundation Professors in the School of Arts and Sciences.
>
> Funding will support the endowed professors' salaries, expenses for their academic activities, and other program elements such as visiting professors, graduate fellowships, academic research, conferences, seminars, and the expansion of the Korean collection in Van Pelt-Dietrich Library.
>
> One chair will be in the humanities, one in the social sciences; and if

28 Yunsook Hong, phone interview. April 14, 2012.

29 "Center offers East Asian resources." (February 28, 1996). Daily Pennsylvanian.

> possible, a third discipline will be determined at a later date, said President Judith Rodin, but Korea is to be the "primary focus of their academic research," she added. (Korean Studies: $5 Million for Chairs, 1997)

Penn and the local community enthusiastically welcomed the support of the Korea Foundation. At the signing ceremony, Major Ed Rendell declared February 5 to be "Jungwon Kim Day" to honor the Foundation's generous contribution to Penn.[30] In 1997, this endowment added to a strong momentum for the continued development of Korean studies at Penn, for Mr. Yong-Hak Park (Chairman of the Yangbak Foundation and Chairman Emeritus of Dainong Group in Seoul), had also established the Y.H. Park Fellowship to support graduate students' research in the humanities, social sciences, international studies, or fine arts within Korean studies in 1994.[31] Additionally, in 1997, Hurst gained the approval of the Dean to found and later head the Center for Korean Studies as an independent center, a directorship that Hurst would fill until 2000. After the minor program in Korean studies was achieved in late 1990s, the department began to search for and fill Korean faculty positions in order to expand the program's resources, establish a strong reputation within the discipline, and ultimately foster a full-scaled Korean studies program at Penn.

5. Building Stability (2000-2009)

The year 2002 marked another new era for the Korean Language Program. Since the KLP was already a complete language program by 2000, the Department of Asian and Middle Eastern Studies wanted the Korean Language Program returned to the department. Shortly after, through the leadership of Cameron Hurst and Victor Mair, all KLP courses (with

30 New grant to fund Korean Studies at U. (1997, February 5). *The Daily Pennsylvanian*.

31 Honors and Other Things. (2000, May 2). *University of Pennsylvania Almanac*, Vol. 46, No. 31.

the exception of Business Korean, which remained under the PLC) were successfully reestablished in the department on par with the Chinese and Japanese Language Programs in 2002. As Hurst's academic discipline was most closely related to Korean studies, Professor Hurst supervised the KLP. There was a similar transition in the leadership within language instruction as well: Dr. Sangkyung Han, once a Ph.D. student in Educational Linguistics at Penn and now Director of the Korean Language Program at the University of Michigan, became the Acting Coordinator of the Korean Language Program in 2000 after Song resigned from the position due to personal circumstances. In 2003, Han became the official Coordinator of the Korean Language Program and continued to strengthen the KLP's position within the department until 2008.

Han was known to be an extremely hard worker, doing his best to strengthen and stabilize the program. Under Han's leadership, the Korean program enjoyed another period of expansion, especially in the areas of upper-level curriculum and staffing. One of his biggest accomplishments was to establish and secure three full-time lecturer positions in Korean. In fact, until 2000, the program had only one full-time professional, and by necessity, many graduate student instructors served as the sole instructor for one or two courses. For example, six instructors taught twelve classes in the academic year of 2003-2004, and seven instructors taught the same number of classes in the academic year of 2004-2005. Even though these graduate student assistants devoted many hours to teaching, the deficiency of full-time teaching staff could not only negatively affect the instructional quality but also deter the development of curricula and the stability of the program in the long run. With the support of the department and the Center for Korean Studies, Ms. Insook Kang and Ms. Ju-Young Han were appointed as full-time Korean language lecturers in 2002 and 2005 respectively. Since then, the KLP has maintained three full time positions.[32] Another of Han's accomplishments was the expansion of the KLP curriculum to include multiple upper-level courses. A fourth-year Korean course, Current

32 *Instructional Research Query Database*. University of Pennsylvania.

Korean Media, was created in the fall semester of 2004. Additionally, in the fall of 2008, the curriculum in Business Korean was modified and divided into two different courses: Business Korean, a fourth year course, and Advanced Business Korean, a fifth year course, to better serve the needs of different students.[33]

In 2005, the program's umbrella organization, the Department of Asian and Middle Eastern Studies, was also divided into two distinct departments by geographic area: East Asian Languages and Civilizations (EALC) and Near Eastern Languages and Civilizations (NELC). Since then, the EALC department has housed three East Asian language programs: Chinese, Japanese, and Korean. After some adjustment in section numbers within lower-level coursework, in the fall 2008 semester, the Korean Language Program offered three sections of Elementary Korean and Intermediate Korean; two sections of Advanced Korean; one section each of two fourth year courses, Current Korean Media and Business Korean; and one section each of two fifth year courses, Advanced Reading Modern Korean and Advanced Business Korean.[34] The enrollment of the Korean Language Program stabilized to around 200 students per year. In terms of student composition, there was a notable increase in the enrollment of non-heritage students in Elementary Korean courses, reaching approximately 60-80% of the beginning level enrollments by the late 2000s.[35] In addition, thanks to Hurst's successful proposal, the Penn Korean Language Program was chosen to host the Critical Language Scholarship Program (CLSP), which was developed as part of the U.S. National Security Language Initiative.[36] The Program was held on the Suwon campus of Kyunghee University in the summers of 2007 to 2009. Through the program, twenty-five students traveled to Korea for the summer to study Korean language intensively, fully

33 Sangkyung Han, written interview. March 16, 2012.

34 *Instructional Research Query Database*. University of Pennsylvania.

35 Sangkyung Han, written interview. March 16, 2012.

36 Ibid.

covered by the CLSP scholarship each year.[37]

While the Korean Language Program was solidifying its curricula and staffing positions, the Korean studies program developed into a full-scale academic program as well. The Center for Korean Studies at Penn, which was established in 1997 to cultivate Korean studies research and education, gradually expanded to cover more specialized areas, thanks in great part to the 1997 KF endowment and matching funds from School of Arts and Science. First of all, two faculty positions in Korean studies were created and filled in the early 2000s. Dr. Milan Hejtmanek, who specialized in Chosôn period history from the fifteenth century to the eighteenth century, joined Penn's History Department as a Korea Foundation Assistant Professor of History in 2000. After completing his Ph.D. at Harvard University in 1994, Hejtmanek taught at the University of California, Berkeley from 1994 to 1995 and later at Harvard University from 1995 to 2000 before joining the department at Penn. During his time at the university, Dr. Hejtmanek enriched the Korean studies curriculum by adding several courses such as Seminars on Chosôn-period Social History, Divided Korea, and East Asian Economic History. He also co-taught a course on the Korean War with Dr. Cameron Hurst.[38] Moreover, Hejtmanek took over the directorship of the Center for Korean Studies from Hurst in 2000 and served until 2007.

After a two-year long search, Dr. Hyunjoon Park, currently a Korea Foundation Associate Professor of Sociology and Education, joined the Department of Sociology in 2005. He received his M.S. and Ph.D. from the University of Wisconsin-Madison in 2003 and 2005, respectively, and he currently teaches courses such as Social Issues in Contemporary Korea. Park served as the Director of the Center for Korean Studies during the 2008 to 2009 academic years. His recent publications include

37 More Options for an Asian Summer. (2007, March 21). *The Daily Pennsylvanian*. Retrieved from. http://thedp.com/index.php/article/2007/03/more_options_for_an_asian_summer

38 Faculty Bios. (n.d.) In *University of Pennsylvania's Center for the East Asian Studies*. Retrieved October 20, 2014, from http://ccat.sas.upenn.edu/ceas/bios-Hejtmanek.shtml

"Globalization, Changing Demographics, and Educational Challenges in East Asia," which he coauthored.[39] In addition, with support from Title VI NRC funds, Dr. Jina Kim was appointed to a three-year position in Korean language and literature in the Asian and Middle Eastern Studies department in the fall of 2004. She offered several courses such as Introduction to Pre-Modern Korean Literature, Screening Modern Korea, and Korean Popular Culture. The fact that Kim's film and popular culture classes attracted substantial enrollment was indicative of Penn students' growing interest in Korean culture.[40] However, these courses were discontinued after Dr. Kim left Penn for the faculty position in East Asian Studies at Smith College in 2007.

In summary, with the leadership of Hejtmanek (2000-2007) and Park (2008-2009), as well as the consistent support of Dr. Hurst, the Korean studies program expanded course listings, improved resources, and increased interdisciplinary collaboration with other academic units, such as the CEAS. First, new courses on a variety of disciplines within Korean studies were developed, adding greater depth and richness to Korean studies at Penn. These courses were related to topics in history (such as Divided Korea, Korean War, Korean History Before 1860, and Korean History After 1860), political science (Korean Political Economy), and sociology (Social Issues in Contemporary Korea and Social Stratification). In addition, Hejtmanek was actively involved in the acquisition and collection of Korean language books, gaining the support of librarian Alban Kojima, NRC funds, and the Van Pelt Library.[41] Furthermore, the new Korean Studies Lecture Series and Philip Jaisohn (Seo Jae-pil) Lecture Series were launched, and thus Penn hosted lectures by famous scholars and researchers on a diverse set of topics relating to the discipline. The Center also sponsored Korean studies events and exhibits, such as the annual Korean-American Women

39 Selected Publications. (n.d.) In *Hyunjoon Park's Homepage*. Retrieved October 20, 2014, from https://sites.google.com/site/hyjpark/home

40 SAS Korean Studies Program Report to The Korean Foundation. July 21, 2006.

41 Milan G. Hejtmanek. *Center for Korean Studies Annual Reports*, AY 2001-2005.

Conference, an exhibition of contemporary Korean architecture, and the "My Korean Mother" photojournalism exhibit.[42]

6. Modern Transitions (2009-Present)

The Korean Language Program experienced significant changes in leadership in the late 2000s and early 2010s once again. Dr. Sangkyung Han, the Director of the Korean Language Program from 2000 to 2008, left the university for a position at the University of Michigan in 2009. Ms. Insook Kang (M.A. in TESOL at Temple University), who began teaching Korean at the university part-time in 1995 and full-time after 2002, was promoted to a Lecturer in Foreign Language in 2008 and also appointed as the Director of the KLP. She headed the program from 2008 to 2011. She left Penn in 2012 and is now teaching Korean at San Diego State University and the University of California, San Diego. Additionally, Haewon Cho (M.A. in Linguistics and TESOL from the University of Washington in 2000 and 2004, respectively, and M.A. in Advertising from the University of Texas at Austin in 1993) joined the Korean Language Program at Penn in 2009 to replace Sangkyung Han's position, and she became Interim Director of the KLP in 2011 and has been serving as the director of the program since 2012. Cho previously taught Korean at the University of Washington and the University of Michigan, and she also co-authored the textbook series *You Speak Korean* with Dr. Soohee Kim and Dr. Emily Curtis from the University of Washington.

The Penn KLP experienced staffing changes as well. Ju-Young Han left Penn in 2007, and Dr. Ihnhee Kim, who got her Ed.D. in Teachers of English to Speakers of Other Languages (TESOL) at Temple University, was hired to replace Ju-Young Han's role in 2007 as a part-time instructor, and she became a full-time lecturer in 2008. Ihnhee Kim left Penn

42 SAS Korean Studies Program Report to the Korean Foundation. August 1, 2007..

in 2014 and now teaches at Northwestern University. Dr. Ji-Young Jung (Ed.D. Applied Linguistics, Teachers College, Columbia University) joined the program in 2012. Jung taught Korean at Rutgers University, New Brunswick and at the Korean Education Center of the Korean Consulate General of New York for three years before she came to Penn. She had also taught French and Korean at other institutions. Ms. Eunice Chung (M.A. TESOL, Teachers College, Columbia University) was the last member to join the Penn KLP team in 2014. She was a Korean lecturer at Boston University from 2012 to 2014 and also taught at Columbia University.

One notable and possibly positive change that happened during this period was that Penn started to hire lecturers through a national search process. It was only in 2009 that Penn conducted a national search to look for new hires in Korean studies. Although the best candidates could likely come from within local communities, as proven by former instructors at Penn, a national search introduced a wider pool of competent teachers nationwide. These new faculty members actively engaged in material development and research on language teaching and learning. Their publications included textbooks, journal articles, conference proceedings, and book reviews. They also participated and presented papers at a variety of nationwide conferences and forums. In addition, they contributed to the field of Korean language education in the United States in various ways. For example, Cho has been serving as an executive board member of the American Association of Teachers of Korean (AATK) and has been a key member of the Korean Honor Society Ad-Hoc Committee for secondary school Korean programs in the United States since 2012. Jung had worked as a key member in the online Korean course development project of the Korean Society, sponsored by Hyundai Kia Motors and the Korean Ministry of Education, Science, and Technology from 2011 to 2013. Kim has also worked as an editorial assistant of the journal *The Korean Language in America* since 2013. In addition, Cho and Jung have been members of the working group for the National Standard-based Curriculum for Korean, a collaborative project of seventeen-member task force and the

American Association of Teachers of Korean (AATK), and they have been working actively to construct a new standard-based curriculum for post-secondary Korean language education.

New directorships and members have brought noteworthy changes to the curriculum of the Korean Language Program and instruction at Penn. The following changes to the KLP have strengthened and improved the curriculum:

(1) A new curriculum map was developed to align the Program with the goals of foreign-language education, as outlined by the National Standards of Foreign Language Learning. In order to accomplish this task, the scope and sequence for each course were re-formed, new learning objectives and outcomes were proposed, and new teaching syllabi and evaluation schemes were implemented for Elementary, Intermediate, and Advanced Korean courses. The curricula for upper content-based courses were either restructured (e.g., Current Korean Media by Kim and Jung and Advanced Readings in Modern Korean by Jung) or redesigned in a structural sequence with specific subjects and topics (e.g., Business Korean and Advanced Business Korean by Cho). There were changes in class times and offerings as well. To enhance students' learning experience, Kang changed the course times of the Elementary and Intermediate Korean courses from two hours on two days of the week (a lingering tradition of the department's past years within the administration of the Penn Language Center) to one hour a day from Monday through Thursday, starting from 2010.

(2) A dual-track system was successfully launched in the 2013-2014 school year. As of fall 2014, Penn's KLP offers separate courses for heritage speakers and novice learners up to the second-year level Korean courses. Two new courses, KORN 131 and 132 (Korean for Heritage Learners I, II), were added to the curriculum, and Ji-Young Jung has been in charge of heritage-focused instruction at Penn.

(3) In addition to the heritage courses, a series of new courses were added to the curriculum, including Online Elementary Korean courses (KORN 011 and 012 summer online) and Business Communication in Korean (KORN 281). Online Elementary Korean courses were successfully launched during the summer of 2013 by Cho and Jung, and a total of fourteen students registered for these two courses, which attracted stu-

dents from Greater Philadelphia, Boston, San Francisco, Mississippi, as well as Hong Kong. Students who responded to the post-class survey appreciated spatial flexibility and were also very satisfied with the quality of instruction. A new upper-level course has also been introduced by Cho: Business Communication in Korean (KORN 281) is offered for the first time in the fall of 2014 for third-year level students. It is the first content-based course that integrates a particular subject area with the Korean language at the third-year level. With this course, Penn has a comprehensive business language course track, which comprises three levels of instruction from the third year to the fifth year.

(4) New online placement and proficiency tests were developed, and the new placement testing system was implemented in the fall of 2013. The system was completed with the use of pre-registration surveys and information testing on the newly constructed KLP website, launched in 2009 and revised in 2014. The new online placement and proficiency tests helped instructors make more accurate and reliable placement decisions.

(5) The KLP faculty members have diligently updated the curriculum to accommodate a diverse student body and changing curricular needs. A series of significant projects to enhance Korean language curriculum and teaching took place with the support of the Teaching Innovation Grants, sponsored by the Penn Language Center and the Kim Program Faculty Research Grant. The material development and research project include the following:

· Online Grammar Practice (Kang, 2008)
· Video Library and Online Exercises Using Video Clips (Cho, 2010-2011)
· Students' Self-Efficacy Survey (Cho, Kim, and Kang, 2011-2012)
· Cultural Literacy Practice through Folk Tales (Kim, 2012)
· Online Korean Language Placement Test I, II (Cho, 2012; Cho and Jung, 2013)
· Multimedia Course Materials to facilitate Beginner-Level Korean Learner's Pragmatic Competence (Jung and Cho, 2013)
· Teaching Materials for Business Communication in Korean (Cho, 2014)
· Flipped Class Materials on Canvas for an Online Elementary Korean (Cho and Jung, 2014)

In the late 2000s, there were many changes in leadership and staffing within the Center for Korean Studies as well as the EALC department. Unfortunately for the Korean and East Asian Studies centers, the EALC department, and the KLP, Dr. Hurst had to take leave from teaching due to personal health problems around 2007. Dr. Paul Goldin, Professor of Chinese Thoughts and Chair of the EALC department from 2007-2013, Dr. Nancy Steinhardt (Professor of East Asian Art and Chair of the department from 2013-present), and Dr. Linda Chance (Associate Professor of Japanese Studies and EALC Associate Chair then and since 2014) have together brought many insights and much assistance to the development of the KLP within the department since Professor Hurst took leave.Additionally, Dr. Frank Chance, a scholar of early modern Japanese art (M.A. in Asian Art History from the University of Kansas, Ph.D. in History of Art from the University of Washington in 1986), has served as the Associate Director of the Center for East Asian Studies since 2002, and he eventually took charge of the major and minor programs in East Asian Studies as well.

Moreover, the Center for Korean Studies and the CEAS lost the leadership of Dr. Hejtmanek, who left Penn to work at Sunggyunkwan University in Seoul, Korea in 2008 and later joined Seoul National University in 2009, becoming the first non-Korean citizen professor of Korean history at SNU. Filling in for Hejtmanek's position was Dr. Eugene Y. Park, a Korea Foundation Associate Professor of History, who joined Penn's History Department in 2009, and soon after became the Director of the Center for Korean Studies, following Hyunjoon Park in January 2010. Professor Eugene Park (M.A. in East Asian Regional Studies and Ph.D. in East Asian Languages and Civilizations in 1993 and 1999, respectively, from Harvard University) previously taught at the University of California, Irvine and is currently offering four courses: Korean History before 1864, Korean History after 1864, Readings in Korean History, and East Asia: Past and Present. Additionally, in 2007, he published his monograph, *Between Dreams and Reality: The Military Examination in Late Chosŏn Korea, 1600-1894*. Eugene Park's history courses, which are cross-listed between the History and

EALC departments, have seen a significant increase in the enrollment of non-heritage students.[43] Soon after he assumed the directorship of the Center for Korean Studies, the name change took place to the Korean Studies Program in the summer of 2010.[44]

Another significant moment for the program came in 2011, when the Center for Korean Studies received an additional six-million dollar gift from Mr. James Joo-Jin Kim. Mr. Kim, a Penn alumnus and the founding chairman of Amkor Technology Inc., a leading independent provider of semiconductors, has been a long-time advocate and supporter of the KLP and the Korean studies programs at Penn, and he is currently an emeritus member of the university's Board of Trustees.[45] Previously, Kim pledged large endowments not only for Korean Studies but also for the Department of Economics and the Wharton School, wherein the James Joo-Jin Kim Professorships in Economics and Business were established. Dr. Randall Wright was appointed as the first James Joo-Jin Kim Professor in the Department of Economics at Penn in 2005, and Dr. Kenneth Burdett was appointed in 2012. Professor Lawton R. Burns, Professor in health care management, is also a James Joo-Jin Kim Professor in the Wharton School.[46] In addition, the James J. Kim Trustee Scholarship was established for undergraduate students at Penn.

During a gathering of Penn alumni in Seoul in 2011, President Amy Gutmann enthusiastically announced Kim's generous gift to Korean Studies at Penn, saying, "Joo-Jin Kim's generosity allows us to significantly expand our Korean Studies Program, building on Penn's interdisciplinary strengths and focusing on Korea within a transnational,

---

43 Frank Chance, personal interview. March 12, 2012.

44 Eugene Park, email correspondence. May 10, 2012.

45 James Joo-Jin Kim Program in Korean Studies Homepage (n.d.) In *University of Pennsylvania.* Retrieved October 20, 2014, from http://www.sas.upenn.edu/koreanstudies/

46 Health Care Management Department Homepage. (n.d.) In *University of Pennsylvania.* Retrieved October 20, 2014, from http://hcmg.wharton.upenn.edu/people/faculty.cfm?id=1503

global context."[47] Thereafter, in early 2011, the Center for Korean Studies changed its name to the James Joo-Jin Kim Program in Korean Studies in his honor. In the same year, the Kim Program also received an anonymous gift of $1.5 million from the Moon family to support a Korean Studies postdoctoral fellowship.[48] Together, these gifts allowed the further development of Korean Studies under Park's leadership by allowing Penn to sponsor research efforts of faculty and graduate students, host several lecture series, and bring post-docs and visiting scholars from a variety of areas to Penn.

The Kim Program in Korean Studies also resumed the Penn in Seoul Program, which provides a unique opportunity for students to study and intern in Seoul, Korea. This program was first started in 1993[49] and revived in 2011. Since then, the Kim Program has been inviting about 15-25 students per year to take courses at SNU's International Summer Institute and to participate in the Penn-in-Seoul Internship Program with various Korean companies.[50] The Penn-in-Seoul Internship providers include Grand National Party, KPMG Korea, LG Fashion, Woori Investment and Securities, and Yes 24.

7. Korean Language Program — Current Status (Fall 2014)

Thanks to the dedication and commitment from former and present Korean instructors, the Korean Language Program at Penn stands

---

47 7.5 Million Gift for Korean Studies Program. (2011, July 12). *University of Pennsylvania Almanac*, Vol. 58, No. 01. Retrieved from http://thedp.com/index.php/article/2012/03/7.5_million_gift_to_enhance_penn039s_korean_studies_program

48 University of Pennsylvania Announces $7.5 Million Korean Studies Gift. (2011, May 23). *Penn News*. Retrieved from http://www.upenn.edu/pennnews/news/university-pennsylvania-announces-75-million-korean-studies-gift

49 SAS Korean Studies Program Report to the Korean Foundation. August 1, 2007.

50 Penn Visit to Seoul National University. (2011, May 3). *Meet President Gutmann*. Retrieved from http://www.upenn.edu/president/meet-president/penn-visit-seoul-national-university

stronger than ever. In the academic year of 2014-2015, the Penn KLP has three full-time Korean language lecturers, Haewon Cho, Eunice Chung and Ji-Young Jung, as well as one part-time instructor, Daniel Kim, who is assigned to the Advanced Business Korean course in the Korean Language Program. The courses offered as of the academic year of 2014-2015 are as follows:

Williams Hall

Course Number	Fall 2014	Spring 2015
KORN 011/012	Elementary Korean I (3)[a]	Elementary Korean II (3)
KORN 111/112	Intermediate Korean I (2)	Intermediate Korean II (2)
KORN 131/132	Korean for Heritage Speakers I (1)	Korean for Heritage Speakers II (1)
KORN 211/212	Advanced Korean I (1)	Advanced Korean II (1)
KORN 311/312[b]	Current Korean Media I (1)	Current Korean Media II (1)
KORN 431/ 432	Advanced Readings Modern Korean I (1)	Advanced Readings Modern Korean II (1)
KORN 281 [b]	Business Communication in Korean I (1)	
KORN 381/382 [b]		Business Korean I (1)
KORN 481/482 [b]	Advanced Business Korean I (1)	Advanced Business Korean II (1)

a The number in the parentheses show the number of sections

b Offered through the Penn Language Center

As shown above, upper-level content-based courses are offered through the Penn Language Center, while the rest of the courses are offered through the department. Currently, with the exception of the School of Engineering and Applied Science, three of the four colleges at Penn have a foreign language requirement for graduation. Both the School of Arts and Sciences and the Wharton School require proficiency in a foreign language equal to four semesters of language study.[51]

Perhaps one of the most unusual strengths that the Penn KLP possesses is its comprehensive course offerings and extensive use of available resources from the Penn Language Center. For lower levels, KLP offers a dual-track program up to the second year level to accommodate students' linguistic background and proficiency. The online summer courses for the beginning level with synchronous lesson delivery were also introduced in 2013, by adopting the model designed in 2009-2010 by Dr. Christina Frei, Executive Director of Language Instruction for the School of Arts and Sciences and the Academic Director of the Penn Language Center, and Dr. Ed Dixon, the Technical Director of the Penn Language Center. This model has been successfully implemented in Gaelic, German, Polish, Italian, Chinese, and Turkish. In addition to the program's provision of solid lower-level courses for novice and intermediate-level students, the KLP offers a variety of advanced courses, ranging from content-based courses such as Current Korean Media and Advanced Readings in Modern Korean to courses on language for specific purposes (LSP) such as Business Communication in Korean, Business Korean, and Advanced Business Korean. These content-based and LSP courses have been offered for over fifteen years: Business Korean was first taught as early as 1993, and Advanced Readings in Modern Korean was first offered in 1997. These courses not only offer students the opportunity to develop their Korean language skills at advanced and professional levels, but they also provide students with access to and knowledge of subject areas that are currently not covered

51 Loheyde, I. Kristin. (1993). "Foreign language teaching at the University of Pennsylvania: A language planning case study." *Working Papers in Educational Linguistics,* Vol. 9 No. 1, p. 105-126.

in the Korean studies curriculum at Penn. Consequently, these courses have been popular for those looking to develop functional ability in Korean that will be applicable to their careers. Students enrolled in Business Korean courses reported that they benefited from learning both advanced Korean language skills and Korean business knowledge, both of which will serve them well in their futures.[52]

As far as enrollment is concerned, the enrollment of the Korean language program has grown rapidly in recent years, reaching about 200-220 students per year. Those enrollments also include a few regional students in the Quaker Consortium, such as students of Bryn Mawr, Haverford, and Swarthmore colleges, in addition to Penn students. The recent trend in Korean language enrollment shows complete recovery from a dip in 2009-2012, when there were significant decreases in the enrollment of heritage students in the lower-level courses due to the implementation of the placement testing system. In particular, the Korean Language Program has enjoyed a sizable increase in the enrollment of non-heritage students, and the total enrollment in lower-level courses has increased rapidly. The enrollment of Elementary Korean I in the fall 2014 semester more than doubled that of the fall 2009 semester. Many non-heritage students are Asian-Americans from China or Southeast Asia, but an increasing share of students are coming from other ethnic backgrounds from all over the world, as both the "Korean Wave" and the nation's rapid economic growth have sparked rising interest in Korean culture. Furthermore, the continuation of Korean language education among non-heritage students beyond the first year level is becoming a growing trend, which has completely changed the landscape of the Korean Language Program at Penn. As of the 2014-2015 academic year, Elementary Korean, Intermediate and Advanced classes are comprised of mostly non-heritage students and a few Korean-American students who are truly novice learners.

In addition, more students have participated in short-term or semester-long study abroad sessions in Korea compared to a few years ago.

52 Course evaluations for KORN 381 and 382.

Many have participated in the Penn-In-Seoul program, and a sizable number of students have chosen to study Korean independently and at prestigious schools such as Seoul National University, Yonsei University, and Sogang University in Korea. Two graduate students have also studied Korean through the Foreign Language and Areas Studies Fellowship in Korea in the past two years.

Another positive trend observed recently is the increase in the number of students pursuing the study of Korean studies as well as the number of students studying the Korean language at Penn. In the academic year of 2013-2014, three students graduated with a minor in EALC with a Korean Studies concentration, and twelve students pursued a minor in a Korean Studies concentration. This is a remarkable figure, considering that in the past, only one or two students per year usually elected to graduate with a minor in Korean.

8. Outlook for The Future

The Penn Korean Language Program's highest priority has been to build upon the strong program of excellence it has achieved thus far and to further strengthen its curriculum to accommodate various needs and interests. The KLP has revamped its curriculum and defined "a scope and sequence of learning," which corresponds to the National Standards of Foreign Language Education as well as the changes in student composition and objectives. The restructured curricular map and heritage track are now successfully implemented and positively viewed by the students at Penn. Enrollment is steadily increasing, especially from the non-heritage population, and the Korean Language Program at Penn is in better shape in many ways than before.

The growing interest in the Korean language and culture has been a great boon to the development of Korean language education nationwide. In the current climate, the establishment of the Korean Studies major in the Department of East Asian Languages and Civilizations is particularly essential for further advancing the Korean Language

Program and Korean studies at Penn. Currently, the EALC department does not have any tenure-track faculty in Korean studies and offers only an EALC minor program in Korean Studies. Penn undergraduates who want to major in Korean Studies typically complete a major in East Asian Studies with a concentration in Korean Studies under Dr. Frank Chance's advising. This major program was established in the fall of 2003 and offered students courses in East Asian studies across disciplines such as social sciences, humanities, and legal studies.[53] Thus far, there have been only two Penn students to complete majors in Korean Studies, mostly due to the dearth of relevant coursework at Penn and the near impossibility of fulfilling requirements outside of studying in Korea and taking relevant courses abroad. The department has offered one-time courses occasionally, contingent upon the budget and available personnel. The Korean Popular Culture course, which was offered in the spring of 2013 by Dr. Matthew Schreibeis (Ph.D. in Music from the University of Pennsylvania), became an instant hit, attracting maximum numbers of enrollment, but it was not sustained due to budget problems. The establishment of the major and the addition of a Korean Studies professorship in the department would greatly contribute to the further advancement of the Korean Language Program and Korean studies at Penn.

As Korea gains more power and voice in the international community and global economy, and as Korean culture becomes increasingly influential beyond Asia, more students will become interested in the Korean Language Program and Korean studies at Penn. The Penn KLP will continue to explore better ways to provide quality instruction for students and will also seek opportunities for formal and informal collaborations with the EALC department, Penn Language Center, Kim Program of Korean Studies, and the Center for East Asian Studies to strengthen Korean studies at Penn.

53 Frank Chance, email correspondence. April 27, 2012.

ACKNOWLEDGEMENTS

Since the Korean Language Program and Korean Studies have been closely tied to each other in terms of their establishment and development, this report covers the history of Korean Studies as well as that of the Korean Language Program at Penn. This report was written based on personal, phone, and email interviews; annual program reports; program review reports; review of data from university catalogues and Institutional Research Query Database; articles from *University of Pennsylvania Almanac, Penn News, and Daily Pennsylvanian*; data from the University Archives; and other relevant materials.

I would like to sincerely thank the following interviewees for their time and valuable input (listed alphabetically by name):

- Frank Chance, Associate Director, Center for East Asian Studies (CEAS), University of Pennsylvania.
- Linda Chance, Associate Professor of Japanese Studies/Associate Chair of the Department of East Asian Languages and Cultures (EALC), University of Pennsylvania.
- Paul Goldin, Professor of Chinese Literature/Chair of the EALC, University of Pennsylvania.
- Peggy Guinan, Assistant to the Chair, EALC, University of Pennsylvania.
- Seung-Gyu Jo, Professor of Economics, Singapore National University.
- Sang Kyung Han, Director of the Korean Language Program, University of Michigan.
- William Hannas, Foreign Language Broadcast Information Service.
- Yunsook Hong, Professor Emeritus of Linguistics, Hanyang University.
- Sunhae Hwang, President, Sookmyung Women's University
- Ihnhee Kim, Assistant Professor of Instruction, WCAS Asian Languages & Cultures Department, Northwestern University
- Chong-Sik Lee, Professor Emeritus of Political Science, University of Pennsylvania.
- Victor H. Mair, Professor of Chinese Language and Literature, EALC, University of Pennsylvania.
- Diane Moderski, Administrator, Undergraduate Affairs, EALC, University of Pennsylvania.
- Eugene Y. Park, Korea Foundation Associate Professor of History/Director of James Joo-Jin Kim Program in Korean Studies, University of Pennsylvania.
- Paula Roberts, Associate Director for Administration, CEAS, University of Pennsylvania.
- Hiroko Sherry, Senior Lecturer/ Director of the Japanese Language Program, EALC, University of Pennsylvania.
- Lada Vassilieva, Administrative Director, Penn Language Center, University of Pennsylvania.

I also thank my student editors, Meghan Dickson and Rachel Lee, for all of their hard work. I would like to give special thanks to Dr. Hye-Sook Wang for initiating her project "Narrative History of Korean Programs in U.S. Colleges and Universities" and for providing me with such a wonderful opportunity to write about the history of the Korean Language Program at Penn. It has been an eye-opening experience for me, and I am truly grateful for this opportunity.

Finally, I would like to express my sincere gratitude to former and present colleagues of the Korean Language Program at Penn for their devotion and contribution (listed by the times of their appointments):

- **Directors/Coordinators**: Kijung Sohn (late 1970s or early 1980s), Yunsook Hong (1984-1985), Sunhae Hwang (1986-1989), Chang Bong Lee (1990-1994), Yongro Yoon Song (1994-2000), Sangkyung Han (2000-2008), Insook Kang (2008-2011), Haewon Cho (2011-present)
- **Full-time Lecturers**: Yongro Yoon Song (1994-2000, part-time/full-time), Sangkyung Han (1994-2009, part-time/full-time), Insook Kang (1995-2012, part-time/full-time), Ju-Young Han (2000-2007, part-time/full-time), Ihnhee Kim (2007-2014, part-time/full-time), Haewon Cho (2009-present, full-time), Ji-Young Jung (2012-present, full-time), Eunice Chung (2014-present, full-time)
- **Graduate Student Instructors/ Part-time Instructors**: Jaehyun Lee (1988-1989), Seungwon Yang (1989-1991), Chul-Hee Kang (1991), Seung-Gyu Jo (1991-1994), WonChul Park (1991-1992), Soohyun Hong (1991-1996), Jayhoon Lee (1991), Jae-Jung Suh (1993-1995), Yongsik D. Bong (1994-1994), Juran Yoon (1994-1995), Joon Jahng (1994-2004), Young-Han Song (1995), Byungseol Byun (1995-1996), Eundeog Hwang (1996-1998), Yong Un Ban (1996-2000), Haewon Kim (1998-2001), Mi Hyon Jeon (2000-2005), Woi-Sook Choi (2000-2003), Myungcheol Kim (2001-2002), Hyun-Sook Kang (2000-2001), Jiyoon Lee (2005-2008), Kyung Hee Lee (2008-2009), Tae-Eun Lee (2009), Naryang Kim (2009)
- **Business Korean/ Advanced Business Korean Instructors**: Seung-Gyu Jo (1995-2000), Edmund Lee (2000-2001), Nam Jae Kim (2001-2002), Wonho Choi (2002-2004), Jungbien Moon (2004-2006), Hong Chong Cho (2006-2008), James Lee Park (2008-2009), Jaesung Choi (2009). Dongho Song (2009), Jeoung Woo Hong (2010), Mee Ryung Song (2010-2011), Hyun Je Kim (2010-2011), Soojin Kim (2011), Sang Byung Seo (2012-2014), Daniel Kim (2014-present)

REFERENCES

7.5 Million Gift for Korean Studies Program. (2011, July 12). *University of Pennsylvania Almanac*, Vol. 58, No. 01. Retrieved from http://thedp.com/index.php/article/2012/03/7.5_million_gift_to_enhance_penn039s_korean_studies_program

Campus Life: Pennsylvania; Oriental Studies to be Renamed after Criticism. (1991, June 16). *The New York Times Archive*. Retrieved from http://www.nytimes.com/1991/06/16/nyregion/campus-life-pennsylvania-oriental-studies-to-be-renamed-after-criticism.html

Center offers East Asian resources. (1996, February 28). *Daily Pennsylvanian*.

East Asia Scholar Robert A. Scalapino dies at 92. (2011, November 4). *UC Berkeley News Center*. Retrieved from http://newscenter.berkeley.edu/2011/11/04/east-asia-scholar-robert-a-scalapino-dies-at-92/

Center for East Asian Studies Homepage. In University of Pennsylvania. Retrieved October 20, 2014, from http://ccat.sas.upenn.edu/ceas/bios-Hejtmanek.shtml

Health Care Management Department Homepage. (n.d.) In *University of Pennsylvania*. Retrieved October 20, 2014, from http://hcmg.wharton.upenn.edu/people/faculty.cfm?id=1503

Honors and Other Things. (2000, May 2). *University of Pennsylvania Almanac,* Vol. 46, No. 31.

James Joo-Jin Kim Program in Korean Studies Homepage. In *University of Pennsylvania*. Retrieved October 20, 2014, from http://www.sas.upenn.edu/koreanstudies/

Korean Studies: $5 Million for Chairs. (1997, February 11). *University of Pennsylvania Almanac,* Vol. 43, No. 21. Retrieved from http://www.upenn.edu/almanac/v43/n21/korean.html

Languages Offered. (n.d.) In *Penn Arts & Sciences*. Foreign Language Study. Retrieved from https://www.college.upenn.edu/language-study

Loheyde, I. Kristin. (1993). Foreign language teaching at the University of Pennsylvania: A language planning case study. *Working Papers in Educational Linguistics,* 9 (1), 105-126.

More Options for an Asian Summer. (2007, March 21). *The Daily Pennsylvanian*. Retrieved from. http://thedp.com/index.php/article/2007/03/more_options_for_an_asian_summer

New grant to fund Korean Studies at U. (1997, February 5). *The Daily Pennsylvanian.*Retrieved from http://www.thedp.com/article/1997/02/new_grant_to_fund_korean_studies_at_u.

Penn to Rename ‘Oriental’ Studies Dept. (1991, December 18). *Philadelphia Inquirer*. Retrieved from http://articles.philly.com/1991-12-18/news/25811476_1_asian-american-students-penn-faculty-asians-and-asian-americans

Penn Visit to Seoul National University. (2011, May 3). *Meet President Gutmann*. Retrieved from http://www.upenn.edu/president/meet-president/penn-visit-seoul-national-university

Profile of G. Cameron Hurst, III. (n.d.) In *Senior Fellow, Foreign Language Research Institute*. Retrieved October 20, 2014, from http://www.fpri.org/about/people/hurst.html

Selected Publications. (n.d.) In *Hyunjoon Park's Homepage*. Retrieved October 20, 2014, from https://sites.google.com/site/hyjpark/home

SNU Hires First Foreign Professor of Korean Studies. (2009, February 2). *Asian Correspondent.com* Retrieved from http://asiancorrespondent.com/23222/snu-hires-first-foreign-professor-of-korean-studies/

University of Pennsylvania Announces $7.5 Million Korean Studies Gift. (2011, May 23). *Penn News*. Retrieved from http://www.upenn.edu/pennnews/news/university-pennsylvania-announces-75-million-korean-studies-gift

The Korean Language Program at the University of Washington: Celebrating Its First Seventy Years

Soohee Kim
The University of Washington

1. Introduction

The year 2014 marked the seventieth year of official Korean language instruction at the University of Washington. With its humble yet critical beginning as a special war-time addition, the Korean language now serves many undergraduate majors and minors in one of the strongest and largest Korean programs in the nation. The program has withstood economic downturns and administrative whims for seventy years, and it has carved a definite place for itself in the field. In its most recent decade of vibrancy, it has produced thirteen Korean language majors and nineteen minors in a five year period (2007-2011), a notable accomplishment compared to a total of six majors in the previous twenty years (1987-2006).

Korean Language Program and East Asia Library in Gowen Hall, University of Washington

The term "Korean Program" at the University of Washington has been the source of confusion due to the dichotomous affiliations of the Korea Studies Program, which is housed in the Henry M. Jackson School of International Studies, and the Korean Language Program, which is in the Department of

Asian Languages and Literature. The program's history runs deep and dates back to the foundation of the Department of Oriental Studies (initially Oriental Subjects) in 1909. The first head of the department, Reverend Herbert H. Gowen (1864-1960), single-handedly taught a wide variety of courses, such as History of Japan, Literature of Persia, Semitic, Sanskrit, Hebrew, and History of Religion, creating a strong foothold in the department and connecting history to literature. After a couple of metamorphoses (as the Department of Far Eastern Studies in 1940, the Department of Far Eastern and Slavic Languages and Literature in 1949), the predecessor of the current department was divided into three entities in 1969: Department of Asian Languages and Literature, Department of Slavic Languages and Literature, and the School of International Studies, the latter of which was later renamed Henry M. Jackson School of International Studies. Since then, language, historical/textual linguistics, and literature courses have been offered by distinct language programs under the auspices of the Department of Asian Languages and Literature. Meanwhile, courses on history, politics, international relations, and others have been offered by the China, Japan, and Korea Studies Programs, which are housed in the Jackson School of International Studies. Since the late 1960s, the Department of Asian Languages and Literature (henceforth, Asian L&L) has provided language instruction in Thai and Hindi (1967-), Vietnamese (1981-), Indonesian (1991-),[1] in addition to its oldest member, Sanskrit, since the late 19th century.[2] Chinese (1926-), Japanese (1928-), and Korean (1944-) now account for the largest student enrollments in the department.

In 1944, the University of Washington (henceforth UW) made a special announcement that "it (except the Law School and the Hospital Division of the School of Nursing Education) had changed temporarily from the quarter to the semester system in order to meet the needs of

1 About. (n.d.) In *Asian Languages and Literature*. Retrieved November 2, 2014 from http://asian.washington.edu/about

2 Mongolian, which began its first classes in the early 1950s, and Tamil, which began with Hindi in 1967, are currently not being taught.

the Navy program,"[3] which started the Korean instruction in the then Department of Far Eastern Studies. Korean was included as one of the Far Eastern languages when an Army Specialized Training Program began at the University of Washington as World War II was nearing its end, initially arranged to provide one-year "proficiency training in the language and a solid background in the nation's socio-economic, historical, and geographical settings."[4] Korean language courses were first offered under rather inconsistent course numbers. The list of initially offered Korean courses included "184 Modern Korean History, 4 Korean Language Intensive A, 4-a Korean Language conversation, 5 Korean Language, 175 Korean language intensive C, 176, 177, 178 Advanced Korean Language,"[5] which were either intensive Korean language courses or general history courses. Although Korean language instruction began in 1943, it became available to civilians and was included in the UW catalogue the following year in 1944. Either way, the UW is veritably one of the oldest institutes, and purportedly the oldest institute, to begin offering the Korean language in the U.S., as evidenced by a collaborative letter signed by at least eighteen faculty members from wide-ranging disciplines such as Sociology, Romanic languages, Far Eastern, Germanics, Geography, Anthropology, History, and Political Science. The letter was a response to the University's apparent intent to desert the newly added Far Eastern offerings due to "housing" shortage issues after a year when the Army Special Training Program ended:

> With the teaching in Japanese, Korean, and Chinese languages and area studies, the University is now making a valuable contribution. *No other university in the country is teaching Korean*, and the number of universities capable of handling a Far Eastern program of this kind is limited. The

3 1944-1945 Catalogue of the University of Washington.

4 Hecker, Felicia J. International studies at the University of Washington: the first ninety years. (n.d.) In *The Henry M. Jackson School of International Studies*. Retrieved November 2, 2014 from http://jsis.washington.edu/jackson/history.shtml

5 1944-1945 Catalogue of the University of Washington.

> University could make a still larger contribution through an extension of the Far Eastern work and the addition of the European program which has been projected. While this work is of paramount importance to the country, it is also of permanent value to the University. The experience which we have gathered in the close cooperation between the various departments concerned and the training of the staff in new methods of teaching will be of lasting benefit to the institution.[6] [emphasis added]

The petition letter by the faculty seems to have been fruitful. George Taylor, then head of the Department of Far Eastern Studies, secured grants from the Rockefeller and Mellon Foundations, which helped the sustenance and expansion of the Korean program. Over the next 70 years, many Korea-related courses were offered, and various Korean faculty members joined the team, some of whom replacing previous positions.

Korean language instruction at the university is divided roughly into two periods: when it was part of the Far Eastern curriculum (before Asian L&L existed) and after the establishment of the Department of Asian L&L.[7] By the time the division occurred, the Korean B.A. degree was solidly in place with literature to support history and social science studies, and the divorce took a great toll on faculty and on both programs over the years.

2. Launching — Harold Sunoo: 1943-1948

Harold Hak Won Sunoo joined the Far Eastern Department in 1943 with an A.B. from Pasadena College to teach the one-year Army Specialized Training Program. Harold Sunoo was hired to teach both Korean

6 Letter to President L.P. Sieg. George Edward Taylor Papers. Special Collections, University of Washington Libraries, Seattle, Washington. (George Edward Taylor was a Professor of Far Eastern History and Politics and Executive Officer of the Department of Far Eastern and Slavic Languages and Literature; he also served as the Director of the Far Eastern and Russian Institute.)

7 There were, however, interims and chapters within each period revolving around the individual researchers and teachers of the time.

and Chinese[8] in the department, and he became responsible for most Korean instruction when the army program ended.

Harold Sunoo

Sunoo was born in Pyongyang in 1938 and came to the U.S. to meet his grandfather, who had come to the States in 1904. At Berkeley, he was an Associate in Japanese and Korean languages, and he was also an employee of the F.B.I. in Los Angeles as a Japanese interpreter as well as a translator in the United States Court of Northern California, Southern Division.[9] For some Korean courses, "staff" was listed as the instructor, which might have indicated Helena Sonia Sunoo, Harold Sunoo's wife, who was a 1937 graduate of San Francisco State College and employed as an acting associate in the Far Eastern Department.

Korean Grammar Textbook by Harold Sunoo

The numbering for the newly added courses was still haphazard, as 42 Korean Civilization and 184 Modern Korean History demonstrate. Most Korean civilization and history courses were also taught by Sunoo. During his tutelage, the Korean major for undergraduate students was established in 1947, and the Korean courses were thus renumbered. The original intensive courses stayed, but new courses were added at the 100 level. Sunoo taught intensive language courses using his own textbook. As for Korean history, in addition to one course created in the previous year (184 Modern Korean History), three more courses were added: 42 Korean Civilization, 92 History of Korea, and 90 History of China. History

8 Such was the claim made by Franz Michael, but when Chinese language was first offered, along with Korean and Japanese, there were two instructors listed for the language: Tweddell, and Ch'eh. Michael might have meant Classical Chinese used in Korean; otherwise, Sunoo also taught Chinese to meet the growing needs of the Chinese program.

9 Franz Michael to Charles S. Hyneman.

of China was described as a "survey of China's history from the earliest times to the present, with emphasis on the development of Korean society." Therefore, students who specialized in Chinese could receive credit as well, initiating a deep-rooted connection between Korea and China curricula at UW. The Korean history survey course was occasionally taught by Frank Goodman Williston, a Wesleyan graduate with a Ph.D. degree from University of Chicago, who joined the Department of Far Eastern Studies in 1943 as an Acting Associate Professor. Williston was a specialist in Far Eastern affairs, particularly regarding Japan and China, and he soon became an exclusive expert in Korea at a time when no one else in the department knew where Korea was.[10]

By 1948, Williston took over and was teaching all Korean history courses, when another teaching associate, Kyung-sun Lee with a B.A. from Korea, joined the department to teach the Korean language, foreshadowing the exit of Sunoo. The shared teaching arrangement between Williston and Sunoo might have resulted in an unintended comparison by students, as one of Franz's[11] letters noted trouble in Sunoo's teachings. Perhaps.

> In 1949, the Board of Regents of the University of Washington fired three tenured professors for their political views: two because they initially denied and then later admitted membership in the Communist Party, and one — Ralph Grundlach, a national figure in the discipline of psychology — who was not a Party member but a radical who was uncooperative with University and state legislature inquiries. Ellen Schrecker wrote that this decision "had nationwide repercussions," not only as the first important academic freedom case in the cold war period but one that also established a model for purges at many universities thereafter⋯. In case of particular interest to the Korean field at UW (an area it has

---

10 David P. Mesler. Dedication to Professor Frank G. Williston. *Journal of Korea Studies*. Volume I No. 2. 1971.

11 Acting Executive Officer of the Department of the Far Eastern Studies, filling in for George Taylor during his absence in 1942-1945. Michael, a German resident alien, pioneered an Army Specialized Training Program in the Department of Far Eastern Studies, and "his loyalty to the American cause was substantiated."

> specialized in since 1945), Allen[12] told the FBI that "although Harold Sunoo appeared to be an innocent dupe of the Party…"[13]

It was the brutal McCarthy era after all. By the time he was finished at the department in 1949, Sunoo had received his M.A. from UW. He went to Prague and received a Ph.D. the next year from the National University of Czechoslovakia in 1950. He has since been in the U.S. as a productive writer and an active advocate of the unification of the two Koreas.

3. In Transit — First Interim Years: 1948-1955

During the next several years, until the arrival of Doo Soo Suh in 1955, Teaching Associate Kyung-sun Lee and Acting Korean Instructor Chang Hei Lee[14] taught all of the Korean courses for the Department of Far Eastern Studies. An array of Eastern Art and Oriental Ceramic Art courses that focused on "Chinese, Korean, and Japanese ceramics from Neolithic times to the present" were added around this time, taught by "Lee," presumably one of the Korean instructors. In 1950, there was a sweeping restructuring of courses by the university, and courses such as Korean Civilization began to be taught for three instead of its initial five credits. The Korean major upgraded the numbers from 104 Korean to 304, 106 Korean to 406, and 92 History to 292 and so forth, with some of them to be counted as graduate credits for both students and faculty alike. Korean language courses remained five credits, and 499 Undergraduate Research was created for three to five and a maximum of fifteen credits. In 1953, Korean veterans started to receive special allowance, but they had to pay their own tuition and fees, which was $25 for residents and $75 for non-residents per quarter at that time. Married

12 The then head of the Department of Far Eastern Studies, who returned from his war time duty in Washington D.C.

13 Cumings, Bruce. *Parallax visions: making sense of American-East Asian relations*. (Durham: Duke University Press, 1999).

14 "Acting Korean instructor" might have meant graduate student then.

students who were veterans of World War II or the Korean conflict were allowed to apply for accommodations in Union Bay Village, the university's family housing project, but students were warned not to rely on immediate housing because of a long waiting list.

Chang Hei Lee, a graduate of Yonsei University, had taught in Korea for three years before coming to San Francisco in 1930 for his education. Initially, he picked peaches and grapes in the farmlands to earn money for travel and tuition, while teaching Korean to first-generation Koreans. He also taught Japanese to university students in California and worked as a translator for the U.S. Overseas Secret Service during World War II, before coming to teach Korean at UW. He had three degrees by then.[15] Lee later became a chemist for the Boeing Company. He was quite productive with his textbook writing during his employment at the university as an acting instructor and published several Korean textbooks, including *Practical Korean Grammar* (1955) and *A First Course in the Korean Language* (1965), which started a long tradition at UW of producing teaching and learning materials for non-heritage learners of the Korean language. Lee also founded Seattle's first Korean church in 1962 and became the first president of the Seattle-Washington Korean Association in 1967. Lee and his wife Kannan Kim ("Mrs. Lee") were considered the "first couple" of the local Korean community.[16] Kannan Kim had attended Ewha University, Korea's first women's university in Seoul, and she started working for the Boeing Company when her husband started there. She began in 1963 as a seamstress, sewing upholstery for the interior of planes. After her husband's death, when her two published memoirs brought in $9,000, she used the proceeds to fund

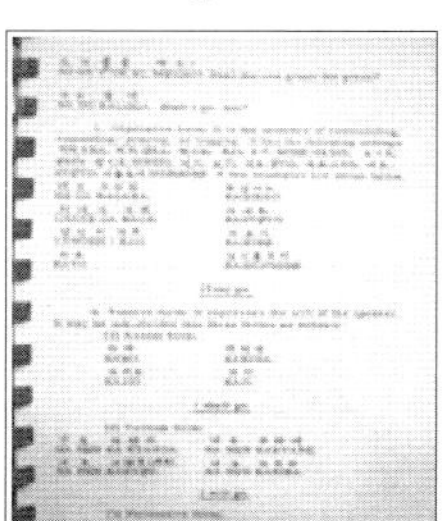

Practical Korean Grammar by Chang Hei Lee

15 Yu, Daeshik. (1983). A Call for the Formation of a Historical Society of Koreans in Washington State. In *Korean American Historical Society*. Retrieved from http://www.kahs.org/history_1.html

16 The two could, of course, not have been the literal "first couple," because according to the 1920 Census, Koreans living in Seattle had grown to thirty-seven.

college scholarships for Korean students.[17] Kim also co-founded the Korean Community Counseling Center and the Korean Language School in 1983 and volunteered at the center until her death in 2004.

4. Smooth Sailing — Doo Soo Suh: 1955-1964

Doo Soo Suh

More people, army men and civilians alike, had seen and heard about Korea by the time the Korean War had ended. Unsurprisingly, Korean Dance and Intermediate Korean Dance courses began being offered for Men's and Women's Physical Education in 1964, and new courses continued to be added to the Korean curriculum after Doo Soo Suh arrived as a Visiting Lecturer in 1955. Doo Soo Suh had received a Bungakushi (M.A. equivalent) in Korean Literature from Keijo Imperial University in Seoul, Korea in 1930, and he completed a Ph.D. program at Columbia University from 1949-52. Upon his arrival, Suh added a barrage of literature courses: 320 Korean Literature in English, which surveys the historical development of Korean literature with an emphasis on the relationship of Korean literature with Chinese and Japanese literature; 501, 502, 503 Korean Seminar; 512, 513, 514 Readings in Korean Documents; 512 Korean Bibliography and References. It appears that he taught all of these courses by himself at least for a decade. He also taught a specially arranged Intensive Japanese class for Chinese-major students.

Suh is fondly remembered by his students and colleagues for his depth and breadth of knowledge in Korean literature, Japanese litera-

17 Merlino, Doug. (2004, June 13). Gloria K. Lee, pioneer among Seattle Koreans, dies at 87. *The Seattle Times*. Retrieved from http://seattletimes.com/html/obituaries/2001955021_leeobit13m.html. Kim went the extra mile to create a Korean community and make newcomers feel welcome; she would go to the airport to greet them and make them meals. For Korean sailors at the Port of Seattle, she would gather a contingent of local Koreans to brew Kimchi and arrange a picnic on the waterfront for them.

ture, and classical Chinese. By the time he came to UW, Suh was a seasoned teacher with a decade of experience as Professor of Japanese literature at Ewha Womans College (now University) (1936-44) and Professor of Korean Literature at Chosun Christian University (now Yonsei University) (1945-1949). Suh also taught for three years as a Visiting Lecturer at Harvard University (1952-55), where he was the first to teach the Korean language and initiated the Korean Studies Program there. Notably, as he was born in the era of Japanese colonial rule, Suh was a native Japanese speaker but was weak in spoken Korean. Students protested at Yonsei University, where he was once a Dean, about his Korean proficiency.[18] He was also rather traditional in his manners, making students bow as he entered the classroom. He gave one-way lectures but was very effective in his teaching, enabling his Chinese students to read Japanese scholarly work on Chinese literature after one year of intensive study; they could thus integrate three languages — English, Chinese, and Japanese — into their research.[19]

In 1965, Dong-A Publishing Company published Suh's *Literary Reader*, which was a 908-page compilation of existing Korean texts put together for teaching purposes. Despite his long-term dedication to training graduate students in Korean literature as a founding father of Korea studies, Suh was never appointed as ladder faculty. Suh's position turned from Visiting Lecturer to Lecturer in 1964, when Fred Lukoff arrived and set a different course from his contemporary Peter Lee, a U.S.-educated scholar, who would produce generations of intellectuals and become the central figure of the Center for Korean Studies at UCLA, the biggest Korean studies program in the continental U.S.[20]

18 Interview with Clark Sorensen.

19 Interview with Taiping Chang.

20 Kim, Keong-il. (2004). *Pioneers of Korean Studies*. Gyeonggi-do (Korea): The Academy of Korean Studies.

5. Respective Paddling In Stormy Seas, Still Getting Somewhere: 1964-1977

Korean Literary Reader by Doosoo Suh

A shift of focus toward the linguistic structure in the study of Korean was on the horizon, anticipating the departmental division in 1969. Many courses were added temporarily, possibly to help the current graduate students finish their work. While newly hired Korean linguist Lukoff was reconfiguring and teaching language courses, history and linguistics courses were taught by visiting scholars. Comparative Korean Linguistics (on Korean dialects and tonetic relationships in Korean) was offered only in 1966-67 by lecturer Maeng-sung Lee, a Korean linguist who was hired for the year.[21] Lee also taught Linguistic Analysis of Middle Korean Texts (on Middle Korean literature from the twelfth through the fifteenth century) that same year. A visitor named Koh (1967-69) taught Korean history courses: 469, 470 History of Korea (a survey of Korean history from earliest times to the modern period), in addition to 567, 568, 569 Seminar in Korean History (selected topics in Korean history and historiography). As he was serving graduate students' needs, Suh taught literature courses for just one year or for alternating years: 521, 522, 523 Modern Korean Literature; 531, 532, 533 Classical Korean Literature (in Hangul up to the twentieth century); 541, 542, 543 Readings in Hanmun Texts (Readings from the 15th to the late 19th C); and 550, 551, 552 Seminar in Korean Literature. In his literature reading courses, Suh used his own book *Korean Literary Reader*, which consisted of an impressive compilation of older Korean poetry, dramas, short stories and even *p'ansori*; texts ranged from *Kumo Sinhwa* to *Hyangga* to *Kuunmong* to short stories published up to 1945. His compilation lacked original interpretations of the texts but certainly served the needs of the time, when Korean literature was barely known

21 Lee was Lukoff's student at the Seoul National University of Education and was invited to be Lecturer while he was writing his dissertation under Zellig Harris at the University of Pennsylvania.

to Americans. The book began with a 115-page "short history of Korean literature" in English. For Hanmun classes, he used Yonsei University's *Daehak Hanmun* textbooks. Suh officially belonged to the Department of Asian L&L, but he still remained affiliated as faculty for the Korean Regional Studies M.A. Program, an interdisciplinary graduate degree program created in 1969. Donald C. Hellmann was the chair of Asian Studies in Jackson School at the time.

James Palais

Along with Lukoff and Suh, James B. Palais was another main faculty member in the Korean Regional Studies Program. After receiving his education from Yale (M.A. 1960) and Harvard (B.A. 1955, Ph.D. 1968), Palais was appointed in 1968 to the Russian and Far East Institute (now Jackson School of International Studies) as Professor in Korean history and later jointly appointed in the History Department. The Korea program thus had three faculty lines: two in Asian Languages and Literatures (Lukoff and Suh) and one in History (James Palais), making it the largest Korea program on the North American mainland at that time,[22] when "most universities with generally good programs in Chinese and Japanese studies made no effort to expand into Korean studies."[23] Upon joining the faculty, Palais drastically changed the course of the Korean history offerings with his scholarship. Regarded as one of the most distinguished scholars in the field, Palais trained and produced a great number of influential Korean historians and politicians in the U.S. and in Korea until his retirement in 2001.[24] Among

22 Sorensen, Clark. History of the Korea Studies Program at the University of Washington. (n.d.) In the *Paull* [sic] *Shin Korea Studies Program and Center for Korea Studies*. Retrieved November 2, 2014 from http://jsis.washington.edu/korea/koreahistory.shtml

23 Interview with Gari K. Ledyard by Charles Armstrong, as appeared in *Pioneers of Korean Studies*. Ibid.

24 Paull Shin (Washington State Senator), Hongkoo Han (Sungkonghoe U), William Donald Smith (government service), Chung Shin Park (Sungsil U), Don Baker (UBC), Kye Seungbum (Sogang U), Son Cheolbae (Sungkyunkwan U), John Duncan (UCLA), Sunjoo Kim (Harvard U), Michael Robinson (Indiana U), Carter Eckert (Harvard), Mark Caprio (Rikkyo U), Michael Allen (Brigham

his students are Bruce Cumings[25] and Hwasook Nam, both of whom later joined the UW Korea Studies Program. Palais also published Occasional Papers on Korea from 1974 to 1977 and the Journal of Korean Studies from 1979 to 1984. He taught all of the new undergraduate history courses, including HSTAS 481 (History of Traditional Korea: Earliest Times to the Nineteenth Century) and HSTAS 482 (History of Modern Korea: 1860 to the present). He also taught HSTAS 582, 583, 584 on Korean History Research (a year-long graduate seminar). Stanford graduate George Beckmann also joined in 1969 as a Professor of East Asian Studies. Beckman was a specialist in Japanese history and later became the director of the Far Eastern-Russian Institute. He helped promote Korean studies, supporting the hiring of Bruce Cumings to fill Suh's position following Suh's retirement.

Protesters demand retention of Korean Lit

The Daily

The Korea(n) program was growing, as it added faculty and courses, becoming more nationally prominent with renowned scholars. Unfortunately, headlines such as "The Korean Program is dissolving!" appeared after the administration's devastating decision not to replace Suh in 1977. Suh's retirement was a blow to both the Korea and Korean programs. Suh had contributed to the program, especially in Classical Korean Literature, for more than two decades (1955-77). Palais, a historian, was an avid proponent of Sino-Korean training, for which Suh had been happily responsible, while his counterpart Lukoff was more interested in modern comparative and structural aspects of Korean and language in general. Lukoff took charge of the Korean Language Program in the Department of

Young University Hawaii campus). Sunhee Yun (Loyola Marymount U), Hwasook Nam (UW), Joshua Van Lieu (LaGrange College) are some of the active scholarly disciples of Palais. Although their majors were different, these two also received Palai's training: Giwook Shin (Stanford U), Clark Sorensen (UW).

25 Bruce Cumings was the only student in the beginning Korean summer courses that Palais taught at Columbia in 1968.

Asian Languages and Literature and built the program in his own vision, but he did a wonderful job. Lukoff saw the change in the wind, and indeed, Chinese characters started dropping out of use in most Korean newspapers and publications by the mid-to-late 1980's.[26]

Was there another literature professor to be hired in Suh's place? As luck would have it, another brilliant historian joined the program to strengthen it even further. The fact that there was no graduate program in Korean Literature was a deciding factor for the hiring of Columbia University graduate Bruce Cumings in 1977.

The Korean community took the loss of the Korean literature position hard, although it was converted into a Korean history faculty position.

> … The University of Washington is one of the few academic institutions in America where both doctoral and master's degrees are conferred in Korean studies. Should the position in Korean literature be discontinued, however, the University can no longer offer Ph.D. or M.A. programs in Korean studies; for, without courses in Korean literature, neither the programs in Korean history nor Korean language programs will be complete…[27]
>
> It would be fatal to the Korean program at the University of Washington if someone who lacks scholarly knowledge of Hanmun and classical Korean literature were to be hired. For this reason, I sincerely hope that you will seek every possible avenue, including advertisements in Korea and Japan, for such candidates. An eminent scholar such as Kim Sa-yop, who is currently teaching Korean language and literature in a university in Tokyo, would be a likely candidate to replace Professor Suh…[28]

26 The 1970 Hangul Only Policy was put in effect during President Park's term, and by the late 1980s, most major newspapers in Korea had stopped using Chinese characters or mixed scripts. Sorensen, the Director of the Korea Studies Center, recalls having to re-learn basic Korean vocabulary when Sino-Korean fell out of use in the 1970s.

27 Letter to President John Hogness, The Washington State Korean Student Association. April 19, 1977.

28 Letter to Turrell V. Wylie then Chairman of the Department of Asian Languages and Literature from Ki Chung Kim, Associate Professor of San Jose State University. March 19, 1977; another letter to Wylie from Professor of Korean History at the University of Hawaii. April 4, 1977; yet another letter from Jongsun Kim, Professor

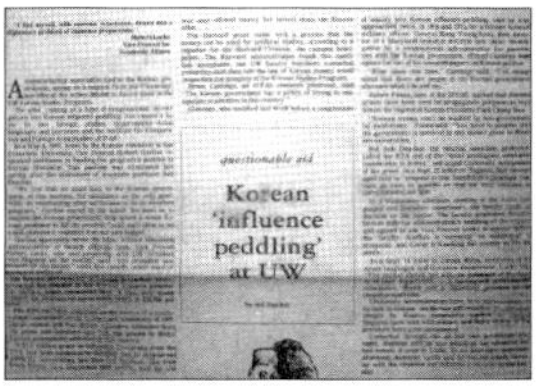
questionable aid
Korean 'influence peddling' at UW

Daily
Hogness refuses Korean aid

There were student protests, petition signings, headlines,[29] and letters requesting a replacement in Korean Literature. The situation became even more complicated when the emeritus Suh told the administration that the Korean Traders Scholarship Foundation wanted to donate an astronomical $60,000 for his replacement. P.J. Koh, a former Lieutenant Governor of the Bank of (South) Korea, had visited the UW campus on September 12th in the previous year in response to the letter written by Vice Provost Robert Garfias to the Korean Consul General in San Francisco as a representative of the Korean Traders Scholarship.[30] Special meetings were held about the matter, as many faculty members were suspicious of the Korean government's intentions. The South Korean government had issued the Emergency Yusin Martial Law in 1972, and the country had been in a full-fledged authoritarianism. Despite the desperate need for literature faculty, Palais most fiercely opposed receiving money from "Park's military regime."[31] Lukoff was not

---

of East Asian History at the University of Rhode Island, dated the same day.

29 Koreans fight to retain professor's position. (1977, April 15). *The Columbia Daily Spectator*.
Protesters demand retention of Korean Lit. (1977, May 17). *The Columbia Daily Spectator*.
Korean students protest staff decision. (1977, May 17). *The Seattle Times*.
Korean Lit Position Frozen. (1977, May 19 and 1977, May 24). *Korea Daily*.

30 Suh to President John R. Hogness, September 22, 1977. More letters by Suh on September 27, 1977 to Hogness and Wylie. Related letter by Hubert G. Locke Vice Provost for Academic Affairs to Turrell Wylie on the same day.

31 Palais later had run-ins with the Korean Consul General in Seattle in the early 1980s. When he and Bruce Cumings showed a North Korean movie on the campus, the Korean Consul General held a party inviting Korean students to prevent them from seeing the film; at least such was the claim by Palais. A quarter century later, when another upheaval erupted regarding the lack of a replacement after his retirement, Palais would request Korea Foundation's support for the Korean studies program at UW, saying that maintaining the program's position as a core center of Korea studies in the U.S. was much more important than his personal

as certain about a flat refusal of the offer, but in the end, the faculty voted unanimously to reject the offer. President John Hogness announced that the refusal of the offer because he was "candidly uncertain of our ability to make a long-term commitment to graduate studies in Korean Languages,"[32] a decision called "a diplomacy problem of immense proportions" by Hubert Locke, then Vice Provost for Academic Affairs.[33] Many more protests and newspaper headlines followed. Technically, however, a literature position in the Department of Asian Languages and Literature was retitled as a history position in the Jackson School of International Studies. This tug of war would haunt the program for generations to come and reappear in the form of linguistics and literature. The letters and petitions would continue until deep into the 1980s.

Nonetheless, the Korea-related programs managed to continue their growth and expansion. The state government was relatively more functional in the 1960s, and the university was able to secure many positions in the Korea and Korean Programs. Cumings was hired following his Ph.D. from Columbia University in 1977. With Palais and Cumings, the UW Korea Studies further concretized its reputation as one of the most competitive Korean studies programs in the nation. Cumings' teaching load was minimal, however, possibly because he was classified as a Research Assistant Professor of East Asian Studies specializing in Korea. Starting in 1982, he co-taught with Palais SISEA 439 Politics of Korea, which was jointly offered as POL S 439. The course was on "Korean politics in the twentieth century, treating political legacy of ancient regime, colonial period, Korean War, and the politics of North and South Korea." Cumings also taught SIS 455 Industry & the State for a year or two until his departure in 1988, and his position was filled by Clark Sorensen in 1989.

The Korean library collection also grew tremendously. In 1969, Yoon-

stance. *Pioneers of Korean Studies.*

32 CU-Korean funding talks resume. (1977, October 5). *The Columbia Daily Spectator.*

33 Korean 'influence peddling' at UW. (1977, September 30). *The Columbia Daily Spectator.*

whan Choi[34] was hired as a Korean studies librarian. Choi had graduated from Seoul National University with a B.A. in Chinese Language and Literature in 1962 and went on to receive a M.L.S. in Library Science in 1969 from Kent State University. In conjunction with Suh and Palais, Choi played a significant role in building the Korean collection, which some perceive to be more important than that of the Harvard-Yenching Institute. The collection is especially strong in pre-modern Korean history, modern social science, and Korean poetry. Sammy Edward Solberg also contributed to the collection; he was a research fellow while working towards his doctorate in comparative literature. Upon receiving his Ph.D. in 1973, he served as assistant to the Director of the Institute at the then Comparative and Foreign Area Studies (now the Henry M. Jackson School of International Studies) from 1973-74. The following year, he was appointed to a part-time faculty position in the American Ethnic Studies and Comparative Literature Departments, where he remained affiliated with UW for 30 years. Solberg wrote an official letter of recommendation for the promotion of Choi.

6. Sailing Steadfast in A Lull — Fred Lukoff: 1977-1989

That a winged genius take up aquatics and swim across the sea was the demand the administration made, placing Fred Lukoff in a department with an unbreakable bond with history and social sciences. The discipline-internal break from the philological tradition of linguistics added fuel to the flame. Reverend Gowen was a man who could teach about Japan, Persia, Sanskrit, and Hebrew, in terms of both the languages and histories. Likewise, Fred Lukoff could have taught Korean, Yiddish,[35] German, Classical Hebrew, and their comparative linguistic structures and histories equally well. He would have been a perfect fit for linguistics, but the Department of Linguistics had only been founded in 1962, with Sol Saporta as its first chair, and no one was full-

34 Also, more recently, known as "Choe."

35 Lukoff in fact gave informal classes in Yiddish for students in the department.

time in linguistics at that time. Even Saporta had a split appointment in Romance languages, and all other members came from Germanic, Anthropology, and Asian Languages.[36] Lukoff tried to meet the needs of the Jackson School of International Studies (JSIS) and his home department of Asian L&L with the creation of reading courses in literary, social, and political areas: KOR 311, 312, 313 Introduction to Korean Writing in Mixed Script, KOR 415 Reading in the Writings of North Korea (later changed to Social Science Literature in Korean), KOR 416 Readings in Korean Narrative and Dramatic Literature, KOR 417 Readings in Korean Journals. He also created and taught a linguistics course series KOR 501-502-503 Seminar in Korean Linguistics, from which many graduate students in the Department of Linguistics benefited. Lukoff, in fact, seemed to have had a joint appointment with the Department of Linguistics, as he listed linguistics courses such as 200 Introduction to Linguistics, 455J Areal Linguistics, 553J Analysis of Linguistic Structures (co-taught with a visiting scholar Allan Keiler). However, the latter two came with the description "offered jointly with the Department of Linguistics," hinting his closer affiliation with the Department of Asian L&L.[37]

In 1969, Lukoff served as Graduate Program adviser in Thomson Hall room 407. The M.A. program in Korean Languages and Literature was available by then, and students were able to arrange a Ph.D. program in Korean language and literature with willing faculty in the Department of Comparative Literature or the Department of Linguistics. Literature and culture courses, such as East Asian Shamanism (for which Suh had been responsible), were taught by visiting scholar Chong-Un Kim

---

36 Interview with Heles Contreras.

37 This might explain the conflicting memory of Heles Contreras, a professor Emeritus who does not believe Lukoff taught in the Department of Linguistics, and that of Benjamin Lukoff, who was certain that his father had a joint appointment in the Department of Linguistics for a few years after he came to UW. Contreras taught in Romance Linguistics, and his interaction with Lukoff may have been minimal, possibly explaining the discrepancy. Fred Lukoff is indeed listed as a regular faculty member for the Department of Linguistics, at least in the 1967-69 UW Catalogue.

from Seoul National University (1982-1984, and again 1984-1985). 302 World Classics of the Orient was also offered around this time and covered great works of Chinese, Indian, Japanese, and Korean literature and philosophy.

Lukoff was a kind, quiet, unassuming man and a brilliant linguist. Born in Shpola (now Ukraine), he moved to Philadelphia as a young child, and he was a native Yiddish-English bilingual.[38] He was also quite proficient in Classical Hebrew, which he learned from Noam Chomsky's father, who was a teacher at the local Hebrew School. By 1945, Lukoff wrote two volumes of a basic Korean textbook for the army, titled *Spoken Korean: Basic Course (U.S. Department of the Army, Educational Manual)*,[39] which predate Samuel E. Martin's *A Quick Approach to Spoken Korean* by nine years. Lukoff was barely 25 when he wrote the books.

Fred Lukoff

He worked at the MIT Research Laboratory of Electronics to work on machine translation under Victor Yngve and wrote a seminal paper "On accent and juncture in English" with Chomsky and Morris Halle in 1956, before receiving his Ph.D. from University of Pennsylvania and joining the Department of Far Eastern Studies in 1964. Lukoff was a prized student of the father of American structural linguistics Zellig S. Harris, who supervised Lukoff's dissertation "Korean Grammar," the first of its kind and written in the framework of structural linguistics. Lukoff edited and reviewed Harris' groundbreaking *Methods in Structural Linguistics* with Chomsky. In his recommendation, Zellig Harris said there were only two students with comparable talent amongst his graduate students, Noam Chomsky and Fred Lukoff, and that Lukoff was a little better than Chomsky.[40] Harris also credits Lukoff's thesis for

38 Email interview with Benjamin Lukoff.

39 Published in by the Linguistic Society of America and the Intensive Language Program, American Council of Learned Societies.

40 This stellar recommendation is cited by those in the Department of Asian Languages and Literature and Jackson School who have been around long enough to

Spoken Korean by Fred Lukoff

inspiring Harris' "Transformation Theory" in his monograph *String Analysis*. After teaching at MIT with Chomsky for a year, Lukoff taught briefly at the Seoul National University of Education and then Yonsei University for seven years, being the first to introduce Modern Structural Linguistics to Korea. During his stay in Korea, he was also entrusted with an English education project and produced some of the first audio-recordings and teaching materials for Koreans.[41] Additionally, Lukoff was appointed the first president of the International Association for Korean Language Education (IAKLE) in 1985.

Lukoff's tie to Yonsei University would last for many years. Many of his graduate students from Yonsei University studied at UW, many of whom became prominent Korean linguists. Benjamin Lukoff remembers his father's students frequently being invited over for meals and gatherings. Their basement was often full of Korean graduate students smoking, drinking, and chatting before they returned to their studies. Lukoff had a deep understanding and love for Korea and its people. He would often help with his graduate students' travels and tuition needs out of his own pocket. Kisim Nam was one such graduate student, who was from Yonsei University and studied Korean linguistics under Lukoff. Nam received an M.A. in Korean linguistics in 1967 from UW and went back to Yonsei University as a professor to teach Korean linguistics from 1977 until he retired. He was one of the most active and prominent public-figure linguists in Korea.[42]

Under Lukoff's leadership, the Korean language program continued to grow. In the wake of the third Korean immigration wave into the U.S.,

---

remember or have heard of Zellig Harris's letter, which accompanied Lukoff's application.

41 Email interview with Kisim Nam.

42 He served as the president of the Korean Linguistics Association (1997), president of the Korean Language Association (1998) and the sixth director of the National Institute of the Korean Language (2001-2006).

the 1.5 and second generation immigrant children were entering UW by the masses. According to the Korean American Historical Society, "[b]y 1970, Washington's Korean-American population was the nation's twelfth largest, 769 of whom were living in King County."[43] In 1980, the Korean-American population jumped to the nation's seventh largest. More than five thousand Korean Americans lived in King County, with two-fifth of them in Seattle. Lukoff arranged different sections for heritage and non-heritage students. There were around twenty-five students in both of the first-year classes and about fifteen students in the second-year class.[44] Graduate teaching assistants taught first- and second-year classes under the supervision of Lukoff, who was in charge of third- and fourth-year classes and graduate courses. Student enrollments in Korean classes were increasing, and as a result, teaching assistants, most of whom were Korean graduate students, were working beyond their 20-hour-a-week legal limit. Lukoff himself was stretched thin with a heavy teaching load and supervising responsibilities for every level of Korean. The problem was discovered and corrected only in 1986 by then chairman David Knechtges, who was shocked at the paucity of resources available for the Korean Program. He took the matter to the dean and secured another teaching assistant position, and an additional graduate teaching assistant position was added a couple of years later.[45]

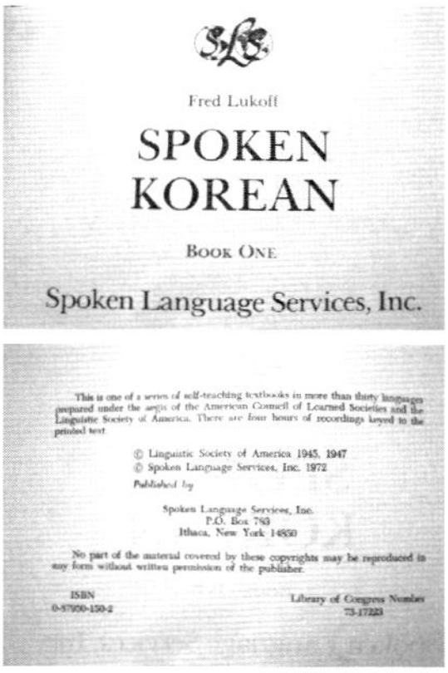
Fred Lukoff
SPOKEN KOREAN
BOOK ONE
Spoken Language Services, Inc.

This is one of a series of self-teaching textbooks in more than thirty languages prepared under the aegis of the American Council of Learned Societies and the Linguistic Society of America. There are four hours of recordings keyed to the printed text.

© Linguistic Society of America 1945, 1947
© Spoken Language Services, Inc. 1972
Published by

Spoken Language Services, Inc.
P.O. Box 783
Ithaca, New York 14850

No part of the material covered by these copyrights may be reproduced in any form without written permission of the publisher.

ISBN 0-87950-150-2

Library of Congress Number 73-17223

During his time at UW, Lukoff wrote several Korean textbooks for non-heritage speakers, including *An Introductory Course in Korean*, *Spoken Korean*, and *A First Reader in Korean Writing in Mixed Script*, solidifying the tradition of strong undergraduate training

43 About KAHS. (n.d.) In *Korean American Historical Society*. Retrieved November 2, 2014 from http://www.kahs.org/about.html

44 Email interview with Song-chul Kim.

45 Interview with David Knechtges.

and textbook-writing for non-native learners at UW. His passing in 2000, four months after the death of his wife,[46] was memorialized with great sadness by many.[47]

7. In Transit — Second Interim Years: 1990-1995

Song-chul Kim

Song-chul Kim, who was hired as a Lecturer in 1990, taught until 1995. He had been a graduate teaching assistant for Lukoff for five years (1985-1990) and received his Ph.D. in Anthropology in 1991.

The program secured one more graduate teaching assistant, and all three taught first year Korean courses. First-year Korean had fifty heritage and twenty non-heritage students; second-year Korean had two sections with fifteen students each in heritage and non-heritage sections. Lukoff's textbooks, including Mixed Script readings, were used for the lower-level courses; the third- and fourth-year courses had about five students each and used selected authentic readings.

Song-chul Kim, now a professor at Inje University, also started a first-year summer intensive course, and around thirty students registered every year. At that time, the student population was predominantly still heritage students. This reality sent a warning sign to administration that the Korean program might be self-serving or at least humoring those looking for easy grades.

At about the same time, Clark Sorensen was hired by the JSIS in 1989. He had received his Ph.D. in Anthropology from UW in 1981 and taught at Vanderbilt University and University of Illinois, Urbana-Champaign before coming to UW. Sorensen concentrated on building the socio-political curriculum of the Korea Studies Program, creating

---

46 Lukoff's wife was a clinical professor of medicine at UW. They had met during Lukoff's teaching at Yonsei University.

47 Obituary by Youngkey Kim-Renaud in LINGUIST List 11.1779.

SISEA448 Modern Korean Society, SISEA 584 Survey of Korean Society, and SISEA 439 Politics of Divided Korea. He also played a heroic role in fundraising and obtaining a position to replace James Palais after his own retirement in 2001. Also, 426 Music of Korea was also added to the curriculum at this time.

Clark Sorensen

In the Korean community, the Seattle Korean Consulate aided the inauguration of the Northwest Korean School Association (NWKSA) in June 1988. NWKSA assumed responsibility for teaching second-generation Korean youth and subsumed more than 100 Korean weekend schools in Washington, Oregon, Idaho, Montana, and Alaska.

8. Charged Clouds over an Empty Sea — Exits and Departures: 1995-2002

Ann Lee was hired in 1995 with a Ph.D. in East Asian Languages and Cultures from Columbia as Assistant Professor of Korean literature in AL&L, and she remained there until 2002.[48] She had taught at the University of Southern California and the University of California at Berkeley before coming to UW. She created more graduate courses in literature for the M.A. program, including Korean 531 Advanced Readings in Modern Korean Literature and Korean 532 Advanced Readings in Traditional Vernacular Korean Literature. In the meantime, the Ph.D. program was officially instituted at the university.

She supervised four graduate students and helped them earn teaching assistantships, and she occasionally taught joint courses that benefited both undergraduate and graduate students. Unfortunately, brilliant scholar as she was, she was another victim of the divorce between JSIS and the Korean Language Program. Her predecessor, Lukoff, had spent nearly a quarter century in the Department of AL&L (re-)building a linguistically strong curriculum for the Korean major and teaching

48 History of the Network for Korean Studies Organizations and Researchers lists the years as 1996-2002.

mainly undergraduate courses he created until his retirement in 1990.[49] Ann Lee, although hired in his place after his retirement, followed the exact opposite direction, re-building the Korean curriculum with a focus on graduate literature courses until her departure. This pendulum was inevitable due to the structural problem of a dichotomous approach to language teaching with only one faculty member, who was simultaneously working in his or her specialization while tending the needs of the Korea Studies Program.

From across the campus, James Palais in JSIS was the most vocal proponent for a pre-modern literature position when Lukoff's AL&L position needed to be filled. Let alone the demand from the brother constituent on campus, as far as the Department of AL&L was concerned, Ann Lee was a good fit. She was a promising scholar, and her era of study went well with that of the Japanese scholars in the program.

While Ann Lee was responsible for mostly graduate instruction, Ikhwan Choe (husband of the Korean Studies librarian at the East Asia Library) was invited as Visiting Lecturer by the Department of AL&L to teach from 1995-99 then again from 2000-01. Throughout the last decade of the twentieth century, Korean educationalists were still scarce. Although he was not a specialist in Korean, Choe was a sophisticated scholar who was well-versed in European literature and benefited advanced-level undergraduate students with his knowledge of literature.

In 1998, Bruce Fulton joined the AL&L faculty as affiliate professor with a Ph.D. in Modern Korean Literature from Seoul National University. He taught upper-level Korean classes with an emphasis in literature and served those who needed Korean courses for their degree. Beginning in 1999, Fulton played a significant role in introducing Korean literature to the local public, inviting celebrated Korean writers for bilingual readings at public libraries, schools, bookstores, and universities. Wan-seo Pak, In-ho Choi. Jeong-hui O, Young-ha Kim, Seong-nan

49 Conflicting records are found in the library catalog, societies to which the scholars belonged, Wikipedia introductions, and obituaries. In this paper, the numbers are provided by the Department of Asian Languages, unless otherwise stated.

Ha and Yu-ju Han have been some of the authors invited for readings, talks, and panels in the past decade. Fulton himself gave many bilingual readings with his wife and co-translator, Chan Pak.

Across campus and overlapping in time with Ann Lee, Soowon Kim (Ph.D. from Brandeis University in Korean and Japanese Syntax) joined the Department of Linguistics in 1994, which by then was independent and strong. After Ann Lee's departure, Kim was asked by the administration about his willingness to jointly teach in the Department of AL&L before his exit from the university in 2003. He had declined. Palais also retired in 2001 but continued to teach part-time through 2005, when he was diagnosed with cancer.

With multiple departures of faculty and dwindling state funding,[50] the program was uncertain about its plans to hire a replacement for the retired James Palais. The Korea (n) programs became the topic of contention yet again, making local newspaper headlines and provoking student protests and petitions.

The expiration of the contract for then Lecturer and Acting Program Coordinator Soohee Kim was also around the corner. Kim, who was on the development committee from 2003-04, began fundraising both locally and abroad to generate awareness about this dire situation. Kim's sister, who was in a Seoul-based band called Haeoreun Nuri, held concerts and began wiring collected donations.[51] The publicity was noted by some of the UW alumni, and Clark Sorensen was contacted for a more systematic community fund-raising effort.

Kim, however, was asked by the administration to stop fundraising efforts for the Korean Language Program, which it thought might

---

50 During the first half-decade of the 2000s, the Department of Asian Languages and Literature added two ladder faculty members in Chinese and in Japanese. Five lecturers were also hired during this period, including one each in Korean, Indonesian, Chinese, Japanese, and Tagalog, the last of which later moved to American Ethnic Studies. Around this time, the Japanese Program began to reach out to community and local businesses and forged a close relationship with the Japanese Consulate in Seattle. In 2005, another lecturer was added in Chinese and one in Urdu, and in later years, Japanese and Chinese added more lecturers.

51 July 13th, 2003. CBS radio. August 11th 2003. *Kyunghyang Newspaper*. September 9th, 2003. *The Korea Times*.

distract the concerted effort that the Korea Studies Program had begun. Regardless, there was a rally on March 1, 2002 in UW's Red Square, with some 300 people participating, including many Korean community leaders. In an interview by Eric Bonham, Clark Sorensen states the following:

> Don Hellman[52] describes the situation by saying, "[W]e had this Senator Paull Shin talking, saying he was going to do everything in his power to find funding for this position. [UW] President McCormick was watching the whole thing happen and pacing back and forth trying to decide what to do." Don Hellman told him that if he has a man who has power from the state saying he is going to do everything in his power to get money for the position then he ought to invite him up to his office. Eventually, Don Hellman, Paull Shin, the mayor of Shoreline and the President met to discuss the possibilities. Later the dean of arts and sciences, Dean David Hodge, informs Clark Sorensen that if he could raise $1 million then they would allow Jim Palais' position to be filled. Dean Hodge said this with the idea that there is no way that it could or would be done and very few people had any belief that it could be done.[53]

Most people thought that Clark would not succeed in raising the money and the program would decline considerably at UW. Even the Korea Foundation denied UW any funding because it did not believe in the program's success. However, Sorensen invited the president of the Korea Foundation, Inho Lee, to see the JSIS Korea program at UW, and when Lee saw the program and the East Asia library in person, she decided that it was too important to not support. She overrode the previous decision of the Korea Foundation and instead offered $500,000 but only if Sorensen could match it. The university gave $250,000, which left $250,000 to be raised. There were fundraising dinners, ads in The

52 Director of the Institute for International Policy, JSIS.

53 The administration around this time was at best nonchalant, if not antagonistic to Korea (n) faculty on campus. With James Palais retiring in 2001, Ann Lee leaving in 2002, and Soowon Kim being contentiously publicized during his tenure review in 2003, there was a sense in the air that Korean faculty was being eliminated one by one.

Korea Times, and even people singing in the subway and at universities in Seoul to raise money for the cause.[54] The community responded with unprecedented support and donations amounting to $150,000. The goal amount was finally exceeded by a donor named George Long, who had graduated from UW with an undergraduate degree in Asian L&L and also an MBA. He wanted to memorialize Jim Palais and gave one of his apartments in Anchorage Alaska to UW, which sold it for about $150,000 and created the position of the Palais Professorship. Paull Shin secured another $500,000, and Clark Sorensen returned to the Korea Foundation to ask for a match. All in all, the Jim Palais Professorship funds went beyond the initial target of one million dollars.[55]

Clark Sorensen helped rejuvenate the UW Korea(n) Program, and through his partnership with Ikhwan Lee, a local Korean community tycoon, a new chapter in UW Korea Studies began. First, it hired Yong-chool Ha in Korean politics in 2004, followed by Hwasook Nam to fill the Palais Professorship position in 2007.

In the Korean community, the Korean government offered another round of funding to start the United Seattle Korean School, which taught elementary through high school students Korean history and language with lessened religious overtones. Ikhwan Lee was selected as the first board chairman, and Kyungsook Baek was appointed as the first principal of the school. The next year, a sister branch was launched in Bellevue for families' commuting ease. The first principal of this school was Boowon Yoon, who was a teacher at a public school in the Seattle District. She currently heads the Korean American Cultural Education Foundation. The launching of the United Korean Schools gathered students and teachers from eight major Seattle churches and six Bellevue churches, leaving intact a strong bond between churches and the school. Its establishment also created a rivalry between the new school and the existing NWKSA schools, which refused to be incorporated. Korean government funding would also scatter, triggering the Korean

54 Haeoreun Nuri.

55 Interview with Clark Sorensen by Eric Bonham.

Consulate to focus its funding on only big schools.[56] The two United Korean Schools currently offer Korean classes to 500 students, from toddlers to adults, on Fridays and Saturdays, and they are affiliated with the Korean American Cultural Education Foundation.

9. A Fleeting Breeze — Scott Swaner: 2003-2005

Scott Swaner

Scott Swaner joined AL&L in 2003 as a postdoctoral fellow on a Freeman Fellowship, and he became Assistant Professor of Korean Literature the following year. Swaner was born in California and moved to Utah during his childhood. He earned his B.A. in English Literature at the University of Utah before going to Korea for missionary work. Swaner received his M.A. from Cornell University and his Ph.D. from Harvard in Korean Literature on a Fulbright scholarship. He was the first student ever admitted in the Ph.D. program to study Korean Literature at Harvard University, and he was awarded a Daesan Foundation Grant for translating Korean poetry upon his arrival at UW. He echoed Lukoff's genuine love for Korean people and the culture, as he was deeply empathetic and pained by the torn history of two Koreas. His understanding of its literature and thought reverberated loudly in his dissertation.[57]

Swaner was well on his way to publishing a book when his tragically premature death came in 2006. His advisor David McCann remembers him as "a wonderful student, passionate about literature, the serious study and performance of it, and above all else, its relationship to the lives of the Korean people who made and read it…"[58] His passion and knowledge in philosophy, esthetics, and literature greatly impacted his students and colleagues in literature. He also initiated the promotion of

---

56 Interview with Da-eun Kwon, Vice-consul of Seattle.

57 Interview with Wookjin Jeong.

58 Obituary. *Salt Lake Tribune* on January 4, 2007.

Lecturer Soohee Kim to Senior Lecturer.

During this period, the Korean collection at UW also grew to some 100,000 volumes (in books alone),[59] attracting scholars worldwide, even from Korea. This growth was due in large part to Hyokyoung Yi, a Rutgers University graduate who came to UW in 2002 as a Korean Studies librarian.[60] Yi has contributed to the pronounced visibility of the Korean Studies Program by continually acquiring books and other materials in the field, in addition to building a tight network between the students and the faculty centered around library services. Yi also worked diligently on Korea(n)-related exhibitions and showcases, annual faculty training, special class lectures throughout the academic year, and accessible web interfaces.

10. En Route — More Interim Years

Two failed attempts to fill the Korean position after Scott Swaner's passing slowed the establishment of a graduate program in the AL&L Korean Language Program. Course changes happened minimally in conjunction with department-wide changes, but at least, Korean 445, an upper-level Foreign Study in Literature, was added. Soohee Kim, now Senior Lecturer, was put in charge as the program coordinator. Under Kim's management, the language instruction part of the program reached its peak. By 2008, among more than 110 universities and colleges that were offering Korean instruction, the Korean Language Program at UW was teaching one of the three largest non-heritage populations in the nation, according to an external reviewer. The UW Korean classes were "bursting at the seams."[61] In 2007, there were 28 students

59 Sorensen, Clark. History of the Korea Studies Program at the University of Washington. (n.d.) In the *Paull (*sic) *Shin Korea Studies Program and Center for Korea Studies*. Retrieved November 2, 2014 from http://jsis.washington.edu/korea/koreahistory.shtml

60 The official position Yi is hired to fill is "Korea Studies" librarian.

61 Ross King. External Review of the Korean Language Program. 2003.

in a second-year class, and "even from the standard of state universities, the class size is overwhelming for any language instruction."[62] In the following years, the number of students who registered for the same course in the autumn quarter remained steadily high: 30 in 2008, 28 in 2009, 21 in 2010, and 27 in 2011, which is more than a modest growth from the 5 students Kim first taught when she created a non-heritage second-year class in the fall of 2000. Nowadays, there are two sections of the second-year class for non-heritage learners, with more than 25 students in each class. The total number of non-heritage students registered in the fall of 2011 for first- and second-year Korean courses alone was 211.

Soohee Kim

Soohee Kim joined the department in 1999 as a Lecturer with a Ph.D. in Linguistics from UW. She overlapped with both Ann Lee and Scott Swaner, intersected with visiting lecturers Ikhwan Choe and Bruce Fulton, worked with lecturers Jeongyi Lee and Inseon Cung, and served three different department chairs. The first major structural change that Kim executed was instituting a dual-track program for heritage and novice students.[63] The dual track program involved three goals: First, to shed the unspoken presumption that Korean language instruction was mainly "self-serving," or allowing unfair grade advantages to Korean-heritage students; second, to serve a broader UW undergraduate population by introducing the Korean language and culture to non-Koreans; and third, to institute rigorous language instruction to produce qualified students for the upper-level curriculum. As the first step, Kim wrote two placement tests and field-tested them with the help of the UW CIDR.[64] Once the placement tests were in place, oral interviews were also required of

62 Sung-Ock Sohn. External Review of the Korean Language Program. 2008.

63 Kim wanted the Korean Language Program to stand as independent; the first thing she did was to begin using the name "Korean Language Program," differentiating it from the Korea (Studies) Program.

64 Center for Instructional Development and Research, now Center for Teaching and Learning.

every student. Initially, *all* students, both heritage and novice, were interviewed one-on-one by Soohee Kim. The process was arduous, but the impact was phenomenal. Heritage students, who did not place out of first-year Korean, were challenged and put work into their learning, and most novice beginners who previously would drop out during the first week of class at the sight of seemingly fluent native speakers, stayed in the classes appropriate to their level, and their numbers kept growing.

Sung-Ock Sohn's external review reveals the following:

> The Korean program at UW demonstrates an excellent model for a dual-track system for heritage and non-heritage learners of Korean··· Unlike most Korean programs in North America in which second (or third) generation Korean Americans constitute 70%-80% of enrollment, the majority of students at UW are from a non-heritage background··· The total enrollment in Korean courses is remarkably high (192 during the fall quarter 2008)··· In spite of the limited teaching staff and lack of a ladder faculty, the Korean language program at UW exhibits some outstanding practices, innovations and initiatives that contribute greatly to their success··· The Korean teaching staff appeared to be dedicated and highly professional with a keen awareness of effective language pedagogy practices. They also demonstrated strong teamwork and collaborative effort···[65]

The key element that contributed to the current level of non-heritage enrollment, however, was the *You Speak Korean!* textbook series, which Soohee Kim co-authored after testing out nearly every available Korean textbook in her classrooms for more than three years.[66] *The You Speak Korean!* series follows the linguistics-based tradition of Lukoff, with a more accessible format with updated content. It is termed by some as a

65 Sung-Ock Sohn. External Review of the Korean Language Program. 2008.

66 The list includes Lukoff's series, King and Yeon's series, Namkil Kim's *Modern Korean*, You and Cho's *College Korean*, the KLEAR series, Yonsei University's reading series, Korea University's conversation book, Ewha Women's University's Path Finder series, and Sogang University's textbook series for foreign learners. Sunmun University's series and Kyunghee University's textbook series are added to the list for volumes 3 and 4.

miracle because of its distinction, and for having been written with no substantial funding. Two reviews are below:

> The textbook series explains grammar like no other books out there, including detailed and nuanced explanation one needs to really grasp the quirks of the language. The YSK series is not only strong as a series, but each individual book and each individual chapter has the gleam and detail of a master craftsman (craftswoman in this case). The grammar notes are less notes and more like full on linguistic lectures (not boring!). Dialogues are so real I hear them VERBATIM in conversation.[67]
>
> It is a major accomplishment and valuable contribution to the fields of Korean studies and KFL pedagogy, full of creativity, originality, humor and sensitivity.···This is definitely the most user-friendly KFL textbook to appear to date.[68]

The series has not been widely used by universities in the U.S. since it is designed for non-heritage learners, and the bulk of learners in U.S.-based Korean programs (70-80%) are still heritage students. Universities that adopted the *You Speak Korean*! series have invariably increased their non-heritage population and managed to expand its programs.[69] The university user base seems to continue to grow, and among them are the University of Georgia, the University of Pennsylvania, Johns Hopkins University, and Yale University. Invaluable to the series were co-authors Emily Curtis, who provided an English native speaker's perspective on grammar explanations with her Ph.D. in Linguistics, and Haewon Cho, who added realistic dialogues and pedagogically-sound exercises, coming with MA degrees in Linguistics and MATESL. The series was selected as a Book of the Year by the Korea Foundation for several years.

Anticipating the arrival of a new graduate faculty member, Soohee

67 Bret Chernoff, James Banfill, Carl Laviolette, Minga Yangze Sherpa.

68 Ross King. Review to Korea Foundation. 2002.

69 University of Michigan, Ann Arbor, was one example, and University of Western Ontario, which has recently added an intermediate level class, is another.

Kim restructured the Korean course-numbering system in 2010-11. Courses such as Korean 301, 302, 303 (first-year non-heritage) and Korean 315, 316, 317 (second-year heritage) were changed to fit a 101-type series, modeled on the school's Japanese and Chinese programs. During the interim, Kim also attempted to integrate innovative ways to strengthen and update the program. One such activity was an experimental internship program in 2006, when the school hosted three undergraduate students majoring in Korean as a Foreign Language at Kyunghee University. Kim's potential contribution was not fully realized, however, as she was responsible mainly for the sustainment and survival of the program during the interim as a non-graduate faculty member. No substantial changes were allowed, and any concrete planning was deemed too risky. The Kyunghee University provisional internship program, as a result, did not continue.

Nevertheless, in 2009, Kim successfully co-chaired the annual conference for 120-plus members of the American Association of Teachers of Korean (AATK). Kim initially turned down the invitation from the president of AATK to co-chair the conference. Mike Shapiro, then department chair, was concerned about her overwork and thus hesitant to endorse the conference. Depending on the term, Kim taught two, three, or four individual courses in both heritage and novice tracks, in addition to occasional seminar courses, which necessitated different course preparations. Due to a lack of upper-level content courses, Kim also sometimes led independent studies (IS) in addition to her regular teaching load, and the number of IS students was as high as ten.[70] Some IS requests were coming from outside the department, including from JSIS students. Soon after, the department limited all IS requests to department majors and the maximum enrollment to four.

Through thick and thin, the program was kept more than afloat, with annual enrollment figures reaching 646 (2007-08), 741 (2008-09), 718 (2009-10), and 668 (2010-11). Moreover, the Korean Language Program came to be known for its students and their levels of competence. Espe-

70 Winter and Spring, 2010.

cially impressive were non-heritage students, whose proficiency levels were "clearly above the typical non-heritage Korean classes taught in leading institutions elsewhere."[71] The notably high levels of language ability were achieved by the language-partner work that Soohee Kim required of every non-heritage student, who was paired with a Korean international student or fluent bilingual Korean-American volunteer. Motivation generated engagement, which turned into competence. The practice also contributed to building international ties and cultural understanding and exchange.

Some have misleadingly ascribed the success of the UW Korean Language Program to Soohee Kim alone, as demonstrated by Sung-Ock Sohn's comment that it was "amazing to discover how a single person can build the entire program so successfully with so little support.[72] The instructional success of the Korean Language Program, however, was owed to many who were involved during this period, especially Jeongyi Lee, who worked tirelessly during her employment at UW. Lee, who joined the program in 2006 with a Ph.D. in Linguistics from University of Georgia, took charge of upper-level language instruction until her departure in 2010. Lee used the *Integrated Korean* textbooks for advanced students and focused her instruction on grammar and vocabulary in written Korean. Students also benefited greatly from Chinese characters included in her curriculum.[73] During her time at UW, Jeongyi Lee did the remarkable three different course preparations with thirteen hours of instruction per week, nine courses a year[74] and did an

71 Eunhee Lee 2005 (Visiting Scholar from Hansung University), Sung-Ock Sohn 2008.

72 Email from Sung-Ock Sohn to Soohee Kim on November 23, 2008.

73 Sohn made a strong suggestion in her review of the program that a Sino-Korean course be created for the curriculum in 2008. Soohee Kim proposed such a course, which was rejected at the insistence of a Chinese faculty member on the curriculum committee that Korean students could take Chinese classes to learn Chinese.

74 This is by no means an ideal arrangement. Any administration expecting a professional instructor to teach more than two courses per term with independent teaching preparation is willing to compromise the quality of education and the instructor's well-being.

unbelievable job of helping the advanced language curriculum flourish.

Jeongyi Lee, now Assistant Professor of Korean at Kennesaw State University, taught for four years at UW and was a full-time lecturer only during the last year due to UW's budgetary constraints, which possibly contributed to her decision to leave the department. As she was teaching and co-teaching four courses and supervising three graduate teaching assistants, Soohee Kim wrote to William Boltz, the department chairman, about her great concern for faculty retention.[75] Many went the extra mile to bring in a full-time Korean Lecturer position, for which Eunyoung Won was later hired.

Jeongyi Lee

Devoted teaching staff was the most important element for the solidity of the program. Graduate teaching assistants at UW also were known for their strong rapport with their students, and students described their teachers in the Korean program as exceptionally encouraging and supportive. In the absence of tenure-line faculty, graduate teaching assistants always willingly assumed heavy teaching responsibilities as far as legal limits could push, and they did a magnificent job.[76] Students who took language classes at UW and elsewhere (including Japanese, Chinese, French, Latin, and more) appreciated that their Korean teachers spent time to make sure the students learned grammar points, leading to a truer understanding of the language.

A similarly emblematic characteristic of the Korean Language Program at UW was its focus on forming a community. Students used various words such as "family," "jeong" (情), "friendship," "friendly,"

75 Email to William Boltz, Soohee Kim, 2010.

76 Graduate teaching assistants that served the program from 1990 to present, alphabetically listed by last name: Hyungjung Ahn, Tae-Youn Ahn, Kyeong-a Cha-Lee, Jung-Im Chang, So-min Cheong, Haewon Cho, Moon-jin Choi, Hojong Do, Jeongwon Hyun, Yong-kil Jeong, Wookjin Jung, Woo-kwang Jung, Hee Seung Kang, Hyein Kim, J-S Kang, Jina Kim, Jiyoung Kim, Keun Hee Kim, Namwoon Kim, Song-chul Kim, Soohee Kim, Sunhee Kim, Sun-mi Kim, Woojoo Kim, Young-Youn Kim, Seung Bum Kye, Meehwa Lee, Jessica Likens, Jeeya Lim, Myungkee Min, David Moon, Jiyun Moon, Seung Chul Moon, Kyoung Ok Noh, Haeree Park, So-Young Park, In Chul Shin, Jeongsoo Shin, Hye-jin Sidney, Jemma Song, Sunhee Yoon.

"inviting," and "happy" to describe their experience with the Korean language at UW, speaking of their excitement to share their learning experience with other students and forge lifetime friendships with their classmates.

The high enrollment in Korean courses remained steady, with 190 students enrolled during the fall quarter of 2008; 168 of them were in first- and second-year classes.[77] Despite its flourishing language classes, the Korean major was suspended in March of 2009 due to the lack of a graduate faculty who could offer content courses, and the program became heavily dependent on foreign study transferred credits. Department Chair Mike Shapiro expressed, "Because of the current financial situation at the University of Washington and the cancellation of a faculty search in the area of Korean literature, admission to the major in Korean language has been temporarily suspended."[78] Shapiro's decision to suspend the major alarmed the administration and strengthened the department's request for a Korean literature position. In 2010, the major was reinstated with the arrival of Heekyoung Cho.

Overlapping in time with Jeongyi Lee during this interim period, Susie Kim taught literature content courses as Visiting Lecturer from 2007-08, and Inseon Chung temporarily joined in 2010 to help fill the void created by Jeongyi Lee's departure. All temporary lecturer positions were at least partly supported by various grants by the JSIS Center for Korea Studies at UW.

Yong-Chool Ha

Yong-Chool Ha joined Korea Studies in 2007 and began teaching in 2008 as the Korea Foundation Professor of Korean Social Sciences. Since his arrival, he taught wide-ranging subjects in Korea Studies, including Comparative Politics, Korean Peninsula and International Politics, Late Industrialization and Social Change, and North Korean Politics. Ha received his Ph.D. in Politi-

77 This is despite the fact that the second-year Korean heritage class was not offered that year partly due to lack of resources.

78 Email request from Department Chair Mike Shapiro to Dean Robert Stacey on March 17, 2009.

Hwasook Nam

cal Science from UC Berkeley in 1985 and had been a professor at Seoul National University before coming to UW. Another professor, Jonathan Kang, taught Korean law in the Asian Law Program for two years from 2006 and 2008. Finally, in 2007, Hwasook Nam joined the faculty as the James B. Palais Endowed Assistant Professor. Nam studied under James Palais until she received her Ph.D. from UW. She taught previously at University of Utah and specializes in the areas of modern Korean history, especially labor, gender, and the social history of postcolonial South Korea. Nam taught HSTAS 582, 583, 584, a year-long Korean History Research Seminar, which she took over from Palais more than a decade ago. Between Clark Sorensen, Yong-Chool Ha, Hwasook Nam, and Wonmo Dong (an affiliate professor and Korean program scholar in residence), the Korea Studies Program offered a variety of Korea-related courses, allowing more options for students in Korea-related majors. In addition to Korean majors and minors from the Department of Asian L&L or Asian/Pacific American Studies in American Ethnic Studies, for example, students majoring in Asian Studies with a Korea Focus from JSIS could also take Korean language classes. Korean majors and minors, in turn, sent students to non-language Korea-related courses to fulfill their requirements, thus stabilizing a desirable symbiotic state between the two entities.

The Korea Studies Program also added two energetic and active staff members, Young Sook Lim and Tracy Stober, the latter hired in 2008 as a Managing Editor of the *Journal of Korea Studies*.[79] Young Sook Lim received her Ph.D. in 1999 from the College of Education at UW in Curriculum and Instruction with a specialization in Bilingual Education. Lim is impressively well-connected in the Korean and local communities due to her extensive educational and work experience. She was awarded federal educational research grants and worked as a bilingual Senior Researcher for the Washington Research Institute from 1998

79 The journal was founded in 1969 at UW. It moved to Stanford from 2004-2008 and returned to UW in 2009.

until 2005, when she began working for UW as the Assistant Director of the Center for Korea Studies. On October 24, 2011, the Center for Korea Studies, headed by Clark Sorensen, succeeded for the second time in getting the Overseas Leading University Program for Korean Studies grant, which brought in an additional $1 million to the Korea Studies Program at the University of Washington.

11. Letting Down The Anchor

Heekyoung Cho

In the new millennium, the AL&L Korean Language Program added two faculty members, Heekyoung Cho and Eunyoung Won. Heekyoung Cho joined in 2010 after teaching briefly at the University of Minnesota and Yale University. She received her M.A. in Russian Literature from Yonsei University and Ph.D. from University of Chicago, specializing in modern Korean literature and culture. Cho is already an energetic new Program Coordinator and has many plans to build the current program, and she currently teaches a reading course and Korean literature courses to an enthusiastic academic Korean community. Eunyoung Won, who previously taught at Harvard University and Columbia University, is a Lecturer who has been in charge of the first- and third-year level language curriculum since 2011. She is developing multi-media teaching and learning materials, starting with the first-year level and later expanding her work to the upper levels.

Eunyoung Won

There will be continued efforts to streamline the program and address the needs of both the heritage population and graduate students from Korea Studies. The program will also create more ties with the local community and K-12 educators, along with better foreign study programs. Heekyoung Cho places priority on buttressing a rigorous advanced-level curriculum, but until at least another ladder faculty member can join the program, Cho is the lone graduate faculty member, and the department may keep the graduate program in Korean language and literature on hold.

In the history of the Asian L&L department, department chairmen, especially recent chairmen David Knechtges, Michael Shapiro, and William Boltz, have gone the extra mile to secure additional graduate teaching assistants and temporary lecturers to sustain the Korean Language Program. Their countless meetings with the Dean of Arts and Sciences and with Clark Sorensen (the Director of the Center for Korea Studies) made possible the hiring of Ann Lee, Scott Swaner, and Heekyoung Cho. Keeping high student enrollments may be a useful strategy, but the future is never certain. With the "Korean wave" and many incoming Chinese students seeking courses in Korean language and culture, Korean enrollments may grow even further. With local policies changing, departments going modular, and language requirements being dissolved, on the other hand, enrollments may decrease. Additionally, obtaining more faculty members, at least another ladder faculty and another lecturer, would be ideal for the UW Korean Language Program. These positions will hopefully be added in due time, but they should not be a goal. The time is ripe for Korean programs and stakeholders to offer more service to the community through independent scholarship and an understanding of a set course for the future, as aptly sung by a poem from the Joseon Period (translation supplied by the author):[80]

> 穿雪野中去
> 不須胡亂行
> 今朝我行跡
> 遂爲後人程

> Through the snow field as I go
> I must not make a random trail.
> The path I leave at today's dawn
> Will soon become another's rule.

80 Some say the poem was written by Korean Buddhist master Seosandaesa 西山大師 (1520-1604); others say it is the poem of Yi, Yangyeon 李亮淵 (1771-1853) from the late Joseon Period.

This essay will close by citing the inaugural speech of Reverend Gowen that the aim of our department is "not to teach opinions, but … to stimulate thought, to aid in the collection of information and the distribution of such means for correct judgment as may be of service."[81]

81 Hecker, Felicia J. International Studies at the University of Washington: The First Ninety Years. (n.d.) In *The Henry M. Jackson School of International Studies*. Retrieved November 2, 2014 from http://jsis.washington.edu/jackson/history.shtml.

ACKNOWLEDGEMENTS

"The Korean Language Program at the University of Washington" is centered around the chronological unearthing of the university catalogues, employment records, enrollment database reports, as well as correspondences found in various special collections archives.

More emphasis was put on the earlier decades of the program's history, partly as there is more information readily available about the recent development of the program. By the same token, the Korea Studies Program was heavily included in this article only through the 1990s since an accurate historical account of the program is now available through the Jackson School of International Studies.

The author has tried her best to keep sentimental self-reflections in check, and the report is a truthful historical account of the program, although the readers will notice occasional inevitable perspectives.

Official documents also showed discrepancies by one year here and there. The University Catalogue, for example, does not publish information until at least a year after the fact, so minor discrepancies in dates are to be expected. All names are written as found in their source Romanization; when the need arose, the Korean government's new Romanization was used.

This historical reconstruction of the Korean Language Program at UW would not have been possible without the great help of William Boltz, who was the chairman of the department when this piece was written. He granted the hourly hiring of Eric Bonham, who assisted the author in the writing. Eric went well beyond anyone's expectations, as much of the information on courses and people came from the raw data he located.

I am also grateful to Clark Sorensen, who eagerly offered information on the Korea Studies Program. Thanks also go to Hyokyoung Yi, our energizer-bunny Korean Studies librarian at the East Asia Library, for her help with special collections in Suzzallo Library; Youngie Yoon for providing me with faculty and graduate student information; and Abby Petty, our former department academic advisor, for impersonating Sherlock Homes in her pursuit of information regarding the Korean major.

I also wish to express gratitude to everyone who generously shared their time to answer my interview requests and/or to provide me with additional resources: David Knechtges, Michael Shapiro, Hwasook Nam, Heekyoung Cho, Eunyoung Won, Joshua Van Lieu, Sungchul Kim, Boowon Yoon, Eunhee Lee, Ritsuko Kurima, Tracy Stober, Bruce Fulton, Heles Contreras, Taiping Chang, Wookjin Jeong, and Jinna Kim.

I would also like to thank the students responding to my call for comments on their experience with the Korean language classes or program at the University of Washington. Those who have graduated or are abroad in Korea include the following: Bret Chernoff, James Banfill, Rob Lauler, Carl Laviolette, Chance Kennedy, Jerome McCuin, Caryl Cavner, Eric Kam. Those who are currently in a Korean class are Minga Sherpa, Yen Do, Ayumi Toyama, Stacy Luong, Michael Uchida, Farah Hushin.

Finally, my heartfelt thanks go to Emily Curtis, who offered comments on various parts of the manuscript. Any errors found are the responsibility and fault of the author alone in compiling and recounting the collected data.

REFERENCES

About. (n.d.) In *Asian Languages and Literature*. Retrieved November 2, 2014 from http://asian.washington.edu/about

About KAHS. (n.d.) In *Korean American Historical Society*. Retrieved November 2, 2014 from http://www.kahs.org/about.html

CU-Korean funding talks resume. (1977, October 5). *The Columbia Daily Spectator*.

Hecker, Felicia J. International studies at the University of Washington: the first ninety years. (n.d.) In *The Henry M. Jackson School of International Studies*. Retrieved November 2, 2014 from http://jsis.washington.edu/jackson/history.shtml

Kim, Keong-il. (2004). *Pioneers of Korean Studies*. Gyeonggi-do (Korea): The Academy of Korean Studies.

Korean 'influence peddling' at UW. (1977, September 30). *The Columbia Daily Spectator.*

Korean Lit Position Frozen. (1977, May 19 and 1977, May 24). *Korea Daily*.

Korean students protest staff decision. (1977, May 17). *The Seattle Times*.

Koreans fight to retain professor's position. (1977, April 15). *The Columbia Daily Spectator.*

Merlino, Doug. (2004, June 13). Gloria K. Lee, pioneer among Seattle Koreans, dies at 87. *The Seattle Times*. Retrieved from http://seattletimes.com/html/obituaries/2001955021_leeobit13m.html

Protesters demand retention of Korean Lit. (1977, May 17). *The Columbia Daily Spectator*.

Sorensen, Clark. History of the Korean Studies Program at the University of Washington. (n.d.) In the *Paull (*sic) *Shin Korea Studies Program and Center for Korea Studies*. Retrieved November 2, 2014 from http://jsis.washington.edu/korea/koreahistory.shtml

Yu, Daeshik. (1983). A Call for the Formation of a Historical Society of Koreans in Washington State. In *Korean American Historical Society*. Retrieved from http://www.kahs.org/history_1.html

APPENDIX A

Ode to the Little Giant in the Pacific

by Soohee Kim

Another storm is expected;
a butterfly or a tree fallen afar five thousand miles
or the earth too hot, by the ocean
whether welcomed or not,
a good cleansing-necessary-calling up a storm.

Old things grow older and neglected,
his decline leading to her prime for a while;
no matter whose body-decaying to fertilize the earth for the season
is beautiful for knowing to go away after its peak,
for it is at ease to come back in some other form.

To the beat of the wind external and disconnected,
waves swaying in crazy dances to wail,
but it has its rhythm as one;
to those who desire from it naught
wind does no harm.

Breathe................
Sink
heavy
like
a bomb................

Mellifluous agitations exaggerated,
Janus in exile;
a notion
a tiny drop of water in a bucket
in my palms.

A storm is expected-
free of wile,
an ocean
'tis an ocean deep,
an ocean calm.

History of the Korean Language Program at Yale

Seungja K. Choi
Yale University

1. The Historic Opening of Korean Language at Yale in 1990

Picture 1. Department of East Asian Languages and Literatures, Hall of Graduate Studies

On the first day of class in the fall of 1990, over 80 students crowded into Harkness Hall, Room 113, many of them overflowing into the hallway. The class was Korean, the first of its kind to be offered at Yale. A combined undergraduate and graduate course, the introduction of the Korean language was received well by many eager Korean-American students. The *New York Times* covered the historic introduction of the class:

> After eight years of student lobbying, Yale College has begun offering a course in Korean language study, and the response has been overwhelming. The administration had predicted that 40 students might take the course, elementary Korean, but more than 80 undergraduates attended the first day, cramming into a room··· Most students in the class are Korean-Americans, interested in "learning the language of their ancestors" said Prof. Samuel Martin, director of the program. (Campus Life)

2. Prelude

The history of Korean language studies at Yale dates back to the Second World War when the study of languages such as Chinese, Korean, and

Japanese were critical to the war effort; thus, resources such as reading materials and classes were in high demand. In 1943, a group of accomplished teachers and researchers formed the Chinese Language School at Yale, which grew into the Institute of Far Eastern Languages (IFEL), to provide training in spoken Chinese for U.S. Army officers.

In 2013, 28 of those Air Force personnel who studied Chinese and Korean at Yale during the 1950s and 1960s returned to the campus. *The Yale News* reported on the veterans:

> The men were once students at Yale's Institute of Far Eastern Languages (IFEL), which had its origins in the Chinese Language School started on campus during World War II to teach Putonghua to U.S. Army officers. The Army chose Yale because of its groundbreaking work in making East Asian languages easier to learn by transliterating them using the Western alphabet, a system known today as Yale Romanization. The Chinese Language School grew into the Institute of Far Eastern Languages in 1947, and its faculty began to develop a radical new approach to learning a spoken language that relied on intensive interaction between students, teachers, and recorded speech. This innovative new system came to be known as the Yale Method. ··· By the early 1950s, when the Korean War broke out, IFEL's primary mission had become the training of U.S. Air Force personnel in Chinese and Korean. Its classes were conducted in a house on Yale's "Fraternity Row" at 215 Park St., which had been purchased by Yale in the 1940s from a bankrupt fraternity. Many of the IFEL "alumni" who returned to campus this September related fond memories of their years in that building, where their intensive language study helped faculty refine and develop the Yale Method. IFEL ceased to exist in 1965, when its classes were folded into Yale's broader language programs. (Bonds, 2013)

In 1946, IFEL expanded its language training to civilians serving in various posts in the Far East, and it additionally began offering courses for enrolled Yale students. Korean was first introduced at IFEL in 1947 and Japanese in 1948. Other Asian languages, such as Burmese, Indonesian, Thai, and Vietnamese, were also eventually added.

In 1947, Elinor Clark Horne, a Yale graduate with an M.A. in Linguistics, received federal funding to institute a Korean language course at IFEL. Air Force students, missionaries, and a few graduate students enrolled. Professor Samuel E. Martin[1] took over the Korean program a few years later with the assistance of Ms. Young-Sook Chang and Mr. Sung-Un Chang. Prof. Martin, who earned an A.B. and an M.A. in Oriental Languages from the University of California, Berkeley and a Ph.D. in Linguistics from Yale University, started teaching in 1950 at Yale in the Department of Linguistics and the Department of East Asian Languages and Literatures.With his passion for Japanese and Korean languages and linguistics, and years of dedicated teaching and research, Samuel E. Martin was a true pioneer and distinguished figure in his field. From 1963 to 1965, he chaired the East Asian Languages and Literatures department, and from 1966 to 1974 he also chaired the Department of Linguistics.

Archived transcripts indicate that the last of the IFEL Air Force students enrolled in the Korean language course in 1961-1962. Academic records show that the Korean program offered a wide range of courses, 12 in total, including Elementary Spoken Korean, Conversational Korean, Intermediate Korean, Elementary Korean I/II, Specialized Conversation I/II, Basic Military Reading, Intermediate Korean Reading, Elementary Newspaper Korean, and Advanced Reading Seminar. With the Air Force's support quickly diminishing and the number of foreign missionaries declining, the Korean language program could not attract enough students and eventually closed its doors. In 1965, IFEL was dismantled, and its language teaching functions were incorporated into the Department of East Asian Languages and Literatures.

The Korean language did not return to Yale until 25 years later, when a growing number of Korean-American students began expressing interest in the course. In 1984, a student-led organization called Korean-American Students at Yale (KASY) was formed to promote the cultural, political, and social interests of the Korean-American student

1 I dedicate this article to Prof. Samuel E. Martin (1924-2009), who was instrumental in establishing the Korean language study at Yale from the beginning and was a pioneer in Korean linguistics.

community at Yale. KASY's mission was to advocate for Korean language classes, and its leaders conducted multiple meetings each year to appeal its case to high-ranking university administrators. In 1990, a private donation enabled the department of East Asian Languages and Literatures to establish a Korean language program, and Professor Samuel E. Martin and Seungja K. Choi, who was then a Ph.D. student in Linguistics, initiated the Korean language course.

Picture 2. Photograph of Prof. Samuel E. Martin and Seungja K. Choi at the ceremony in Beinecke Rare Book & Manuscript Library in which Prof. Martin was awarded the Republic of Korea Presidential Medal of Honor for Distinguished Cultural Contributions (*Pokwan munhwa hwuncang*) in 1994.

This essay will examine the trajectory of the Korean language program at Yale, from its beginning to the present. We will reflect on key aspects of the program's three periods; introduce the Center for Language Study, its Fields program, and the Richard U. Light Fellowship, which play important roles in promoting Korean language study at Yale; and finally take a glance at Korean-American student organizations that promote academic, cultural, political, and social interests of the Korean-American community.

3. The Beginning: 1990-1999

Based on enrollment trends, among other factors, the last twenty-four years fall into three stages: the beginning period (1990-1999), the middle period (1999-2009), and the revival to the present (2009-).

In the beginning period, the program only offered two levels, Elementary Korean K115 and Intermediate Korean K135. Dr. Seungja Choi, who earned a B.A. in English Literature from Yonsei University, an M.A. in Linguistics from the University of Toronto, and a Ph.D. in Linguistics from Yale University, taught both levels with the help of teaching assistants and Prof. Martin, who provided a grammar lecture session once a week. Average total enrollment for this period was 55. While the two levels fulfilled the standard requirements for foreign language proficiency and basic communication, they did not meet the needs of advanced students with higher Korean proficiencies, which was possessed by many Korean-American students.

A third-level course could not be established without additional teaching resources. However, Dr. Choi, as the only instructor, found a solution: By creating an intermediate level course with a different number, K136, more students could enroll and learn at various levels. Twice a week, all students met for a grammar session, and three times a week they were divided into 2-3 sections, in which teaching assistants conducted drills. Despite constraints, total enrollment each semester in this period ranged from 52 to 69. As the demand for Korean courses saw consistent growth, the Korea Foundation and Yale established a $1 million fund to support the program in 1995.

In 1999, a third-year course, Advanced Korean K150 I, was created when Dr. Jaehoon Shim, who had earned a Ph.D. in history from the University of Chicago, joined the faculty. He taught Advanced Korean I and a course on Korean history until he left Yale in 2002. In 2003, Dr. Angela Lee-Smith, who earned a Ph.D. in Korean Linguistics from Sangmyong University and taught for many years at the Sogang Korean Program and Brown University, joined the faculty. Thus, a solid foundation was laid for future growth of the program.

4. The Middle: 2000-2009

As many researchers note, an obstacle that most Korean programs at U.S. universities faced was the mix of heritage and non-heritage learners. This issue had to be addressed in order to establish an effective program. Non-heritage learners could be intimidated by Korean heritage students with prepossessed language knowledge and often times withdrew from class within the first week. After a few years of attempting to manage this disparity in the Elementary Korean classes, the department established two distinct tracks for heritage and non-heritage students in 2006, with different names and learning materials. This change led directly to a significant increase in non-heritage learners enrolled at the Elementary level after 2009. Between the period of 2000-2009, however, the program saw relatively low enrollment, with an average 35 students each semester.

5. The Revival and The Present

The Korean language program, one of three East Asian languages offered by the Department of East Asian Languages and Literatures along with Japanese and Chinese, has grown into a full-fledged program. The current faculty consists of Dr. Seungja Kim Choi, who also served as Director of Language Instruction in East Asian Languages until 2014, and Korean Coordinator Dr. Angela Lee-Smith. From 2011 to 2014, a Title VI grant also provided funding for a visiting lecturer from Sogang University to join the faculty each year. However, the visiting lecturer program has since closed, causing two courses (third year non-heritage track K150 and one semester of Advanced Korean, K153) to end.

After a stagnant few years, the program saw an increase in enrollment, from an average 35 in 2000-2008 to 55 in 2009. The increase can be attributed to the addition of a fourth-year course (Korean 154) in 2007, a Korean Film course (Film/Korean 251), and a considerable surge in non-heritage track Elementary Korean students. In the fall of 2010, enrollment in Elementary Korean almost doubled from 13 to 28. Various factors contributed to the rise in enrollment, including the impact of *hallyu* (the "Korean Wave"), the new non-heritage track courses, and opportunities for study abroad provided by the Richard U. Light Fellowship.

Currently, the program offers first through fourth-year courses. The non-heritage track offers two levels, first and second year courses, while the heritage track begins at an intermediate level, followed by two levels of Advanced Korean, K152 and K154. While first, second, and third-year courses are intensive, meeting five hours a week, the fourth-year course (K154) is a hybrid between online and classroom teaching, and it meets only once a week. K154, introduced in 2007, was designed for advanced readers and writers whose proficiency surpassed the three-year mark. Students in the K154 course are often those who were educated in Korea for some years in elementary or junior high school, or students who possess very advanced speaking proficiency but lack advanced reading comprehension and writing abilities.

Although only two levels of courses are offered for non-heritage learners, students who complete the second year course on the non-heritage track can continue on to Advanced Korean K152/K153/K154 after one summer and a semester of study abroad. In addition to the courses described above, Independent Tutorial (Korean 470) is available for students with advanced Korean language skills who wish to engage in concentrated reading and research on material not otherwise offered in courses.

6. Korea-Related Courses

Since East Asian Languages and Literatures majors are offered only in Chinese and Japanese literatures, Korea-related courses are scarce at Yale. One course, however, called Literary Modernization in Japan and Korea and taught by Prof. John Whittier Treat, explores Japanese prose fiction, modern Korean novels in English translation (e.g., Yi Kwangsu's *Maybe Love, Heartless*, Yi Sang's *Phantom Illusion, Wings*, Ch'ae Man-shik's *A Ready-Made Life*, Yom Sang-seop's *Three Generations*, and Kim Tong-in's *The Photograph and the Letter*), the impact of the West, Japanese colonization, and the relation of social changes to cultural ones. Prof. John Treat earned an M.A. and Ph.D. from Yale University and has served as East Asian Languages and Literatures Department chair. One of his two book projects currently underway, titled *Too Close to the Sun*, is a study of pro-Japanese Korean intellectuals under the Japanese occupation.

Another Korea-related course offered from 2005 to 2009 was Korean/Film 251, Korean Cinema from 1961, taught by Dr. Seungja Choi. The goal of the course was to understand the significance and aesthetics of contemporary South Korean cinema in the context of themes such as history, nationhood, gender, class, and modernization through a select series of post-1960 South Korean films, whose periods ranged from the Golden Age in the early 1960s through the New Korean Cinema Age in the 1980s and 1990s to the present. The films chosen for examination reflected the dynamic changes, ideological issues, and collective experiences in contemporary Korean society and cultural life.

Other Korea-related courses have been offered occasionally by the Political Science department as well as the Council on East Asian Studies' post-doctoral program. These courses include Politics in South and North Korea; Approaches to Korean Archeology; Tracking Contemporary Asian Cinema; Gender in East Asian Art History; Understanding North Korea; Mapping Korea in East Asia; History and Memory in East Asia; Translation and Modern Literature in East Asia; A Cultural History of Modern Korea and Japan; History and Tradition in Modern Korea; Japan and Korea: A Transnational History; East Asian Cinema and Transnational Tropes; Korea Before 1876; Trauma and Collective Memory in Modern Korean Literature; Location and Dislocation in Modern Korean Literature; Development and Democracy in East Asia; Gender and Ethnicity across Japan, Korean and the United States; Competitiveness, Industrialization and Economic Development in East Asia: A Case Study of Korea; Self and "Other" in China, Japan, and Korea; China, Japan, and Korea in the Early Twentieth Century; and The Military in Traditional Korea.

7. The Center for Language Study and Richard U. Light Fellowship

Aside from the Department of East Asian Languages and Literatures, the Center for Language Study and the Richard U. Light Fellowship play crucial roles in the advancement and promotion of Korean language study at Yale. The Fields Program, which is housed under the Center for Language Study, provides students the opportunity to pursue advanced-level language study within the context of their academic areas of focus. Fields is a highly individualized, non-credit, discipline-specific language study program, which funds and coordinates language partners, mentors, coaches, coursework, instructional materials, field experiences (such as internships, assessments of language proficiency), and portfolios.

The Richard U. Light Fellowship is an important study abroad fellowship that promotes East Asian languages at Yale. Dr. Richard U. Light saw East Asia's growth as an opportunity for Yale students to bring fresh perspectives and keener insights to both their studies and their eventual leadership roles in society. Dr. Light thereby reasoned that students should gain foreign language ability while immersing themselves abroad. To that end, he created a fellowship that fully funded such opportunities.

The Richard U. Light Foundation began funding the Richard U. Light Fellowship at Yale in 1996. Since then, the Light Fellowship has steered Yale's efforts to internationalize its campus culture by providing nearly 1,000 students with fully-funded opportunities to pursue intensive language study in East Asia. Through the Light Fellowship, Yale students of exceptional promise are granted funding (for transportation, tuition, room and board, and incidentals) for the advanced study of Chinese, Japanese or Korean at approved sites in China, Taiwan, Japan, and South Korea. There are five Korean language sites approved by the Light Fellowship in Seoul: Ewha Womans University, Korea University, Seoul National University, Sogang University, and Yonsei University. Each year, over 15-20 Yale students are given the tremendous opportunity to further their language studies in Korea, and immerse themselves in the culture.

I conducted interviews with Light Fellowship students about their experience studying abroad in Korea. Andrea, a junior year heritage learner majoring in psychology, shared her story:

> I was exposed to Korean at home, but never made an effort to speak Korean. In high school, I studied Spanish, so I intended to continue Spanish at Yale. Sitting in a Spanish class one day, I heard a Korean teacher's voice "Annnyonghaseyo!" I got homesick, and wanted to learn Korean. I thought, "Maybe I should learn my mom's native tongue." I enrolled in Elementary Korean at the end of course selection period. I spent one summer in Seoul at Sogang University program, totally immersed in Korean. I found my Korean identity, half American, half Korean. It was comforting that I was not totally isolated.

The following is an excerpt from her blog while she was studying Korean at Sogang University, in Seoul:

> My mom moved to the States in her early 20's after marrying my American father, and since then has graduated from college in the States despite her limited English capabilities, and raised my brother, sister, and me as a single mother after my parents' divorce. My siblings and I all have varying degrees of Korean comprehension, but none of us speak Korean. My mom came to America without friends or family (outside of my dad), and for the first five or so years, didn't have a school or workplace to meet anyone at. It must have been lonely. I'm also starting to realize what a huge barrier language can be. Being able to better understand my mother's Korean words makes me feel that I now better understand her Korean thoughts. When I was able to understand my mom's native tongue, I realized how my mother is smart and I had an incredible bonding experience with mother. After one year of learning, I was able to bond with relatives in Korean.
>
> In the future, I really plan to use Korean in personal life. Now I use exclusively Korean with my Mom.I have a strong connection with my Korean heritage. I will even pass it on to my children. I am extremely interested in the welfare system of children in Korea and I will explore that area.

After her experience at Sogang University, Andrea became confident that she could master Korean, and she is planning to work as a lawyer for children's welfare.

Roger, another student who studied abroad, is a very determined economics major who became interested in Korean through high school friends. Here is an excerpt from his blog about studying at Sogang University through the Light Fellowship:

> Today was a relaxing day. I spent a good chunk of my time studying in a cafe up near Ehwa [sic] Women's University. I love just sitting in cafes. I enjoy overhearing others' conversations, feeling the comfort of being near so many people, and allowing homework to fit in to my time to chill out alone. I sit in, on average, one cafe per day. As someone who tends to hit the library alone at Yale, this is a nice change of feel for me. It also gives me an opportunity to explore: there are cafes everywhere in this city, and I can bring my homework to any one of them. Today, exploring was fairly local, and I really liked the area near Ehwa [sic]. It was funny to see the abundance of female clothing and hair salons, and of course, it was not surprising to see very few men in the cafe I was in.

However, not all Light Fellowship study abroad trips were successful. Some students traveled to Seoul to discover that they did not connect with the Korean culture or people, and found the language too difficult.

8. Korean-American Student Organizations at Yale

Korean-American students at Yale are active in academic discussions and involved in social and cultural activities through several student organizations. The Contemporary Korean Studies Society (CKSS) was formed in August 2012 by five students; it was the first student-led organization on campus with a specific interest in modern Korea studies. CKSS promotes academic discourse among students and faculty regarding Korean current affairs within the context of East Asia and the world. In 2012, among other activities, CKSS conducted academic roundtables on important topics such as territorial disputes in East Asia, North Korea, and modern day Korean culture. Students with an interest in not only Korea, but also China, Japan, and East Asia were invited to contribute to meaningful and insightful discussions. CKSS also hosts Master's Teas, inviting prominent speakers to share their views on East Asia, as well as Korean food-making sessions, movie screenings, and K-pop dance parties.

The Korean-American Students at Yale (KASY), as mentioned earlier, was established by students to support the Korean-American community at Yale. In the nearly 30 years of its existence, KASY has grown in both size and influence, but it still remains dedicated to its founding principles.

In addition to KASY and CKSS, there is a Korean Drum Troupe called Unity and a Korean foreign students group called *Hanppuri*. Founded in 1991, Unity is dedicated to preserving the arts of Korea and raising cultural awareness. The troupe practices and teaches traditional Korean music, and it performs several times a year, both on and off-campus.

CKSS and KASY collaborated to establish a task force called the Korean Studies Initiatives with the following mission statement:

> The Korean Studies Initiative at Yale is a student-run initiative to establish a Korean Studies program at Yale University. We are pushing for a Korean concentration within the East Asian Studies major, a tenure track professorship that focuses on Korea under the supervision of the East Asian Studies department, and more classes in the area of Korean studies. We believe that Korean Studies is an indispensable asset to the study of East Asia as well as the current role that Korea plays on the global level.

Despite such enthusiastic efforts of the Korean-American students, Yale seems far from establishing a Korean studies program beyond its existing Korean language courses.

REFERENCES

Bonds, Robert. (2013, September 26). Air Force vets who helped pioneer Chinese language study at Yale return to campus. *Yale News*. Retrieved from http://news.yale.edu/2013/09/26/air-force-vets-who-helped-pioneer-chinese-language-study-yale-return-campus

Campus Life: Yale; Course in Korean Draws 80 Students On Its First Day. (1990, September 23). *The New York Times*. Retrieved from http://www.nytimes.com/1990/09/23/style/campus-life-yale-course-in-korean-draws-80-students-on-its-first-day.html

APPENDIX 1. Korean Language Courses

Non-Heritage Track		Heritage Track	
Course Title	**Course Content**	**Course Title**	**Course Content**
K110/K120 Elementary Korean I/II	A beginning course in modern Korean. Pronunciation, lectures on grammar, conversation practice, and introduction to the writing system.		
K130/K140 Intermediate Korean I/II	Continued development of skills in modern Korean, spoken and written, leading to intermediate-level proficiency.	K132/K142 Intermediate Korean for Advanced Learners I/II	Intended for students with some oral proficiency but little or no training in Hankul. Focus on grammatical analysis, the standard spoken language, and intensive training in reading and writing.
* (K150/ K151) were closed in 2014		K152/ (K153) Advanced Korean for Advanced Learners *K153 was closed in 2014	An advanced course in modern Korean. Reading of short stories, essays, and journal articles, and introduction of 200 Chinese characters.
		K154 Advanced Korean III	An advanced language course designed to develop reading and writing skills using Web-based texts in a variety of genres. Discussions, tests, and intensive writing training in class.

APPENDIX 2. Biography of Samuel E. Martin

Important Roles Outside of Yale:

1958-62 ACLS Committee on Uralic and Altaic Studies: Secretary
1959-61 Linguistics Society of America: Executive
1972 Papers in Japanese Linguistics: Editorial Board
1978-80 Korean Linguistics: Editor and Editorial Board

Honors and Prizes:

1972 Sumitomo Faculty Research Grant
1980 NSF Grant
1979 Japan Ministry Education: Invited Scholar
1982 Korea-USA Centennial Program Committee Award
1983 Japan Foundation: Visitor's Grant
1994 Republic of Korea: Presidential Medal of Honor for Distinguished Cultural Contributions (*Pokwan munhwa hwuncang*)
1999 *Tongswung* Academic Foundation: First Place Award

Korea-related Publications:

1951 Korean Phonemics. Language 27: pp 518-533
1954 Korean Morphophonemics. 64 pp. Baltimore: William Dwight Whitney Series
1968 A Korean-English Dictionary (with Yang-Ha Lee and Sung-Un Chang). 1902 pp. New Haven, Yale University Press
1975 A Reference Grammar of Japanese (revised 1983). 1190 pp. New Haven: Yale University Press
1983 Beginning Korean (revised 1980) (with Young-Sook Lee). 575 pp. New Haven: Yale University Press
1992 A Reference Grammar of Korean. 1032 pp. Tokyo: Tuttle

APPENDIX 3. Biography of Elinor Clark Horne

Elinor Clark Horne received an MA in Linguistics from Yale, where she taught Linguistics, Japanese, Javanese, and Korean. She published four books on these languages, including the only existing Javanese-English dictionary. At Dartmouth and at various community colleges in the Upper Valley, she has taught courses in Linguistics and traditional folktales, as well as in expository writing and critical thinking.

History of Korean Language Education at the Defense Language Institute

Sahie Kang
Defense Language Institute

1. Introduction[1]

It is essential to discuss Korean language education within the federal government of the United States before discussing it in the context of the Defense Language Institute. The U.S. government recognizes the need for foreign language proficiency among its officials, such as diplomats, foreign area officers, and other personnel, who respond to language-related missions. Because foreign language education at regular colleges and universities in the United States generally aims to develop academic skills and does not meet the needs of the government, the U.S. government has been specializing in foreign and second-language teaching and learning within several government institutes over the past 70 years.

The Defense Language Institute's history started with the Army Language School, which was founded during World War II. In its early stages, the objectives of Korean language education and those of thirty other foreign languages were related to national defense and focused on listening skills for cryptologists rather than on global communicative skills.[2] Prominent teaching methodologies in the early stages included

---

1 This manuscript is written based on DLI's command history.

2 The objectives of DLI's foreign language education are as follows: "The major DLIFLC goal is to ensure that graduates meet the requirements of the agency that has assigned them to foreign language study. Students must therefore be provided instructional programs that are responsive to the foreign language needs of a wide variety of military positions throughout the world. DLIFLC programs must meet high standards so that functional language skills can be developed for professional

the audio-lingual method, which made intensive use of language laboratories.[3] Since then, the Korean program at the Defense Language Institute has evolved due to the changes of second language acquisition principles and theories, as well as international affairs related to the Korean Peninsula.

2. The Birth of the Korean Language Program

After World War II, the first American troops were deployed to Korea in September of 1945, and the Department of Defense realized that there was "no country of comparable significance concerning which so many people are ignorant."[4] In the same year, the Korean language program at the Military Intelligence Service Language School at Ft. Snelling, Minnesota was the first Korean language program at the Department of Defense. There were a few Korean-American students enrolled, including a Korean-American Army officer named Captain Kelvin Kim, who was from Oakland, California. At that time, the same institute had already been teaching the Japanese language to over a thousand Japanese-American students. The Korean program ran for several months in the fall of 1945, producing thirteen graduates in March 1946. Beyond that time, however, the program did not continue.

In the spring of 1946, the Department of Defense decided to move the Military Intelligence Service Language School from Minnesota to its current location in Monterey, California. The following year, in 1947, the school was renamed the Army Language School.

The Army Language School opened a new era of government-sponsored institutes of higher education that focused on foreign language

use in real-world communication situations. Individual opportunities for learning are provided for all students on an equal basis." http://www.dliflc.edu

3 DLI distinguishes between two different listening skills: interactive and non-participatory.

4 "…there is no country of comparable significance concerning which so many people are ignorant." McNaughton (1990)

education, and it started hiring faculty members across 20 languages, including Korean. At the same time, Mr. Raymond S. Yun, a government employee at the Presidio of San Francisco, was tasked to launch a Korean Program in San Francisco. At that time, a few Korean language textbooks were available from Korea, but the faculty in the Korean department decided to develop textbooks internally to address the needs of Korean language education at DLI. In the following year, 1948, there were six Korean language instructors who were teaching Korean to 16 students, some of who were Korean Americans. At that time, the introductory Korean course was an intensive, year-long course, which was the longest language course allowed at DLI.

3. The 1950s

Interest in Korean studies was not high until the Korean War began in 1950, when the U.S. government needed an unprecedented number of Korean language experts. Moreover, there were only two Korean experts in the Far East Command under General MacArthur. Due to a lack of Korean experts, Japanese linguists who graduated from the Military Intelligence Service School were sent to Korea during the Korean War. Korean linguists were so rare that these Japanese linguists worked with Koreans, who had a command of Japanese and Chinese, in order to interrogate Chinese prisoners of war. Until the ceasefire agreement of 1953, the 501th Communication Reconnaissance Group was stationed in Korea and increased the number of linguists to 1,600, including many Korean linguists.

During the Korean War, the U.S. government struggled to find qualified teaching staff for the Korean language. Because of a lack of instructors, only about 100 students were enrolled in the Korean program, and their proficiencies were not very noteworthy.

After the Korean War, in 1955, the Korean program ranked as the third biggest program at DLI after Russian and Chinese. There were about 70 Korean teaching faculty members teaching over 300 students.

At that time, the U.S. Air Force also sent many airmen and women to DLI and Yale University to learn the Korean language.

After the Korean War, the U.S. and South Korea signed the Mutual Defense Treaty in 1954, and most U.S. troops were removed from the Korean Peninsula. In 1958, the number of Korean students had decreased to 157, and more than half of the Korean instructors were released from DLI. Afterward, the Korean program was maintained with about 30 faculty members until the end of the 1980s.

Despite the reduction in the number of students and faculty in Korean, the program continued piloting courses of various lengths, including a 9-month course in 1955 and an 18-month course in 1957. Naturally, developing curriculum to meet the needs of the students was an ongoing project. Military language materials were introduced, including many audio clips produced at the recording studio at DLI. At that time, the Korean textbook published by Yale University was also used. In regard to student assessment, the first version of the Army Language Proficiency Test (ALPT) was developed and implemented for Korean (and other languages) to measure students' proficiency gains at the end of each language course.[5]

In the 1950s, only seven universities in the United States taught Korean language courses. In the 1960s, there were three Centers for Korean Studies: programs located at Harvard University, the University of Hawaii, and the University of Washington, with a total student enrollment of just 12.[6] The Korean studies program at Harvard was the only one partially funded by the federal government. By comparison, there were 10 Japanese studies institutes nationwide, and nine of them were

5 DLI students take a variety of achievement tests and proficiency tests during the course. The final graduate tests are proficiency and performance tests.

6 *Korean Studies Guide*, ed. by Richard Marcus (Berkeley, CA: University of California Press, 1954); *US Army Handbook for Korea*, American University, Department of the Army Pamphlet (Washington, DC: Government Printing Office, 1958); *The National Interest and Foreign Languages*, rev. ed. by William R. Parker (Washington DC: US National Commission for UNESCO, 1957), p. 120; *Resources for Language and Area Studies, A Report on an Inventory of the Language and Area Centers Supported by the National Defense Education Act* of 1958, Washington, DC: American Council on Education, 1962).

funded by the federal government, with a total of 958 students. There were also 11 Russian studies institutes, which were all funded by the federal government, with a total student enrollment of 4,025.

While Korean studies and Korean courses were rarely taught in colleges and universities, DLI continued to teach Korean to over 100 military students using the most recent method at the time, the audio-lingual method. DLI was equipped with the most up-to-date language laboratories, which were fully utilized in Korean classrooms. Each student was provided with portable cassette recorders to record their own speech. Thus, speaking was the main language skill on which DLI focused during this time, and students had mandatory speaking-oriented field training exercises. Additionally, a Korean refresher course was established for graduates in 1981.

4. The 1960s

In 1963, it was reported that about 400 Korean linguists were working in the federal government, which was less than 50 percent of the number of Japanese and Chinese linguists. The Korean program at DLI published revised textbooks for the basic course, and in 1970, it also published area studies textbooks.

The Army Language Proficiency Test, which was developed and used in the 1960s, was replaced by the Defense Language Proficiency Test II (DLPT II), which was developed by the Educational Testing Service (ETS) in New Jersey. The test was created not only for Korean but also for all other languages taught at DLI at the time. DLPT II was developed mainly to check knowledge of grammar and vocabulary, but it was not effective in evaluating students' proficiency levels.

In the 1960s, the federal government started discussing the importance of listening and moved away from an emphasis solely on speaking. In 1965, the Air Force Chinese-Mandarin Aural Comprehension Course at Yale University was adopted by DLI, which in turn influenced the development of the Korean language curriculum. The Korean curriculum focused mainly on non-participatory listening skills over a 12-month course. The curriculum was found to be ineffective after three years, however, and the Korean program was reorganized to emphasize all four basic language skills: listening, reading, speaking and writing.

In 1967, DLI began appointing non-commissioned officers who served in the field for several years and graduated from the basic program as Technical Language Assistants (TLAs). Later, the title of the position was changed to Military Language Instructor, and these officers assisted civilian faculty members in teaching special military jargon.

By the end of the 1960s, tensions between North and South Korea were quite high. In December 1967, armed North Korean insurgents intruded on the area surrounding the Blue House, the presidential residence in Seoul. Furthermore, in January 1968, the American Navy vessel Pueblo was hijacked by North Korea while it was on its first mission in the East Sea. At that time, some of DLI's Korean graduates were among the kidnapped sailors, and it was reported that their Korean proficiency level was not good enough to resolve the situation. In April of 1969, a U.S. Navy aircraft was shot down by North Korean aircrafts in the East Sea, and several of DLI's Korean graduates were lost. After these incidents, the U.S. government published North Korean area studies materials separately from South Korean area studies materials. Such incidents also led to an increase in the number of students enrolled in the Korean program at DLI. For the next three years, until the end of 1971, the number of Korean students enrolled was 350.

5. The 1970s

In early 1970, the U.S. policy for East Asia changed radically. President Nixon signed the first diplomatic relations agreements with China in 1970 and withdrew U.S. ground troops from Vietnam in 1972. In 1971, on the other hand, President Nixon also withdrew one of the two divisions that were stationed in Korea. Consequently, the number of cryptologists for North Korea decreased in 1972, and the number of

Korean enrolled students plummeted from 350 to 76, resulting in a dramatic decrease.

In the early 1970s, the final learning objectives for foreign language learners were introduced in the federal government, especially for cryptologists. These final learning objectives were the standard for curriculum development and classroom instruction. This was a time when DLI paid close attention to the quality of curriculum development through professional and academic approaches, and it established an independent training development division in which language curriculum development was done independently of schools. At the same time, various language departments, including the Korean department at DLI, continued revising and supplementing existing materials. During the same period, DLI contracted out several language textbooks with other universities, including a Korean textbook that was developed and published by Bonneville Research Center in Provo, Utah. The textbooks were found to be inappropriate, however, because the content was lifted from previous textbooks in DLI's Korean program.

The 1970s was the period when the Department of Defense went through budget cuts after the Vietnam War and the military draft ended. Consequently, DLI closed its main office in Washington D.C., and DLI in Monterey became the main campus. Although the overall enrollment at DLI decreased in the 1970s, the Korean program maintained 200-300 students per year.

By the end of the 1970s, DLI's Training Development Division decided to concentrate on listening skills based on NSA's evaluations and guidelines, and it developed the New Korean Aural Comprehension Course. This listening course was for a 37-week intensive listening-only program that was reduced by 10 weeks from the original 47-week basic course. The course focused mainly on listening in the language laboratory and eliminated speaking activities. The same listening course was implemented in other language programs, but not surprisingly, it was welcomed by neither the faculty nor the students. Moreover, the outcome was a failure in general proficiency as well as listening proficiency.

6. The 1980s

By the end of the 1970s, U.S. security policy toward Korea changed due to the reevaluation of North Korea's threat by the intelligence community. In 1979, the Soviets hijacked a Korean Air civilian plane, and in 1983, the Soviets shot down yet another Korean Air flight, resulting in the death of all 269 passengers. These two incidents led the Department of Defense to reevaluate threats during the Cold War. At that time, the U.S. and Korea Joint Command was established, and it began the annual Team Spirit military training in South Korea. At the same time, South Korea's economic and political growth was noteworthy because of the end of the military dictatorship and of the hosting of the 1988 Olympic Games.

Accordingly, the number of Korean students enrolled increased in the early 1980s, while more Korean programs were opening in many other universities in the United States. In 1984, DLI developed Language Maintenance and Refresher courses, which followed the German model to help Korean linguists who were working in the field after their basic course.

In 1979, Korean student enrollment was over 450, new faculty members were recruited, and an additional Korean department was added to the existing one. In 1982, DLI added the third Korean department to the branch campus in San Francisco.

In the 1980s, DLI started new efforts for more effective foreign language education. First, DLI decided to close the Aural Comprehension courses due to their lack of efficacy. At the same time, DLI decided to move away from the audio-lingual method, which also was proven to be ineffective for helping students gain true functional ability in the target language. Proficiency Oriented Methods were also finally introduced. In 1979, DLI received official academic accreditation by Accrediting Commission for Schools Western Association of Schools and Colleges, and it continued to test and implement the most current foreign language education techniques and principles. For proficiency-oriented curriculum and instruction, for example, communicative teaching methods were emphasized. Consequently, curriculum and evaluation went through significant design changes. In the middle of the 1980s, Korean departments decided to develop new Korean textbooks, and in 1983, it compiled new modules based on communicative teaching methods. These new modules were piloted in the Korean department in the San Francisco branch campus.

With the new textbooks, Korean departments experimented with the length of courses; it extended 47-week courses to 60-week courses (which had 18 students) and maintained 47-week courses with one more class hour per day (which had 28 students). However, the outcome of the comparison did not lead to any reasonable conclusions due to so many variables. At the same time, in 1986, DLI established a new 5:1 student to teacher ratio. Korean departments also gained ten students for every class to which two faculty members were assigned. Each department had about 20 faculty members teaching the 47-week intensive Korean basic course under the supervision of a chairperson. At the end of 1980s, the team-teaching system was implemented, whereby each department had 3 to 4 teaching teams, each of which consisted of 5 to 6 faculty members teaching 30 students in three separate classes.

In the early 1980s, DLPT II was replaced by DLPT III, which was considered to be a more proficiency-oriented assessment tool than DLPT II. In 1986 and 1987, about 23 percent of Korean graduates scored ILR level 2 in Reading and Listening, even though the graduating goals were still ILR level 1+.[7]

1986 was a very meaningful year for the government's funding of language education because the Inter Language Roundtable proficiency guidelines were finally announced and published for all foreign languages. With the ILR proficiency guidelines, foreign language education in DLI and in the government became more standardized in regard to teaching and learning objectives. Ultimately, standardized evaluations and their tools were developed based on the guidelines.[8]

---

7 ILR level 2 is described as "limited working proficiency."

8 ILR Proficiency Guidelines.

At the same time, the Oral Proficiency Interview (OPI) was developed and implemented, and a few Korean faculty members were certified to conduct official OPIs.

In the middle of the 1980s, student enrollment in Korean departments rapidly increased and reached 584 in 1986. At that time, about 1,500 DLI Korean graduates were stationed in Korea. The rapid increase in student enrollment led to the recruitment of many Korean faculty members, and the third Korean department was added in the Monterey campus. Altogether, there were four Korean departments, including the one in the San Francisco branch. After the San Francisco branch closed, all four Korean departments resided in the Monterey campus.

At that time, the government emphasized implementing job-and mission-related language education in all language programs. Thus, the new learning materials for the Military Enhancement Program were based on the 16 different performance skills specified in the Final Learning Objectives.[9] In 1988, 40 percent of Korean students graduated with ILR level 2s in Reading and Listening.

At the end of the 1980s, DLI started video tele-training for Korean and other languages in the initial format of distance learning. The curricular materials for the VTT were developed using Macintosh computers. At the same time, a new version of DLPT IV, with multiple-choice questions, began to be developed.

In 1989, Korean gained independence as the eighth basic language school at DLI due to the continued increase of students and faculty members. At the same time, the Korean school aimed for an 80 percent success rate in ILR level 2s in Reading, Listening and Speaking by 1995. Due to the closer alliance of the U.S. and South Korea after the unification of West and East Germany, in addition to the end of Cold War in 1989, the importance of Korean language was reevaluated and recognized, and the DLI leadership required the Korean school to be prepared for future challenges.

9 Some of the performance skills described in the final learning objectives were translations, obtaining gists, transcriptions, and so on.

7. The 1990s

In the early nineties, the proficiency goals for basic language program graduates were raised to ILR Level 2s from 1+. Accordingly, the Defense Language Proficiency Test II was implemented. Since DLPT IV was purely a proficiency test using multiple-choice question types, there was a need for more effective curricular materials to help students prepare for such tests.[10] The textbooks developed in the eighties did not push students to ILR level 2s, and thereby both the materials and the Korean language in the materials were outdated. Therefore, the Korean school implemented the Myongdo Korean textbooks in 1992, but it stopped using them after one year due to the textbooks' inability to meet the DLI's teaching and learning needs, as student outcomes were not improved after using Myongdo. Accordingly, the Korean school started a curriculum development project with a team of six selected faculty members. The project ran for three and half years and resulted in the publication of 14 books with 56 lessons in the summer of 1997. These textbooks moved away from traditional teaching principles and applied the most up-to-date second language principles for adult learners, leaner-centered approaches, and lessons to enhance higher-order thinking skills.[11] It also incorporated activities focusing on proficiency as well as performance objectives. The project used Task Based Language Instruction, problem-solving activities in small groups, and content-based instruction. Moreover, a variety of authentic materials were introduced from the early stages and for all four language skills (reading, listening, speaking and writing), which were integrated into most activities, so students were exposed to comprehensive approaches every hour.[12] At the end of each unit, a bridge activity was introduced

---

10 DLPT IV is not related to any curriculum because it tries to check the true proficiency of the language learner, regardless of the materials with which he or she learned the language.

11 Generally, DLI applies the same principles for curriculum development in different languages.

12 Authentic materials are written and oral texts produced by native speakers

as a scenario-based and task-based activity.

The Korean basic course curriculum was successfully completed in 1997, and it was used until 2012, when the textbooks were updated. It was recognized as the most successful curriculum development project in DLI's history and has become the model curriculum for Chinese, Russian, and Arabic curriculum development. As the new textbooks were implemented at the end of 1996, the course length for category 4 languages (Korean, Chinese, Japanese, and Arabic) was extended to 63 weeks in order to reach ILR level 2 requirements.[13]

Additionally, the Korean school gradually recruited more professional faculty members with higher degrees and academic credentials in the 1990s. The strong quality of faculty, implementation of new curricula, and extension of the course length resulted in the improvement of students' proficiency levels, and 80 percent of Korean graduates had an over 80 percent ILR level 2/2+ success rate.

During the 1990s, the Korean school, together with the Russian school, planned and implemented two-week total immersion programs in an isolated facility.[14] Since immersion was still at a very early stage in the nineties and the length of the program was so short, the outcome was not overwhelmingly positive. However, the program made students feel confident in their ability to use the language outside of their classrooms. Some Korean graduates who were stationed in Korea attended Yonsei University's Korean Language Enhancement and Assessment Program during that time. The number of students enrolled in Korean schools continuously increased, and the fifth Korean department was added in December 1998. In 2000, faculty members numbered 120, whereas students numbered 600. At the same time, the need for OPI testers increased, so about 35 OPI testers were trained and certified after

for native speakers.

13 The U.S. federal government categorized foreign languages into four different categories based on difficulties for native speakers of English. Korean belongs to Category 4 (along with Arabic, Chinese, and Japanese), which is the most difficult language category for native American English speakers.

14 This is called "Joint Language Training Exercise" (JLTX).

a two-week workshop and one probationary year.

In the nineties, DLI put more emphasis on teaching culture, history, and area studies in addition to foreign languages. The basic Korean course provides 45 college credits for 15 different courses, including 6 credits for culture and area studies.

DLI also emphasized academic counseling for each individual student. The faculty members received training from the Faculty Development Division regarding academic counseling. The training allowed them to identify students' learning styles and strategies to help students become aware of their own best learning methods. In the middle of the nineties, a diagnostic assessment was developed to identify these areas in a more systematic way.

As mentioned before, more professional faculty members with PhDs and MAs in languages and related fields were hired in the nineties, especially since DLI transitioned from a civil service system based on congressional and presidential approval to a faculty personnel system with tenure positions in 1996.

8. 2001 to Present

In the new millennium, the Korean language, alongside the Arabic language, gained more attention from the U.S. government. In 2001, the sixth Korean department was added, and 150 faculty members were teaching over 700 students in the Korean School. Due to the growth of the students and faculty, in February 2002, the school was divided into two divisions: Asian II and Asian III. At that time, each school had three Korean departments, with 70-80 faculty members teaching about 350-400 students. After the division, the number of students continued to grow until the end of 2007, when each school had about 120 faculty members teaching about 400 students in four Korean departments. Ultimately, the total number of Korean faculty members was about 240, and students numbered about 800. After 9/11, DLI continued to gain more attention from the Department of Defense and the federal government, and the budget was increased accordingly.

Classrooms were equipped with high-tech educational technologies and related software. For instance, in 2002, all of DLI's classrooms were equipped with Smartboards, with which students could view target language TV channels and internet materials at any time. Consequently, all of the audio materials and cassette tapes were transferred to digital materials. At the same time, all students were provided with MP3 players until 2006, by which time they were replaced by iPods. Later in 2010-2013, with the network's migration to the Apple system, students and faculty members were also provided with iPads and MacBooks equipped with learning management tools such as Blackboard and Sakai. Implementation of educational technology generally motivated the more technology-savvy students, while faculty members who were not skillful with computers had some difficulties.

After 9/11, DLI also implemented the Proficiency Enhancement Program to meet higher proficiency goals (ILR level 2+/3), and it had to hire more faculty members to maintain a small student to faculty ratio, which was 3:1. After implementing the Proficiency Enhancement Program in early 2007, each classroom ended up with six students.

In 2000, DLI developed upper-range DLPTs for languages such as Korean, Arabic, Spanish, Chinese, and Russian that rated 3+ and 4.[15] In 2007, DLI's Directorate of Evaluations and Standardization started developing DLPT V and gradually implemented the completed test in different language programs. In October 2011, Korean DLPT V was the last one to be implemented. It is noteworthy that 15-20 percent of the Korean DLPT V covers questions on the North Korean dialect. In 2004 and 2005, DLI ran initial immersion programs internally, and Korean schools implemented immersion programs lasting 1-3 days. At the end of 2005, two Korean schools started in-country immersion programs, one at Korea University (Asian II) and one at Sogang University (Asian III). Additionally, more OPI testers were trained and certified due to retirements and growing needs. In 2002, ACTFL (American Council

15 Level 3 was the maximum rating given by the lower-range DLPTs.

on the Teaching of Foreign Languages) began cross-certification of a few DLI testers with the ACTFL OPI protocol. From then on, DLI and ACTFL OPI divisions have been working together to standardize the protocols.[16]

At the end of 2007, two Korean schools received several class cancellation notices and faced downsizing in the summer of 2008. At the end of March 2009, the two Korean schools were merged into one school (Asian II), with about 160 faculty members. As of October 2014, Korean Basic School (Asian II) has about 120 faculty members and 400 students in six different Korean departments.

In 2001, DLI established the Directorate of Continuing Education, which later expanded to four different schools: the School of Intermediate and Advanced Resident Education, the School of Distance Learning, the School of Extension Programs, and the Division of Field Support. The Directorate has multi-language programs, including Intermediate and Advanced Korean as well as Distance Learning programs. Currently, Intermediate and Advanced Korean resides in the School of Resident Education at the Directorate of Continuing Education and has 9 faculty members who are led by a chairperson and who teach an average of 20-25 students per year. Four Korean faculty members are in charge of Korean Distance Learning through the Broadband Language Training System and Mobile Training Team. The proficiency goals for the Intermediate Korean program is ILR level 2+ and ILR level 3 for the Advanced Korean program.

In August 2009, the Dean of Resident Education began the Advanced North Korean Dialect Materials Development Project with four project members. In August 2010, it completed 42 units of content-based web-deliverable learning materials, aimed at levels 2-4. These materials were well received by students, graduates, and faculty members of Korean, and they are still utilized in intermediate and advanced classrooms

16 The Oral Proficiency Interview was started by the federal government in the 60s. After the proficiency guidelines were completed in 1986, the American Council on Teachers of Foreign Languages started a similar OPI system based on ACTFL's own proficiency guidelines, which are very close to ILR level descriptions.

within and beyond the government.

9. Concluding Remarks

As mentioned earlier, the federal government has been taking a leading role in Korean language education for the last seven decades. This effort has been re-emphasized by National Security Language Initiative, which is a program introduced by President George W. Bush on January 5, 2006 at the U.S. University President's Summit to develop the foreign language skills of American students, especially in "critical-need" foreign languages including Korean. The initiative certainly brought more attention to Defence Language Institute and its language programs. Therefore, the Korean program at the Defense Language Institute Foreign Language Center continues to support the language professionals in the Department of Defense with most up-to-date teaching methodologies and principles of foreign language education.

REFERENCES

Applegate, R. (1996). Korean language sustainment program. *GLOBE, 19 (7)*, 11-13.

Boylan, P. & Kang, S. (1995). Syllabus design for the less commonly taught languages, *Korean Language in America*, 1, 3-12.

Latest News & Events (n.d.) In *Defense Language Institute: Foreign Language Center*. Retrieved from http://www.dliflc.edu.

DLI Command History.

Herzog, M. & Soh, A. (1997). Korean Language Program improves curriculum. *GLOBE, 20 (6)*, 7-8.

Kang, S. (2005). Korean Language Education in America. In International Association of Korean Language Education (Ed.), On *Korean language education III: Its history and prospects* (pp. 463-495). Seoul: Hankukmunhwasa.

Korean School (2001-2012). Annual Command History, Defense Language Institute Foreign Language Center, unpublished manuscript.

Mcnaughton, J. C. (1990). A history of the Korean Language Program at the Defense Language Institute, unpublished manuscript.

______ (1996). Korean Language Program evolves with the times. *GLOBE, 19 (7)*, 15-16.

Sampson, K. (1997). Sustain, maintain, survive. *GLOBE, 20 (6)*, 9.